Kick the Bucket and Swing the Cat

The *Balderdash & Piffle* Collection of English Words, and Their Curious Origins

ALEX GAMES studied Classics at university and now teaches Latin. He has been a comedy critic, travel and feature writer for newspapers from the Financial Times to the Evening Standard, and has written comedy for BBC Radio One, Four and Sky TV.

VICTORIA COREN is a well-known freelance journalist. She writes weekly columns in the *Guardian* and the *Observer*, and she has written two books, *Love 16* and *Once More With Feeling*. She presents *Balderdash & Piffle* and several televised poker series.

Balderdash & Piffle is made by award-winning independent production company Takeaway Media

takeaway

Kick the Bucket
and
Swing the Cat

The *Balderdash & Piffle* Collection
of English Words, and
Their Curious Origins

Alex Games

BOOKS

takeaway media

This book is published to accompany the television series *Balderdash & Piffle*,
broadcast on BBC2 in 2006 (Series 1) and 2007 (Series 2).
Series produced by Takeaway Media.

Executive Producer: Neil Cameron (Series 1), Archie Barron (Series 2)
Series Editor: Archie Barron (Series 1)
Series Producer: Caroline Ross Pirie (Series 2)

10 9 8 7 6 5 4 3 2 1

Published in 2008 by BBC Books, an imprint of Ebury Publishing.
A Random House Group Company.

Text © Takeaway Media Ltd and Alex Games, 2006; Alex Games 2007

The Random House Group Limited Reg. No. 954009

Addresses for companies within the Random House Group can be found at
www.randomhouse.co.uk

A CIP catalogue record for this book is available from the British Library.

ISBN 978 1846076107

The Random House Group Limited supports The Forest Stewardship Council
(FSC), the leading international forest certification organisation. All our titles
that are printed on Greenpeace approved FSC certified paper carry the
FSC logo. Our paper procurement policy can be found at
www.rbooks.co.uk/environment

Mixed Sources
Product group from well-managed
forests and other controlled sources
www.fsc.org Cert no. TT-COC-2139
© 1996 Forest Stewardship Council

Commissioning editor: Martin Redfern
Project editors: Eleanor Maxfield & Nicholas Payne
Designer: seagulls.net
Production controller: Antony Heller

Printed and bound by CPI Cox & Wyman, Reading, RG1 8EX

Contents

Note: Words and phrases discussed and/or defined in the text appear in **bold** type and are all listed in the index. Foreign words appear in *italic* type.

Foreword

When I was a child, I made a list of my favourite words. Ferret.
Tinsel. Quagmire. They were my top three.

I made the more traditional lists too: boys I liked, Barbie
outfits, revenges to be exacted on horrible schoolteachers. But,
while teachers and Barbies dominate our lives for a limited
period of time, and boys become far less enigmatic with
exposure, words remain mysteriously fascinating for ever. I still
think I picked a good three. Ferret, tinsel, quagmire, all of them
strange and perfect in their various ways. 'Ferret' squirms slightly
as you say it: a mischievous, wriggly little word. 'Tinsel' is sharp
and silvery against the teeth. You can get bogged down in
'quagmire', with its juicy start and claggy centre.

This is why there is no such thing as a perfect translation. The
precise relationship between a word or phrase and its meaning is
peculiar to every language.

You might say to a friend, 'I'll see you at teatime', meaning only
an approximation of four o'clock. But tucked away inside the
word 'teatime', to a British ear, is a chill winter afternoon:
darkness outside, a little orange glow around the streetlamps, and
a pile of hot buttered crumpets on a table by the hearth. (And
tucked away inside the word 'crumpets' is a little parade of
Victorian prostitutes, from the time when the word came to
mean an attractive woman, for reasons which I can't possibly
spell out here.)

Your plan, when you meet this friend at teatime, may involve
neither chill winds nor tea, and I certainly hope it doesn't involve
prostitutes. But every time you use an English word, it whispers a

little story. Words are like the best sort of grandparents: still engaged and busy in the modern world, but full of colourful tales about the place they were born, the years of their youth, and the job they used to do. The question is, are we always listening? The reason I wanted to work on the series *Balderdash & Piffle*, when I usually consider myself far too fat and croaky to appear on television, is the opportunity it offered to investigate some of our more curious words and phrases at first hand. TV producers usually ring up and ask whether I might like to be a guest on their hilarious new panel game, pressing a buzzer and competing with stand-up comics to shout one-liners at a slightly frightened audience.

But this one said: 'Let's hire a Mini and travel to the birthplace of "codswallop" and "ploughman's lunch".' It was an irresistible adventure. Off we could go to... ferret out the truth. World-class Scrabble players, I have read, are familiar with literally thousands of words without knowing their meaning. The letters are simply point-scoring symbols, and definitions don't matter. This is one of approximately fourteen reasons why I will never be a world-class Scrabble player. I can't imagine hearing a new word without wanting to know its meaning, and knowing its history is even better. We can understand our own history, as a nation, through these little tales.

When you know your etymology, the words 'ferret out' should summon you immediately back to 1580, when gamekeepers sent half-tame ferrets down rabbit holes to flush out their tasty occupants. The word 'ferret' itself, coming from the Old French *fuiret* and previously the Latin *fur, furis* (a thief), speaks to you of people moving across Europe in ancient times, bringing their languages with them and noticing, even then, that there is something suspicious and untrustworthy about ferrets. 'Look at zem,' some Old French wordsmith must have muttered, 'Like leetle thieves.' Except he probably thought it in French.

It must surely be worth knowing as much of this stuff as possible. Unlocking the history of words gives so much more weight, colour and poetry to every conversation we have. Why not let images of sixteenth-century gamekeepers dance in the mind, and sixteenth-century wives cooking delicious rabbit pies, rather than letting 'ferret out' become a flat one-dimensional phrase with no further meaning than its figurative one? Why not keep those stories alive?

After the first series of *Balderdash & Piffle* (and thanks to the sterling work of amateur detectives all over the country, who helped us to investigate the history of words and phrases), forty-three changes were made to *The Oxford English Dictionary (OED)*. Why are we so proud of that? It's partly because the English language is our greatest national treasure, and there is a pure satisfaction in recording it correctly. If you are the kind of person who enjoys the neatness of a finished crossword, the solving of a riddle, or the clear explanation at the end of a Sherlock Holmes mystery, you will know immediately why we yearn to make sure that the dictionary's entries and dates are completely accurate.

But there is more to it than a geeky desire for properly ordered facts. The history of our language unlocks the history of our culture. Those dictionary changes that our wordhunters helped to make after the first series included ante-datings for the words 'balti', 'cocktail' and 'cool', as well as the phrases 'chattering classes', 'on the pull' and 'smart casual'. In tracing the first entry of these terms into the English language, we discover when we first started to act, speak, eat, drink or think in certain ways. They are little souvenirs along the path of social change.

Group words into themes, and we can learn even more. Consider 'bung','swindle' and 'Glasgow kiss'.Why do we use such jolly alternatives to 'bribe','defraud' and 'head-butt'? Having one cute,colourful term for a violent or criminal act is a linguistic quirk.Having three begins to tell us something about ourselves. Our love of this colourful slang is connected to our fondness for TV characters such as Del Boy,Arthur Daley,the Mitchell brothers and Norman Stanley Fletcher.Why are we so ready to enjoy the lighter side of crime?

The English language is equally full of light-hearted terms for madness:'bonkers','bananas','one sandwich short of a picnic'. Such phrases sound rather old-fashioned these days alongside the trend for more serious jargon inherited from America:'bipolar', 'therapy','post-traumatic stress'.Tracing a dateline for the demise of one lingo and the rise of the other reveals the genesis of a more sombre and sympathetic society.For better or worse?That is surely not for the amateur lexicographer to say.Delving into the history of comical phrases,such as 'spend a penny 'or 'kick the bucket',we can think about when and why the concept of euphemism took hold.Or rather,when and why it changed;the ancient Greeks used *euphemismos* to avoid ill omens.We do it to be socially 'nice'.Were we never able to discuss sex,death and bodily functions frankly? Or was there a particular moment in our history when,like Adam and Eve after eating the apple,we suddenly felt ashamed and started draping everything in fig leaves? If we can discover the exact dates when these fig-leaf phrases were born,we will know more about the history of human behaviour.

If you ask me,the most delightful words from our Wordhunt are those that are (unfortunately) put-downs:'wally','pillock', 'plonker' and 'prat'. Looking at them all together,enjoying their humorous sound, inspires one to wonder why there is so much more linguistic pleasure to be had from insulting people than praising them. It isn't just TV and restaurant critics who find this to be true; it's everybody. Are we all awful? (At least it was the Germans, and not we, who coined a special word for 'malicious enjoyment of the misfortunes of others' – *schadenfreude*.)

And there may be no better way to demonstrate how wordhunting unlocks our cultural history than by tracing the language of sexuality. The *OED* currently traces the word 'kinky' (in the sense of adventurous sexual practices) back to 1959. If that was indeed the year that experimental sex reached the conversational mainstream, thus requiring its own adjective, then we can almost hear the liberation of the 1960s banging at the door. But if our wordhunters can help us to push it back earlier, that will force us to look again at the 1950s, or even the 1940s. It would mean that, in those supposedly grey decades, people didn't talk exclusively of rationing and the weather.

When did the dark, technical term 'sadomasochism' become the everyday shorthand 'S&M'? If you think about it, there must have been a moment when people started talking about this tendency so often that they needed to say it more quickly. The linguistic change signifies a notable shift in moral outlook and social conversation. The date of that shift can tell us a lot about our parents – or grandparents.

I'll be honest: I am hoping not to spend too much time thinking about the possibility of my grandparents' dark sexuality. Nevertheless, I am excited about unlocking the secrets of our language to find out more about the people we are, and the people we have historically been.

Part One

Introduction

*H*uman beings have their limits. We can't soar gracefully
through the air like an eagle, nor can we swim unaided to
the ocean floor like a sea-lion and stay there for hours without
surfacing. Our night vision is hopeless compared to that of an
owl. Most of us can't run as fast as an over-excited spaniel, let
alone a cheetah, and we can't change colour according to our
environment. Our skin blisters in the sun, we get frostbite if we're
too high up a mountain, and our young are helpless if left to fend
for themselves during their first ten years or so.

So far, then, the prospects for the human race are not bright, so
what exactly are we good at? Well, we can talk. And we can write
and read. We may not be able to talk to the animals, but we can
talk about them, and we can talk to each other; and our capacity
for self-awareness, for encoding and decoding complex
messages, our love of playing games and debunking each other
marks us out as distinctive. Of course, some of us are better than
others at speaking our own language, but not being a fluent
speaker is no obstacle to holding high office (just ask the current
occupant of the White House). So it isn't purely the quality of our
speech that counts. In different ways we all have the capacity for
writing, and it is that capacity that separates us from the other
species with which we share the planet.

There is, inevitably, a bit of a battle to be named the world's
earliest writing centre. We know that the Sumerians of Uruk in

southern Mesopotamia – modern-day Iraq – were keeping
records of goods and services as long ago as 3400–3300 BC. In
Abydos, 400km (250 miles) south of Cairo, ancient Egyptian
hieroglyphics at the tomb of King Scorpion recording linen and
oil deliveries have been dated to between 3300 and 3200 BC.
Then, in May 1999, it was disclosed that archaeologists at a site
called Harappa in Pakistan had found deliberately-incised marks
on pottery which could date back to 3500 BC. The first forms of
writing, at any rate, emerged over 5000 years ago. It wasn't pure
literature, then, and it took some time before language evolved to
achieve the subtlety of Homer's *Iliad* (and then 2750 years later,
Nuts magazine) but it all proves that our ancestors were adept at
communicating with their fellow beings.

The hunger for language is rooted in our culture. The
inarticulate speech of small children is known as **babble**, a word
that, if not purely imitative of the way babies speak, may be
related to the biblical tower of Babel. In that famous story from
Genesis, the peoples of the world came together to build a tower
so that we could have a squint inside God's living-room, and God
– in a striking blow for the right to privacy, which nearly all
subsequent celebrities would gladly endorse – knocked the
whole project on the head, not with the soon-to-be conventional
weaponry of thunder, lightning, disease or slaughter, but with a
much wilier ruse. He cast them down with language: one
morning, they all woke up unable to understand what each other
was saying. End of tower.

The Babel story is one way the ancient world explained the
incredible variety of tongues, but these days, our towers reach
not up to the sky, but horizontally, across different communities.
As long as we're not trying to puncture the heavens, language can
be a formidable means of generating consent. Consequently,

words themselves have taken on a variety of different meanings over the years.

Meaningful noises

Words are our most valuable currency, and over the years they have taken on a host of different meanings. Anyone skilled with words is known as a **wordsmith**, a sense borrowed from the days of blacksmiths, forges and anvils, as they hammer new words out of flexible letters. We give our **word of honour**, or we say that someone is **as good as their word**. In the City of London, the Stock Exchange has operated since its founding in 1801 on the principle of **My word is my bond**, a motto which – Latinized into *Dictum Meum Pactum* – was incorporated into its coat of arms in 1923. Two simple words, 'I do', can commit two people to each other for life when uttered as part of a marriage service. But words can also fail us, and we can be lost for them. They can be honeyed or twisted. They can send us to war, or move us to tears.

Words have power. Prayers are recited every day for the living and the dead, for the rulers and the weak. As religion evolved, some faiths created names for their God so sacrosanct that they cannot even be spoken: so now the fear is not of a physical tower ascending to heaven, but of a simple word on the lips of a mortal scraping the heavenly underbelly by its mere utterance. Words have political significance. To talk of Madras or Calcutta these days is to betray that you are locked in a Raj-like time warp: in modern India you must talk of Chennai and Kolkata. Salisbury used to be the capital of Rhodesia; now Harare is the capital of Zimbabwe. You can say **cant** and **wink** on the radio or TV in Britain at any time of the day, but if you change one letter in either of those words, the broadcaster's switchboard will light up with complaints and hundreds of angry letter-writers will reach for their pens or keyboards. Being **stuck for words** is a dilemma. **Verbal diarrhoea**, on the other hand, is a condition that the hearer is usually able to diagnose a lot faster than the speaker. But, then, isn't the **gift of the gab** said to be a blessing? The power of words is indisputable. In the beginning, after all, was the word. And it will probably be there at the end, too.

Starting at the beginning

This book is about words and where they come from. It's not a dictionary, an encyclopaedia, a manual or a textbook. Nor is it about grammar, punctuation or style, though all those elements come into the story at various points. It is an unashamedly personal selection of words which have undergone interesting and unexpected journeys on the way from what they originally meant to what they mean today. It is not intended as an academic study, and it steers well clear of scholarly dialect or specialist language, though we have taken pains to ensure that our definitions and etymological[1] explanations are correct. It is, rather, a bit like a chat show in which the guests are not people with products to plug – that really would be shameless – but words with interesting stories to tell. The only make-up we have resorted to is an element of **bold type** so that it's easy for you, the reader, to identify the notable word or phrase. And the only time we shall allow ourselves to pause for a glass of water is at

---

1 Etymology – the study of the original meaning of words. *Etumos* – true (Greek). For 'Ology' – see Chapter 8, page 206.

the end of the book when, out of sheer goodwill, we shall add a list of further suggestions, to help you to take your investigation of the subject a stage further.

But don't feel you have to. After all, any fluent English speaker has thousands of words at their fingertips – or, rather, on their tongue. Among friends, colleagues or family, most of us are capable of astonishing fluency. We can talk – frequently for hours – without having to consult a dictionary, thesaurus, vocabulary book or grammar primer. William Shakespeare is said to have had a working vocabulary of between 17,000 and 20,000 words. The linguistics expert David Crystal estimates that most modern professional people have a vocabulary of around 50,000 words. So we're all experts, and we are all authorities, though few of us will write plays as good as Shakespeare's. Some of us might make the odd boob on paper, or when typing, but essentially we have an entire dictionary in our heads.

For most British people, English is their mother tongue. But even further afield, English is an amazingly successful language. It is spoken and taught the world over, frequently by people who have never even been to Britain. English is the most popular second language in the world, which goes some way towards explaining why most British people have such an appalling record when it comes to speaking other people's languages. Across the world, English is the language that most people want to learn. There are more Chinese speakers than the approximately 375 million people who use English as their mother tongue, but most of them are in China. English is the most widely spoken language in the world today, used regularly by over 700 million people in over 100 countries. A recent survey found that more than four-fifths of all international organizations use English as either their main, or one of their main, operating languages, and that more than 80 per cent of all internet home pages are written in English.

Unpacking the language

The power of words derives from their extraordinary economy. Here is a three-word sentence, just about the simplest unit of sense that you can get:'Petrol prices soar'. A mere three words, yet each word comes pre-bundled with an entire world of implied meanings.The words conjure up an image of a fully operational world behind those sixteen letters: we may think of petrol stations and long queues, or oil tankers on the oceans. It doesn't matter what we think of: words draw pictures in our heads. And we can do our own predictive texting too. If we had to choose a word to come after 'petrol', many of us (based on our past experience) would probably choose 'prices'. And, to complete the sentence, many of us would be more likely to choose **soar** than 'plummet'. Words relate very directly to the associations that we have already made with them in the past. We also have a sense of familiarity with certain word groups, which is why more of us – at least in Britain – would choose 'soar' than, say, **escalate**. We all have a mental thesaurus, and we are combing through it all the time, making choices in search of the best word to communicate meaning.

Learning such associations is a natural process for children, but acquiring them in a new language at a later age can be difficult. Nonetheless, more people are studying English than ever before.The British Council estimates that English has official or special status in at least seventy-five countries, with a total population of over two billion.The appetite for English is growing fast because it is still the language of business, technology, finance, medicine, travel, scholarship and, to a lesser extent, the media. There are various reasons for this, and they don't all relate to Britain's imperial past or to America's cultural and economic dominance. English is a hard language to master, but an easy language to pick up in some basic sense. Grammatically, it doesn't have complicated final forms or rules about agreement based on declensions and conjugations. Learning English is a national obsession in some countries, such as Japan. Across Europe, most schools teach English as a compulsory subject, but the evidence suggests that most pupils need little encouragement to learn the language of J-Lo, Eminem, Craig David and Brad Pitt.

Fashion aside, the English language is a fascinating subject even for native speakers, and relevant to us all in our daily lives. Take the word **run**, for example. *The Oxford English Dictionary* (*OED*) entries for both noun and verb forms stretch to over 55,000 words, or sixty-one pages – the length of a short novel. Hardly surprising, though, when you think of the number of possible meanings. A sprinter **runs**, and so does a wet nose. An escaped prisoner is **on the run**, but a **play can run to** three and a half hours. A cricketer **makes runs**, but can be **run out**. An invalid looks **run down**, perhaps from an attack of **the runs**, while a new car needs **running in**. Commodity speculators might trigger a **run on** oil, which leads to us **running up** quite a bill at the petrol station. Are you being evasive? You're giving someone the **run-around**. Didn't hear what was said? **Run it by me** one more time.

Precision matters

Choosing the right word can make all the difference between making sense and causing offence – or worse. There is a marked difference between **bumping into** an old friend, and **bumping**

off an old friend (or enemy), and it is one that just about all native speakers of English appreciate. Learners, no matter how adept, have to acquire this skill, and it can take time. A German friend recalls asking a well-known British actor what he thought of the charitable event that they were both attending. Unfortunately, though, instead of asking him, 'What do you **make of** events like these?' she asked, 'What do you **make out of** events like these?' and was surprised when he gave her a very moody stare.

We all know the advice given to a journalist that 'Dog Bites Man' is no story. 'Man Bites Dog' is news. In English, word order is vital to making sense. Imagine if you saw a newspaper headline that read: 'Pet Shops Run Out of Hamsters.' It wouldn't raise many eyebrows. We might pause to wonder what caused this sudden dearth of pouched rodents. Possibly a flurry of school projects or an unguarded comment by a teen idol who happens to like them. It's not a major event, at any rate. But change the word order, and the story becomes much more dramatic: 'Hamsters Run Out of Pet Shops.' Now that's news!

You can have great fun looking up words in a big dictionary. English has hundreds of colourfully disparaging terms, so let's look at two words in the title of this book: **balderdash** and **piffle**. Neither is particularly common these days, and in essence they mean the same thing: 'twaddle'. But what history lurks behind these words?

First we'll look at the *OED* entries for them, which show in miniature the skill of the lexicographer,[2] the technical term for someone who writes or compiles dictionaries.

----

2 Dr Johnson, in his *Dictionary* of 1755, clearly relished defining the word as 'a writer of dictionaries; a harmless drudge, that busies himself in tracing the original, and detailing the signification of words'.

balderdash, *n*.

†**1.** ? Froth or frothy liquid. *Obs*.

    1596: Nashe *Saffron Walden* To Rdr. 11 Two blunderkins,
hauing their braines stuft with nought but balder-dash. 1599:
–*Lent. Stuffe* 8 They would no more…have their heads washed
with his bubbly spume or barbers balderdash.

The entry tells us first that the word 'balderdash' is a noun. The †
means that the definition is obsolete (no longer used in that
sense). This is reinforced by the question mark, indicating that
the editors were not sure of the meaning from the available
evidence, and the abbreviation 'Obs'. The earliest definition,
therefore, however uncertain, is of a 'Froth or frothy liquid'.

Next comes the evidence from the printed page. The earliest
quotation found to back up the definition is from 1596. The
author is named as Nashe, and in the *OED*'s online version, an on-
screen hyperlink takes us to the *OED*'s Bibliography, which tells
us the author's full name, Thomas Nashe, and gives a short list of
his works – 15 in all – including the one cited above, *Have with
you to Saffron-walden*. 'To Rdr' means 'to reader', so this
quotation can be found in the part of the book entitled 'To The
Reader.'

Thomas Nashe was born in 1567 and died in 1601. Clearly the
word had not yet taken on its modern meaning. The second
quotation is from the same author (indicated by the long dash):
Nashes Lenten Stuffe from 1599. He obviously liked the word
'balderdash' a good deal: we are left wondering what barbers did
with it. Was it drinkable, or somewhat like a shampoo or rub?

Those who are, by now, intrigued by Thomas Nashe and can
get to their local library might be interested to see more of his
contribution to the English language. Using the online *OED*'s
Simple Search button, we can draw down a list of the English

words for which Nashe is named as the 'first cited author'. It comes to a very impressive 705. Although not much known these days, Nashe was obviously a master of offensive words: **dish-wash** was used first by him, in its literal sense and as a term of abuse. Other Nashe words include **conundrum, helter-skelter, grandiloquent, harlequin, impecunious, silver-tongued** and – you saw it here first – **dildo**.

To be a first quoted author in the *OED* is a considerable feather in any writer's cap, and Nashe's score puts him in elevated company. Geoffrey Chaucer has 2018 entries to his name, William Shakespeare has over 1700, Jane Austen has exactly sixty and Charles Dickens has 262.

The second definition of 'balderdash' looks like this:

> †2. A jumbled mixture of liquors, e.g. of milk and beer, beer and wine, brandy and mineral waters. *Obs*.
>
> 1611: CHAPMAN *May-day* III. Dram. Wks. 1873: II. 374 S'fut winesucker, what have you fild vs heere? baldre~dash? 1629: B. JONSON *New Inn* I. ii, Beer or butter-milk, mingled together … It is against my free-hold … To drink such balder-dash. 1637: J. TAYLOR (Water P.) *Drink & Welc*. (Worc.), Beer, by a mixture of wine hath lost both name and nature, and is called balderdash. 1693: W. ROBERTSON *Phraseol. Gen.* 198 Balderdash; of drink; Mixta Potio. **b.** *attrib.* 1641: HEYWOOD *Reader, here you'll*, etc. 6 Where sope hath fayl'd without, Balderdash wines within will worke no doubt. 1680: *Revenge* v. 68 Ballderdash Wine.

Here we meet such writers as George Chapman, Ben Jonson, Jeremy Taylor and William Robertson. We see the variety of ways in which the word was spelt, as well as archaic spellings of other words, such as 'filled', 'us' and 'here'. And we can also see that the word now applies to something drinkable, probably cheap grog, the sixteenth-century equivalent of Tennents Extra or McEwans.

In the next two definitions, the word has set out on what we will soon recognize as a familiar journey from a physical object to something more abstract or figurative.

> 3. *transf.* A senseless jumble of words; nonsense, trash, spoken or written.
>
> 1674: MARVELL *Reh. Transp.* II. 243 Did ever Divine rattle out such prophane Balderdash! 1721: AMHERST *Terræ Fil.* 257 Trap's second-brew'd balderdash runs thus: Pyrrhus tells you, etc. 1812: *Edin. Rev.* XX. 419 The balderdash which men must talk at popular meetings. 1849: MACAULAY *Hist. Eng.* I. 351, I am almost ashamed to quote such nauseous balderdash. 1854: THACKERAY *Newcomes* I. 10 To defile the ears of young boys with this wicked balderdash. 1865: CARLYLE *Fredk.* Gt. II. VII. v. 287 No end of florid inflated tautologic ornamental balderdash.

There, within that short paragraph, are some of our finest writers: Andrew Marvell, Thomas Babington Macaulay, William Thackeray and Thomas Carlyle, as well as the lesser-known Nicholas Amherst, all brought together for a purpose that they could never have anticipated: to attest to the same sense of 'balderdash' as the one in which the *Edinburgh Review* uses it.

And in its final definition, 'balderdash' comes to mean:

> 4. *dial.* Filthy, obscene language or writing.

Without any further examples, the *OED* follows this with a longish discussion of the etymological origins (historical formation and development) of 'balderdash'. It suggests that although the first two definitions mean 'frothy talk' or 'a senseless farrago' or 'jumble of words', the majority of etymologists have taken the third meaning as the original. From this point, they have sought to locate its roots in languages beyond these shores. They find the English dialect word 'balde', meaning 'to use coarse language', but they want more, so continental Europe is scoured for a time when the language mulch was in a more formative state. The linguists peer into our muddy shared linguistic past. They see the Dutch word *balderen*, meaning 'to roar, thunder'. Cousin or coincidence? Next they see the Norwegian *baldra* and Icelandic *baldrast* or *ballrast*, which mean 'to make a clatter'. Possibly. Back to the UK, perhaps, where they note the Welsh word *baldordd*, meaning 'idle noisy talk, chatter'. That explains the 'dash' part of the word too, though another linguist conjectured a reference to 'the froth and foam made by barbers in dashing their balls backward and forward in hot water'. Quite what the barbers were trying to achieve by doing this with their balls, or indeed which balls they were doing it with, remains a mystery. Whatever it was, though, the practice has, mercifully, fallen out of favour amongst contemporary barbers.

Meanwhile, here is the great American writer H.L. Mencken (1880–1956) scornfully dismissing the prose style of US president Warren G. Harding (in office 1921–3):

> He writes the worst English that I have ever encountered. It reminds me of a string of wet sponges; it reminds me of tattered washing on the line; it reminds me of stale bean soup, of college yells, of dogs barking idiotically through endless nights. It is so bad that a sort of grandeur creeps into it. It drags itself out of the dark abysm of **pish**, and crawls insanely up the topmost pinnacle of **posh**. It is **rumble and bumble**. It is **flap and doodle**. It is **balder and dash**.

How about the other word from our title? The *OED* entry for 'piffle' takes us straight to the verb form, as follows:

piffle, *v. dial.* and *slang*
intr. To talk or act in a feeble, trifling, or ineffective way.
    1847–78: HALLIWELL, *Pifle*, to be squeamish or delicate.
1896: KIPLING *Seven Seas, Mary Gloster* (1897) 146 They piddled
and piffled with iron; I'd given my orders for steel! 1897:
Sunday Times 2 Jan. 6/7 Their defence is sound, and their
attack altogether good, save a tendency to 'piffle' in front of goal
at times.

That's more straightforward. Dialect, slang, an intransitive verb
(one having no object, such as 'to stand', as opposed to a
transitive verb, such as 'to push', which needs to push
something). We note with interest some lines from Rudyard
Kipling. It's also relevant that the popular press, here in the shape
of the Sunday Times, has a crucial role to play in the citing of
sources. Who, though, is Halliwell? James Orchard Halliwell
(1820–89) was a much-admired Shakespearean scholar, who
went up to Trinity College, Cambridge, aged seventeen. Widely
regarded as a genius, his fame so preceded him that he was
granted access to Trinity's unique collection of priceless
manuscripts. Some months after his admission, the college
discovered that over a dozen of them had gone missing. The
culprit was Halliwell, and his punishment earned him a spell
not in Dartmoor High Security Prison but – possibly worse –
Jesus College, Cambridge, where he remained a great scholar
and married the daughter of the eccentric book hoarder Sir
Thomas Phillipps. Here, then, within the skein of a simple
word, a thumbnail sketch of an entire family history emerges.
Phillipps described his own appetite for manuscripts (written

on vellum[3]) as that of 'a perfect vello-maniac', so the two men were obviously well matched, even if Sir Thomas may have had to check his son-in-law's pockets before he let him leave.

The entry continues:

> Hence **piffle** *n*., foolish or formal nonsense; twaddle; trash; also used as a derisive retort; **piffler**, a trifler, a twaddler; **piffling** *vbl. n.* and *ppl. a.*

> 1890: *Sat. Rev.* 1 Feb. 152/2 If there is … a certain amount of the 'piffle' (to use a University phrase) thought to be incumbent on earnest young princes in our century, there is a complete absence of insincerity. 1900: O. ONIONS *Compl. Bachelor* ii. 18 He'd talk a lot of piffle, wouldn't

> he? 1914: 'HIGH JINKS, JR.' *Choice Slang* 16 *Oh piffle*, an exclamation denoting inconsequence of the subject in question. 1920: 'B.L. STANDISH' *Man on First* xviii. 127 'The Hawks have the lead on us, still.' 'Piffle!' said Cady. 'We'll even things up to-morrow.' 1959: ELIZABETHAN Apr. 10/1 I gave you a bar of chocolate on the train from London. So piffle! 1892: *Star* 14 July 1 The nervousness of the other juvenile and titled piffler. 1896: *Westm. Gaz.* 4 Dec. 2/1 Lord; but this chap is dull… Dull! He's a perfect piffler. 1864: MRS. E. LYNN LINTON *Lake Country* 309 Pyklin an' pyflin, thoo gits nowt doon. 1894: *Westm. Gaz.* 21 May 2/3 He seems … to have convinced himself that he is an old man, and settled down to a piffling eld. 1916: 'BOYD CABLE' *Action Front* 17 You don't think a pifflin' little Pip-Squeak shell could go through *his* head? 1927: *Daily Express* 26 July 3/4 The Bench consider that this is a piffling offence, and … that a warning would have been sufficient. 1927: *Observer* 13 Nov. 10/4 The mechanical parts of the moving-pictures are superb, but the imaginative and

---

3 Calfskin that has been soaked, limed, shaved, stretched and dried – a type of parchment.

intellectual parts are piffling. 1963: *Times* 12 June 8/7 The sum
involved was piffling compared with the firm's £25m. a year
turnover. 1973: J.WAINWRIGHT *Pride of Pigs* 56 The lesser hooks
being pulled in for the piffling crimes, while the big boys work
the blinders.

Here is a veritable treasure trove of quotations, all shrouded in
the mysterious and sometimes exotic wrapping paper of history.
We find university usages, exclamations, the word standing on its
own or joined to others. We see a dialect spelling, sporting
journals, financial news, war titles, obscure diaries, political
journals and film reviews: a body of evidence spanning a period
of 83 years.

About this book

The appeal of words is that most of them have been around for
a great many years, and, like any sprightly senior citizen, have
travelled a bit, seen a lot and have some good stories to tell.
As soon as you start looking at words, you find that they have a
tendency to veer off in the most curious directions. In fact, this
book could equally have been called *Make & Do* or *Tea &
Biscuits* or *Rhubarb & Custard*. They all bring their own
histories with them, and all are worth the chase. It is about our
fascination with language, especially with the English language.
It aims to show how English has consistently refashioned itself,
or been refashioned, throughout its long history. At every stage
of its development, though, the questions we really want to ask
are: how does English reflect the period in which it was used, and
which words from *that* time do we still use?

The chapters of this book are arranged by themes. In part one,
we deal with the origins of the English language and the varied

influences that have shaped our vocabulary over time. Whenever you look out of a window, you are looking straight through a word with Viking roots, and one that represents a victory over two other contenders for the same title. Originally, or at least from 890 (the time of King Alfred, and we have the documents to prove it) to about 1225, we used to look through **eyethurls**. This word was comprehensively trounced by the Middle English **fenester** (not a million miles from the French **fenêtre**, which shows how close the two languages once were), which made its pitch between at least 1290 and 1548. In 1225, the same year of the eyethurl's last recorded appearance, the word **window** made its first appearance: as perfect an act of baton-passing as a 4 x 100-metre relay team. It originated from the Old Norse **vindauga**, which in turn came from **vindr** (wind) and **auga** (eye), which was clearly what you would have experienced had you stuck your head out of a window before supplies of glass were readily available in the thirteenth century.

Within the linguistic churn that this book covers – from Anglo-Saxon to Estuary English – we look at the epic poem Beowulf, which is still scaring the faint-hearted over a thousand years after it was written. We find out a little about Celtic place names, and how important it was to have the right ending, such as **–dunum**, and Saxon endings such as **–ham** and **–stead**. And we also meet some Norman barons who brought French across the Channel, and the scholars who reintroduced Latin to Britain.

We look at some of the early attempts to standardize the English language, such as Dr Johnson's Dictionary. When Johnson turned his London garret into the production office for a book that would 'fix the English language', he little knew that it would take him and his small team eight years. But the work they eventually produced – late, over-budget, packed with idiosyncrasies and as lively and provocative as the man himself – was one of the greatest cultural works of the eighteenth century. Following on from this, we look at the extraordinary labour that went into the compilation of the *OED*, a project begun just over a hundred years after Johnson's publication and that took seventy years to complete. We look at the pioneering work of Frederick Furnivall and Sir James Murray on the *OED* in the mid-nineteenth century and at the present-day *OED Online*, available since 2000.

The Bible – the book that Christians and atheists alike constantly quote, although they may not know they're doing so. No matter how staunchly secular they are, many people pepper their speech with biblical expressions, 'such as 'out of the mouths of babes", which comes from the book of *Psalms*. If they talk of **sticking to the straight and narrow** or see something as a **sign of the times**, they are quoting the book of *Matthew*. If they try to be **all things to all men** or **suffer fools gladly**, they are quoting *Corinthians*, and if they **fight the good fight** or **scorn filthy lucre**, they are borrowing from the book of *Timothy*.

Similarly, the words of Shakespeare live on in daily speech, from **what the dickens** (*The Merry Wives of Windsor*) to **a foregone conclusion** (*Othello*). The expression **all Greek to me** is borrowed from Julius Caesar, and **playing fast and loose** comes from A*ntony and Cleopatra*. And so it goes on: **cold comfort** is from *King John*, **making a virtue of necessity** is from *Pericles*, and the first recorded use of the word **obscene** is in *Richard III*. Without Shakespeare, would we be using words such as **accommodation**, **assassination**, **barefaced**, **countless**, **courtship**, **dwindle**, **eventful**, **fancy-free**, **lacklustre**, **laughable**, **premeditated** and **submerge**? Perhaps not, as Shakespeare popularized them, if not invented them.

Words can mean the same or something quite different, depending on where your feet are planted on these islands. We chart the journey that English took within the British Isles, and the endless varieties of English within Britain. In the past, varieties of dialect speech may have been exploited for comic purpose, and it may even have been thought that standard English would one day supplant the huge wealth of accents and dialects that have given English its colour and character. Fortunately, we have moved away from such ideas, and every variation in speech is now welcomed as part of the family. Whether we wear **trousers** and **trainers**, or **kecks** and **pumps**, whether you say 'Do you know?' or 'D'ye ken?', we now recognize that the heart of a language is nourished by its extremities.

All communities feed the body, in the broadest sense of the word. Words that were coined by the Black Community form a discrete language, but many of its distinctive words – from **irie** to **massive**, from **skanking** to **spliff** – which were coined behind a wall of racial separation, have leaked out and entered the mainstream. Black English, with its roots in creolized forms of English from the days of slavery, has always had a two-way relationship with the mainstream English language. So whereas a word such as **mambo** comes from Cuban Spanish and then Haitian Creole, words from other gated communities – be they children, women, gays – are entering the English language at an unprecedented rate. Such communities are gated because access to them is not guaranteed, but the gate can be opened at will, and that's when words – whether invented or with a meaning specific to that community – slip out.

When British explorers travelled the world, they brought back far more than commodities and strange animals. New terms came too, including the Arabic words **cotton**, **marzipan** and **sherbet**. From Calcutta in India came **calico**, while **gauze** came from Gaza, **ombudsman** from Sweden, **molasses** from Portugal, **tycoon** from Japan and **hoard** from Turkey. These words and many others have given English its fascinating variety.

Just as secular people use the Bible, so non-sportsmen and women use the language of sport. Some sports are ancient, but their language remains young. For example, if you've ever been **hoodwinked**, you may not have known that you are using a falconry term that is at least 200 years old. It derives from the practice of covering a falcon's face with a hood so as to remove the prey from its talons. Similarly, the word **boozing** is related to the Middle English word **bowse**, the term used to describe the drinking action of a bird of prey.

We use sporting language all the time, even when we're sitting down. If you've ever **crossed a line**, **hit the ground running**, **hit a bullseye** or **fallen short of your mark**, you are employing a phrase that was created in a very different context. If you've ever been the **butt** of someone's joke, that's an archery term. The old sports have the deepest roots. Don't confuse today's **quarrel** with the one from 1350, which meant 'a short, heavy, square-headed arrow or bolt, formerly used in shooting with the cross-bow or arbalest'. And if you've ever been told to **brace yourself**, **bracing** is what used to be done to a bow to make it strong enough to take the arrow.

Popular entertainment is responsible for producing a long list of words in common currency. The **64-thousand dollar question** was originally a catchphrase from American television. A boxing manager called Joe Jacobs was the first to utter the immortal words 'we was robbed' when his boxer Max Schmeling lost on points to Jack Sharkey in 1932. If you say **pass** when you don't know the answer to something, you are using a word which came into prominence on the British quiz show *Mastermind*.

Of course, if it hadn't been for science and technology, we wouldn't have had telly in the first place. We have drawn thousands of words from science, and many are still in daily use. Anyone who says they **went ballistic** is using an eighteenth-century term that reflects that age's fascination with projectile science.

When something passes the **litmus test**, or reaches a **critical mass**, even when we get to boiling point, we are drawing on scientific vocabulary. And if you **park your tanks on someone's lawn**, or **bring up the rear**, or feel **outflanked** or **ambushed**, you're conscripting military language for non-military purposes. As we shall see, this happens more than we might have expected.

As we scan the wilder shores of language, we must look at the furthest coast of all: taboo words, swear words, obscene and profane language, and words that are designed to hurt. Words uttered in anger or passion: the mysterious origins of the word **fuck** and its ruder medieval equivalent of **swive**. Why, when Mrs Patrick Campbell said the word **bloody** during the first night of George Bernard Shaw's *Pygmalion* on 11 April 1914, the event was marked with sensational newspaper headlines. The history of swearing and of blue language occupies a distinguished place in word history.

A more shameful place is rightly given to racist and derogatory language. Some of these pejorative terms have now been appropriated by the intended targets. **Queer**, **dyke** and **nigger** are obvious examples; 'damn kids' has not undergone the same transition.

Whizz, bang! Ouch! Er… we regress to the most basic language of all – words that are almost non-words, but that are nonetheless a vital part of our vocabulary. When we say things go **pop** and **splash**, we are using onomatopoeia, an elaborate word for describing the most basic of sounds – the sounds of the world around us. From the external to the internal, we come to the sounds we make. We all know how it feels to stub a toe, but when did that inchoate shriek of pain crystallize around the four-letter word **ouch**? And then there are other words, all sharply expressive in their way but with more coherent and complex meanings.

The French philosopher Voltaire (1694–1778) said that 'if God did not exist, it would be necessary to invent him.' That may also be true of nonsense words. Once they have been created, they are so evocative that it's hard to imagine a world without them. Oscar Wilde demonstrated this when he borrowed Lord Bunbury's name and turned it into an excuse for not doing things. From the pages of the *Beano* to *The Lord of the Rings*, we take a look at made-up language that with time and use has become 'real'.

Words of the month, the week, the day, the year, 'it' words, jargon, lingo, slang, the word on the street, in the club, on the net – some have stuck with us, others we have shrugged off as trends move on. Looking at each decade from the early twentieth century to the present, it may come as a surprise to learn just how old some slang words are. We may not often say something we like is 'the bee's knees' these days, but **wicked** is common currency. Yet both entered the language in the 1920s. You may wish to know the words that were judged our favourites in 1980, and how the rather harsher realities of life in modern Britain caught up with a similar survey twenty years later. This is the history of the way we speak – pins on the map for future linguists to follow.

And that leads us to those historical black holes of the dictionary: those mysterious words marked 'origin unknown' or 'etymology obscure'. The public is invited to get digging, and to share its findings with the editors of the *OED* in a search for the earliest verifiable usage of words in the English language.

In part two, we look at several areas of life that seem to inspire a playfulness which other areas simply lack. Take dogs, for example. If you had to scribble down on a scrap of paper any word or phrase that contained a reference to dogs in the English language, from **dogged** to **dog-eared**, it's a fair bet that one scrap of paper would not suffice. Having assembled this mass of phrases – a regular **dog's dinner**, you could say – you might begin to ask: where did all these come from? Why do we refer to dogs whether describing ruthless competitiveness (**Dog eat dog**) or the scuffed appearance — **dog-eared** – of a book? What is it about our attitudes towards dogs that lead us to plunder their world for expressions with which to understand our own lives? The answers to all these questions and more can be found in the chapter entitled *Man's best friend*.

And it isn't just the humble hound. Dogs are external beings whose behaviour mirrors, however distortedly, our own. But we are also very good at not saying what we ought to be saying. There is a chapter on Mental Aberration in which the word **mad** is barely mentioned: such is our tendency to tip-toe around the subject. We also round up a whole bunch of terms that allude to 'bodily functions' – going to the toilet, sex, death and drunkenness - without once mentioning what the activity involves. There are phrases drawn from the worlds of the

Fashionistas and petty crime, famous sayings uttered by or about the famous, infamous or not-so famous. We have also made right **pillocks** of ourselves by going to the trouble of exploring some of the *Put-downs and Insults* with which we have added salt to our language over the years.

Finally, tucked discreetly at the end of the book, there is a chapter entitled *X-rated*. It should be fairly clear to which area of human activity this refers – parental control is recommended, in other words.

This book is for anyone who is interested in talking, reading, writing or hearing English. It is not a textbook or a scientific book – it is for the general reader. And it aims to be part of a broader debate, in which it forms part of the BBC series from which it is drawn. Readers are encouraged to take up the challenge, to join in the public craze for language that is sweeping the nation, just as garden or home makeovers or unblinking studies of self-publicists stuck in a jungle have fascinated the public until now. Websites about words are attracting new viewers all the time. In today's **zeitgeist** – one of those foreign words that has bedded down nicely in modern English – words are cool, and books, websites, newspapers and magazines all feed on and profit from the British love affair with its language.

From the soaraway success of Lynne Truss's *Eats, Shoots and Leaves* to Michael Quinion's invaluable *POSH* and Susie Dent's fascinating *Larpers and Shroomers*, an abiding interest in the spoken and written word characterizes our fascination with the crucial and the trivial, and is as popular with bloggers and rappers as it is in the columns of the *Spectator*. Word-searching is a dangerous and rather delicious addiction, but one that is open to everyone. The English language is currently the scene of the nation's favourite quarry. 'Digging a hole' can sometimes be a synonym for getting yourself into deeper and deeper trouble, but not on this occasion. If you need any further encouragement, just grab a spade and start digging. Happy reading!

Chapter One

Our Mongrel Tongue

*T*he English language is a great borrower of words. But once it's borrowed them, it likes to hang on to them, and there they stay, like migrant workers, working productively under new economic conditions. English is basically a Germanic tongue, but it has cross-pollinated ceaselessly for centuries, and is correspondingly multi-faceted. Sir James Murray, the first and arguably still the most renowned editor of the *OED*, began classifying the English language in 1884. Having noticed that English frequently contains a whole series of words to describe the same thing, he began to compile lists of English words in terms of their 'register' or tone. The four registers he devised are illustrated in the following example. A priest might describe a bride as looking **euphoric** or **elated** on this joyous occasion (literary), while she tells him she is **happy** (common). She might then tell her friends that she is **chuffed** (colloquial), unless she is in Liverpool, where she might be **made up** (slang). Each synonym has its proper time and place in a sentence, and a native English speaker will automatically know when to use which particular word.

Each word is equally 'correct' of course, and, as a lexicographer, Murray was naturally most interested in describing the richness of the English language and the vast range and diversity of the synonyms themselves. But one way of deciphering meaning or register is to study the numerous linguistic sources from which the synonyms derive. A word's history may not give its current meaning, but it can help to understand the nuances with which each word in English is now imbued. 'Euphoric' is classical Greek in origin and therefore likely to have entered the language via religious scholars during the Renaissance. 'Elated' is Latin, which came into English with William the Conqueror, whose coronation in 1066 was conducted in both Latin and French – the source for 'joyous'. The word 'happy' derives from the Old Icelandic word 'happy', one of a group of languages including Old Norse which was spoken in Scandinavia by the Vikings, and particularly the Norwegians, until about AD 1000 and which is still closely connected to modern Icelandic. No one really knows the origins of 'chuffed', while 'made up' is Shakespearean, but didn't come to mean 'chuffed' until as late as 1956. The scholar Geoffrey Hughes gave an example of the nature of our mongrel tongue in the following diagram:

Anglo-Saxon:	a	to the		of the English
Norman French:	guide			language
Latin and Greek:		lexical history		

Adapted from: Geoffrey Hughes, A *History of English Words*, Blackwell, 2000

This multi-layered representation goes some way to revealing why our language, with all its versatility and subtlety, is such a linguistic soup. Every word becomes a time capsule, containing its own past within itself. To understand the nature of the mongrel, we need to travel back to the dawn of Englishness.

The Celts

'Britain, formerly known as Albion, is an island in the ocean, facing between north and west, and lying at a considerable distance from the coasts of Germany, Gaul and Spain, which together form the greater part of Europe,' wrote the Venerable Bede (c.673–735) in his *History of the English Church and People*, completed in 731. He entered the monastery of St Paul in Jarrow, Northumberland, at the age of seven, and went on to become a renowned scholar, composing over thirty books in Latin, which was still the primary language of monastic scholarship. In Bede's day the British Isles were an ethnic melting pot and the people divided into five main groups: 'At the present time there are in Britain, in harmony with the five books of the divine law, five languages and four nations – English, British, Scots and Picts.' Bede points out that Latin, 'by the study of the Scriptures', is the fifth grouping since it is 'common to (whom we would now call Celts) who gave their name to the land'.

But despite writing in Latin, Bede firmly believed that it was important to translate important religious texts into the new, fully merged language of the people. The first translation of his book into this language – Old English – is said to have been made by or under the influence of King Alfred the Great almost 150 years later as an inspiration for his English subjects and an acknowledgment of the quality of the Venerable Bede's writing. (It is, incidentally, the linguistically gifted King Alfred who is credited with one of the first recorded appearances of the word **Englisc** in his late-ninth-century translation of another Latin work – Pope Gregory's *Pastoral Care*. Who was the last British monarch who could have undertaken either of these tasks?) Judging by the number of other texts that Bede would have had to consult, it strongly suggests that the island's speakers were at least bilingual at the time, and that this was considered the norm, or even a bare minimum.

There are those who, for political reasons, now use the word Anglo-Saxon as if that were the beginning of British culture. In fact, the Anglo-Saxons were an invading race, who displaced the original natives of this land, along with their language and culture. The first-known inhabitants of these islands were the Celts, who also travelled to Scotland. They were followed, in about the fourth century AD, by a tribe called the Picts, who had arrived from Ireland, since the Irish inhabitants (who spoke Gaelic) would not allow the Picts to live there. The Picts used an alphabet called Ogham, which consisted of a series of scrapes into stone. It was hard work and it doesn't truly survive in any other form except runic artefacts. The *OED* now contains no words directly derived from Ogham, though some are listed as 'recorded in an Ogham inscription'. One is **neve**, which turned into 'nephew'. Another is the **O'** prefix in Irish names.

Julius Caesar attempted to invade the islands and tame the Celts in 55BC, but he was unsuccessful. Almost a hundred years later the Emperor Claudius tried again. The Celts dispersed and retreated north and westwards, but maintained links with the Romans, coexisting relatively peacefully and speaking their respective languages, with the Celts presumably speaking Latin too for trade purposes. Almost 400 years later, however, the Roman Empire began to collapse and a power vacuum was created at the heart of it. The troops hastily withdrew to Rome in the early fifth century and the Celts began to be attacked from the north by the Scots and the Picts (who finally merged in 850 and thenceforth spoke a unified Scottish tongue).

In 494 the Celtic king Vortigern turned to the Anglo-Saxons (modern Danes and Germans) for military assistance. These tribes spoke a wide range of different Germanic dialects, and whole new linguistic threads were now added to the native British tongue. One of these Germanic tribes in particular had been referred to by the Romans as the '*Angli*', and within 150 years of their arrival, the whole area of their invasion became known as **Englaland** (land of the Angles).

As Bede was to recount some 300 years after the event, the Angles and Saxons, led by the 'brother-commanders' Hengist and Horsa, arrived in three long ships in 449. The tribal groupings were, in fact, relatively straightforward geographically, with the Angles from Denmark arriving along the northern half of the east coast, while the Saxons from northern Europe came aground along the Thames and the south coast. It may not be surprising that the invaders took some time learning to communicate with the locals, but it is possible that the invaders could not even understand each other. They had a common oral heritage, but wildly varying pronunciation and vocabulary. There were dozens of different localized dialects, and their influence spread rapidly through central, southern and northeastern England, generally along major rivers. The Celts remained in Cornwall, Wales and Cumbria, while the Angles occupied most of eastern Britain (modern-day East Anglia) and the east Midlands. The Jutes, who came from Jutland in modern-day Denmark, occupied the land east of the River Medway, southern Hampshire and the Isle of Wight. The Germanic Saxons settled in southern England west of the Medway, particularly along the south coast, the Thames valley, and the western Midlands around the River Avon in Warwickshire. Of the invading Germanic tongues, Frisian (from an area around the modern Netherlands) was probably the tongue closest to modern English. The Frisian for a **broomstick**, for example, is *bromstich*.

Very few Celtic words survived to be passed on in normal speech. An enormous number of place names have Celtic prefixes or suffixes, and these, logically, steadily increase from the east to the west of England and into Wales and Cornwall, since these were the places to which the Celts fled. The Celtic family of languages today includes Breton, Welsh, Manx, Scottish Gaelic, Irish Gaelic and Cornish, but all surviving Celtic words in modern English are related to geography and landscape – the hills they walked upon, the streams they crossed and the paths where they led their herds. Celtic words really are the roots of Britishness, from **cwm** (valley) to **tor** (hill). There are a few words of dubious Celtic origin, such as **bin** (receptacle), which may actually derive from the early Latin word *benna*, while **ass** probably comes from the Celtic word *assen*, but equally may be from the Latin word *asinus*.

The reasons for the almost total disappearance of Celtic remain, frankly, mysterious. It is just about possible that the rural Celtic way of life had so little in common with the Anglo-Saxons that they simply didn't need their vocabulary, or that life was so similar that the Anglo-Saxons already had a word for everything they needed. Or that, just like the subsequent Normans, the Anglo-Saxons considered the Celts too 'common' to use their vocabulary, or, conversely, so closely integrated into the now disgraced Roman Empire that they wanted nothing to do with their language. It is also true that since almost all the Celts who resisted the invasion were evicted across the Welsh border, the Anglo-Saxons may simply not have come into much contact with their vocabulary.

Aside from geography, the only other major area of influence of Celtic on Old English was, rather surprisingly, in first names. The Anglo-Saxon nobility adopted Celtic first names with great relish. Caedwalla was the king of Wessex in 685, while Caedmon was a seventh-century stable boy who became England's first Christian poet. It may simply be that the Anglo-Saxons liked the sound of the new names (all of which began with 'C'), but still, noble Celtic names must have been socially acceptable. It remains even more of a mystery, therefore, why so little else from the culture survived.

The vocabulary left by the retreating Roman soldiers, however, made somewhat more of a mark. Where the Celts had inhabited hills and valleys, the Romans had constructed long-lasting buildings (and roads), and the names for these remained common currency. *Strata*, for example, meant a 'paved street' – more durable than the humble 'road' – so Britain's Roman roads had names such as Icknield Street, Ermine Street and Watling Street, the last extending 180 miles between London and Chester. Chester itself came from the Latin word *castra*, meaning a 'camp', which resurfaces in Chichester, Cirencester, Lancaster and Worcester.

Latin also gave us important words, such as **wine** (from *vinum*), which led to Britain's proud tradition of wine-making, or at least wine-drinking. In that first visit of the Romans to Britain, not a great many words changed hands before the invaders limped back to mop up the remnants of the Roman Empire, which had imploded owing to a combination of factors, including lead poisoning and incest. We moulded *cucina* into **kitchen** and took on many Latin loan words in that department, such as *caseus* (**cheese**), *pisum* (**pea**) and *prunus* (**prune**). The much-debated **cheap**, originally a noun rather than an adjective, meaning a 'bargain', is generally recognized to have derived from the Latin *caupo* (a petty trader), a few of whom can still be found trading at Cheapside in London. As well as commercial terms, we also borrowed Latin units of measurement. The Latin *uncia*, meaning 'one-twelfth', became the Anglo-Saxon 'unce/ince', and the Modern English 'ounce/inch'. But the Romans did metric too: *millia* meant a thousand paces, which we transformed into the (non-metric) 'mile'.

As these examples show, the first generation of Latin words were one or two-syllabled, and related very specifically to the Britons' basic needs. More complicated constructions, and the more complex thought processes that they conveyed, would come later. This process, however, was effectively restricted to the southern part of these islands when Emperor Hadrian, during the course of his AD 122 imperial tour, glanced north and decided that a wall was needed to protect the soft southerners from the hairy hordes. The wall took six years to build and stretched 117km (73 miles) from Wallsend on the Tyne to Bowness-on-Solway in the West. South of this line, Latin words are more common in the English tongue.

The Angles

According to the Venerable Bede's history (which may not be strictly accurate since it was written 300 years after the events it describes), the Anglo-Saxon invasion actually refers to three distinct groups of people: Angles, Saxons and Jutes. The Anglians headed north, from where the Northumbrian and Mercian dialects derive. The Saxons, including the West-Saxons in what became known as Wessex, went south. The Jutes headed for Kent, where the Kentish dialect became a particularly hybrid linguistic soup, since the Romans had made their biggest mark there, too. Numerically, there were more Saxons than Angles, but the Angles, in true German style, must have got up especially early as they were first in line when it came to naming the country 'Englaland' in Old English, since shortened to 'England'. The true pronunciation of the country's name is 'Eng-a-Land', recalled most accurately in our national football chant. The most common theory of how England got its name is that early Latin writers used the term *Angli Saxones* as an easy way of distinguishing them from the 'Old Saxons' on the Continent and that, as in many double-barrelled names, only the first half stuck.

Under the Anglo-Saxons a further wave of place-naming occurred, with the ending –**ing** denoting a Saxon founder. Buckingham, for example, breaks down as 'the home of the sons of Bucca', where the Old English 'hám' means 'home'. It also appears at the front of such place names as Hampstead or Hampton. Nottingham, meanwhile, was first settled in pre-Roman times and was originally called *Tigguo Cobauc*, which means 'a place of cavy dwellings'. Nottingham's modern name, however, derives from later settlements that were built by Anglo-Saxon invaders after AD 600. These settlements were named after their chieftain – Snot – who brought his people together in an area of the city where the historic Lace Market can now be found. This place became known as Snotingaham – 'the home of Snot's people'. While most of the '–ing' towns were in the southeast of England, the words **Sussex** (a contraction of South Saxon), **Essex** (East Saxon) and **Middlesex** are also Saxon words. The word **Saxon** itself comes from the word *seax* (sword). There is a district called Angel in the province of Schleswig in Germany, and this may be where the original Angles came from.

The Anglo-Saxon language soon became known as **English** (Bede refers to a monastery 'namned on Englisc' – named in English – and King Alfred, who coined the term, used it in a treaty between the English and the Danish). We now refer to this early Anglo-Saxon language as Old English, and by this time its vocabulary included such words as **dog**. The *OED* really has no idea where this sprang from, although it was originally written 'docga'. At the time, the generic name for a dog, as in many other Teutonic (generally German) languages, was *hund* (later 'hound'). The *OED* says that the 'English dog' was used to mean a powerful breed or race of dogs. But the word was clearly a winner since, by about the late sixteenth century, in the days before quarantine, the animal had spread all across Europe. The Danes, Dutch and Germans were referring to *dogge*, the Swedes to *dogg*, the Italians, Spanish and Portuguese to *dogo*, and even the French to *dogue*.

When we compare certain basic Anglo-Saxon and Latin words, we see that even though they come from the same roots, they have mutated along different lines as English developed. Latin began its existence in England as the language of political power, and this would have made it the language of choice for the educated and the aspirational. Even the Celts had taken some of the early learning on board, since the Welsh *eglwys* (church) came from the originally Greek *ecclesia*, and *ysgol* (school) from *schola*. This trend also touched Old English – it is even possible that aristocratic Britons continued to use Latin as their chosen tongue long after the Romans had left and the Anglo-Saxons arrived. In church environments, of course, Latin never stopped being used, which led to it acquiring the cachet of 'educated speech'. Latin words were used for plants and animals, domestic goods, business matters, law and medicine. As monks began to need new words for new areas of study, over 60 per cent of the later imports from Latin were specifically scholarly or technical, while native Anglo-Saxon words were vaguer and much better, therefore, for poetry and metaphorical speech. The Latin word *sol* became **sun**, so the Anglo-Saxons gradually extended it to words such as **sunshine** and metaphorical uses, such as **sunstruck**. *Sol*, meanwhile, took on a strictly technical usage in words such as **solar**.

For these reasons, the illogical, anti-rational and purely emotive terms in English are predominantly drawn from Anglo-Saxon sources. Such English words as **murder**, **kill**, **steal** and **lie** are all direct, even brutal. Latin, meanwhile, the language of authority and discipline as opposed to the language of the street and the tavern, gives us the rather judicial-sounding **homicide** and **mendacity**. Similarly, compare Old English **sweat** with Latinate **perspiration**, **shit** with **defecation**, **fucking** with **copulation** and it's clear which word-base has a well-earned reputation for earthiness, directness and rudeness.

The word **woman** is from Old English, as is the word **man**, but their stories are more intertwined than that. *Man* is common in Germanic languages and means both a 'human being' and a 'male person'. In addition, Old English had two words – **wer** and **wif** – which meant 'male human' and 'female human' respectively. 'Wer' lives on only in **werewolf** (man-wolf), but is a cousin of the Latin word *vir* for man (see Virtue, page 53). In Anglo-Saxon times 'man' and 'wer' were used interchangeably. The idea, then, that it is sexist to use the word 'man' to describe both men and women is etymologically incorrect since 'man' was originally a root word that implied all humankind.

The word 'wif' is still used today, of course, as **wife**. In Anglo-Saxon usage, however, 'wif' was a much more general term and meant any woman, not just a spouse, and words such as **midwife** are derived from this usage. Coming as it did from the Anglo-Saxon rather than the Latinate **dame** or the later Anglo-Norman **mistress**, it was a distinctly lower-register term. It was most often applied to women who worked in humble occupations, such as **ale-wife**, **fish-wife**, **apple-wife** or **oyster-wife**. And these women told stories that became known as **old wives' tales**. Meanwhile, the Old English word **wæpman** meant a 'human with a weapon', and **weapon** was coarse slang for the penis from about 1000 onwards (and probably long before). The female equivalent to 'wæpman' was **wifman**, and from this Anglo-Saxon root we get the modern 'woman'.

Originally a Germanic tribe, the Angles settled in Britain and formed the kingdoms of Northumbria, Mercia and East Anglia, eventually giving their name to the whole 'English' people. When King Alfred used the Old English word **rad** in the year 888, it meant 'the act of riding on horseback' or a 'journey on horseback'. From 900 to 1600 it meant 'incursions', in the same sense that **inroads** still carries, and from 1300 for a good 500 years it had the sense of a 'sheltered piece of water', somewhere near the shore, where ships could be anchored safely. It was not until the seventeenth century that the word began to take on its present meaning of a channel down which people, horses or carriages could pass. And many Anglo-Saxon words have had a similarly long journey to get to their present point. It is a tribute to the patience and curiosity of generations of lexicographers that we can trace these words back to their earliest origins.

The Danish presence was felt here as long ago as the eleventh century and also made its mark on the English language. When King Canute (actually Cnut, since he was a Dane) sought to prove his humanity by failing to stop the waves, it would not have been surprising if the word **drown** had flashed across his mind, since that word may likely have come from Old Norse. Caring little for the monasteries, the Danes came to be known by the Gothic word **heathen**, meaning 'heath-dweller', or non-

Christian. It may also be related to the Greek word *ethnos*, meaning 'nation'.

It is not always easy to decide whether a word is Norwegian or Danish in origin, but linguists are reasonably certain about their early Scandinavian origins (see Chapter 6, page 174). **Addle** used to mean 'stinking urine' – something to consider the next time you call someone **addle-headed**. **Boon** meant a 'prayer', and **busk** meant 'to prepare oneself' or 'get ready'. Other than that, the great Danish linguist Otto Jespersen reckoned that Danish and Norwegian or Old Norse were pretty inseparable at the time. It is worth noting, for the tone of the vocabulary, that Old Norse gives us **raid** and **ransack**, as well as the word **Viking** (*vik* means a 'creek', rendered into Old English as 'wic' (a settlement), which is still visible in place names such as Greenwich.

The Vikings

The received wisdom about the Vikings is that they were brutes. They sacked the holy island of Lindisfarne in 793, razed the Venerable Bede's own monastery at Jarrow in 794 and generally set the tone of the period known as the Dark Ages. The best known of the English kings who tried to oppose these murderous, pillaging Danes (and the only one who achieved some measure of success) was Alfred the Great, who reigned from 871 to 899. His best battleground triumph was in 878 at Edlington in Lincolnshire, and in that same year, in the Treaty of Wedmore, he handed over to the Danish chief Guthrum an area northeast of Watling Street, which was thereafter ruled by Danelaw. In Yorkshire, therefore, a large proportion of place names now end in the Old Norse suffix of *-by*, which denoted a town or settlement (e.g. Grimsby, Derby, Rugby, Whitby and Denby – 'town of the Danes').

Norse terms were also used to make geo-political divisions, such as the *thridings* (third parts) found in Yorkshire, now called the **Ridings**. The Watling Street line worked well as a linguistic separator, and its effects are still noticeable. North of it, hay is still raked into **stacks**; south of it, they are called **ricks**. The Old Norse *stithy* is an Anglo-Saxon *anvil*. Old Norse children *lake*, while Anglo-Saxon children *play*. North it's **mun**, south it's **must**. Northern lads and lasses have **lugs**; southern boys and girls have **ears**.

The Normans

The next invaders were the Normans, who came over with William the Conqueror in 1066. These Normans had once been Vikings who settled in the Pas de Calais and around Normandy. They immersed themselves so deeply in the local language that almost no Norse words survive in northern French, apart from some remaining place names. Just as Lancashire has Breck and Iceland has Laugarbrekka, both from the Norse word *brekka* meaning 'a slope', so too does Normandy have Bricquebec. Boothby in Cumbria and Lincolnshire is derived from the word *búth* meaning shelter. Compare Búthir in Iceland, and Elbeuf in the Seine-Mar. Then there's Fulby in Denmark, Lincolnshire's Fulbeck, and northern France's Foulbec, all of which come from the Norse word *full* (foul). *Sund* means 'strait', still visible in the French Sund de Chausey, or Haraldssund in the Faroe Isles. The word *cliff* gives us Cleethorpes and the French Clitourps. There are at least thirty such places, at a conservative estimate.

The French nobility very quickly became the English nobility too, not least through a process of cross-Channel marriages. Their influence on the English language has been enormous, but the strain of French they spoke was not Parisian French. Linguists call it Anglo-French, and it was one of the most successful linguistic imports ever conceived: three-quarters of the 10,000 words that sprang up during the Middle English[1] period are still in use. In fact, it was not until Henry IV came to the throne in 1399 that England had a king whose mother tongue was English. The Normans had engineered a complete cultural takeover.

In England at that time there was almost no middle class. Either you were a member of the French-speaking nobility, or you were a peasant who spoke Old English. Therefore, common trades, such as **miller**, **blacksmith**, **cobbler**, **ironmonger** and **shoemaker**, have Old English names, whereas the more skilful jobs, such as **tailor**, **painter** and **carpenter**, are Anglo-French.

Titles at Court

Anglo-Saxon	Norman
King	
Queen	
	Prince / Princess
	Duke / Duchess
	Marquess / Marchioness
Earl	Count / Countess
Lord	
Lady	
	Viscount / Viscountess
Baron	
	Baronet

---

1 A translation of the term coined in 1819 by the great German linguist Jacob Grimm, to denote the English language between Old and modern English, i.e. from 1100–50 to about 1450–1500.

And the Anglo-French **butcher** originally meant someone who dealt in he-goat, from the Old French for he-goat, *boc*.

King and **queen** are native English words, but almost all the appurtenances of royalty, including the word **royalty** itself, are on long-term loan from the French, in recognition of the fact that French was the language of the court – which is another French word.

The word **crown** is an Anglo-Norman formation, on loan from *corune*, *coroune* or *corone*. The word *real* (royal) lingers on in such terms as **real estate**, **real tennis** and **Real Madrid**. Other words that we adopted include **realm** and **country**. The original meaning of 'country' sounds so far-fetched as to be speculative, but the *OED* states that it comes from the Middle English 'contre(e, cuntre(e' and that the Old French *cuntrée*, *contrée* took that meaning from the Latin preposition *contra* (against), as in 'contrary'. And the country is precisely what lies opposite when you look out at it.

French also permeates our government. The word **exchequer** comes from the Old French *eschequier*, which derives from *scaccarium*, the medieval Latin word for a **chessboard**. This is believed to be because the accounts were originally kept using counters on chequered tablecloths that resembled chessboards.

The head of state in Great Britain still uses an old French form of words, 'La Reyne le veult' (The Queen wishes it), when giving assent to an Act of Parliament.

Government, regulation and arbitration all became definably French, even when satisfactory measures had been in place before. The word **thing**, for example, one of the most basic words imaginable, had an original meaning far more nuanced than today. The general assembly of Iceland, the oldest parliament in Europe, was called the Althing, and most Scandinavian countries or their settlements, such as England prior to the Norman Conquests, gave that name to their assemblies, public meetings or legislative council. In Old English a 'thing' was a meeting or an assembly, such as a judicial assembly, court or council. By the year 1000 it was the case itself, a matter brought before a court of law. Then it became a cause or a reason, but even from 897 onwards it could mean 'that with which one is concerned'.

As long ago as the seventeenth century, the grammarian John Wallis (1616–1703) made the point that animals are English in life, but become French upon death.

Alive	Dead
ox, cow, calf, sheep,	beef, veal, mutton, pork,
swine, boar, deer	bacon, brawn and venison
(all Anglo-Saxon words)	(all loans from French)

The standard explanation for this duality is that the ordinary people were busy looking after the animals, so they used everyday terms to refer to them, while the nobility used their own language to describe what ended up on the table in front of them. The poor folk looked after the live animals and so named them in their own tongue, while the nobility got to eat them at banquets and feasts, and so named them in theirs; hence the split.

The list of French words that relate to cooking is huge, from **boil** and **fry**, to **sausage**, **soup** and **jelly**. 'To boil' – not to be confused with the impeccably Old English 'suppurating tumour' sort of boil – means 'to pass from liquid into a gaseous state' and has been around since at least the early thirteenth century. And **toast** comes from the French *toster*, meaning 'to roast' or 'grill'. The humble **breakfast** is English. The more sumptuous **dinner** and **supper** – as well as 'feast' – are loans from French.

Anglo-Norman, the French which the first invader barons spoke, eventually died out, to be replaced by a more courtly, Paris-influenced French. But the linguistic hierarchy maintained itself, with French still being used by the upper classes, and Anglo-Saxon or Old English words with approximately the same meaning being used by those lower down the social scale. In fact, almost the entire class system of aristocratic Britain was imported from France, including many of the titles (see page 49). It also gave us words for the sorts of behaviour that might be expected in such an environment, such as **courteous**, **noble** and **refined** (from the French *raffiner*).

The Old French word *dangier* means the sovereignty of a *dominus* or 'lord', so if you wrote in 1450 'I am gretly yn your danger', that meant you were at someone else's disposal. Although it had existed as early as 1225, the word evolved during the fourteenth century to mean the 'power to inflict damage'. A 1611 translation of the Book of *Matthew* talks about being 'In danger of the judgment', with the sense of 'liability', but within the same decade (1300–10) the word is capable of meaning any of a dozen slightly different things. Not until William Caxton became the first person to set up a printing press in England in 1476 (and thereby began to standardize language) does **danger** come to mean 'exposed to peril', and later the peril itself. The new rulers became the new generals too. The words **war** and **peace** are from French, as are 'battle', 'arms', 'officer', 'soldier', 'navy', 'lieutenant' and 'sergeant'.

In the earliest version of the poem *Sir Gawain and the Green Knight*, dating from around 1400, the English is as follows:

> *And alle his **vesture** verayly watz clene **verdure**,*
> And all his clothing truly was completely green,

*Both the **barres** of his belt and other blythe stones,*
  Both the bars of his belt and other bright gems,
*That were richely **rayled** in his aray clene*
  That were richly arranged in his elegant dress
Aboutte himself and his sadel, upon silk werkez
  About himself and his saddle, upon silk embroidery
*That were to tor for to telle of **trifles** the halue*
  That were too hard for to tell of details the half
*That were **enbrauded** abof, with bryddes and flyzes,*
  That were embroidered upon it, with birds and flies,
*With **gay gaudi** of grene, the golde ay inmyddes.*
  With bright verdant hue of green, the gold always in the
  middle.

A comparison of these two extracts shows that the English poem contains numerous words deriving from French: **clothing** (*vesture*), **truly** (*verayly*), **green** (*verdure*), **bars** (*barres*), **arranged** (*rayled*), **details** (*trifles*), **embroidered** (*enbrauded*), **bright** (*gay*), **verdant hue** (*gaudi*). What is interesting is that even though the translation has opted to take most of these words back into Anglo-Saxon, they live on in other forms, such as **vestments**, **verily**, **verdure**, **gay** and **gaudy**.

Words such as 'clergy', 'romance', 'sport', 'beauty' and 'authority', demonstrate the dominance of the French language in terms of power, religion and the arts in England at that time. And these words have continued to define British life and culture for centuries. The English word **mercy** and the French *merci* (thank you) both come from the early Latin *merces*, meaning 'payment' or 'wages', which by the sixth century came to mean 'pity', 'favour' or 'heavenly reward', and eventually 'thanks'. It is interesting that a word that started out with commercial overtones acquired religious connotations as life became more Christian, then once again became secular. In a more domestic context, the Old French *cloke* or *cloche* (**bell**) is the source of the word **cloak**, the two objects having a similar shape. The same word is also the root of the English word **clock**, when time was measured by the sound of a bell.

Virtue has a similarly intricate history. It began life as a manly sort of word derived from the Latin *vir* (**man**) and hence *virtudo* (**manliness**, valour, worth), and more specifically the power inherent in a supernatural being. Over the years it began to denote the idea of chivalry and 'a secular sense of moral attainment' at a time when the Church was the self-appointed guardian of all pastoral, intellectual and spiritual matters. Gradually, virtue became associated with honour and, eventually therefore, with maidenliness and virginity. The Latin word for 'man' had thus switched sexes in English, and had now become specifically associated with women.

But it was with the adoption of classical Latin words that Middle English became a truly expressive medium. During the fourteenth and sixteenth centuries, Latin words, and Greek words that had been incorporated into Latin, flooded into the English language. With the start of the Renaissance (a revival of art and learning according to classical models) in fourteenth-century Europe, the vocabularies of the various European languages exploded across the Continent, and English was particularly receptive to them. Having already adopted many French words, England showed little resistance to adopting other foreign words. It isn't always clear whether words such as **consolation**, **solid**, **infidel** and **infernal** came direct from Latin or were imported via French.

Streamlining

As Middle English accelerated away from its Alfredian roots, its grammar changed too. Although our concern here is not with grammatical developments, it is worth looking very briefly at the effects of these changes. One was that the English language began to lose its inflections. These are the endings that every verb or noun required in Latin and Greek, and without which their meaning is lost. It is generally considered that this process began when the British started trading with the Anglo-Saxons and they needed to be able to understand each other quickly. It didn't really matter if you got the wrong ending; as long as you picked the right root noun or verb, everyone could understand you, so word endings began to disappear. Suddenly, English grammar was relatively easy. Non-native speakers could do business even if they got their words in the wrong order – people knew what they meant and that was the main thing. English had become a language of communication rather than perfection, and this was to add an important new dimension to its history.

Compared to the grammar of most other European languages, English grammar is a model of simplicity, and this gives our words much greater mobility. If you were to ask what part of speech the word **work** is, the answer could be any of the following:

> **Verb:** 'I work very hard.'
> **Noun:** 'I love my work.'
> **Adjective:** 'The meeting was work-related.'

The flexibility that the single word form offers to English users is immensely valuable. In previous ages three separate spellings would have been needed to reflect the word's different role within each sentence. Those spellings were therefore liberated, and free to be used in more creative ways.

There are whole categories of words that can be used in two if not three ways. Somehow, English has liberated many words from their original meanings and given them functions that are subtly different from their strict application as nouns. Take one group of words: animals. People have been **taking their dogs for a walk** since the year 1050, and they have been **dogged by scandal** since before Shakespeare – 1519 is the earliest citation in the *OED*. The media can **hound** a celebrity to distraction (usage first recorded 1528), or a chess player could be **foxed** (1611) during a game. Some people **parrot** what they hear (1596), and in 1632 Philip Massinger asked, 'Why should you **ape** the fashions of court-ladies?'

Similarly, many parts of the body can also be used as verbs:

To arm (1205)	**To thumb** (1593)
To shoulder (*c.*1300)	**To elbow** (1605)
To head (*c.*1300, originally to decapitate)	**To hand** (1610)
To eye (1583)	**To stomach** (1523, originally to be offended)

This usage, which is called 'conversion', lent ever greater flexibility to English language writers, but this would be anathema[2] to a Greek or Latin scholar since classical language is all about rigidity of grammar. There are, of course, many Latin words that have been retained in their original forms – **gratis**, **genius**, **prima facie**, **et cetera**, **memento** and **limbo** – unlike

---

2 A Greek word, originally meaning 'Anything accursed, or consigned to damnation' (1526).

those earlier words – cheese, wine, pound and inch – that were refashioned and partially de-Latinized. Thousands of other words show what linguists call **assimilation** (a Latin word). **Allegory**, for example, from the Greek *allegoria*[3], entered English via Latin. The Venerable Bede described Britons at one point as a *perfida gens* when they refused to accept the teachings of St Augustine. **Perfidious** entered the language in the second half of the sixteenth century, when it meant 'deliberately faithless; basely treacherous' and led to the eighteenth century phrase 'Perfidious Albion', of which, no doubt, Bede would have approved.

Geoffrey Chaucer

The poet Geoffrey Chaucer (*c*.1342–1400) is notable for his sensitivity to the different registers of Middle English. The beauty of his language was that while he drew primarily from native words, he could also plunder French or Latin words when required. Proof of his popularity is that he was the first commoner ever to be buried in Westminster Abbey. His wit was admired by all the educated classes, despite the fact that his verse was plugged with profane and obscene words: **fart**, **arse**, **piss**, **shit**, **queynte** (cunt) and **swive** (an old version of 'fuck', see Chapter 9). Chaucer was sensitive to changes in language ('*and wordes tho / That hadden prys, now wonder nyce and straunge / Us thinketh hem*"...and words which previously had prestige, now seem odd and unfamiliar to us' – *Troilus and Criseyde*, Book II, 21–4), and his was one of the last voices of Middle English, but he was also one of the first writers in the language to use the various

---

3 *Allegoria* ('speaking otherwise than one seems to speak') – *allos* (other) and *agoria* (speaking).

registers of it selectively to create mood and character. He understood that the newly formed, hybrid English could now reach a range of expressions that would have been previously unimaginable. He uses words such as **governaunce** and **plesaunce**, which had only just joined the English language, while also managing to incorporate French borrowings and, in the finest tradition of the new English language, simply made up words when he couldn't find anything suitable. He gave us **autumn**, **edifice** and **ignorant**, but he also took advantage of the sheer fluidity of the English language and its new grammatical flexibility to experiment with words like 'beblot', 'achatour' and 'acheck', which haven't survived the test of time quite so well. Chaucer knew that he could bend the language almost any way he liked and his audience would simply enjoy it more.

It was also true that a variety of words in southern English would still not be comprehensible to someone in the north of the country, and in 'The Reeve's Tale' Chaucer becomes the first-known Englishman to ridicule a northern accent in writing. 'Ham' says the character when he means 'home', 'gang' for 'gone' and 'na' for 'no'. The wealthy southerner's mockery of the rustic northerner had begun, and confidence in the use of English as a medium of expression was running high. Despite his mocking of the comic north, Chaucer was particularly concerned that everyone in his native country should be able to read or understand what he had written, despite the immense regional diversities in the language. His final words in Troilus and Criseyde were the rather tremulous:

> *And for there is so gret diversite*
> *In Englissh and in writyng of our tonge,*
> *So prey I God that non miswryte thee…*

The fifty remaining handwritten copies of *The Canterbury Tales* attest to the fact that Chaucer was well known during his lifetime; even the future King Richard III was familiar with his work. *The Canterbury Tales* has been in print constantly ever since the first two editions produced by Caxton at the end of the fifteenth century, and it would, no doubt, have alleviated Chaucer's fears to know that a mere hundred years after his death the elements of the language had come together to such an extent that they were more or less recognizable as modern English.

Chapter two

Dr Johnson's Big Idea

*W*e are surrounded by dictionaries these days. You can buy a
dictionary of just about anything, from insults to Igbo,[1]
but 250 years ago the choices were not quite so broad.
Dictionaries[2] tell us a great deal about how language is evolving.
The process is continuing today, and, if anything, is happening
faster than ever.

The publication of a dictionary is a rite of passage for a
language, and English was no exception. For centuries the English
language had been a snotty-nosed child, running around the room
shouting anything that sounded funny. It had taken massive
liberties with spelling, and if you had asked it for the etymology of
a particular word, it would have stared at you as if you were mad.
But with the passing into print of the first dictionaries, a different
mood set in. Those early lexicographers must have surveyed the
mess and decided that enough was enough.

Dictionaries proper are of two kinds: they either translate

----

1 One of the languages of southern Nigeria.
2 Dictionary, *n.* 1. a. A book dealing with the individual words of a language
(or certain specified classes of them), so as to set forth their orthography,
pronunciation, signification, and use, their synonyms, derivation, and
history, or at least some of these facts. First recorded use 1526.

from one language to another, or they define words within the language itself. The second category is the more recent.

Given the reputation of the English language, you might have thought that Britain would have taken to dictionaries as willingly as it embraced hearty breakfasts, dogs and imperialism. In fact, compared to our Continental cousins, Britain was a bit slow off the mark. Even though there were some 642 books known as dictionaries in print before 1746, the standard was, at best, questionable. One of the more authoritative efforts was A *Table Alphabeticall of Hard Usual English Words*, written (or, more accurately, compiled) by a schoolteacher called Robert Cawdrey. Published in 1604, it contained 2521 'headwords' or main word entries, and is considered the first single-language dictionary ever to be written in English.

Many more compilers were prompted to follow Cawdrey in drawing up a guide for 'Ladies, gentlewomen, or any other unskilfull persons', in which were gathered and explained the mass of strange or 'hard' words that literature, science, medicine and the arts were introducing into the language. Cawdrey also wrote about 'far journied gentlemen' coming home from their travels who then 'pouder their talke with over-sea language'. It may have been in response to this that the dictionary was written.

Despite his pioneering work, some of Cawdrey's definitions don't quite pass muster. His definition of **allude** as 'to speake one thing that hath resemblance and respect to another' is masterful, but would the explanation of 'allegation' as 'alleging' have shed much light? Among other dictionary-makers, simple definition proved even more elastic, with one defining **dog** as 'a common animal, known to all'. That definition, inadequate though it is, goes to the heart of the difficulty in compiling a dictionary. How do you define a dog? (See Chapter 1, page 43.) The idea must have seemed impossible to most people. Why should anyone need to define a dog, for goodness' sake? You'd know what a dog was even if you'd never been bitten by one.

But as lexicography took shape, people began to feel that a word was not properly dressed unless it had been defined, or **spelled**, or perhaps we should say 'spelt', since the issue of a universal spelling model arose after William Caxton brought the printing press to Britain in 1476 and the paths of written and spoken English began to diverge. In speech, most people from the same area pronounced **wife** (see Chapter 1, page 45) the same way, but it could be spelled – and frequently was – as either 'wyf' or 'wif'. The same goes for **little**, which could be written 'lytyl' or 'lityl', or 'good' as 'goode'. It was the emergence of printing that created a need for a standard, but not necessarily simplified, system of spelling words.

As to the other function of a dictionary – once we know what a word is, we can also say what it isn't. We can prise apart words with related meanings – **fierce** and **savage**, for example. How do they differ? A dictionary makes us think hard about the job that words do. It is also a form of word census: by naming the words in use, you also count them.

Across the Channel, other countries were doing just that. The Accademia della Crusca, which is still the national language academy of Italy, was the first such institution in Europe, and the first (in 1612) to produce a record of the words then in use in its national language. The Académie Française, created by Cardinal Richelieu under Louis XIII in 1635, was charged with 'defining the French language'. The French language police are still at it. In July 2003, concerned that the English word **email** was becoming too widespread in the French tongue, they chose the Québécois word *courriel* instead. It is now government policy that this be used.

Wish them luck, or read about their progress online, on what the French, with impeccable spelling, refer to as '*un blogue*'.

The Italian and French efforts at recording their languages – the *Vocabolario* and the *Dictionnaire* respectively – were nothing if not thorough. Each was the product of intense scholarship. The French, for example, used an army of forty word-pickers, who agreed the spelling for 5000 words – around a quarter of the words then in use. By contrast, Cawdrey had produced just over 2500. Both the French and Italian dictionaries were bigger than ours. Clearly, something had to be done.

It is somehow appropriate – and very British – that the work that came to represent the best of British lexical scholarship was cobbled together in eight years, on the cheap, in a rush, and was largely the work of one man with five or six helpers. And yet it was immediately acclaimed as a work of genius, and still is to this day.

Another virtue of a dictionary is that it represents a contemporary snapshot[3] of the language – overlooking for now that the word snapshot did not come into common use until the latter half of the nineteenth century. It distinguishes between words that are in common usage, and words that are on the way out. In the process, it tells us a lot about who we are. And in eighteenth-century Britain, a lot of people were interested in finding out. The question was: who would do the best job?

Cometh the hour

Samuel Johnson (1709–84) defines **genius** as 'a man endowed with superior qualities'. He later defines **monster** as 'something

----

3 Snapshot, 1808: 'A quick or hurried shot taken without deliberate aim, esp. one at a rising bird or quickly moving animal.' 'An instantaneous photograph, esp. one taken with a hand-camera.'

out of the common order of nature'. In truth, he was better qualified than most to define those words, since he was both. Born in the Staffordshire town of Lichfield, which also gave us Erasmus Darwin, the polymathic grandfather of Charles, and, more recently, the M6 toll road, Johnson may not seem like an obvious choice for what is now regarded as one of literature's most serious and high-minded commissions. His father was a bookseller, and the young Samuel suffered from poor eyesight and trouble with his ears. A voracious reader, it was said that he 'tore the heart out of books', often handing them back to their owners badly mauled. After attending Lichfield Grammar School, where he was beaten repeatedly by John Hunter, the Latin master, he went up to Pembroke College, Oxford in 1728, but came down fourteen months later when his money ran out. Like many writers and journalists, financial crises came very easily to Samuel Johnson.

Arriving in London, he began to make friends with his impressive wit. Many of his verbal exchanges were collected by his trusty biographer James Boswell (1740–95), whose *Life of Samuel Johnson* (1791) extended to 1500 pages. Johnson was a grandiose, clubbable man, dining with other heroes of the age, such as the great actor David Garrick, whom, incidentally, Johnson had taught at the school he founded in Edial near Lichfield. In 1764 Johnson helped found the Club, later renamed the Literary Club, whose members included other A-list[4] writers, such as Edmund Burke and Adam Smith.

In company, Johnson was vastly entertaining, with enormous

----

4 **A-list**, *n*. 1. The first in a series of lists, esp. lists ranked in order of preference or significance. (1890). 2. *n*. orig. *U.S. A*ny (notional) list comprising only the most celebrated, sought-after, or high-ranking individuals, esp. in the entertainment industry or the media; a social, professional, or celebrity elite.

social stamina and the endless curiosity of the self-taught intellectual. But he also drank more than was wise, wore himself out with late-night carousing, and suffered frequent bouts of depression, especially during the course of his not-often-consummated marriage to the ailing Tetty. Hard-working and meticulous, from 1738 onwards he had contributed to almost every edition of a publication called the *Gentleman's Magazine*, writing foreign and domestic news and book reviews. These articles had gone down well in literary London, establishing him as a man of letters whose scholarship was beyond doubt.

He received another step up towards his great challenge when, in 1740, he was employed by a bookseller called Thomas Osborne, who had paid the vast sum of £13,000 to buy the library of Robert and Edward Harley, the first and second Earls of Oxford. The library contained 50,000 books, 250,000 pamphlets and 7000 volumes of manuscripts. Johnson worked alongside Edward Harley's personal librarian, William Oldys, and the two men produced a catalogue of the collection. According to another of his biographers, Sir John Hawkins (1719–89), 'while he was engaged in so servile an employment [he] resembled a lion in harness'.

Osborne was not terribly interested in reading the books he had bought, but he had a shrewd idea that they might fetch him some cash. Johnson and Oldys busied themselves in documenting the thousands of volumes being put up for public sale. In fact, the auction itself was a disappointment, but Johnson must have been able to study just about every important dictionary that European scholars had produced until then. Of the many lessons Johnson learnt, one was that a proper English dictionary ought to illustrate its definitions with quotations so that readers could see the context in which a word had been used. Second was the good lexicographical habit of arranging words into 'headwords' by taking a main word and then giving its various definitions. If it sounds surprising that anyone should not have organized a dictionary in that way, bear in mind that most dictionaries until then were not arranged in alphabetical order, and that some were alphabetized only by the first two letters of each word.

His career and ambition were both advancing equally when he was approached by a small committee of publishers and booksellers, and asked if he would undertake to compile – though Johnson preferred to use the verb 'write' – a dictionary of the English language. In three years. The committee members' motives were varied, but all agreed that its main purpose was to standardize the language. English was becoming unregulated: it was time to bring it into line. The historian of the Royal Society, Thomas Sprat, had expressed a wish to see a 'mathematical plainness' about the language. Gentlemen also tabled their desire to guard 'propriety' against the advance of 'elegance'.

Some felt or hoped that the dictionary would prevent slippage of the tongue. Already the language of Chaucer was almost unrecognizable to some speakers, and the writer and essayist Alexander Pope (1688–1744) was not the first to voice the fear that if steps were not taken, his books might be incomprehensible to future generations. So self-interest played a part in bringing about the work. The enthusiasts knew that it would be their writings that would benefit most directly from the coverage. When Johnson defined the word **opulence**,[5] for

5 Opulence – defined by Dr Johnson as 'Wealth; riches; affluence', 'There in full opulence a banker dwelt,/Who all the joys and pangs of riches felt;/His sideboard glitter'd with imagin'd plate,/And his proud fancy held a vast estate.' (Swift)

example, he added an illustrative quotation from the works of Jonathan Swift, the creator of *Gulliver's Travels*. Even though the two men had their differences, Swift must have been delighted to see himself thus **name-checked**.[6] The branding opportunities were almost endless.

To most learned minds, the Latin dictionary was the main source of reference for English words; they found nothing odd in seeking definitions of English words in Latin. Indeed, Latin was a valuable reference point for writers, since spoken Latin was a finite entity and could thus be studied under a microscope.[7] Johnson, though, rejected Latin as being insufficiently inclusive. He wrote his dictionary in English, though he agreed that the English language should be purged of 'solecisms and improprieties, and made as unchanging and authoritative as Latin'.

One by one, the country's top writers had lent their weight to the idea of a new national dictionary. For the former poet laureate John Dryden (1631–1700), a dictionary would restrain some writers who 'corrupt our English idiom by mixing it too much with French'. Johnson's approach would have pleased Dryden, as he wrote in the preface that he had taken the decision not to include any proper names, nor foreign words that any authors may have introduced through 'ignorance of their own, by vanity or wantonness, by compliance with fashion, or just of innovation…'

The great essayist Daniel Defoe (1660–1731), author of *Robinson Crusoe* and *Moll Flanders*, traveller, dissident, satirist

----

6 Name-check, v. trans. To mention or acknowledge by name. 1986 City Limits 16 Oct. 42 'Namechecking The Cat In The Hat gets you no hipster points at all once the club has closed down.'

7 Microscope – defined by Dr Johnson as 'An optick instrument, contrived various ways to give to the eye a large appearance of many objects which could not otherwise be seen.' (Attested from 1651)

and failed civet-breeder, had in 1697 condemned the proliferation of lewd terms. Johnson doubtless agreed with him. There is no **fuck** in the dictionary, nor **cunt**, **shit** or **wanker**. We are permitted a discreet **fart** ('Wind from behind'), as well as the respectable **piss** (it's in the Bible) and **bum**, **arse** and **turd** (which aren't). But there is no room for **penis** or **vagina**.

Johnson was offered £1575 to write the dictionary. As his annual income at the time was £100, much of it swallowed up on medical bills and opium for poor Tetty, a grand and a half was a fortune (and still more than some publishers pay their authors 250 years later). Johnson signed the contract on 18 June 1746. Then, in true writer's style, he blew much of the cash by moving his wife and servants into a comfortable, three-storeyed house in Gough Square, off Fleet Street, and settled down to his task.

One up on the French

Around the time that Johnson embarked on his labours, he had an exchange with the Revd Dr William Adams, the former master of his old college. 'This is a great work, Sir,' said Adams. 'But how can you do this in three years?' Johnson replied that he was confident that he could. 'But,' said Adams, pressing him, 'the French Academy, which consists of forty members, took forty years to compile their dictionary.'

Johnson's reply is a classic of its kind, and one that should not be repeated south of Dover. 'Sir, thus it is. This is the proportion. Let me see; forty times forty is sixteen hundred. As three to sixteen hundred, so is the proportion of an Englishman to a Frenchman.'

Johnson's working methods were scrupulous, and he hired six fact-checkers. The work must have been tiring, for Johnson throws us a playful hint of this when he gives an example to define the word **dull**: 'To make dictionaries is dull work'. And yet he was passionate about it. When he had finished the work, he wrote in the preface that 'The English dictionary was written with little assistance of the learned, and without any patronage of the great; not in the soft obscurities of retirement, or under the shelter of academic bowers, but amidst inconvenience and distraction, in sickness and sorrow.' It sounds almost like 'in sickness and in health'. For those years, it must have seemed to Johnson as if he were married to the English language.

Boswell described the great man's working methods, though the two men did not meet until after the dictionary had been published, by which time Johnson's reputation was secure. His own library had proved inadequate, so he begged and borrowed volumes from booksellers or friends. This supply of goodwill began to erode when the volumes were returned in a generally worse state than they had been received. On one occasion, for example, his friend Garrick lent him his very rare quarto edition of Shakespeare. When Johnson returned it, it had been torn to shreds.

Johnson began by consulting and rewriting entries in existing dictionaries. But at some point he changed his approach, and instead sought out individual works of literature. It was from these that he assembled his list of words, which he then defined. He marked vertical lines against passages that he wanted to cite, underlined in black lead pencil the word that each passage was illustrating, and wrote in the margin the letter of the word. Then one of his trusty amanuenses would copy out the relevant passage and score through the letter to indicate that it had been included. When friends objected to finding marks in their books, Johnson is said to have claimed that they could remove the marks by rubbing them with breadcrumbs.

The struggle to finish

It was not long before Johnson began to run out of money. Of the various members of the nobility who were tapped with a view to providing funds, the most promising was Philip Dormer Stanhope, fourth Earl of Chesterfield, with whom Johnson enjoyed reasonably good relations. In August 1747 Johnson published his *Plan of an English Dictionary*. This was his manifesto in which he set out his credentials and his aims for the work. It was also intended to warn off anyone else who was considering something similar; this would give Johnson more time in which to complete his work, which, it was now clear, would not be completed within the three-year deadline. The new lexicographer sought to challenge the foundations of previous works. He criticized the lack of authority in the selections and definitions of words in existing dictionaries, and announced his ambition to standardize the spelling and pronunciation of words. The dictionary's 'chief intent', he wrote, must be 'to preserve the purity, and ascertain the meaning of our English idiom'.

A dedicatory note to Lord Chesterfield praised the Earl's 'vicarious jurisdiction'. In describing his aims for the dictionary, he promised to select 'words and phrases used in the general intercourse of life, or found in the works of those whom we commonly style polite writers'. He goes on, 'My idea of an English dictionary [is one] by which the pronunciation of our language may be fixed, and its attainment facilitated; by which its purity may be preserved, its use ascertained, and its duration lengthened.' Johnson seemed to believe that he was ensuring the very survival of the English language.

Noting the illogical way in which **fox** and **ox** become **foxes** and **oxen** in the plural, he acknowledges that 'English poses some peculiarly stubborn problems.' Among the most intractable are an irregular spelling system, which only began to be standardized in the fifteenth century. Twenty-first-century foreign language students may share with eighteenth-century lexicographers a sense of shell shock (see Chapter 8, page 212) at our profusion of synonyms. We also have numerous examples of polysemy, a word which could net you an extra fifty points if used judiciously during a game of Scrabble, but which means 'the phenomenon of a single word with numerous meanings', as in 'bear' (to carry) and 'bear' (large, hugging, furry animal).

The *Plan* was published and immediately provoked a storm of interest from critics. Johnson was encouraged by this, but his funds were running low, so he went to see his patron, Lord Chesterfield. Unfortunately, in one of those administrative cock-ups that persist to this day, the noble lord was out when Johnson called, and thus unable to advance him the cash. Johnson did not take this well. To make things worse, some months before the dictionary was about to be published, Chesterfield wrote a rather insipid endorsement of Johnson's efforts, languidly stating that 'I hereby declare, that I make a total surrender of all my rights and privileges in the English language, as a free-born British subject, to the said Mr Johnson, during the term of his dictatorship'.

The gesture was not appreciated. Johnson fumed to a friend, 'I have sailed a long and painful voyage round the world of the English language; and does he now send out two **cock-boats**[8] to tow me into harbour?' On 7 February 1755 he composed and sent a letter to Lord Chesterfield that, even now, makes one wish

---

8 Cock-boat – a small ship's boat, esp. the small boat that is often towed behind a coasting vessel or ship going up or down river. Often used typically as the smallest or lightest of floating craft.

the floor could open up and let the unfortunate peer disappear inside it.

> Seven years, My Lord, have now past since I waited in your outward rooms or was repulsed from your door, during which time I have been pushing on my work through difficulties of which it is useless to complain, and have brought it at last to the verge of publication without one act of assistance, one word of encouragement, or one smile of favour. Such treatment I did not expect, for I never had a patron before…
>
> Is not a patron, My Lord, one who looks with unconcern on a man struggling for life in the water and when he has reached ground encumbers him with help? The notice which you have been pleased to take of my labours, had it been early, had been kind; but it has been delayed till I am indifferent and cannot enjoy it, till I am solitary and cannot impart it, till I am known and do not want it.

When his dictionary came out, the word **patron** was defined as 'one who countenances, supports, or protects. Commonly a wretch who supports with insolence, and is paid with flattery.' Patronage cuts two ways.

A warm reception

The first, two-volume edition of Dr Johnson's *Dictionary* was published in 1755. The title-page reads: 'A Dictionary of the English Language: in which the words are deduced from their originals, and illustrated in their different significations by examples from the best writers.' It seems obvious these days, but back then it was still novel to define a word by tracing it back to its first verifiable example. Even more, to source each word by citing an example from the body of literature was revolutionary for its time.

'It is the fate of those who toil at the lower employments of life, to be rather driven by the fear of evil, than attracted by the prospect of good, to be exposed to censure, without hope of praise, to be disgraced by miscarriage, or punished for neglect, where success would have been without applause, and diligence without reward.' So begins the preface to Johnson's *Dictionary*. Long on commas, short on full stops, it reveals the extraordinary combination of swagger and self-pity that defined its author. Johnson continues:'Among these unhappy mortals is the writer of dictionaries; whom mankind have considered, not as the pupil, but the slave of science, the pioneer of literature, doomed only to remove rubbish and clear obstructions from the paths of Learning and Genius…'

Removing rubbish from the paths of Learning and Genius. If the task demanded the skills of a thoroughly professional street-cleaner, it was lucky for the English language that Johnson had been born with a broom in his mouth. We do not know the full list of all the authors that he consulted, though he made no secret of his admiration for the Bible, Shakespeare, Pope and William Law (1686–1761). Quotations abound, though some contain slight inaccuracies, which suggests that Johnson swottishly inserted them from memory without bothering to double-check. But he must have used other dictionaries and encyclopedias. 'I have been cautious lest my zeal for antiquity might drive me into times too remote, and croud [*sic*] my book with words now no longer understood,' writes Johnson, justifying his decision not to search too far back in history. He decided to go no further than the works of the poet Sir Philip Sidney (1554–86), who died in Holland, aged a mere thirty-two, but achieved immortality through works such as the *Arcadia* and his *Defence of Poetry* – and through being Johnson's **back-stop**.[9]

Johnson's *Dictionary* may have provided the basis for all subsequent works, but it also differs significantly from them. For one thing, Johnson himself is a constant presence, often using the word 'I' in a manner that would never be tolerated today. The noun **spot** is defined first as 'a blot', then as 'a taint'. For the third definition, Johnson writes: 'I know not well the meaning of spot in this place, unless it be a scandalous woman, a disgrace to her sex.' Johnson had no editor but himself. His five Scottish researchers were unable to prevent him defining the word **oats** as 'a grain, which in England is generally given to horses, but in Scotland supports people'.

Johnson was sending himself up when he defined **lexicographer** as 'a harmless drudge' (see Introduction, page 18). Drudge he may have been, but he was no slouch. He and his team produced some 42,773 definitions, with approximately 110,000 quotations to back them up. Not quite the whole language: the letter X was ignored on the grounds that 'X is a letter, which, though found in Saxon words, begins no word in the English language'. **Bourgeois** and **champagne**, being foreign words, suffered a similar fate: besides, Johnson was always more of a 'port' man. His entries are also notably scant on areas in which he was less than interested: the word **sonata**, for example, is dismissed merely as 'a tune'. He acknowledged the efforts of scholars such as Francis Junius (1589–1677) and Stephen Skinner (1623–67) for their work on 'Teutonick' (German dialects),

---

9 Back-stop – originally a mound of earth or a now obsolete fielding position in cricket. First recorded use, *Suffolk Chronicle* 1819: 'They were deprived of two of their best bowlers, and a back-stop.' First figurative recorded use in *Lady Sings the Blues* (1956), the memoirs of Billie Holliday: 'Tony kept my job open. He offered to backstop me with the money I needed.'

though he was not exactly filled with praise for them.'Skinner is often ignorant, but never ridiculous,' he writes.'Junius is always full of knowledge; but his variety distracts his judgment, and his learning is very frequently disgraced by his absurdities.'

As an example, Johnson cites, with much derision, Junius's attempt to relate **dream** to **drama**, 'because life is a drama, and a drama is a dream'. Of his own (better) efforts, Johnson comments approvingly that 'My search, however, has been either skilful or lucky; for I have much augmented the vocabulary.' The book contained errors too, of course. Boswell noted that **windward** and **leeward** were both defined as 'towards the wind', and that **pastern**[10] was described as 'the knee of a horse'. When a woman once challenged Johnson as to how he could have made such a mistake, his reply was refreshingly forthright: 'Ignorance, Madam, pure ignorance.'

Given Johnson's character, some might have expected every page of his *Dictionary* to reflect his boisterous nature. In fact, he reins himself in. With his emphasis on usage, he starts with the most practical and accessible meaning before advancing towards the more far-flung or metaphorical. Words such as **cant**, **hypocrisy**, **judge** and **bookseller** – in which he might have let off a few fireworks – are defined with a straight face. Where derivations elude him, he confesses, 'I know not whence derived'. At other times, though, his caustic nature emerges. A **stockjobber** is described as 'a low wretch who gets money by buying and selling shares in the funds'. **Excise** is 'a hateful tax levied upon commodities, and adjudged not by the common judges of property, but wretches hired by those to whom excise

---

10 Pastern, pre-1400, though attested earlier in the now obsolete sense: 'A shackle attached to the foot of a pastured animal, esp. an unbroken horse.'

is paid'. A **fortune teller** is 'one who cheats common people by pretending to the knowledge of futurity'.

At times the *Dictionary* is a medical source book, which reflects the concerns of its time: **colick**, for instance, is accompanied by a 228-word description by John Quincy, a member of the Royal College of Physicians around 1721, which ends 'most commonly to be treated by nephriticks and oily diuretics, and is greatly assisted with the carminative turpentine injection in the anus'. Then again, he can sound almost tender when he defines **embryo** as 'the offspring yet unfinished in the womb'. See also, however, a **pessary**, defined as 'an oblong form of medicine made to thrust up into the uterus upon some extraordinary occasions'.

Author's quirks

Johnson's definitions and quotations tell us something of his political and religious views.

Leader: '4. One at the head of any party or faction: as the detestable Wharton was the leader of the Whigs.'

Popery: 'For corruptions in doctrine and discipline…the most absurd system of Christianity.' (Quotation from Swift)

Protestant: 'One of those who adhere to them, who, at the beginning of the reformation, protested against the errors of the Church of Rome.'

Royalist: 'The old Church of England royalists, another name for a man who prefers his conscience before his interests, are the most meritorious subjects in the world, having passed all those terrible tests, which domineering malice could put them to, and carried their credit and their conscience clear.'

Tory: 'One who adheres to the ancient constitution of the state, and the apostolical hierarchy of the Church of England, opposed to a Whig.'

Whig: 'The name of a faction.'

Spreading the words

Johnson congratulates himself for including a great many compound words formed with prefixes, such as **after**, **fore**, **new**, **night** or **fair**, for which, he says, 'I have endeavoured to make some reparation for the universal negligence of my predecessors'. At other times, thirty-three in all, he even quotes himself as source material for quotations. Some he labels, while others are ascribed to 'Anonymous'. One quotation, listed as Johnson, is actually lifted from Pope's *Essay on Man*, and another quotation seems to have been made up entirely. In his preface, Johnson is bracingly honest about the difficulties under which he laboured, and it is hard not to feel sympathy for him. Describing his undertaking 'to pierce deep into every science' and 'enquire the nature of every substance of which I inserted the name', he concludes with regret that 'these were the dreams of a poet doomed at last to wake a lexicographer'. With such words, he seems to be waving farewell to the body of work that he would leave behind, whether drama, fiction or biography. 'The work, whatever proofs of diligence and attention it may exhibit, is yet capable of many improvements,' writes Johnson. And yet he seems to have reconciled himself to the notion of change. Later, he writes:

> When we see men grow old and die at a certain time one after another, from century to century, we laugh at the elixir that promises to prolong life to a thousand years; and with equal justice may the lexicographer be derided, who being able to produce no example of a nation that has preserved their words and phrases from mutability, shall imagine that his dictionary can embalm his language, and secure it from corruption and decay...

There was no sign of corruption or decay in the language that he so famously delivered just over 250 years ago. Indeed, to judge from his inclusion of words such as **giglet** (a wanton), **fopdoodle** (a fool), **dandiprat** (an urchin) and **jobbernowl** (a blockhead), he may have sought out persons of questionable character, such as market traders or cardsharps, to discover the **chav** vocabulary of the times (see Chapter 5, pages 152-3).

There is also the famous story of Johnson being rebuked by two respectable old ladies for including obscenities in his *Dictionary*: 'Ah, my dears,' he teased, 'so you have been looking for them!'

The publication of Johnson's great work was an undoubted success. As James Boswell wrote thirty years later, 'The world contemplated with wonder so stupendous a work achieved by one man, while other countries had thought such undertakings fit only for whole academies.' Johnson was for a while able to bask in a certain amount of adulation. His friend David Garrick wrote a congratulatory poem to him in the *Public Advertiser*, which described Johnson as 'a hero of yore'. *The London Magazine* and his own *Gentleman's Magazine* – the latter across eight pages – were positively gushing. There were critics, including the economist Adam Smith, who felt that the *Dictionary* was insufficiently grammatical. But even he had to concede that 'when we compare this book with other dictionaries, the merit of its author appears very extraordinary'.

It had been Samuel Johnson's original intention to 'fix' the English language. In the process, however, he himself was, to some extent, 'fixed'. Inevitably, the book changed his life, turning him into a celebrity. His most recent biographer, Henry Hitchings, reports that whereas his name was being mentioned once or twice in the English press during the 1750s, by 1765 it was occurring between ten and fifteen times a month. Johnson went on to produce a valuable edition of the works of Shakespeare, and to take his place in London society as one of its most esteemed wits. He was given an honorary doctorate by Trinity College, Dublin in 1765, having only, and somewhat grudgingly, been awarded a retrospective degree by his old university (after much politicking by his friends) in 1755. His biographical work *The Lives of the English Poets* (1779–81) was his final literary achievement, but his *Dictionary* provoked dozens more to publish books on grammar, language and etymology. Johnson triggered a printing craze, and not just in Britain. His *Dictionary* was translated into French and German, and it was essential reading for lexicographers in the Netherlands, Sweden and Portugal. A friend of his called Giuseppe Baretti even modelled his own Italian dictionary of 1760 on Johnson's work.

In 1855, just over a hundred years after Johnson's *Dictionary* was published, the first moves were made towards compiling what would eventually become the *OED*. The first edition of the *OED* retained just over 2000 Johnsonian quotations, which were marked (J.). As part of the ongoing revision of the *Dictionary* for its third edition (currently underway), the accuracy of each one of Dr Johnson's literary quotations is being checked, just in case the good doctor's pen – or imagination – might have got the better of him. On its website, the *OED* notes that its own first edition made considerable use of Johnson's *Dictionary of the English Language*, quoting at length both from the first and from subsequent editions. 'These were accepted on Johnson's authority, but we are now checking the quotations in their original sources,' states the *OED*, quietly acknowledging that not all of Johnson's 708 quotations are equally reliable. The *OED* editors have once again asked the British public for their help in tracing quotations. So far, it has been a huge success: at the last count, only nineteen quotations remained to be identified (see box, page 80).

A volume of Johnson's *Dictionary* was famously flung through a shop window in Chiswick by an outraged Becky Sharp in Thackeray's *Vanity Fair* (published 1847–8). References to it appear in Laurence Sterne's *Tristram Shandy* (1759–67), Elizabeth Gaskell's *Wives and Daughters* (1866) and Herman Melville's *Moby Dick* (1851), and in several works by Charles Dickens, Wilkie Collins and Jane Austen.

Compared to Johnson's *Dictionary*, most modern lexicographies are sober, severe, maybe a trifle bloodless. Johnson's book, into which he poured so much of his legendary energy, is a work of literature in itself, and a revealing commentary on his own times, which is ironic, given Professor John Carey's description of him as 'the only famous writer who is better known for what he said than for what he wrote'. More than 250 years after it first appeared, Johnson's *Dictionary* remains a publishing phenomenon. It also contains a great deal more jokes than its French or Italian counterparts.

Are they accurate?

Here are some quotes from Johnson's *Dictionary* for which The *OED* is seeking verification. Can you help? (The 'a' before some dates is for *'ante'* – 'before')

1. **1727** J. Arbuthnot, *Tables Anc. Coins*, The Romans had the art of gilding … but some sort of their inauration, or gilding, must have been much dearer than ours.

2. **a1626** Bacon, The chymists have a liquor called water of depart.

3. **a1682** Sir T. Browne, The fullest good … the most beatifying of all others.

4. **1651** Ld. Digby, *To Sir K. Digby*, The slightest part that you excel in is courtliness.

5. **a1714** Geddes, In some monasteries the severity of the Clausure is hard to be born.

6. **a1676** M. Hale, Some will have these years to be but months … yet that reduction will not serve.

7. **a1661** B. Holyday, All that are recusants of holy rites.

8. **a1661** B. Holyday, In a superexaltation of courage, they seem as greedy of death as of victory.

9. **a1661** B. Holyday, Is it the purity of a linen vesture, which some so fear would defile the purity of the priest?

10. **a1640** H. Peacham, A blue stone they make haver or oatcakes upon.

11. **?a1602** W. Perkins, If a man be lopping a tree and his ax-head fall from the helve…and kills another passing by; here is indeed manslaughter, but no voluntary murther.

12. **a1700** Salmon, The pine-apple is one of the tropical fruits.

13. **a1586** Sir P. Sidney, Euryalus taking leave of Lucretia, precipitated her into such a love-fit, that within a few hours she ghosted.

14. **a1698** W. Temple, A lady said of her two companions, that one was more amiable, the other more estimable.

15. **c.1675** A. Walker, The two great aims which every institutor of youth should mainly and intentionally drive at.

16. **?16..** White, It is not an idol ratione termini, in respect of termination; for the religious observation thereof is referred … to the honour of God and Christ.

17. **1676** R. Wiseman, *Several Chirurgicall Treat.*, Either anasarcous or ascitical.

18. **a1728** J. Woodward, A*ttempt Nat. Hist. Fossils*, Another was very perfect…and more sinuated.

19. **1711–14** *Spectator*, He carves, displays, and cuts up to a wonder.

Chapter Three

From 0800 Number to Zyxt

*T*he following paragraph contains some recent additions to the grandest literary project currently being undertaken in the English language:

> I'm having a **bad hair day**. I was **surfing** in this **chat room** and when I **logged on** I got a load of **spam**, and it's, like, **24/7**, what is wrong with you? And there was this **webcam**, some guy was giving it the **full monty** and I thought, I don't know, this really makes me feel **cyberphobic**. But then, **doh**! Time's up.

Meet some of the new recruits to *The Oxford English Dictionary*, the ongoing publication that is, according to the Oxford University Press, 'the accepted authority on the evolution of the English language over the last millennium.' The word 'doh' is defined as 'expressing frustration at the realization that things have turned out badly or not as planned, or that one has just said or done something foolish', which pretty well fits how Homer Simpson uses it in the cartoon series that spawned him. The *OED* adds: 'also (usu. mildly derogatory): implying that another person has said or done something foolish'. This illustrates, in a nutshell, what the *OED* does. It watches, notes, quotes and defines. It can take years for a word to be accorded recognition, but when, in

July 2001, the *OED* added such phrases as **acid jazz**, **zero tolerance** and **snail mail** to its pages, it was the official sign that they had passed into the language.

The *OED*, which currently begins with an entry for **0800 number**, is a true twenty-first-century creature, but it was once a grand Victorian project. It did not, however, begin in Oxford. By the mid-1850s, the jaunty, even somewhat pompous, self-assuredness of Dr Johnson's *Dictionary* was no longer appropriate for a more scholarly age. In June 1857, three linguists – Herbert Coleridge, Frederick Furnivall and the Rev. Richard Chenevix Trench, Dean of Westminster – all frustrated with the dictionaries of English then available, formed an 'Unregistered Words Committee' under the auspices of the London Philological Society, and, with the help of a few dozen other interested scholars, set about identifying the words and meanings that even the best of the dictionaries then available failed to cover. Before their findings could be reported to the society, however, Trench delivered two devastating papers on the subject of 'Some Deficiencies in Our English Dictionaries', eloquently setting out the true nature of the problem under seven headings:

> Incomplete coverage of obsolete words
> Inconsistent coverage of families of related words
> Incorrect dates for earliest use of words
> History of obsolete senses of words often omitted
> Inadequate distinction between synonyms
> Insufficient use of good illustrative quotations
> Space wasted on inappropriate or redundant content

The challenge of addressing these problems could best be tackled, Trench argued, with the help of the public. He envisaged a vast army of readers combing the pages of all the available published works, searching for quotations to back up definitions, just as the German reading public had done for the brothers Grimm – Jacob and Wilhelm – with their dauntingly authoritative *Deutsches Wörterbuch*, a dictionary that they had produced in 1852 when they weren't trawling for their other obsession: folk tales such as 'Rapunzel', 'Hansel and Gretel' and 'Rumpelstiltskin'. Once again, it was keeping up with our Continental cousins that stung the British into action.

Within a few weeks of Trench's papers, the Philological Society decided to widen the scope of the project enormously: the aim was now to collect evidence not merely for words previously 'unregistered' by other dictionaries, but for *all* the words of the English language, past and present. Readers would be encouraged to copy out passages that illustrated the actual uses of certain words, and to send these quotation slips to the editor. The work would be called A *New English Dictionary* (*NED*), and it amounted to a call for a complete re-examination of the language from Anglo-Saxon times onward.

The new dictionary would comprise four volumes and 6400 pages. It would include all the English language vocabulary from Early Middle English (AD 1150) to the present day, as well as any earlier words that earned a place. The dictionary's supporters were confident that the task could be completed in ten years. That, it soon emerged, was somewhat naive.

Founding fathers

The Rev. Richard Chenevix Trench was central to the project in its infancy, but he had a calling, and his ecclesiastical sense of duty took him to Dublin. Instead, Herbert Coleridge, grandson of the poet Samuel Taylor Coleridge, became the dictionary's first editor. A brilliant man, full of radical ideas, he published his plan for the work on 12 May 1860. He wanted to divide the dictionary into three parts: one for common words, including **slang** and **Americanisms**; the second for technical and scientific terms; the third to consist of an etymological appendix.

Coleridge's home became the *NED*'s first editorial office. A grid of fifty-four pigeon-holes was arranged that could accommodate 100,000 quotation slips. In April 1861 the first sample pages of the dictionary were published. It would have been fascinating to see the rest of Herbert Coleridge's dictionary, but that hope – together with the three-part plan – was cut cruelly short when he died, aged only thirty-one, in 1861. As in life, his death owed much to his beloved Philological Society, since he had attended a meeting after having been caught in a downpour. A chill set in and turned to consumption, from which he did not recover. He never stopped working, though. His last words were said to be, 'I must begin Sanskrit tomorrow'.

The mantle of editor passed to Frederick Furnivall, then aged thirty-six. He was a great linguist and passionate about language, but lacked the grafting temperament needed for such a job. Furnivall took his eye off the ball, frequently resting it instead on an ever-increasing number of highbrow, literature-related societies, and on an army of young female admirers, whom he cultivated with great energy. For a while, the project began to founder. He was not good at keeping in touch with his assistants, and some of them gave up on him, or assumed that the whole undertaking had run out of steam, or money, or both. Furnivall lost track of the whereabouts of hundreds of thousands of contributors' slips. One complete set of quotation slips for words starting with H was eventually traced to Florence, taken there by an American scholar who thought he would like to work on them there and in his house in the Tuscan hills. There were other close shaves. Q turned up in Loughborough and Pa in a stable in County Cavan, where some of the slips were assumed to be waste paper and burnt.

Furnivall also introduced a young man called Kenneth Grahame to the joys of rowing. This inspired Grahame to write his immortal tale of waterborne life, *The Wind in the Willows* (1908), about the friendship between a mole, a rat and a toad. Aged eighty-two, Furnivall, that ever-youthful, bright-eyed pedant – the inspiration for Grahame's Ratty – was still sculling up to 30km (20 miles) on the river every day.

Knowing that the *NED* could never come to fruition with himself at the helm, Furnivall approached some other scholarly men – Henry Sweet and Henry Nicol – in the 1870s, but they said no. Finally, though, in 1879, the Philological Society struck lucky for two reasons. It found a suitable publisher – Oxford University Press (OUP) – and an editor, called James Murray.

Editor extraordinaire

Murray was born near Hawick, Roxburghshire, on 7 February 1837. A compulsive reader, he was more or less fluent in Italian, French, Catalan, Spanish and Latin. He also spoke Portuguese, Provençal and Vaudois (as spoken by the inhabitants of Vaud, Switzerland). He was 'tolerably familiar' with Dutch, Flemish, German and Danish, knew a little Celtic and some Slavic languages, had obtained 'a useful knowledge' of Russian, and could manage some Persian, Sanskrit and Hebrew. He was also familiar with the thirteenth-century dialect of Aramaic known as Syriac, and could decipher the ancient script of Mesopotamia.

In 1870 he became a teacher at Mill Hill School in North London. In 1876 he was approached by Macmillans, the publishers, to edit an English-language dictionary. This came to nothing, but his name was then put forward as a potential editor of the Philological Society's dictionary. In 1879 – by which time he was also president of the society – contracts were signed, and it was then that the dictionary really began to take shape.

The complexities of the English language made the task formidable, involving as it did the examination of seven centuries of the language's development. Five years after he took over, Murray's team published the first instalment of the *NED*: A–Ant. It was clear that this was not going to be a short-term project.

Murray was able to conceive the project on the grand scale that befitted it. He also took seriously the task of organizing the thousands, and ultimately millions, of quotation slips, enlisting the assistance of his wife and their eleven children. Murray worked not from home, but from an iron outbuilding that he called ('first in sport, and then in earnest') the Scriptorium.[1] It contained a lot of bookshelves, 1029 pigeon-holes, but no pigeons.

Murray issued an appeal, asking readers to report 'as many quotations as you can for ordinary words'. He felt that readers who had taken up the Philological Society's invitation to join in the Reading Programme and send in quotations had concentrated too much on esoteric vocabulary. (For instance, readers had collected about fifty examples of the word **abusion**, but only five examples of the much more widely known and used word **abuse**.) Murray's 1879 'Appeal to the English-speaking and English-reading Public' was much broader in scope than previous

----

1 Scriptorium: 'A writing-room; specifically the room in a religious house set apart for the copying of manuscripts.'

appeals. It was printed in newspapers, and some 2000 copies were widely circulated to bookshops and libraries, not just in Britain but in North America and the British Colonies. 'Anyone can help,' he wrote, 'especially with modern books.'

There were numerous other knowledgeable, enthusiastic and dedicated contributors upon whom Murray could call, and many of them submitted thousands of quotations. James Platt Jr, for example, was a prolific philologist who, although he worked in London, spoke many non-European languages. He had said that anyone who could learn twelve languages would have little difficulty in mastering a hundred, but he was so famously shy that he was said to be a man who had 'learnt a hundred languages and forgotten his own'. He must have had some capacity for speech, though, because he often visited London's opium dens in search of linguistic variants – and only that, we are assured – as well as offering himself as a guide to foreigners on the streets of London, just so that he might soak up some of their language and usages. He worked in the City, and visited the library of the British Museum every day to take out a book – in those innocent days when the British Museum library lent some of its stock. He would return it the next day for another title. When Platt died in 1910, aged forty-nine, Murray was distraught. 'I know no one, and cannot hope ever to find any one,' he wrote, 'to whom I can send any strange alien word and say "What language can this belong to?" with a very sure and well-founded expectation that in a day or two there will come an illuminating answer.'

Several women became champions of the 'Big Dictionary', as the project was informally known. Miss Jennet Humphreys of Cricklewood personally sent in 18,700 quotations, somewhat ahead of Miss E.F. Burton of Carlisle's 11,400, and the extraordinary Thompson sisters, Edith and E. Perronet, who sent in over 15,000 and did invaluable work on the proofs. All these were pored over and sorted by Murray's team of helpers, or, in many cases, opened first by his children, who all developed prodigious vocabularies as a result of their association with the project. Some of the lady contributors found it quite bracing even to correspond with a gentleman.

Another of Murray's principal contributors was Dr Fitzedward Hall, a professor of Sanskrit who had lived in India. After his return to London he had an argument with Professor Goldstücker of the Philological Society, and allegations were made that he was a foreign spy and a drunkard. Piqued, he went to live in Suffolk, where he accused a local clergyman of ruining his marriage, and became a virtual recluse. But he spent between four and six hours each day proofreading the *NED*, adding comments gleaned from browsing in his own extensive library. When Hall became ill, Murray broke the habit of a lifetime's formality by ending his letters to him 'yours very affectionately'. In the preface to the published work, Murray acknowledged the important part Hall had played: 'there is scarcely a page to which he has not added earlier instances of words or senses'.

Trials and tribulations

Murray had frequent and spirit-sapping arguments with the Oxford authorities, which are discussed in *Caught in the Web of Words* (1977), a book written by his grand-daughter Elisabeth. But a more recent book, *Lost for Words* (2005), by the Oxford academic Lynda Mugglestone uses previously unseen documents to throw more light on the struggle over the compilation process. Decisions about what to include and what to exclude, as well as how to define what was included, were the source of much grief among the editorial team. Murray antagonized his colleagues, and was on notoriously bad terms with some of the loftily named 'delegates' of OUP, the university dons who oversaw the press's business and who were effectively his bosses. Some had no time for scientific terms, and many took a dim view of the slang, **jargon** and Americanisms that many readers were contributing. They wanted to limit the range of definitions and the illustrative quotations he sought, and they wanted the work finished sooner rather than later.

Elisabeth Murray and Lynda Mugglestone both describe the constant battle between Murray's perfectionism and the more commercial and pragmatic instincts of his publishers. The delegates, who were senior academic staff from Oxford University, had, in today's parlance, a very hands-on[2] attitude towards the dictionary. To the dismay of Murray, many got close – too close, in his opinion – to the text itself. Murray records arguments with them in which he pleads that there is no such thing as a 'good' or 'bad' linguistic source. And yet they were not placated. Complaints of 'too many scientific words' arose at a Delegates' Dictionary Committee on 10 May 1883. 'Should not the quotations illustrative of modern literary words be taken from great authors,' they asked, 'and the language of newspapers banished?' It's a commonly heard complaint. One wonders whether the speakers had in mind the lofty pronouncements of *The Times*, or was that, too, fair game? Lynda Mugglestone quotes an apoplectic note from Murray's colleague, the phonetician Alexander Ellis, that 'The delegates contracted to print the dictionary – not to edit it'. Murray and his more enlightened

----

2 The phrase 'hands-on', meaning to take part directly in something, is sourced by the *OED* to a *Sunday Times* article from 1969 that refers, in fact, to a computer training scheme in schools.

contemporaries were running ahead of the bull of academic opinion, and being roundly gored in the process.

Murray's problems were not merely with the dictionary's content, however. The project had begun slowly, with less than one letter being published in five years. At that rate, it could be decades, if not several centuries, before the whole work was complete. Speed was important, especially to the publisher – whether they expected to make a profit on the venture or not – and yet the work was such a serious undertaking that its pace could not be hurried. Murray was almost inventing the process of modern lexicography. He and his team were nothing less than pioneers – nothing this ambitious had been attempted before. No wonder it was slow going at first.

The delegates' frustration was, in part, due to their desire to present the academic world with a work they knew was eagerly awaited. Learned journals and popular newspapers alike were united in their praise of each fascicle[3] that appeared, hence the unconstrained impatience in notes sent to Murray, such as, 'The dictionary is *wanted* by students *now*' (January 1887). No doubt the announcement that the work was in preparation had aroused a frenzy of anticipation. All they had to do now was to produce the book and the prize would be theirs, yet it was a long time coming. The delegates were aware of Noah Webster's masterful *American Dictionary of the English Language* (1864), a work against which Murray's work was, at times, larger by a proportion of 16:1. OUP had decreed that the proportion should be no more than 6:1, but that was an impossible demand. By drawing an arbitrary line, some words would inevitably be ruled out, yet the

---

3 Fascicle, 1647: 'A part, number, "livraison" (of a work published by instalments).'

original intent had been to include a biography of every word in the language. A compromise was eventually reached: they would proceed at eight times the size of Webster's dictionary.

Thanks to scholars such as Lynda Mugglestone, who in her research had access to the *OED* archives, we too can stumble on the quotations that were, perforce, invented by Murray on rare occasions. The illustrative quotation 'Such responsibilities are not **abdicable** at will' was written to support the word 'abdicable', and came not from literature but from Murray's own pen. The reason? The researchers knew its meaning, but could not find a text to back it up. 'He gives good dinners, but I don't think much of his **cellar**' performs the same function under the heading 'cellar', where the word stands for 'wine-cellar'. But such cases, like really good wine, are rare – and in any event, the word existed and must therefore be dealt with. But what happened when a word's very existence was debated? On one occasion, Murray entered into correspondence with a reader who upbraided him on his use of the ungainly word **advertisemental**. Murray hit back that although the reader might not like it, he personally liked it as much as **testamental**, **ornamental**, **monumental** 'or any other –mental'. His point was that 'The dictionary does not advise you to say so, it merely records the fact that such has been said.'

The matter of subjectivity is, of course, a crucial issue for an editor of dictionaries. Murray coined his own term, **nonce-words**, for words apparently used 'only for the nonce', i.e. once. A similar term as used by the Greeks, who had a word or two for most things, is *hapax legomenon* (a thing once said), though the one-off word **graiomania** (a mania for all things Greek) never made it. Murray was happy to dispatch many of these singularities to the paper-bin, even when he met them in proofs.

Questions of Victorian taste determined other choices. The word **condom** (see Chapter 8, page 204) was omitted on grounds of taste, and the word **clap**, for 'venereal disease', was labelled 'obsolete in polite use'. **Bloody** was defined by Murray in 1887 as 'now constantly in the mouths of the lowest classes, but by respectable people considered "a horrid word", on a par with obscene or profane language, and usually printed in the newspapers (in police reports, etc.) "b——y"'. We should not point mocking fingers at Victorian prudishness: a classical scholar wrote to Murray about the word **cunt**, 'It must in any case be inserted.' Other scholars, including the headmaster of Murray's old school in Roxburghshire, felt it should be included because it was a good old English word of Teutonic origin. And yet Murray had the final word: the first edition contained no entry for 'cunt'.

The original pioneering voice behind the dictionary, Richard Chenevix Trench, had deprecated scientific terms, seeing them as mere 'signs' or 'tokens' and not relevant to a work of literary reference. Murray did his best to include as many as he could, but the dictionary could not keep up with the rapid pace of scientific advancement in the nineteenth century. Murray frequently complained that he was being asked to make judgements, often on matters of spelling or pronunciation, forcing him to protest that 'I am not the editor of the English language'. And yet, when push came to print, he had to cast his vote.

Raw ingredients

The procedure for getting quotations into the *New English Dictionary* remained standard for over a century. The first step was for quotations to be collected by readers participating in the

Reading Programme. Initially, they were asked to produce quotations for 'remarkable' words, although this was changed in time to accommodate the specific needs of the editor (known by Murray as his **desiderata**[4]), to reflect a concern that there must surely be an earlier reference that would give a fuller history of a particular word. After these were submitted to Murray each quotation was written out on a small (6 × 4-inch) index slip, and a reference added to explain the source of each quotation. Each slip was then filed alphabetically according to the word noted by the reader so that the lexicographers could refer to them as they worked on the dictionary. The Scriptorium was soon receiving around 1000 slips per day. By 1882 its shelves were groaning with a combined total of 3.5 million slips.

For a while, OUP had been pressing Murray to move to Oxford to be closer to the heart of the project. Somewhat reluctantly, Murray finally conceded, and the family moved to Banbury Road in 1885, together with the Scriptorium – which he got builders to half-sink into the ground so as to minimize noise and disturbance to the neighbours. The Post Office obligingly installed a new letter-box outside his house. OUP also felt Murray needed the help of a deputy. Henry Bradley, a man who was reputed never to have uttered an ungrammatical sentence, was appointed as an assistant in 1886. He became an independent editor in 1888, working in a room of the British Museum in London, and later in Oxford.

The Scriptorium became an essential stop on the tourism trail for a certain type of visitor. Victorian celebrities, such as the writer Mark Twain, asked to visit the Murray residence in Banbury Road, as did Lord Gladstone. The great Victorian

----

4 Plural of Desideratum, 1652: 'Something for which a desire or longing is felt.'

Mad about words

When 2000 copies of Murray's first appeal to readers were distributed
to bookshops and news-stands, one came to the attention of a retired
assistant surgeon of the American army called Dr William Chester Minor.
Minor was a lover of books, and he wrote to Murray offering to help.
The work he sent in was exemplary, and from around 1880 or 1881
he became one of the Scriptorium's most valued, efficient and prolific
correspondents. Minor had plenty of money, which he put to good use
in buying parcels of rare and historical books, but it was not until after
several years of regular and cordial correspondence that James Murray
asked permission to visit him at his home in Broadmoor. However, the
extraordinary and uncomfortable fact was that Minor was an inmate of
Broadmoor's criminal lunatic asylum, having shot dead a man in Lambeth
in 1872. They met several times after that, becoming close friends, and
Minor did much invaluable research for the dictionary.

   Rational by day, at night Minor's mood changed and he suffered
dangerous delusions about his own safety, being convinced that he was at
risk of injury from murderous Irishmen. He also suffered terribly from
sexual fantasies, which he did his best to cure in 1902 when he cut off his
own penis with the penknife that he normally used for slicing open uncut
pages. Minor eventually returned to Washington DC, and died in 1920.

statesman was somewhat surprised to find the door opened by a
young man clutching a knife, but there was no cause for alarm: it
was just one of the Murray children, who happened to have been
helping his mother in the kitchen.

   The reason the dictionary took so long to finish is that James
Murray insisted on having the phrase 'on Historical Principles' in
the title. Far from listing merely a guide to pronunciations,
definitions and Latin, Greek and other roots where applicable, and
not content with listing just those words that stretched back to AD
1150 – which would have been a monumental enough
undertaking – Murray undertook to cite passages that illustrated
how every term had been used in a given sense over the

centuries, including the earliest known record of each word's appearance.

The material that became *The New English Dictionary*, subsequently known as *The Oxford English Dictionary*, was drawn largely from the 5 million examples of words and phrases that had been sent in via the Reading Programme. These included extracts from novels, newspapers, magazines, scientific and philosophical treatises, manuscripts and other documents covering written English from Anglo-Saxon times until the early twentieth century. In its scope, ambition, confidence, thoroughness, seriousness, dedication and determination, it was a truly Victorian undertaking.

First edition facts

Proposed extent: Initially 4 volumes, 6400 pages
Actual extent: 10 volumes, 15,490 pages
Proposed completion time: Ten years
Actual completion time: 70 years (from approval date)
Publication date: 19 April 1928
Pages edited by James Murray: approx. 7200
Number of entries: 252,200
Word forms defined and/or illustrated: 414,800
Contributors (readers): est. 2000
Quotations submitted by contributors: approx. 5 million
Quotations used in dictionary: 1,861,200
Authors represented in quotations: 2700
Works represented in quotations: 4500

Murray never lived to see the project through to completion. He died in 1915, having overseen the publication of A–D, H–K, O–P and T, nearly half of the finished dictionary. Bradley died in 1923, having edited E–G, L–M, S–Sh, St and W–We. Two additional editors, who had been working alongside Murray and Bradley, ensured that the work continued smoothly. William Craigie had joined the staff in 1897, becoming editor in 1901, and was put in charge of N, Q-R, Si-Sq, U-V and Wo-Wy. C.T. Onions joined in 1895, becoming editor in 1914. He oversaw the remaining pages, Su-Sz, Wh-Wo and X-Z.

If Murray was the Moses who didn't live to see the promised land, Onions and Craigie were the joint Joshuas who led the tribe in. The last fascicle of A *New English Dictionary on Historical Principles* was published in April 1928 and cost twelve shillings and sixpence. The full set, consisting of 125 fascicles, sold for between fifteen and fifty guineas, depending on the binding. Here, at last, was the English language complete. Well, not quite. The word **bondmaid** (a slave girl) went missing from the 1887 fascicle (Batter-Boz) in which it should have appeared after its paperwork was lost. This embarrassing omission was amended in the next edition.

And yet, bound or unbound, the English language was far from being - in the words of Samuel Johnson - 'fixed'.

Keeping it fresh

Even as the first edition was being prepared for publication, it was clear that new information was becoming available all the time and deserved to be incorporated into the great work. But how to include it when the book was already published? In 1933 OUP published a single-volume supplement to the dictionary, containing new words, and new meanings and senses of words already listed. Alongside this, the original dictionary was reprinted in twelve volumes and formally given the title that it still holds - *The Oxford English Dictionary*. But a living language never stops evolving. The harsh fact is that a dictionary is antiquated on the day of its publication. It had been forty-four years since A–Ant had been published, and though ants had not in themselves undergone fundamental structural change, the editors knew that the updating had to begin immediately. To some, this might make the job of compiling a dictionary seem Sisyphean.[5] But lexicographers are made of sterner stuff.

The background to the second edition is that a decision was made to expand the 1933 supplement, since it was recognized that the dictionary was now in great need of updating. At that time, according to the *OED*'s present-day team, no thought was given to a new edition. The man chosen to oversee this, in 1957, was Robert Burchfield. Onions was still around, although he was eighty-four that year. The work was expected to take seven to ten years. Once again, this proved wide of the mark. Burchfield's new supplement took twenty-nine years and spanned four volumes, which were published between 1972 and 1986.

Supplementary facts

The following figures relate to the supplement produced between 1972 and 1986.
Proposed extent: 1 volume, 1300 pages
Actual extent: 4 volumes, 5730 pages
Proposed completion time: 7 years
Actual completion time: 29 years
Publication date: Vol. 1, 1972; vol. 2, 1976; vol. 3, 1982; vol. 4, 1986
Number of entries: 69,300
Number of quotations: approx. 527,000

---

5 Sisyphus was a character in Greek myth who had to roll a rock up a mountain. Every time he got near the top, the rock rolled down again and he had to start from the bottom. It was a thankless task.

In 1989 the *OED* combined the first edition with the 1933 supplement and the 1972–86 supplementary volumes, and added about 5000 new entries. Some light revision across the alphabet was also done. The second edition of twenty books contained just over 615,000 definitions and 2.4 million quotations. This edition contained a greatly enhanced selection of twentieth-century vocabulary – hardly surprising since the century had only just got going as the first edition was nearing completion. The dictionary maintained a Reading Programme so as to monitor modern English, and many more scientific and technical terms were added. The work also took on a more global aspect, reflecting the increased interest in and significance of words from North America, Australia, New Zealand, South Africa, Asia and the Caribbean.

Second edition facts

All the figures below relate to the 1989 edition and should be regarded as approximate.
Proposed extent: 20 volumes
Actual extent: 20 volumes, 21,730 pages
Publication date: 1989
Weight of manuscript: 62kg (137lb)
Ink used to print complete run: 2830kg (6243 lb)
Words in entire text: 59 million
Number of printed characters: 350 million
Different typographical characters used in text: 750 (660 special, plus 90 on regular keyboard)
Equivalent person years used to key in text: 120
Megabytes of electronic storage required for text: 540
Number of entries: 291,500
Longest entry: The verb 'set', with over 430 senses explained in 60,000 words
Number of etymologies: 219,800
Number of quotations: 2,436,600

In 1971 OUP published the entire thirteen-volume 1933 *OED* in a compact edition of just two volumes, housing them in a sturdy box. Each page reproduced four pages of the old edition, so the magnifying glass that was supplied in a pull-out drawer at the bottom of the box was essential, even for those with good eyesight. The second edition (*OED2*) went on sale in 1991 in a compact edition, with nine original pages to one page, and a stronger magnifying glass.

The digital dictionary

The second edition became available on CD-ROM in 1992, whereupon more than 60kg (132lb) of paper were replaced by about 550 megabytes of text on a disk weighing just a few grams. The *OED* was now increasingly becoming an electronic product. Paper editions were still in demand, but new realities were coming into play.

In March 2000 the *OED Online* became available to subscribers as part of the £34 million revision programme that began under chief editor John Simpson in 1993. Since then, on any given day, some seventy scholars, research assistants, systems engineers and project managers, as well as about 200 specialist consultants and readers, have worked on this project. Estimates of a completion date for what will be *OED3* are conservative, which is probably wise, given how wide of the mark all the earlier dates were. There is at present no estimated end date, as this depends on a number of factors. New technology, new evidence and new developments in the worldwide use of English are rapidly changing the picture. But the rate at which revised and new words are being published has risen by 150 per cent since online publication of the third edition began.

With the revision process starting in earnest in 2000, the online database that contains the whole of *OED2* is being updated quarterly. Every word and every definition – most of which have been left unchanged since they went into the first edition – will eventually be subjected to the intense scrutiny of Oxford's team of lexicographers. The online revised text is an ever-expanding third edition, in continuous publication until completion. Revision started at M because by mid-alphabet the original editors were sure of their style, and had enough quotation evidence as well. 'As editors who were learning how to revise the dictionary,' writes Penny Silva of the *OED*, 'we felt that we needed a secure base for our work on the text. Also, M is a representative letter: it includes large, old words (such as make, man, may and might), and also many words borrowed from other languages.'

It is possible that the *OED3* will never be printed conventionally, but will only ever be available electronically. That will be a decision for the future, when it is nearer completion. The *OED* went online in March 2000 to rave reviews. Writing in the *Observer* newspaper, literary editor Robert McCrum welcomed it, excitedly describing his first encounter with the *OED*'s cyber version as 'a vivid reminder that we are living through a second Gutenberg revolution'.[6] There are two sides to *OED Online*. First is an open-access information site that contains news, history, educational resources and a generalized help area. Second is a closed, subscription-only area that houses the internet version of the dictionary, known as *OED3*.

The main, open site is the public face of the *OED*, and would

----

6 Johannes Gensfleisch zur Laden zum Gutenberg (c.1398–1468), a German metal-worker and inventor, developed a printing press with moveable type. Books could then be printed at a rate never known before and resulted in an information explosion in Europe.

take several days or weeks to explore properly. Schoolchildren will be drawn to its educational site, which contains word stories, links and quizzes. General readers might want to scroll through the history and significant facts of the *OED*, or read through one of the many newsletters that the dictionary has been producing since January 1995. The policy of openness suggests confidence and accessibility, and the striking design of the pages complements, albeit electronically, the grandeur of the original Victorian project. Indeed, it's difficult to stay on one page without the eye being distracted by a link to another, just as consulting the 'hard copy' of the *OED* inevitably led to a paper-chase from one word to another.

But it is the dictionary itself that is the shining star of the *OED Online* project. The current annual subscription rate is £195 plus VAT, so for about £50 per quarter readers can see for themselves how the *OED* has entered the twenty-first century. Aside from the bells and whistles of technology, this is a work that has wholeheartedly grasped the opportunity to revise its original definitions, and to present an English language that is truly global. Lynda Mugglestone, in *Lost for Words*, recollects William Craigie's original definition of **white man** as 'a man of honourable character such as one associates with a European (as distinguished from a Negro)'. Ouch. *OED2* rephrased that as 'a man of honourable character (such as was conventionally associated with one of European extraction)'. The original entry for **negro** referred to 'black skin, black woolly hair, flat nose and thick protruding lips'. The draft revision from September 2004 takes us on a condensed historical journey through the word's meaning, touching on the **black power** movement of the 1960s, organizations such as the United Negro College Fund, and 'positive contexts', such as baseball's Negro Leagues. One comes away with a sense, more than ever before, of having learnt something. Now, the *OED* can expand to fill all the available space necessary to encapsulate a word's meaning. They also have all the time in the world.

OED3 is a versatile and adaptable tool. If you approach it with one thing in mind – let's say to look up a word such as **justice** – you can find a response within seconds. The search brings up both the noun and verb senses of the word. The noun page opens up to reveal the headword on the right. On the left, you can choose whether to display an alphabetical list of those words that precede and follow it, or you could show a date map of all the other words that came into the English language in the same year – 1137. The only other word from that year is **crucet-hus**, which means 'a house of torment'. The following year, 1138, gave us the noun **letch**. The entry for 'justice' has a good many quotations. If the author of the quotation is underlined, a simple click will take you to a bibliographical chart containing all that author's works, once again surrounded by alphabetical forebears and successors. The overall impression gives the reader, scholar, researcher or idle browser a powerful sense of immediacy. Here we are, with our noses pressed right up against whole generations of words. Although the original bound edition of the *OED* had charm and authority, it had become unwieldy, and pages became creased and damaged with use. There can be few scholars who would not welcome the functional flexibility that *OED3* offers.

The Simple and Advanced search buttons allow readers to search with pinpoint accuracy. You can check spelling and punctuation, look for a word within a definition, an etymology or a quotation, or search for a word within a particular year. You might want to see all the quotations used from a particular author in the *OED*, or to see which quotations have been used from, say, *Hamlet* (sixty-three in total). All these features are available at the click of a mouse. The result – a twinning of nineteenth-century meticulousness with twenty-first-century computer sophistication – is a mouth-watering prospect for anyone who has ever wondered how words fit together. The *OED Online* is a serious research tool that has been made available to the ordinary reader.

Oxford University Press has not abandoned the paper-based dictionary. The idea of a concise dictionary was first mooted by Frederick Furnivall in 1862. As with other planned works, it took a long time to materialize, but finally, in 1911, the first edition of *The Concise Oxford English Dictionary* (*COD*), edited by H.W. and F.G. Fowler, was published. This popular volume has since passed through two editions and reached its eleventh printing in July 2004. It contains more than 240,000 words, including over 2000 *COD* debutantes, such as **plasma screen**, **speed dating** and **sexing up**, which reflect the smaller dictionary's responsiveness to developments in the English language. It also has an expanded list of words from around the English-speaking world, as well as boxes offering advice on usage and a section of 100 special word histories.

Another OUP project, *The Shorter Oxford English Dictionary*, is one of the great oxymorons of publishing because it's still longer than most other dictionaries. Its two volumes are a tenth of the size of the first *OED*, but as the entries are shorter it contains a third of its words. It was prepared for publication by William Little, H.W. Fowler and Jesse Coulson and revised by C.T. Onions. The first edition was published in February 1933 after work had begun in 1902. The aim of *The Shorter OED* was to gather together all the words that have been in general use in English since 1700, as well as the language of Shakespeare, the Authorized Version of the Bible and works by Edmund Spenser (*c*.1552–99) and John Milton (1608–74); two-thirds of the entries in the great

OED were removed. The fourth edition was published in 1993 and the fifth in September 2002. It contains many new words yet to be added to the full *OED*, such as the modern usage of **text message**. The list of people whose works have been quoted includes Helen Fielding and Quentin Tarantino.

Other reduced dictionaries include *The Pocket Oxford, The Large Print Dictionary, The Oxford English Reference Dictionary* and *The Visual English Dictionary*, and there are also children's dictionaries, such as *The Oxford School Dictionary of Word Origins*. OUP publishes over 4500 books a year, so somewhere within that mass of information is the right title for every taste.

Meanwhile, *OED Online* pushes on. It aims to clear up the discrepancies of the past and to incorporate an ever-increasing number of new words – approximately 900 a year entering the language at present estimates. All printed sources are currently acceptable, which modern readers will recognize as a thoroughly contemporary attitude towards the printed word. Few dictionary editors would have to face the concerted hostility to journals and periodicals against which James Murray battled, and readers might be surprised to see that some supposedly topical words have an older lineage than they imagined. At last scholars have the technology to take on these challenges. The benefits are immediate, enormous, wide-ranging and fun.

It would take a while to piece together all the quotations sourced to our most famous playwright. A search on William Shakespeare brings up 3566 entries, and the abbreviated '*Shakes*.' – abbreviations were used for some particularly well-known authors – produces even more: 26,106. It's certainly true that Shakespeare's influence has been felt far and wide across the English language, but could any other work match his? Possibly the Bible. The next chapter looks at them both.

Chapter Four

Desert Island Texts

Considering how much is said about how dumb we are all meant to be getting, it is amazing how much we quote the Bible and Shakespeare – those staples of any visit to a desert island – in daily life. If you have ever talked about the **promised land**, if you have occasionally felt **bloodthirsty**, said that someone had **iron in their soul** or felt **at death's door**, you will have been quoting straight from the Old Testament. If you have ever **licked your wounds**, if you have **suffered fools gladly**, been **in fear and trembling**, suspected that something could be a **double-edged sword**; if you imagined yourself in a **bottomless pit** or thought your outfit covered a **multitude of sins**, then you are quoting the New Testament. Phrases like **high-minded**, to be **beside oneself**, **old wives' tales** and **a sting in the tail** were not originally in the Bible, but gained much popularity from being repeated therein. And if you have ever **held up a mirror to nature**, been **hoist with your own petard**, given the **devil his due**, or **stood on ceremony**, then you have been spouting pure, unadulterated Shakespeare. Perhaps we are all far better read than we thought we were.

By the Book

The early history of the Bible in translation – both the Old and New Testaments – is a tale of overlapping re-translations. In the early years of the first millennium after Christ, extracts were translated by the monk Caedmon and the Venerable Bede. Some psalms were rendered into English in the ninth century. The flowering of scholarship in northeast England towards the end of the tenth century produced the Lindisfarne Gospels. A similar flowering in Winchester produced Aelfric's translation of the first seven books of the Old Testament.

John Wyclif (c.1330–84) was born in Richmond in North Yorkshire and studied at Oxford. The two translations from Latin of the Bible associated with his name (1382 and 1388) are the first complete English versions of the Scriptures, though scholars disagree on how much was Wyclif's own version. The second version is both cleaner and clearer.

William Tyndale (c.1495–1536) studied at both Oxford and Cambridge. His translation of the New Testament is the first based on the Greek text. His 1530 translation of the Pentateuch (Genesis to Deuteronomy), which he followed with the Book of Jonah, were made, at least in part, from the original Hebrew, though other classic texts, such as the Vulgate, Erasmus's Latin version and Martin Luther's Bible were also consulted.

Miles Coverdale's translation of the Bible – from Luther, the Zurich Bible, the Latin Vulgate (c.404) and with some debt to Tyndale – was printed in 1535 and reissued in 1537. Amid an explosion of interest in translations of the sacred text and the development of the printing industry, other versions include Matthew's Bible (1537), Taverner's Bible (1539) and the Great (or Cranmer's) Bible of 1539, which was sponsored by Henry VIII.

The Authorized Version, the most famous English translation

and generally known as the King James Bible, was commissioned in 1604 and published in 1611. Although it was meant to be based on the Bishops' Bible of 1568, it is, in essence, Tyndale's text, with an occasional nod to Wyclif. Much of the wording that became famous through the King James Bible was Tyndale's own, including 'Let there be light', 'Am I my brother's keeper?', 'The powers that be', 'Blessed are the peacemakers', 'The signs of the times' and 'Eat, drink and be merry'. Tyndale was conservative: only 120 of our words owe their first recorded usage to him. Nevertheless, we are also indebted to Tyndale for his first-time use of compound phrases, such as 'broken-hearted', 'fellow-soldier', 'house-top', 'long-suffering', 'rose-coloured', 'sea-shore', 'stumbling-block', 'two-edged' and 'wine-press'.

But let's start at the beginning. When we think of the Book of Genesis, most of us remember the Adam and Eve story, the Garden of Eden, the Tree of Knowledge and, of course, the **apple** that Eve ate, gave to Adam... and the rest was downhill all the way. The problem is that apples are unjustly maligned, since apples were not specified in the text itself. The guilty couple merely ate of the tree's fruit. The specification of the tree is thanks to generations of painters, who must have sensed that 'Eve handing a generic fruit to Adam' or 'Eve tempting Adam with a satsuma' lacked a certain something.

Moses referred to apples in a poetic passage near the end of Deuteronomy (32:10) when, in a sentimental mood on the bank of the Jordan river, he reminds the tribe of Israel that the Lord cared for them and kept them as the **apple of His eye**. Here, the apple has nothing to do with Granny Smiths or Coxes. From Old English onwards, the word 'apple' had another, purely biological meaning, as in the **pupil** of the eye. This phrase is repeated in the book of Zechariah (2:12), when God assures Israel of His divine protection by assuring them that 'He that toucheth you toucheth the apple of His [i.e. God's] eye'. The same Hebrew word, you might think, but no. This time, the writer uses a different Hebrew word for 'pupil' or 'apple', and one that occurs only once in the entire Old Testament. *Bavah* shares a sense with the Arabic word *bab*, which means 'gate', as in *Baby*lon. The meaning is the same, though: the 'eye' – or the 'pupil', which is its direct translation – is the gate to the soul. Bear in mind also that those early English translators were translating from the Latin, with no reference to the original Hebrew text.

There is more fruit in the book of Ezekiel (18:2), though this prophet's tastes were rather sharper: 'The fathers have eaten **sour grapes**, and the children's teeth are **set on edge**.' In fact, Ezekiel has borrowed verbatim a turn of phrase coined by his senior partner in prophecy, Jeremiah (31:28), though it seems that even then the phrase had achieved proverbial status.[1] The verb originally used for 'to set on edge' means literally 'to blunt or dull', which is certainly what sour grapes – mentioned in the original version – do to the teeth. These days 'to eat sour grapes' means to deride something that you can't enjoy, in such a way that no one else will want to enjoy it either: a somewhat self-defeating operation.

In his seminal work on language and translation, *After Babel* (1975), the literary critic George Steiner, during a discussion of 'the innocent finality' of ancient poetry, writes almost enviously about how ancient texts such as the Bible and the writings of Homer could use such metaphors because – although he doesn't quite put

---

1 We also owe the phrase to Aesop (sixth century BC) in one of whose fables, 'The Fox and the Grapes', a fox could not reach some grapes and so declared them to be sour – to prevent anyone else enjoying what he himself could not eat.

it like this – they had got to the metaphor cupboard first. 'To them, metaphor and simile had been novel, perhaps bewildering suppositions. That a brave man should be like a lion, or dawn wear a mantle the colour of flame, were not stale ornaments of speech but provisional, idiosyncratic mappings of reality.' For a modern equivalent, imagine, in the very early days of football commentary, saying admiringly, 'Well, at the end of the day it's a game of two halves,' and being loudly applauded for your eloquence.

As well as fruit, the Bible is full of words for dangerous predicaments. One is to **escape by the skin of one's teeth**, which comes from the Book of Job (19:20). The King James translation reads: 'My bone cleaveth to my skin and to my flesh, and I am escaped with the skin of my teeth.' Some have suggested that Job's teeth had been ground down to his gums, or that this was the very barest form of escape, rather like surviving by a **hair's breadth**, almost tantamount to not escaping at all – which was clearly the predicament that Job felt he was suffering from.

The Bible had its share of grumpy old men. 'Can the Ethiopian change his skin, or the leopard his spots?' asks the prophet Jeremiah (13:23) in one of his (many) deeply pessimistic moments. Jeremiah, you felt, was not one of life's cheerier types, which is perhaps why Victorian wine merchants, hunting for colourful names to give their outsize and novelty bottles, chose the name of a different biblical figure – evil King **Jeroboam** – to denote a large bottle that holds four normal bottles of sparkling wine or six regular ones.[2] He may have been a byword for depravity, but at least he knew how to throw a party, as did evil

----
2 Although the *OED* quotes *The Daily News* from 27 July 1889 to the effect that a Jeroboam contained 10 or 12 ordinary bottles.

King **Rehoboam** (six bottles of champagne) and the not-at-all-evil **Methuselah** (the equivalent of eight standard bottles).

There are more **lions** in the Book of Daniel, prompting one of the most long-lasting images in the Bible, when Daniel's friends Shadrach, Meshach and Abednego are cast by the Babylonian king **Nebuchadnezzar** (twenty bottles, still or sparkling) into a fiery furnace for refusing to bow down to his image. Three chapters later there is more trouble when Daniel himself is cast by King Darius into a lion's pit. (Not Darius's fault, say his spin-doctors – see Chapter 7, page 180 – Daniel was the victim of a palace coup, and Darius the innocent party.) In any event, Daniel survived without a scratch, and even changed places with the plotters, who met the bloody end that they had intended for him. So a more accurate definition of **to be in the lions' den** should really be 'to emerge triumphant, against apparently impossible odds, and to turn the tables on your former pursuers'.

Daniel is not quite out of trouble yet. His next challenge was Belshazzar's feast, at which the equivalent of a good many jeroboams, rehoboams, methuselahs and nebuchadnezzars were drunk. Belshazzar was in fact Nebuchadnezzar's son, and the party he threw – let's not mince words, it was an orgy – was famously interrupted by a hand that suddenly appeared and wrote with one finger upon the wall. In fact, the words **writing on the wall** are nowhere mentioned in the text, but the biblical commentaries are confident that the inscription, which was all Greek[3] to Belshazzar's wise men and enchanters, but which was actually in Hebrew letters, was displayed as follows, to the confusion of the king's interpreters:

----
3 SHAKESPEARE, *Julius Caesar* (1601): 'He spoke greeke … those that vnderstood him, smil'd at one another, and shooke their heads: but … it was Greeke to me.'

```
S U T M M
Y Ph K N N
N R  L E E
```

Start in the top right-hand corner and read down to the E. Then
move up to the adjacent M and read down again, and so on.

You need to add a few vowels because Aramaic letters are
mostly consonants, but what you should end up with (Daniel
5:25) is MENE MENE TEKEL UPHARSIN. The phrase has been used in full
by authors such as Charlotte Brontë, William Gladstone and D.H.
Lawrence in the sense of an obscure omen or a warning of
impending disaster for the following reason. The Aramaic word
menë is a play on the word *manneh*, which is a coin. *Tekel* is the
Aramaic for the Hebrew word *shekel*, also a coin, and the noun
pharsin is the plural of *peres*. A *peres* is worth half a *manneh*,
but also signifies the word *peris* (divided) and *paras* (Persia). No
wonder the enchanters and the astrologers were scratching their
heads. Daniel's interpretation was as follows. The repeated word
MENE means 'God has numbered your kingdom and brought it to
an end'; TEKEL means 'you have been weighed in the scales and
found wanting' – another memorable phrase that we still use
today; and UPHARSIN means 'your kingdom is to be divided
between the Medes and the Persians'. Not surprisingly, we don't
often use the words MENE MENE TEKEL UPHARSIN to describe the
imminent demise of a regime of which we disapprove, but the
phrase 'the writing on the wall' has come to mean, as the *OED*
puts it, 'warning signs of impending disaster'. As for Belshazzar,
he tried to change his ways. He clad Daniel in the finest clothes,
and doubtless the party died away and the guests made their
excuses and left. And later that night Belshazzar learnt what
Daniel's interpretation meant when he was slain. Still, he

achieved wino-immortality, since a **balthazar** (a corruption of his name), contains sixteen bottles, still or sparkling, which must be some consolation.

As a source book for unfeasibly large bottles of wine, the New Testament is disappointing, but a treasure trove in all other respects, especially phrases involving minerals. In the Sermon on the Mount in the book of Matthew, for example, in a passage thickly studded with ringing phrases, Jesus declares to his followers 'Ye are the salt of the earth…' (5:13). **Salt** was a crucial substance in the ancient world, ever since Lot's wife turned to look at the destruction of Sodom and Gomorrah and found herself transformed into one half of a condiment set. The line continues, '…but if the salt loses its flavour, how shall it be seasoned?' But how can salt lose its flavour? One way is by being spilt and mixed with other things. In other words, Jesus is telling his believers to keep themselves pure in thought.

In its biblical use, the phrase **salt of the earth** implied a select group of people. It evolved, perhaps inevitably, to refer to the powerful and wealthy, those who gave the world its flavour. Salt has also been used for thousands of years as a preserving agent, and that usage was applied to a class of people who were seen to preserve life on earth by their wealth and power: namely, royalty and aristocracy. In the twentieth century, though, it has been democratized, and its original moral qualities reinserted. It now means, in effect, a **geezer**,[4] a decent person from any class. **Down to earth**, you might say, though that phrase dates from the early twentieth century, perhaps from a time when the possibility of

----

4 **An** 1885 dialect pronunciation of 'guiser' (chiefly Scotland and the north) 'one who guises' (1488), a masquerader or mummer. As geezer, 'A term of derision applied esp. to men, usu. but not necessarily elderly; a chap, fellow.'

flight had become stronger. Salt also recurs in phrases such as **to be worth one's salt**, though you might want to take that one with a **pinch of salt** – or at least, you would have done since the first recorded (non-biblical) use of the phrase in 1647.

Matthew also contains the famous declaration 'You are the light of the world' – same idea – and follows this with another memorable turn of phrase: 'Neither do men light a candle, and put it under a bushel, but on a candlestick.' This means that if you were to hide your light under a bushel, you wouldn't be able to see it, which would be a bad thing. But what is a **bushel**? It certainly has nothing to do with a bush, since if you hid your candle under one, the whole thing might go up. A bushel is a measure, approximately 36 litres (8 gallons), or a container for that same amount – and not a drop of wine. The modern usage came into common currency in the sixteenth and seventeenth centuries, so whenever someone tells you that you're **hiding your light under a bushel**, they're quoting from the book of Matthew.

The imagery of flames and light – not surprisingly from a man who said 'I am the light of the world' – fills the New Testament. Matthew again (15:14) tells us that Jesus said 'if the blind lead the blind, both shall fall into the ditch'. **Blind** is a common Teutonic adjective. (Ask any Latvian and they will tell you that the verb *blendu* means 'I do not see clearly'.) A crude contemporary version of **the blind leading the blind** is a T-shirt bearing the slogan 'I'm with this idiot…'.

On a not dissimilar theme, we might note that President George W. Bush quoted the book of Matthew when declaring his **war on terror**. 'He that is not with me is against me', was Jesus's uncompromising message in Matthew (12:30). George Bush said much the same on 6 November 2001, when he said 'You are

either with us or you are against us in the fight against terror.'
Of course, the president was hardly the first politician to dip into
his Bible in search of a suitable sound bite. 'We've gone the **extra
mile** in arms control, but our offers have not always been
welcome,' said President Ronald Reagan on 14 November 1985,
with reference to the nuclear arms race that the Unites States and
the Soviet Union were still fighting. He wasn't the first to talk
about mileage in this way. The British comic actress Joyce
Grenfell, in her 1979 autobiography *Turn Back the Clock*, wrote
of 'Working like a beaver / Always with a smile / Ready to take
the rough and the smooth / To **go the extra mile**.' But it seems
unlikely that the president's speech-writers had studied the
works of Joyce Grenfell. In fact, the phrase occurs in odd writings
from the mid-nineteenth century onwards, but it was with
Reagan that the phrase 'extra mile' entered the political
vocabulary and never really left it. Again, the inspiration comes
from the book of Matthew (5:41), in which Jesus says, 'And
whosoever shall compel thee to go a mile, go with him twain.'
Jesus was talking about the requirement to love your enemy. It
was a Christian response to provocation and violence, suggesting
that one should be prepared to go to any length to secure peace.

This, incidentally, is just two verses after the injunction to
turn the other cheek, which was not a policy option favoured
by the Reagan administration, nor any US government since. And
in between those two verses, Jesus also advises that the response
to someone who takes away your coat is to let them have your
cloak.[5] The Scottish novelist Tobias Smollett, in *Humphrey
Clinker* (1771), as well as coining the non-biblical phrase **not**

----
5 'And if any man will sue thee at the law, and take away thy coat, let him
have thy cloak also.' (Matthew 5:40).

room enough to swing a cat, also wrote 'He would **give away the shirt off his back**', which was the exemplum for those who can't help giving until it hurts.

On the subject of politicians, it is worth pointing out that when Neville Chamberlain returned from Berlin on 30 September 1938 to a country gripped with war panic, he told them that he had brought them **peace in our time**. That phrase, as many people in those days must have known, was borrowed from the Book of Common Prayer. Just under a year later, he was announcing that Britain was at war.

'Beware of false prophets, which come to you in sheep's clothing, but inwardly are ravening wolves,' says Jesus (Matthew 7:15). The idea of a **wolf in sheep's clothing**, with or without false prophets, is as much in use now as ever. And as the gospel of Matthew reaches its climax, we meet Pontius Pilate, the Roman governor of Judea from AD 26–36. Pilate made his decision about the fate of Jesus and then famously **washed his hands**, saying, 'I am innocent of the blood of this person' (27:24). Since then, the imputation of guilt has, to some extent, melted away, in that you can say 'I'm washing my hands of the whole business' without it being inferred that you have thereby sentenced an innocent man to an agonizing death. And when we say something will **all come out in the wash**,[6] it implies that the truth will eventually emerge, which at least represents some sort of ethical vindication for the whole laundering process.

The book of the Apostles contains that memorable phrase **kicking against the pricks**. This has a remarkable history, far from the brief burst of schoolboyish sniggering that it might

----

6 Kipling, actually. 'An' it all went into the laundry, / But it never came out in the wash.' (*Five Nations*, 1903).

occasion. The remark was made, twice in the same book (9:5), by Jesus to Saul, later Paul, who, because he didn't know any better, had been persecuting Christians. A **prick** is actually a 'goad' – a wooden shaft, sharply pointed at its end – which is used by tillermen to keep oxen walking in a straight line. The oxen might try to deviate from the course by 'kicking against the prick', but the more they did so, the more the tillermen, working in the field, would drive it against the poor beasts' skin. The expression originally meant to resist authority even if you harmed yourself in the process. These days it means, more generally, to be **recalcitrant** or just plain **bolshy**. Kevin Mitchell of the *Observer* newspaper got that sense of futile aggression about right in May 2005 when he described Manchester United fans burning an effigy of their new owner Malcolm Glazer as an example of 'to kick against the pricks'.

Have you ever said **in the twinkling of an eye**? That's from the Bible too. In 1535 the priest and translator Miles Coverdale (1488–1568) published the first complete Bible to be printed in the English language, which contained the line from Psalms 30:6, 'His wrath endureth but the twincklinge of an eye.' Ever since the early fourteenth century it had meant not just the action of blinking, but a tiny amount of time too. Geoffrey Chaucer (see Chapter 1, pages 63–5) had used it for the same effect, and Shakespeare would return to it in *The Merchant of Venice*. Corinthians, written by the arch spin maestro Paul, abounds with drop-dead[7] phrases. It is, for example, one of the first places where you would find the phrase **puffed up**. It's there in

----
7 Drop-dead, American, colloquial: 'Stunning, striking, exceptional; breath-taking, heart-stopping.' First cited in 1962 in the *New York Herald Tribune*: 'Fashions from Florence not drop-dead... For almost the first time in history Simonetta failed to deliver an absolutely drop-dead collection.'

Tyndale's translation of Colossians 2:18, 'puft vppe with his flesshly mynde', and Coverdale wrote, 'Knowlege puffeth a man vp, but loue edifyeth' (1 Corinthians, 8:1).

The saying **My body is a temple**, so beloved of health faddists, has a holier origin than most Reiki practitioners might have imagined. Jesus said it first, or Paul wrote it, anyway, in 1 Corinthians 6:15. The Authorized Version gives 'Know ye not that your bodies are the members of Christ?' But more modern versions prefer 'temples' – and that seems to strike the right chord. And, of course, your body cannot be said to be ready to **fight the good fight** (1 Timothy, 6:12) unless it is in peak condition. One way to do this is to **gird your loins**. This expression is everywhere in the Bible, both Old and New Testaments. To **gird** means 'to put a belt around the waist', in other words, to prepare for exertion, the loins being the part of the body between the pelvis and the ribs.

St John's Gospel reminds us what to do when we're being judgmental: 'He that is without sin among you, let him **first cast a stone**.' (8:7) In fact, the last two words are missing from this quotation, which should end 'at her', since Jesus was arguing with a crowd who wanted to stone an adulterous woman. From one stone to an even bigger one: Paul, in 1 Corinthians (13:2), wrote the memorable exhortation: '...though I have all faith, so that I could (re)**move mountains**, and have not charity, I am nothing'. Moving – or removing, depending on the translation – mountains is an enviable occupation, and one that still exists, as then, in the imagination.

And for those trapped under the relocated mountain? A painful death, probably, that will lead them to **give up the ghost**. The Bible translators may not have been the first to put it this way, but in 1388 the scholar John Wyclif (c. 1330–84) translated

Matthew 27:50 as, 'Jhesus eftsoone criede with a greet voyce and gaf vp the goost'. Jesus also 'gave up the ghost' in Mark, Luke and John. Another ghostly phrase that post-dates the Bible is 'Williams hadn't the **ghost of a chance** with Tom at wrestling' from *Tom Brown's Schooldays* (Thomas Hughes 1857).

By the Bard

Whereas Wyclif, Tyndale, Coverdale and the other great Bible translators were rendering sacred texts into the most formal language, to be spoken in church at births, marriages and deaths, Shakespeare's linguistic daring was created for that most despised of settings – if you were a Puritan – the popular theatre. At the end of the Anglo-Saxon period of British history – before about AD 1100 – the size of the lexicon (the total number of words in use) was around 50,000. By the end of what is known as the Middle English period it had doubled, and it would double again in early modern English. The current *OED* has about 400,000 **lexemes** – 'a word in the most abstract sense, as a meaningful form without an assigned grammatical role; an item of vocabulary' – in actual use (and 100,000 marked as obsolete or obsolescent). Shakespeare's output ran from 1588 (*Love's Labour's Lost* and *Titus Andronicus*) to *Henry VIII* in 1613. During this amazing, life-long burst of creativity, he coined many words that we use to this day, as well as many – **acture, anthropophaginian, bepray, besort, conceptious, fustilarian, irregulous** – that have not lasted quite so well.

Shakespeare, like Chaucer, gave vent to a full range of dialect voices, and he likewise made much of the contrast between learned and common speech. Shakespeare's word play was endless, not least because of the lack of grammatical inhibition that English was beginning to show. When Cleopatra said of Antony, 'He words me, girls' (V.ii), we understand that she is being chatted up. This is the first recorded use of **word** as a verb (1608). Similarly, and again for the first time, Antony talks of being **windowed** (IV.xv), in the sense of being shown off or exhibited. (It was thirty years before a different writer would use it to mean 'to furnish with windows'.[8]) Many of these words enter the dictionary as one-offs, as if only Shakespeare's daring or **pedantry** – he invented the words **pedant** and **pedantical** – could have put them there. But many more phrases have lodged themselves permanently in our mental phrase books, so much so as to appear at times almost clichéd. We may not know the original context in which the phrases were used, but there are so many in daily use that it **beggars[9] all description**, to quote again from *Antony and Cleopatra* (II.ii).

How much Shakespeare is there in daily English? 'Thereby hangs a tale' we could say, quoting from Act Four of *The Taming of the Shrew* (1596) (IV.i), where the phrase first appears. He evidently liked this turn of phrase, as he used it again two years later in *The Merry Wives of Windsor* (I.iv). At moments of heightened emotion, it seems, we often reach for a phrase of Shakespeare's. If you're feeling happy, you might echo Pistol, the friend of Sir John Falstaff in *The Merry Wives of Windsor*, when he says, 'Why then **the world's mine Oyster**, which I, with

----

8 That man was the Earl of Essex's favourite spy Sir Henry Wotton (1568–1639), the man who defined his job of ambassador as 'an honest man sent to lie abroad for the good of his country.'
9 The origin of the word 'beg' could come from a thirteenth-century order of friars called Beghards or Beguins, who carried no money and relied on charity. They were known as 'mendicants', from the Latin *mendicare*, meaning 'to beg'.

sword will open' (II.ii), perhaps hoping or expecting to find a pearl lying within.

Someone who rarely felt so benevolent in that same play was Mistress Page, who at one point splutters 'I cannot tell what the **dickens** his name is' (III.ii), invoking an old name for the Devil. If there was an earlier **devilkin** or **deilkin** from which this is derived, none has turned up, but later in the seventeenth century the word is used to curse, as in **the dickens take you** or **go to the dickens**, and if someone has **played the dickens**, they have caused mischief or havoc.

Falstaff is the cause of raised tempers in *Henry IV Part Two* (1597), when an exasperated Mistress Quickly demands that Falstaff be arrested. 'For what sum?' asks the Lord Chief Justice. 'It is more than for some, my lord,' she says, misunderstanding, 'it is for all, all I have. He hath eaten me out of house and home: he hath put all my substance into that fat belly of his.' (II.i) **To eat someone out of house and home** passed rapidly into the language, but the two words 'house' and 'home' have somewhat different CVs. Both are Old English, and first recorded – in the Anglo-Saxon poem *Beowulf* and the Lindisfarne Gospels – within a hundred years of each other at the turn of the first millennium AD. **House** could be connected to the verb 'to hide': both have a sense of private space. 'House' was used in *Beowulf* to mean 'a building for human habitation; esp. a building that is the ordinary dwelling-place of a family'. But we also find other formations, such as **almshouse**, **lighthouse** and **workhouse**. **Home**, by contrast, meant 'A village or town' in the year 900, or 'a collection of dwellings; a village with its cottages'. A **home from home**, as used in the 1400s, is cosier than a house could ever be. 'England is my home,' someone might say emotively. They wouldn't say, 'It's my house,' unless they didn't speak English very well.

And if the Lord Chief Justice had lost his temper with both Falstaff and Mistress Quickly, he might well have said **a plague on both your houses**, which were almost the dying Mercutio's last words in *Romeo and Juliet* (III.i) (1592). Having been struck under the arm, he repeated that curse three times, while admitting that he was **peppered** (i.e. not long) for this world. 'Plague on't,' wrote Jonathan Swift (1667–1745) in one of his pamphlets. The word **plague** is Greek (*plaga*), meaning 'stroke' or 'blow'. The *OED* cites it as a borrowing from Latin, reinforced by French. **Plague, pestilence** and **infection** all came into the English language via the Latin Vulgate translation of the Bible of AD 405.

We noted earlier that apples bob up all over the Bible. They feature in Shakespeare too. If anyone has ever been described as a **rotten apple**, the reference is to *The Taming of the Shrew* (I.iii). 'Faith, as you say, there's small choice in rotten apples,' says Hortensio, referring to the rather poor choice between marriage to Katharina the shrew, and being whipped at the high cross every morning. And Antonio in *The Merchant of Venice* refers to Shylock as A **goodly apple rotten at the heart** (I.iii). (Apples can be good too, of course. New York has prided itself on being the **Big Apple** since 1921, when horse races were held in the city, and the 'big apple' became the term for the prize, which later spread to mean the city itself.)

There are plenty of other such expressions in *The Taming of the Shrew*. The word **shrew** is believed to be related to the shrew mouse, which was held to be unlucky, as a manual from 1545 which is quoted in the *OED* suggests: 'a kynde of myse called a shrew, whyche yf it goo ouer a beastes backe, he shall be lame in the chyne'. There is an old German[10] word *schröuwel*, which

---

10 Middle High German, to use the proper linguistic description.

means 'devil', and Chaucer may have used it in that sense too, but 'shrew' did not originally imply 'woman'. Around the year 1250, and for centuries after, it meant 'a wicked, evil-disposed, or malignant man; a mischievous or vexatious person; a rascal, villain'.

We know that Chaucer also used the term 'shrew' to denote a scolding wife, but another strange transformation in the word's meaning came in the sixteenth century, when it drew near to the word **sheep** in an unflattering sort of way. A country writer called Thomas Tusser wrote in a 1573 husbandry manual, 'Now be she lambe or be she eaw, Giue me the sheepe, take thou the shreaw'. Another writer, John Lyly, wrote in 1580 that 'although the virgin were somwhat shrewishe at the first, yet in time she myght become a sheepe'.

Cleopatra, another feisty woman, invokes lettuce rather than apples in *Antony and Cleopatra*, when she refers to 'My **sallad dayes**, When I was greene in iudgement, cold in blood' (I.v). Just like a good fresh lettuce should be. Professional wordsmith Michael Quinion, in his word column on Salad Days, writes: 'for Shakespeare a salad wasn't just lettuce with some dressing, but a much more complicated dish of chopped, mixed and seasoned vegetables (its name comes from the Latin word for salt)'.

But, as we know, Shakespeare can be **hot-blooded** too. 'Now the hot-blooded Gods assist me!' shouts Falstaff in *The Merry Wives of Windsor* (V.v), as he springs on to the stage with horns on his head and ready for love. And, sure enough, within minutes he was in trouble of his own making, which is a somewhat different way of saying what was described by Alonso and Trinculo in *The Tempest* as being **in a pickle**, a reference to drunkenness (V.i).

'What's here?' says Arragon in *The Merchant of Venice* (1596). 'The portrait of a **blinking** idiot.' (II.ix) At that time this epithet simply meant 'winking' or someone with weak eyes. A 1914 edition of the *Scotsman* newspaper oversaw the word's transition into a minor swear word: 'One Guardsman … declared … that His Majesty seemed to carry the "blinking Army List in his 'ead".' More famously, in *The Merchant of Venice*, the Jewish moneylender Shylock demands his 'pound of flesh' (IV.i), a phrase that has come to stand for the unjust and relentless pursuance of any debt. No wonder that Antonio, from whom he sought repayment, was unwilling to satisfy the debt, but would the word 'sorry' have **stuck in his throat**? If it had, Antonio would have been quoting from *Macbeth* (1605), when the eponymous anti-hero returns to his wife in Act Two after she had told him to **screw your courage to the sticking-place** (I.vii) so that he could murder Duncan, King of Scotland. 'I had most need of blessing, and "Amen" stuck in my throat,' says Shakespeare's tormented hero (II.ii). Ever since, more words than ever have been sticking in people's throats.

It all ends rather messily, of course, and there is very little **milk of human kindness** (I.v) in evidence by the time Birnam Wood is relocated in Dunsinane. But still, **Come what come may**, as Macbeth says (I.iii) in one of his many asides, and from which later generations extracted the second 'come'.

Shakespeare was generous with his good lines: he liked baddies to sound well-spoken too, and in *Othello* the dastardly Iago jokes darkly – one could almost say he crows, in the circumstances – 'I will wear my heart upon my sleeve for **daws** to peck at' (I.i). 'Daws' are small crows, more commonly jackdaws. *Othello* has a wealth of other marvellous allusions to the dark side of human nature, such as the **green-eyed monster** of jealousy (III.iii), from green's meaning of 'sickly or bilious'. The play has other famous phrases, such as **pride, pomp and**

circumstance (III.iii), from which we have since lost the first word, and **foregone conclusion** (III.iii), though commentators have not been able to agree whether the word 'conclusion', as used here by Shakespeare, means 'a final result', 'an experiment' or 'the outcome of a discussion'.

Hamlet, the play about the University of Wittenberg's most illustrious and ill-starred ex-student, gave more phrases to English than any other play. We could make several paragraphs out of well-known *Hamlet* expressions, from **more in sorrow than in anger** (I.ii) and **to the manner born** (I.iv), to being **cruel to be kind** (III.iv), **in my mind's eye** (I.ii), **suspecting foul play** (I.ii), **holding the mirror up to nature** (III.ii), and being **hoist with your own pétard** (III.iv). It's worth noting that a 'petard' is defined in the *OED* as 'a small engine of war used to blow in a door or gate, or to make a breach in a wall, etc.'. The word owes its origin in part to the French word *petard*, which is from the verb *péter*, meaning 'to break wind'.

The tide of change

The works of Shakespeare and the books of the Bible represent a high point – perhaps a 'golden age' – in a language that is, for the most part, more or less recognizable as modern English. They wrestle with great moral issues, but they are also full of the most fantastic stories. On the BBC Radio 4 programme *Desert Island Discs*, castaways are invited to choose a favourite book, 'as well as the Bible and Shakespeare', as if there might not be enough to keep them occupied with just those two works alone. There are 791,328 words in the King James Bible, and 884,647 in Shakespeare. That's a grand total of 1,675,975 words, which should be enough to keep most readers gripped between the time it takes for a potential rescue boat to get from one side of the horizon to the other. And yet, of course, the marooned guests of *Desert Island Discs* always ask for one extra book – and they would probably light a fire and wave if they looked up and saw any chance of rescue. Why? Because human beings are curious and they always want something more.

But language did not stop evolving just because it had reached a stylistic high point, so we continue our exploration of English, not in the hands of great writers, but with snuff merchants, carpet traders, fabric printers, roof tilers, circus promoters, vegetable packers and make-up appliers. And if there's a boat on the horizon, it'll just have to wait.

Chapter Five

Local Lingo

Volume one of Joseph Wright's *English Dialect Dictionary*, containing the letters A–C, was published in 1898. The sixth volume, T–Z, came out in 1905. In between the first proper word **aam** (chill) and the last, **zwodder** (drowsy) is the most comprehensive attempt ever made to bring together the dialect words of the English language, and it is reasonably clear what was at the back of Wright's mind. In the introduction to the first volume he explains that the book is intended to be a museum for dialect words, but also, to some extent, a mausoleum. 'It is quite evident from the letters daily received … that pure dialect speech is rapidly disappearing from our midst,' he wrote, 'and that in a few years it will be almost impossible to get accurate information about difficult points.' He obviously hadn't met any 'chavs'.

Wright cannot have anticipated the upsurge in regional pride that took place in the latter years of the twentieth century. Regional speech is now regarded as one of the glories of the British Isles. A few generations ago, if you travelled the length of the country, you would have been exposed to a pick-and-mix selection of independent strains of speech, in which words and phrases, accents and emphases differed from place to place, sometimes from street to street. The BBC Voices Survey (www.bbc.co.uk/voices) keeps track of our changing English language, recording people from all over the country and charting the many different ways of saying different things. For example, Professor Paul Kerswill of Lancaster University has a page in which he describes the changing accent of Reading, whose older citizens have the Berkshire accent, which, as he says, sounds West Country to many people, while young people reflect the influence of the London accent.

In a sense, the survey is carrying on the tradition established by the *Survey of English Dialects*, an information-gathering project that was created by Harold Orton and Eugen Dieth in 1946. By October 1950 they were ready to take their model questionnaire out on the road and put their carefully composed queries to local people in a wide variety of places. In all, 313 localities were chosen, usually not more than 25km (15 miles) apart, in villages with a fairly stable population base. Those interviewed, says *The Cambridge Encyclopedia of Language*, 'were natives of the locality, mainly male agricultural workers, with good mouths, teeth and hearing, and over sixty years of age'. The interviewees were asked up to 1300 questions about farming, animals, housekeeping, weather and social activities. Over 404,000 items of information were recorded.

The *Survey of English Dialects* was published in four volumes between 1962 and 1971, culminating in *The Linguistic Atlas of England* (1978). As an example, they were asked what word they would use for **snack**. The answers were traced in all their dizzying variety across England from Cornwall to Northumberland: in all, forty-two alternatives were offered, from 'progger' (around Dover or Felixstowe) to 'ten-o'-clock(s)' on the

Scottish border. Around the Wash the most common word was 'lunch'; in the southwest tip of Cornwall it was 'crust', but further north in the county they found 'crib'. In Devon they came up with 'nammet(s)'. Other words offered around the country included 'bagging(s)', 'bait', 'beaver', 'dew-bit', 'docky', 'dowen', 'jower', 'lowance', 'minnin-on', 'nummick', 'snap', 'tenses' and 'tommy'. All this in a country just larger than the US state of Pennsylvania.

Has all this diversity disappeared, or resurfaced in another form? Walk into any shopping centre today (having remembered to take off your **hoodie**) and you will see how **dialect**[1] has to some extent given way to **sociolect**.[2] Whereas dialect is geographically specific, sociolect groups people together not by where they live but by how they speak. Sociolects are linguistic subcultures: groups of kids right across the country could all be saying 'ayrie' if the word catches on.

We should note, though, that the word 'dialect' is a disputed term, and that languages, as well as people, can make war. Before Yugoslavia dissolved into anarchy, Serbian and Croatian were regarded as dialects of the Serbo-Croatian language. Several years later, after hundreds of thousands of deaths and some hasty paper shuffling, they were carefully regarded as separate languages. You might even call 'dialect' a dirty word, though we might use **reasty** as a Black Country substitute for 'dirty', or a wonderful Orcadian (Orkney) word **skyuimy**. These days the word **variety** is preferred to 'dialect', as if the d-word were pejorative: is Scots a language or a dialect? Is Brummie a dialect or an accent? Is

----

1 Dialect, 1577: 'One of the subordinate forms or varieties of a language arising from local peculiarities of vocabulary, pronunciation, and idiom.'
2 Sociolect, 1972: 'A variety of a language that is characteristic of the social background or status of its user.'

anyone down south hard enough to find out? The dialect map is shrinking, but it is still a tapestry of the English tongue.

What's in a burr?

A rough sounding of the letter *r; spec.* the rough uvular trill (= French *r grasseyé*) characteristic of the county of Northumberland, and found elsewhere as an individual peculiarity. (Writers ignorant of phonology often confuse the Northumberland *burr* with the entirely different Scotch *r*, which is a lingual trill: see quots. 1835, 1873.)

   1760 FOOTE *Minor* (1781) Introd. 9 An Aunt just come from the North, with the true NewCastle bur in her throat. 1805 R. FORSYTH *Beauties Scotl.* II. 57 From [the Tweed], southward as far as Yorkshire, universally all persons annex a guttural sound to the letter *r;* a practice which in someplaces receives the appellation of the Berwick *burrh*. 1835 W. IRVING *Crayon Misc.* (1849) 240 He spoke with a Scottish accent, and with somewhat of the Northumbrian 'burr'. 1873 J.A.H. MURRAY *Dial. S. Scotl.* 86 The northern limits of the *burr* are very sharply defined, there being no transitional sound between it and the Scotch *r*. Along the line of the Cheviots, the Scotch *r* has driven the *burr* a few miles back, perhaps because many of the farmers and shepherds are of Scotch origin. 1876 GREEN *Short Hist.* i. §3 (1882) 25 The rough Northumbrian burr.

   b. Hence, *loosely*, A rough or dialectal pronunciation, a peculiarity of utterance.

   1849 C. BRONTË *Shirley* iv. 39 'A Yorkshire burr … was … much better than a cockney's lisp.' *Ibid.* III. ii. 41 Your accent … has no rugged burr. 1867 A.J. ELLIS *E.E. Pronunc.* I. i. 19 Each district has its burr or brogue. 1874 FARRAR *Christ* II. lix. 348 Betrayed by his Galilaean burr.

North, south, east and west

Henry Higgins, the professor of linguistics in George Bernard Shaw's *Pygmalion* (1913), was fascinated by accents in the same way that rubber-neckers[3] can't help staring at car crashes. 'Hear a

---

3 US slang. As verb: 'To crane the neck in curiosity, to gape; also, to look around, to sight-see' (1896). As noun: 'Someone who stares; an inquisitive person; a sight-seer, a tourist' (1899).

Yorkshireman, or worse, hear a Cornishman converse, I'd rather hear a choir singing flat,' he harrumphed in *My Fair Lady*, the film based on the play. And yet all of us speak some form of dialect English, even when we don't know we're doing so. Take **grockles**, a pejorative term for 'holidaymakers'. Many of us may have used the word ourselves. It is marked in the dictionary as 'origin uncertain', but its first recorded use in the *OED* was in the October 1964 magazine *Films & Filming*, which mentions 'life's drifters who wend their way down to these resorts to make an easy living off the "grockles" (holidaymakers) during the four months of the summer season'. Since that appearance, it has blossomed, along with caravans, until the *Daily Telegraph* in August 1986 could poke fun at **grockle fodder** (fish and chips), **grockle bait** (the merchandise sold in souvenir shops), and **grockle nests** (camp sites). That same paper got the summer of 2004 off to a typically bilious start by describing the queues of caravans on the road in the West Country as the start of the **grockle-hutch season**. Meanwhile, Norfolk was described as 'an unusual mixture of the trendy and **grockle-ridden**, alluding to tasteful bungalows shoved next to caravan sites virtually falling off cliff-tops.

Of course, there's no use grizzling over a bad press. **Grizzle** originally meant 'to show the teeth; to grin or laugh, especially mockingly'. The following examples, gathered from the *OED*, make it pretty clear that the word was a West Country coinage:

> Grizzle: 1746 *Exmoor Scolding* Tamzen and Thee be olweys ... stivering or grizzling, tacking or busking. 1837 Mrs Palmer *Devonian Dialects* The ould man grizzled: No sure, lovy, zed he, I ne'er had the leastest inkling for such a thing. 1880 *West Cornwall Glossary* 'What's the g'eat bufflehead grizzling at?' "He grizzled at me; he was as vexed as fire.'

One hundred years after the first reference to 'grizzle', it has moved away from its local base, and its meaning. By 1842 it means 'To fret, sulk; to cry in a whining or whimpering fashion' and has made it into a book of Kentish dialect.

Heading up towards Wales, in Hereford, you might still hear someone say 'Have you heard the **charm** in the garden?' Trace that one back a few hundred years and you would find a reference to Milton's *Paradise Lost*: 'Sweet is the breath of morn, her rising sweet, / With charm of earliest birds' (IV:642). *The New Shorter OED* also lists the noun or verb **chirm** as, for example, 'the sound of birds singing or children chattering': the two sounds are probably more easily distinguishable these days, since birds – lacking thumbs – have not yet acquired the skill of using a Gameboy.

For almost every area of Britain there is a dictionary of local dialect. Many of these were compiled during the nineteenth century, and are smaller, localized versions of Joseph Wright's *English Dialect Dictionary*. Anticipating Harold Orton and Eugen Dieth's *Survey of English Dialects*, they paint a unique picture of a landscape that was still largely rustic but must have been disappearing almost as fast as the book was being completed. A good linguistic guide to the area might tell you that in Ludlow, for example, 120 square metres (144 square yards) of coppice wood make a **lugg**. And an old farmer might be able to point to twenty-four sheaves of corn and describe them as a **thrave**.

But dialect words do not have to be obscure, still less obsolete. Many, with very specific regional origins, now enrich all our tongues. One reason that we have so many words is that we freely use synonyms from all over the UK. In the Midlands, for example, the young William Shakespeare might once have played in a **yard** as opposed to a **garden** or **garth**; the last of these is still used in some eastern and northern parts. (In fact, they are all connected at the roots. The ancient word *gard* or *gart* means 'an enclosure'.) 'Yard', from the same word root, meant 'a twig' in Old English (*c.* AD 950). Then around AD 1000 it meant 'a staff' or 'walking stick' and, during the same period, the stick was laid on the ground and used as a measurement. The French word *verge* also means 'stick' or 'cane', and was introduced by Edward III in 1353, when French units were all the rage, but the English word came back into fashion, and **verge** (which originally, before 1400, meant 'penis') went on to mean a sceptre. Its sense of 'edge' or 'margin' is fifteenth-century.

The *OED* has **manky** meaning 'skittish horse', from **mank** ('a hesitation; a fuss, to-do'). It also has 'manky' meaning 'bad, inferior, defective' and notes that it is 'of uncertain origin', but it might be connected to the Brummie word meaning 'heaving with maggots'.

Brummies also claim **conk** as their own, perhaps as a figurative application of the word 'conch', which comes from the French *conque* (shell). 'Conk' has a spirited literary ancestry stretching back to the early nineteenth century and means 'nose' or 'face', though these days it has comic book associations, being the word that accompanies custard pies and pratt-falls. During the nineteenth century **to conk someone** was to punch them on the nose. In the twentieth century – and perhaps in response to such an assault – **to conk out** meant to faint. In the Midlands, however, **to conk** means to talk, chat or gossip, from an eighteenth-century verb meaning 'to cackle like geese'. And **chelp** is the Midlands or northern term for impudence, as in 'I want you on your best behaviour when the grandma and grandpa get here; any of your chelp and you'll be grounded for the week.'

From Lincolnshire to Cumbria, in parts of Britain that were occupied by the Danes and Norwegians, **beck** means a 'brook' or 'stream'. But there are other rivulets of meaning attached to 'beck'.[4] You could make a sign or nod your assent to someone in Scotland by **becking**, a shortened form of the verb 'to beckon', which led to the expression about being at someone's **beck and call**. Scots writer John Arbuthnot (1667–1735), who came to be Queen Mary's personal physician, used it to mean 'curtseying': 'I must stand becking and binging'.[5] He was a friend of writers such as Alexander Pope and Jonathan Swift, and wrote a satirical pamphlet called 'The Art of Political Lying'. Dr Johnson described him as 'The most Universal Genius'.

Central Northamptonshire fifty years ago was no place for a left-hander. The word **cack-handed**, which means 'clumsy', was reserved for them. This disgraceful slur starts badly and gets worse, since the word **cack** means 'shit' in most Germanic languages – as in the sentence, 'I was so nervous I was cacking myself' – so 'cack-handed' is the equivalent of saying that one had shit on one's hands. In the same region, **clod-hoppers** was a rather deft play on the word 'grass-hopper', and is an example of many instances where country life was an easy target for mockery. These days a nasty newspaper critic might describe a rather **leaden-footed** performance of Beethoven's *First Symphony* as **clod-hopping**, but around 1690 'clodhopper' was a slightly mocking word for a ploughman. The *OED*'s first definition is 'one who walks over ploughed land; a ploughman

---

4 'Beck' is also the name of an agricultural implement used for dressing turnips and hops, and a large shallow vessel or tub used in brewing and dyeing.
5 From *Law Is a Bottomless Pit* (1712). 'To binge' meant 'to fawn' right through to the nineteenth century.

or agricultural labourer; a country lout; hence, a clumsy awkward boor, a clown'. By 1836, 'clodhoppers' had come to refer to the ploughman's shoes. The word implies a yokel making slow progress across a field of clods or lumps of earth. Charles Dickens in *Martin Chuzzlewit* (1843) writes of 'A common, paltry, low-minded, clodhopping, pipe-smoking alehouse'. **Clod** is a fourteenth-century variant from 'clot', the word for 'a lump of anything, especially blood'. What a difference a 'd' makes.

The past will out

It may be news to some that the first official female police constable in the country came from Grantham. Her name was Edith Smith and she joined the force in August 1915. More familiar is the name of another public servant supplied by Grantham: Margaret Thatcher. In April 1983 in the House of Commons, the Labour MP Denis Healey tried to goad the prime minister by asserting that her plans for a June election proved her desire to **cut and run**. The Iron Lady cut him down with the following retort: 'Oh, the right honourable gentleman is afraid of an election is he? ...''Fraid, frightened, **frit**!' This last word was pure Grantham – dredged up from her roots in a moment of high emotion.

The most familiar northern English dialects are those spoken in Yorkshire, Lancashire, Cumbria and Tyneside. These make much greater use of original Angle vocabulary – about 80 per cent, as opposed to the more diluted 30 per cent down south. Yorkshire is still the place to go to hear the second person singular pronoun **thou** used with a degree of regularity, and words such as **aye** and **nay** are still heard a lot when 'yes' and 'no' are standard. Family words are different: northern speakers, and Scots especially, will say bairn for 'baby', and you'll find a **lad** or **lass** (boy or girl) playing, again in the yard (not garden) – at least in those houses that had yards. Scandinavian agricultural vocabulary survives in words such as **pike** (a small stack of hay).

In York it must be reassuring for visitors from Denmark, Norway and Iceland to see streets called Walmgate, Coppergate, Stonegate and Skeldergate, since the word for 'street' in those countries is *gata*. **Skeldering** – 'a cant term of obscure origin' attested from 1601 – means 'to live by begging, especially by passing oneself off as a wounded or disbanded soldier', which gives you some idea of the quality of folk who used to congregate in that street. York's **gates** should not be confused with its gateways, which are called bars; nor should its **bars** be confused with its pubs, which, reassuringly, are called pubs.

Modern northern writers are not scared of taking traditional language and making dialogue that manages to be both antiquated yet recognizable to a contemporary reader. In, for example, *The Blackpool Highflyer* by Andrew Martin (2004), every page emits an unmistakably Yorkshire flavour. 'You look **all-in**,' says one character. 'Will you **give it here** for a moment?' says another. Someone else says, '**Frame** yourself, man!' in the sense of **pull yourself together**. One truculent character says, 'I was **blowed** if I was going to tell him the truth'. When people don't believe something, they say, '**Get away**.' And when something good happens, they say, 'You must be **chuffed**.' With that last word, Martin is visiting the sight of a 1960 literary skirmish, since two novels, published in that year, contained absolutely contradictory definitions. Auberon Waugh's *The Foxglove Saga* used it to mean 'pleased': 'He was chuffed at this new monumental skive he had discovered.' Whereas in David Storey's *This Sporting Life*, when Frank Machin says, 'I felt pretty chuffed with myself,' he means the complete opposite: displeased or disgruntled.[6] Despite the classic status of Storey's novel, Waugh's positive meaning has won through. During the nineteenth century a **skive** was a hard-working tool, used for cutting or polishing diamonds. In 1829 a **skiver** was a 'person who split leather' – there are references to this profession from Newcastle-upon-Tyne and Ayrshire. But 'skiver' came to mean 'one who avoids work; a shirker; a truant' in military slang from the early twentieth century, perhaps from the French *esquiver*, meaning 'to dodge or slink away'.

In Lancashire and many other areas, a comical euphemism for 'dying' is to **pop one's clogs**. We have written evidence of **clog** meaning 'wooden shoe' from the fifteenth century. In the seventeenth century **to clog** meant to put wooden soles on shoes, as a blacksmith shoes a horse. The *OED* says it was common in the north of England and the south of Scotland during this period for people to take their shoes to the **clogger**, who would 'clog' them for the winter. To this day in Scotland a 'clog' is a 'heavy block, especially of wood, fastened to the legs of a person or animal to impede motion'. (We can be certain that clog-dancing owed nothing to this definition.) That notion of impeding motion now applies to traffic getting **clogged up** during peak periods, which might cause some people to start 'mithering'.

According to the *OED*, to **mither** means 'to complain or moan'. It's related to the word **moider** from the Irish *modartha*, meaning 'dark, murky, morose'. In 1587 'mither' meant 'to confuse', but confusingly, by 1828 it meant 'to work very hard', which is pretty confusing. Then it meant 'to babble or ramble',

---

6 Why not gruntled? Because the verb 'to gruntle' means 'To utter a little or low grunt. Said of swine, occas. of other animals; *rarely* of persons.' In use 1400–1855.

and by 1847 meant 'to smother, muffle up; to encumber, burden'. A year later it had the meaning 'to bother, pester, worry, irritate'. Then it meant 'to ramble, be delirious; to "go on"; to complain, make a fuss, whine', as in this 1998 example from the *Observer* newspaper: 'The throng of pale grey Brummie lawyers sipping champagne and mithering ... about how poor they are.'

In Liverpool, the affectionate appellation **wack** as a familiar term of address, like 'pal', was attributed to Ringo Starr when it first appeared in a 1963 Beatles fan magazine (this was at a time when Merseyside speech still needed subtitles in some parts of the country). If you were feeling **chordy** anywhere near Merseyside, you would be feeling 'moody' elsewhere. The derivation is uncertain, and surely not derived from the eighteenth-century word **chordee**, defined by the *OED* – though they have more sense than to try to make a connection between the words – as 'a painful inflammatory downward curving of the penis', which would put anyone – or most men – off their chips. The same city gave us **scally**, which is defined by the *OED* as 'a young working-class person (esp. a man); *specifically* a roguish, self-assured male (esp. from Liverpool), typically regarded as boisterous, disruptive, or irresponsible'.

New dialect words are coming into the language the whole time, but some are not as new as we might think. After Liverpool's dramatic win on penalties against AC Milan in May 2005, their inspirational captain Steven Gerrard expressed his delight at goalkeeper Jerzy Dudek, whose goal-line antics – wobbling his knees and swaying from side-to-side – had evidently psyched out the AC Milan penalty takers. Gerrard said he was **made up** (see Chapter 1, page 36) for the thousands of fans who had travelled to Istanbul. That expression[7] has been in use since at least 1956, when it meant 'assured of success or happiness…'. A long time before, it meant 'of a person: consummate, accomplished' as used by Shakespeare in Timon of Athens (1616): 'Know his grosse patchery … Yet remaine assur'd that he's a made-up Villaine' (V.i).

In the north of England if you feel 'tired' you'll say you're **jiggered**. The noun form, jigger, has two separate meanings in the

---

From battleground to boardroom

Does anyone still use the word **slughorn**? You might hear it if you were eavesdropping on military leaders, since it is a variant of 'war cry', which goes back to at least 1513. The cry usually included someone's name, as in 'Advance, McDonald!' and was known generically as a **slogan**. Since the eighteenth century it has lost some of its belligerent overtone, and is now used in advertising – odd bedfellows perhaps, not unlike a redundant miner who has found employment in the fast-food industry.

---

7 Which the *OED* says is 'Irish English and British regional (esp. Liverpool) English.'

OED. The first means 'someone who dances a jig' and the second is a type of tropical flea. Perhaps when the flea had stopped jigging it was exhausted – hence the word 'jiggered'. In other parts of Yorkshire you might use the word fligged for the same purpose. Over to the northeast, Geordie and Northumbrian words are more than 80 per cent Angle (Danish) in origin, so, for example, the Geordie phrase **gannin yem** (going home) would be perfectly understood by a Norwegian. The phrase **Ah wes pelatick**,[8] meaning anything from 'I enjoyed myself' to 'I was completely smashed, bladdered, pissed, etc.', may not yet have travelled far outside the city walls, but *Viz* comic, which is still produced in Newcastle upon Tyne, has popularized such sayings as, 'Join the army cos all the birds are **gagging** for squaddies'. Even better if they are **bonny** (good-looking), but less likely if they're **canny** ('knowing, sagacious, judicious, prudent; wary, cautious').

Present-day Scottish writers have proved themselves to be among the most dynamic and exciting writers today. Liz Lochhead, A.L. Kennedy, James Kelman and Irvine Welsh have all explored their Scots heritage differently. 'Sae the Kirk Assembly are makkin' a mountain oot o' a **mowdie**-hill,' writes Lochhead in *Mary Queen of Scots* (1989), using the Scots word for 'mole'. She also used the term 'fuck-me shoes' in her 1985 book *True Confessions & New Clichés*. The only printed predecessor was David Bowie's 1974 album *Diamond Dogs* which had 'fuck-me pumps'. Welsh, in *Trainspotting* (1993), throws in phrases such as 'Dinnae really ken the boy. Only likesay run intae the gadge a couple ay times since we were **ankle-biters**, ken?' 'Ankle-biter' was first used to mean 'small child' in an 1850 issue of *Harper's Magazine*. And Welsh, who has an honourable forty-one

---

8 Etymology a total mystery.

quotations to his name in the *OED*, was on the money again where we find the following:'I open my overcoat and flap it to see if the **ming** is as steadily rancid as I imagine it to be' (*Filth*, 1998).

Minging, in the sense of 'stinking', (attested from 1970) is one of the twentieth century's less attractive words. It used to be an alternative to **mingling**, which lasted from Old English to the mid-nineteenth century. It was also an Old English alternative to the etymologically distinct warning word **mind**, as in 'Mind you don't do that', and later went from 'looking out' to simply 'remembering', but by the eighteenth century that use had gone too. **Meng** merits an honourable mention in the 1923 *Roxburghshire Word-book*, where it is defined as 'human excrement'. It might be related to another early nineteenth-century word, **ming**, meaning 'the ingredients mixed with or substituted for tar in sheep-smearing', but whether that was its true parentage or not, **minger** ('an ugly or unattractive person, esp. a woman') has come to be a particularly nasty insult, as internet discussion themes such as 'My wife is a minger: should I run away to Thailand?' can attest. Could ming in some way be a distant relative of the word minge, meaning vagina and believed to be a Romany word?

Cockney Rhyming Slang is the romantically preserved language spoken in a small area of East London, historically by people born within the sound of the bells of St Mary-le-Bow. It is spoken by young and old alike. Theories abound as to how the language originated: most likely is that it was a code system devised to keep small-time criminals from having their plans overheard. The word 'head', for example, was referred to as a 'loaf of bread', and then – as sometimes happened to further outfox nosy parkers – just 'loaf'. In the same way, 'talk' became first 'rabbit and pork' and then just 'rabbit'. Stairs have long been referred to as 'apples and pears', 'trouble (and strife)' is 'wife', and the phrase 'Would you Adam and Eve (believe) it?' has almost slipped into modern parlance. 'Alligator', as in 'See you later alligator' is originally rhyming slang. 'Barnet fair' stands for hair. 'Khyber pass' means 'arse' and 'mince pies' means 'eyes'. Admittedly, few of these words have much to do with small-time crime, though one is the word **scarper**, which has two roots – the Italian *scappare*, to escape, and the rhyming slang 'Scapa Flow', to go.

Evolving English

Regional English has entered a new and vibrant phase. Old English words are now mixing things up with the language of Britain's multicultural communities. 'British Asian adolescents may sound more British than Indians in India, but they just don't sound as British as their white counterparts,' wrote Rashmee Z. Ahmed of the *Times of India* in April 2004. He noted that Britain's second-generation Indians are revelling in their bilingual ethnicity, pronouncing ordinary English words, such as **goat**, **kill** and **face**, in a recognizably Indian way, and that they never go to see a **film**:'to British Asians, it's always a **fillum**'. (A pronunciation popular too in parts of Scotland and Ireland.) But for immigrant communities from that part of the world, their language is peppered with Indian words such as *gora*, a term for a white person, and *chuddies* (underpants). And wherever large numbers of British Asians live alongside the white community, linguistic co-habitation starts to take place. Asian English is a genuine sub-language, with words such as **innit**, which is short – though not that short – for 'isn't it', often appearing at the end of a sentence, where a full stop might do the same job on paper. The website urbandictionary.com quotes three exemplary snatches of dialogue:

> 'Shane's got that new Nokia phone, innit?' 'EastEnders was wicked tonight, innit?' '... and then she fell on her arse. That was well funny, innit?'

A recent study for the BBC Voices Survey found that the once traditionally cockney sound of London's East End was being influenced by the area's Bangladeshi community. Young white men in particular are starting to say *nang* (good), *creps* (trainers) and *skets* (slippers) in imitation of their neighbours. Other cultures are feeding into the mix too. Black English is a sub-language of many sources, and much of its vocabulary involves taking English words and, basically, having fun with them. At the beginning of the fourteenth century, **to big** meant 'to dwell in or inhabit', and in parts of Northern England and Scotland 'to big' still means 'to build'. In black British English, though, to **big up** means 'to talk up, praise or promote' something or someone – compare with 'large it' (see Chapter 11, page 268). **Irie**, developed from 'all right', is a word with a West Indian lilt, meaning 'nice' or 'good'. The slightly more confrontational **facety**

– a more intensive way of pronouncing the US slang word **feisty** – means 'bold', sometimes 'rude'. Someone who is **dissing** you (being disrespectful) could be said to be 'facety'. And anyone keen to show off their **Bimmer** (a nickname for BMW cars, which may have begun in the black community) will probably have an ample selection of **bling**. 'Bling' is not yet recognized by the *OED*, but rap and hip-hop street fashion have created this 'echoic' word, which mimics the chinking sound made by the wearer of a large amount of flashy gold jewellery.

For anyone who joins a gang, crew or **posse**, the last of these is shortened from the Latin *posse comitatus* (the force of the county), meaning 'a body of men raised and commanded by the sheriff'. As the word edged towards crime, the *OED*'s first sighting of it comes from the *Daily Gleaner*, based in Kingston, Jamaica, which reported in 1986 that 'Police have identified the largest and most feared Jamaican gangs as the "Shower Posse" … and the "Spangler Posse".'

Dialect can become a very emotive subject. **Chav** was named buzzword (see Chapter 11, page 256) of the year in 2004 by the linguistics expert Susie Dent in her book *Larpers and Shroomers*. Its prominence arose in part from the website chavscum.co.uk – 'A user's guide to Britain's new ruling class'. The behaviour of chavs is broadly anti-social. Many are regarded as **council** (on social security). Chavs wear baseball caps, trainers, branded shirts and jackets, preferably Burberry. The Chav Freebies website www.chavfreebies.co.uk offers wristbands, horoscopes and a dating service. Its 'Chav Bling' page – a sublime coupling of two linguistic sub-groups – offers a broad range of high street jewellery, all at the very reasonable prices you would expect.

The word 'chav' has caused huge debate in linguistic circles. It's possible that it comes from the Chatham area of Kent, where a lot of chavs live and don't exactly work. In the opinion of language scholar Michael Quinion, the word probably comes from the Romany *chavi*, meaning 'child', which has been in use since the middle of the nineteenth century. The word then went underground for about 150 years, only to resurface and haunt us all. In Newcastle, chavs are called **charvers**. They too wear fake designer and sports gear, are usually from poor backgrounds, and frequently get into fights with other youth groups, such as **goths**.[9] A website called Charver Central (www.newcastlestuff.com/charver) contains the following urban tale:

> I was on the back seat of a 38 bus heading for the West End, when two charver lasses parked themselves next to me. They were talking about last night, when one asked the other how she'd got on with Scott.
>
> 'He took me behind the Youth Club and we had a snog. Then he put his hand straight up me skort.'
>
> 'He nivva! What did y'dee?'
>
> 'Ah smacked him rund the heed and telt 'im, "Where's your fuckin' manners? It's tits first!"'

'Chav' may not be a beautiful word, but it is very much alive and with us. No doubt Joseph Wright would have been excited to come across it.

Revenge of the regions

Contemptuous of the linguistic anarchy that he observed all around him, George Bernard Shaw addressed the decline of

----

9 Once a Germanic tribe who invaded the East and West in the third to the fifth centuries. Now the name for someone whose fashion sense and choice of music celebrate a mood of horror, darkness and the supernatural.

English in his play *Pygmalion* (1913) as Europe was about to dissolve into a different and even more murderous form of anarchy. In the introduction he wrote, 'The English have no respect for their language, and will not teach their children to speak it. They spell it so abominably that no man can teach himself what it sounds like. It is impossible for an Englishman to open his mouth without making some other Englishman hate or despise him.'

Shaw's character Henry Higgins was modelled on the real-life Henry Sweet (1845–1912), one of the founders of the British School of Phonetics. As Higgins hangs around the streets of Covent Garden, he winces at what to his ears are the mangled vowels of the various coster-mongers and barrow-boys. His views had changed little by the time the play was filmed as *My Fair Lady* in 1964. 'Remember that you're a human being with a soul and the divine gift of articulate speech, that your native language is the language of Shakespeare and Milton and the Bible. Don't sit there crooning like a bilious pigeon,' he chides the flower seller Eliza Doolittle. To Higgins, the nearer one's speech was to standard English, the better one's chances of social advancement. 'Hear them down in Soho Square dropping aitches everywhere. Speaking English any way they like,' he chants.

'You, sir, did you go to school?' he asks one man. 'What do you tike me for, a fool?' the man hits back. 'No one taught him "take" instead of "tike",' says Higgins, but the man did learn to speak the way he did, just as Higgins learnt to talk posh. We think very differently about cockney speech these days. We still don't have many top officials in government dropping their aitches and minding their apples and pears, but nor do we have as many old Etonian accents in Cabinet. The main accent down south has become known as Estuary English, and the Mayor of London himself, Ken Livingstone, is a prime example of the species.

Higgins observes, 'It's "ohh" and "garn" that keep her in her place. Not her wretched clothes and dirty face.' The faces are cleaner these days, but the accent has not been scrubbed up that much.

The study of linguistics has moved on since the days of Henry Higgins. In December 2000, Australian researchers at Sydney's Macquarie University revealed their findings – in which they had compared the vowel sounds of the Queen's annual Christmas broadcasts over a period from the 1950s to the 1980s. The analysis revealed that the Queen's pronunciation of some vowels had drifted towards what is generally known as Estuary English – the term which comes from the Thames Estuary bordered by Kent and Essex, where this accent predominates. Her Majesty's pronunciation of 'had', for example, used to rhyme with 'bed', but now the 'a' was becoming more prominent and less like the sort of upper-class speech which used to be called 'cut-glass'. Whether this was conscious or not – an attempt by the Queen to 'get down' with the people or merely the inevitable result of fewer people talking that – the verdict seems to be that even the Queen doesn't speak the Queen's English.

Maybe this is a touch sweeping. The Queen's English, along with other similar terms like Oxford English, BBC English and Received Pronunciation (RP),[10] is a specific accent, and Estuary English seems to be influencing them all. But there was nothing pure about the Queen's English: it mangled all sorts of alien vowel sounds, such as 'hice' for house and 'clorth' for cloth. Nor was it enshrined that way for centuries. John Walker, in the 1791 preface to his *Critical Pronouncing Dictionary and Expositor of the English Language*, writes that 'The best educated people

----

10 Received pronunciation – the pronunciation of that variety of British English widely considered to be least regional, being originally that used by educated speakers in southern England.

in the provinces, if constantly resident there, are sure to be strongly tinctured with the dialect of the country in which they live.' So if Her Majesty has taken to pronouncing investiture 'investicher', or, for that matter, 'Eschery English', it proves how wise Samuel Johnson was when he realized that any attempt to 'fix' the language is doomed to failure.

So far we have been looking inwards, at the development and evolution of English words within the British Isles. But there has been an enormous influence on the English language from other countries and languages, and we need to address that too.

Chapter Six

Global Lingo

*L*anguages don't care which other languages they talk to, and the English language has for long been as chatty as the most up-for-it Club 18–30 holidaymaker, willing and eager to get to know the locals wherever on the globe it pitches up. Part of the trajectory of that journey was caused by imperial swell, as the British Empire gave fresh hope to several generations of red ink suppliers, but, given its promiscuity while abroad, the English language has proved remarkably good at making long-term relationships. Linguistic borders are porous, and the process normally rubs both ways, but English has absorbed enormous numbers of foreign words and phrases, some of which are heard more often on the lips of foreign-born English speakers than in the language of their origin. Our strongest connection is to our European neighbours and occasional enemies. But the other languages form a shadow world map that betrays the thud of British boots – whether military or mercantile – across the world for several centuries.

Arabian nights

What is the connection between a nineteenth-century British officer's off-duty clothing and a legal decision? The clue lies in the

Arabic word *fatiya*. In its basic form, that verb means 'to be youthful or adolescent'. But a more complex form of the same verb means 'to give a formal legal opinion' – from this comes *fatwa* – and a personage whose opinions are always listened to is a **mufti** (a legal expert entitled to pronounce on religious matters). From there, British soldiers overseas seem to have been rather struck by the resemblance, in dress terms, between an off-duty officer's wardrobe of dressing-gown, tasselled smoking cap and slippers and the costume of a *mufti*, so they named their non-uniform clothes after this legal grandee.

Another expression used by British Servicemen, but not recorded until the Second World War, was to have a **shufti** (look), which comes from the Arab *shufti*, meaning 'have you seen'.

Arabic has made a huge contribution to English, largely thanks to merchants, who were continually crossing trade routes between Europe and the Middle East, and who brought hundreds of Arabic words into the English language. Another, perhaps stranger, journey takes us from eye-liner to the local pub. The Arabic verb *kahhala*, pronounced with a slightly harder than usual H, means 'to rub, paint or smear with kohl'. **Kohl** was – and still is – used by women in the East to darken the area around the eyelids. Such femmes fatales as Jezebel and Cleopatra must have made use of this bewitching substance to cast their spell over men. In some societies, they even used to throw the substance into their eyes to give them extra sparkle. Arabic verbs can be pressed, squeezed or manipulated into all sorts of shapes, and *kahhala* was moulded into *kuhhūl*, meaning 'spirit'. The spirit in question, which was much in use when attached to the products of distillation, came to be known in medieval Latin as **alcohol**.

Given the prominence of alcohol in British society, it might seem like a slur on our national pride that the word 'alcohol' is not originally British. Consider, furthermore, that the Koran can be read as distinctly ambivalent about – if not downright hostile to – alcohol. But that is an example of what happened when British explorers met people of different races and traditions. Ideas spread, and words were one of the currencies for that encounter.

Another seemingly impeccable English word is **admiral** or the 'ruler of the Queen's Navee', to quote from Gilbert and Sullivan's *HMS Pinafore* (1878). In fact, it's not that impeccable, since it comes from the Arabic words *amiir al-bahr* meaning, literally, 'commander (*amiir*) of the (al) sea (*baHr*)', which was the title that the Arabs created for the leader of their navy after he had conquered Spain and Sicily. This phrase was successively adopted by the French, Genoese and English (under Edward III) who all apparently misunderstood the individual parts of the phrase and thought that the definite article *al* meant 'sea'. Eventually, the English dropped the final word *bahr* – because they didn't know it meant 'sea' – and, around 1500, ended up with a new official title that, somewhat eccentrically, meant 'commander of the', or *amir-al*. And, partly because the letter 'a' often stood for the Latin preposition *ad* (e.g. 'admirable'), the 'a-' soon changed to 'ad-' and we were left with a stump of a word, with nevertheless sweeping powers over an entire fleet.

Many other originally Arabic words retain their original *al*. One example is **alkali**, the salty substance at the other end of the pH scale from acid. The word was anglicized from the French *alcali* and is derived from the verb *qalay*, which means 'to fry or roast in a pan'. You might have guessed by now that **algebra** is ultimately from Arabic, but did you know that in our earliest sighting of the word, from 1541, it means 'bone-setting'? A mere ten years later, however, it refers to mathematics. How so? Algebra was introduced into Italy, and thence the rest of Europe, by the Arabs, who had come across it in ancient Babylon, Egypt and India. Its old meaning continued for a while in Spain, where in medieval times a bone-setter was called an *algebrista*, a 'restorer' of bones, which was precisely the same effect mathematicians were expected to have on jumbled piles of numbers.

Alchemy, which came into the language via Old French and medieval Latin, is that branch of science in which medieval scientists vied to turn base metals into gold. It originally comes from the noun *al-kīmīā*, though there is much dispute as to whether that comes from an early word for Egyptian art, or the Greek verb *cheō*, which means 'I pour', an action that is integral to the pursuit of chemistry. Alchemy was a risky science, or, to put it another way, a hazardous occupation, which is coincidental, since the word **hazard** is ultimately Arabic – again from the French. William, Archbishop of Tyre in old Antioch (*c*.1130–*c*.1185) – the city that gave us beautiful dyes – claimed that the city's name came from the siege of a castle called Hasart or Asart in Palestine. It was used in the sense of a game of dice, played as long ago as 1300, and vulgar Arabic gives us the word *az-zahr* or *az-zār*, meaning 'die', the singular of 'dice'.

The city of Mosul, which came to prominence during the American-led invasion of Iraq in 2003, was once famous for something altogether different – the lightweight cotton fabric that was made there: **muslin**. By the nineteenth century, that term had come to represent the women who were inside the cloth. In his rakish novel *Pendennis* (1850), William Thackeray (1811–63) includes the line, 'That was a pretty bit of muslin hanging on your arm – who was she?'

Iraq's neighbour Iran is another world-famous fabric producer in its own right, and **taffeta** from that country figures in our written records as long ago as 1373. Chaucer, in the prologue to *The Canterbury Tales* (1386), describes 'A Doctour of Phisik ... In sangwyn and in pers he clad was al / Lyned with Taffata and with sandal.'[1] In early times it would have been 'a plain-woven glossy silk of any colour'. Shakespeare took it to mean something florid or bombastic in *Love's Labour's Lost* (1588), when Berowne the suitor, trying to impress the ladies, renounces refined speech – 'Taffata phrases, silken tearmes precise' (V.ii) – while using precisely the same refined speech.

Our love of **sugar** is at least partly to blame for the current global epidemic of obesity, and that addictive substance has been around a very long time. Arabic is stuffed with words for sweet things. The verb *shariba* (to drink) gave us **sherbet**, **sorbet** and **syrup** – all via French. The relationship between the English 'sugar' and the Arabic *sukkar* is clearer in Spanish (*azucar*) and Portuguese (*assucar*). The word 'candy' has also been involved with Arabic at some point, via Persian, since the Arabic *qand* refers to what's left when you boil cane sugar. Alongside all this sweetness it is worth adding that *tabib isnaan* – which has not made its way into English – is the Arabic for 'dentist'.

From dessert we make our way to **desert**, for which the Arabic word is *badu*. *Badawi* means 'desert dweller', of which the plural is the rather better-known *bedouin*. Another plural Arabic word that we know well these days – though with a singular sense in English – is **assassin**. Most word-watchers go along with the *OED* derivation, which puts it all down to drugs.

The story sounds so far-fetched that it might just be true. The *OED* traces it to a tribe of 'Ismaili sectarians, who used to intoxicate themselves with hashish or hemp, when preparing to

---

1 'He wore scarlet and blue/ lined with taffeta and fine linen.'

dispatch some king or public man'. There is certainly a verb, *bhasha*, which means 'to mow' or 'cut'. In a slightly stronger form, it means 'to smoke hashish'. Sure enough, the noun *mah'shash* means 'hashish den'. But the noun mih'ashsha means 'a tool for weeding'. This has nothing to do with smoking weed.

'Assassin' was defined in the *OED* as 'certain Moslem [*sic*] fanatics in the time of the Crusades, who were sent forth by their sheikh, the "Old Man of the Mountains", to murder the Christian leaders'. The old man in question was Hassan ibu-al-Sabbah, a renegade Persian, who controlled a bunch of Ismaili separatists in the eleventh century, capturing the castle of Alamut, south of the Caspian Sea, in 1090.

Marco Polo visited the area in 1273, about 150 years after Hassan's reign. According to him, the old man sent his followers into a beautiful garden, where he gave them hashish to drink, which knocked them out for three days. 'When these young men woke and found themselves in the garden with all these marvellous things, they truly believed themselves to be in paradise.'

The only problem with these etymologies is that they may not be right. The Old Man of the Mountains was not an Arab, but a Persian, so the word 'assassin' should be Persian rather than Arabic in its roots. Is it possible, then, that the assassins were not followers of hashish, but of Hassan? Also, Hassan's religious views on intoxicants should have barred such narcotic indulgence. Besides, if they believed in the cause, he surely didn't need to drug them. The idea that a mysterious, charismatic, mystical man would take to the mountains and inspire hundreds of followers to risk all, even their own lives, for a cause... well, who would ever imagine that such an unlikely thing could come about?

Indian takeaway

Alongside the British debt to Arabic stands our legacy from the Raj, the name given to the period of British rule in India. Britain's first ambassador, Sir Thomas Roe, presented his credentials to Jehangir, the Mughal[2] emperor, at Delhi in 1615 amid the first stirrings of British interest. History is sparing on the details of their meeting: was the maharaja sitting out on his verandah? Was Sir Thomas wearing jodhpurs? We may never know, though we do know that in the years since then, Britain's Indian take-away included words borrowed from Hindi and the subcontinent's other languages.

There was no doubt that the British and the Indians, though at times at each other's throats over the years, were in a sense spiritually entwined. Many words were coined by the British army, who had distinctly mixed feelings about the whole experience: pleasure at the country and people, horror at the climate, and the fact of being separated from their loved ones by a huge sea voyage. Naturally, one of the things they talked about obsessively was how much they missed Blighty (England), but it says something about the experience of being away that the very word they used for the old country was Hindi/Arabic in origin.

The Hindi word *bilāyati* is related to the Arabic word *wilāyatī*, both of which mean 'foreign', especially European. As usual, the great British Tommy was not adept at pronunciation, but he excelled at adapting foreign words. The famous *Glossary of Anglo-Indian Words and Phrases* by Sir Henry Yule and A.C. Burnell, popularly known as '*Hobson-Jobson*'[3] (1886), records

----

2 Or, formerly, Mogul: 'The name given to the heads of the Muslim dynasty founded by Zahir-ud-Din Muhammad Babur (1483–1530).' The Mughal empire stretched across much of the Indian subcontinent between the sixteenth and nineteenth centuries.
3 The title derived from an 'Anglicized form of the repeated wailings and cries of Muslims as they beat their breasts in the Muharram procession.'

bilayat pan, or 'European water', a reference to the usual name for soda water in British-ruled India. Another was *bilayati baingan* for the tomato, at that time unknown in India. Such were the terms used by Indian soldiers to describe the strange things that the 'white devils' had brought with them, and sure enough the compliment was returned. Perhaps the English liked the fact that the Hindi word smacked of that English word 'blighted'.

The present-day word sleuth Michael Quinion maintains that Blighty didn't pass into common usage until the First World War. The music-hall songs of the period have that poignant urgency: 'Take me back to dear old Blighty,' wrote A.J. Mills, Fred Godfrey and Bennett Scott in their famous 1916 song. 'Put me on the train for London town. Take me over there, Drop me anywhere: Liverpool, Leeds, or Birmingham, well, I don't care!' There were other songs from the same period that also hailed Blighty, but these have not stood the test of time so well.

It's also possible that the surprisingly recent word **bloke** – only in use since about 1850 – derives from the Hindi word *loke*, meaning 'man'. We don't talk about taking a **dekko** (look) so much these days, but it is an adaptation of the Hindi *dekho*, which is the imperative of *dekhnā*, to look.

The British loved Indian architecture, particularly the **bungalow**. This word comes from the Hindi *banglā*, meaning 'belonging to Bengal'. It was originally a one-storeyed house, with tiles or thatch on the roof, first in Bengal and afterwards throughout India. According to the authors of *Hobson-Jobson*, it was 'the most usual class of house occupied by Europeans in the interior of India'.

India's less formal dress code was also popular with the British. **Pyjamas**, from an Urdu word, were a form of loose drawers or trousers tied round the waist, worn by both men and women in India, and especially popular with Sikhs and Muslims. Anglo-

Indians[4] took to wearing them to sleep in, adding a matching jacket. 'It is probable,' say the authors of *Hobson-Jobson*, 'that we English took the habit, like a good many others, from the Portuguese', who also had a substantial presence in India.[5]

India was the source of many fabrics. 'Bought my wife a **chintz**, that is, a painted Indian **callico**, for to line her new study,' wrote Samuel Pepys in his diary on 5 September 1663. The *OED*'s first citation dates from 1614. The Hindi word *chint* comes from an even older Sanskrit word *chitra*, which means 'variegated'. 'Calico' itself comes, of course, from the Indian city of Calcutta, from where so many of the fabrics were shipped back to Britain. And the wild goat of Tibet, if you can catch it, gives up its wool – along with that of the Kashmir goat – to be made into the costly fabric known since 1822 as **cashmere**.

Many more words became common currency in Britain, such as **khaki** (dusty), a Persian word that passed into Urdu and became forever associated with the dull, yellowish-brown fabric of the British army in India. Perhaps that dust was also responsible for another import from Hindi – *čāmpo*, which was the imperative form of *čāmpnā* (to press). We anglicized the word into **shampoo**, but in the eighteenth and nineteenth centuries it was much closer in meaning to 'massage'. A 1762 account of the process by a British traveller to the East Indies contains the understandable reaction: 'Had I not seen several China merchants shampooed before me, I should have been

---

4 British people who made India their home, or people with mixed European and Asiatic parents.
5 The Portuguese reached India well before the British. The globe-trotting Vasco da Gama landed in Calicut (now Kozhikode) on 20 May 1498, and trading terms began shortly after. The southern area of Goa remained a Portuguese possession until December 1961 when Indian forces reunited it with the rest of the country.

apprehensive of danger.' And John Badcock, in his *Domestic Amusements* (1823), writes: 'We had long ago seen negroes employed in percussion upon their Barbadean masters, by whom it is termed "Champooing",' at which time it was part of the Turkish bath process. In 1829 it was described in the journal *Health & Longevity* as 'friction with the hand', but at around the same time, the experience of a shampoo changed from a dry one to a wet one, and newspaper advertisements for 'shampoo liquid' started to appear in British magazines in the 1860s.

Did that shampoo do a **pukka** job? We'll never know, but pukka, in the sense of 'good' has been popularized by the celebrity chef Jamie Oliver and he is not far off using it in its original sense, since *pakkā* is a Hindi word, meaning 'ripe, mature or cooked'. In Hindi it is most often contrasted with *cutcha* (imperfect, slight), a term that Jamie might perhaps have used to describe just how awful he thought school lunches were.

The British brought back many exotic things from India, though few are more surprising than the expression **big cheese**, meaning 'an important person'. This in fact comes from Persian via the Urdu word *chiz*, meaning 'thing'. According to *Hobson-Jobson*, the phrase was a common one, as in 'These cheroots are the real chiz.' Since people had already been saying 'the real thing' as an expression of admiration, there may have been an element of linguistic interplay. And what of that popular dish, the **curry**? The *Oxford Dictionary of the English Language* cites the Tamil word *kari*, which means 'sauce'.

One of Anglo-India's most famous words, but one that did not come to the attention of the editors of *Hobson-Jobson*, is **doolally**. This is defined by *The Times English Dictionary* as 'out of one's mind or crazy'. But the story of how it came to be so is interesting. The full phrase is **doolally tap**, and is British army slang, originally named after the town of Deolali, near Bombay. There the British bought a military sanatorium in which to treat soldiers who had really seen enough of India. The word *tap* is Urdu or Persian for 'fever'. F. Richards, in his book *Old-Soldier Sahib* (1936), wrote that 'Time-expired men sent to Deolalie [*sic*] from their different units might have to wait for months before a troop-ship fetched them home... The well-known saying among soldiers when speaking of a man who does queer things, "Oh, he's got the Doo-lally tap," originated, I think, in the peculiar way men behaved owing to the boredom of that camp.'

Everybody salsa

From the land of the curry to the land of the tortilla chip, typically topped with melted cheese, linguistics experts have puzzled long and hard over the origin of the word **nacho**, until an enterprising *OED* researcher came across a story about a Mexican chef, Ignacio Anaya, whose name was shortened to 'Nacho'. He lived in a small Mexican town called Piedras Negras, just across the border from Eagle Pass, Texas, and he is credited with creating the first nachos in 1940 for a group of women who asked the chef to make something for them to eat with their cocktails.

Aztec civilization dominated Mexico and Central America for centuries, and Aztecs were growing the *tomatl*, as it was then called in the Nahuatl language, as early as AD 700. The Aztecs of Central America called it *xitomatl*, and wild Central American tribes called it *tomatl*. Tomatl, xitomatl... xitomatl, tomatl... let's call the whole thing off: **tomato** emerged as the compromise candidate. At first, people were suspicious of eating it, since it belonged to the same botanical family as deadly nightshade, but once the usual tests had been run and no mothers-in-law, force-fed on nothing but tomatoes for a week, had gone belly up, it became an essential part of our diet.

Before curry became so popular, the British national dish was, of course, chips. The **potato** was said to have been imported by Sir Walter Raleigh (*c.*1552–1618), though these days scholars are leaning more towards Sir Francis Drake (*c.*1540–96) as the importer of this vegetable. Within thirty years of their arrival in Britain, potatoes were such a craze that they had been referred to by Shakespeare in *The Merry Wives of Windsor*. They were, it seems, an older version of Viagra, noted for their power to enhance love-making. 'Let the sky rain potatoes,' declares Falstaff as he attempts to ravish Mistress Ford, 'and hail kissing-comfits and snow eringoes.' ('Kissing-comfits' were like sweet mints, and 'eringoes'[6] were supposedly an aphrodisiac. They also reduce flatulence: just the thing when going on a date.)

West meets East

In a satisfying meeting of cultures, those Aztec tomatoes mentioned above were later used in China to make a sauce that we now all eat with our fries. However, the name of that sauce, **ketchup**, is one of the most disputed words around, and no matter how many times you thump the bottom of the dictionary in a bid to sort out the mess, when you look at the other end, nothing seems to come out. Amid such confusion, one strong possibility is the Amoy (Chinese) dialect word *kôechiap* or *kê-tsiap*, which means 'the brine of pickled fish or shellfish', and which may have been an early ingredient in the sauce. Or was it the Malay word *kēchap*? When the Dutch came to China, they

----

6 Or eryngo: 'The candied foot of the Sea-Holly, formerly used as a sweetmeat.'

found the sauce, ate it, bought the company and spelt it *ketjap*, which is as near to today's word as you would wish to be.

Following our palates around the world, we say **chin-chin** as a pre-drink toast because we are copying the Chinese, who use the salutation ts'ing ts'ing. The first surviving British reference is from 1795 by a British traveller, Michael Symes. Some thirty-nine years later, in 1834, the *Canton Register* newspaper was recording the use of **chop-chop hurry**, which is pidgin English, from the Chinese *k'wâi-k'wâi*. The same usage survives in chopsticks, since 'chop' is pidgin for 'quick' and *k'wâi-tsze* means 'nimble boys' or 'nimble ones', which no Chinese person could have said if they had seen an English diner struggling to eat gracefully with chopsticks.

Chinese society had for centuries been highly ritualized, and one of the customs that particularly caught the eye of many a British explorer was the act of prostrating oneself before the emperor or the local bigwig. This involved the supplicants stretching out so low on the ground that their forehead grazed the earth or floor. This act of extreme respect or submission, even worship, is known in Chinese as the *k'o-t'ou*, coming from *k'o* (knock) plus *t'ou* (head). The Greeks tried the same thing, but called it *prosgenesis*. That never caught on as a phrase nearly as well as the English adapted version, which became a noun, first recorded in 1804, then a verb, to **kowtow**. Nowadays it means to be an all-round crawler, but it has nobler roots.

The Japanese and Chinese hierarchy went all the way up to the heavens. When the Chinese brought together the words *ta* (great) and *kiun* (prince), the Japanese reshaped it into *taikun*, meaning 'great lord or prince', the title given to the Japanese shogun. The most famous Westerner to be called a **tycoon** was Abraham Lincoln (1809–65): the name stuck to him for a while, since when it has been popularized, and is now more often applied to people who have amassed huge business fortunes, from Rupert Murdoch to Bill Gates.

Out of Africa

In 1900 the pink parts of the world map, which indicated the extent of the British Empire, included much of Africa, so we have acquired many words from that huge continent. The Swahili word **safari**, meaning 'an overland journey or hunting expedition, especially in Africa' (*Collins Concise Dictionary*), comes originally from the Arabic word *safara*, meaning 'to travel'. At first these (purely hunting) expeditions usually took place on foot in East Africa. Since then tourism has turned them into an opportunity to view or research wildlife in a game reserve. Instead of carrying a dead animal home slung between two poles, the supreme mark of courage is now to sit in your jeep while a curious monkey snaps off your radio aerial.

These days, four wheels are the main form of transport throughout Africa, but the word **trek**, originally from South Africa, came from Afrikaans (the Dutch spoken by early settlers), and in 1849 meant 'to make a journey by ox wagon'. It now means a long overland journey, whether on foot or in a vehicle. Nowadays the word can have more frivolous uses, as in 'I had to trek all the way to the supermarket', where the word 'safari' doesn't have the same comic potential. The original *Star Trek* TV series ran from 1966 to 1969 and featured the first interracial kiss on American network television, in the episode 'Plato's Stepchildren', which aired on 22 November 1968. In this episode, Captain Kirk (William Shatner) kissed Lieutenant Uhura (Nichelle Nichols). The studio at first demurred, wishing to spare the blushes of white people watching in states such as Alabama and

Tennessee. It was even suggested that Uhura kiss Mr Spock instead because he was, after all, only a Vulcan, but in the end Kirk and Uhura kissed, which marks the end of an arduous linguistic journey for the Afrikaans word that gave the TV series its title.

Such a kiss would not have been possible on TV screens in South Africa in 1968, where the **apartheid** regime still had twenty-six years to run. The word *apartheid* is Afrikaans for 'separateness', from the Dutch word *apart*. The system of apartheid was imposed by the government in 1948 and referred to the 'segregation of the inhabitants of European descent from the non-European (Coloured or mixed, Bantu, Indian, etc.)'. The *Cape Times* wrote in 1947: 'It is always easy to discern the immediate benefits or comforts conferred on the apartheid-minded Europeans, but impossible to discern the benefits conferred on the non-Europeans.'

Africa was at one time known as the Dark Continent because it was mysterious and little known to outsiders. Part of its mystery stemmed from its cults and rituals, of which **voodoo** is probably the best known. We talk liberally about voodoo these days, but this form of religious witchcraft originated in the Dahomey area of northwest Africa, and was later transported to the West Indies (especially Haiti) and the southern states of America through the slave trade. Since then 'voodoo' has evolved to refer to dodgy practices, such as **voodoo economics** (1980).

Some people, of course, think it's all a load of **mumbo-jumbo**, which seems to derive from the Mandinka word *maamajomboo*, which was, says the *OED*, 'the name of a mask or masked dancer representing a cultic society and participating in religious ceremonies'. It has been terrifying British people ever since 1738. There was also a Haitian Creole voodoo ritual dance – a modified version of the rumba – called the **mambo**. But the after-life of the word **jumbo** is still more extraordinary, since it was the name given to an unusually large elephant that was kept first in Paris and then, for seventeen years from 1865, in the London Zoological Gardens (now Regent's Park Zoo).

This popular, benign, hard-working animal gave rides to thousands of children, and he was still growing when he came to the attention of the American circus promoter P.T. Barnum. In 1882, Barnum bought the elephant for $10,000 and brought him to the United States. Just one year later *Harper's Magazine* was describing a humble cicada as 'the Jumbo of crickets, and just as black'. Jumbo was very popular in the USA and Canada, but after a mere three years he was hit by a train as he was being loaded into a carriage in St Thomas, Ontario, and died. We still remember Jumbo, though, every time we have a **jumboburger** (hopefully never) or fly in a **jumbo jet**.

And another thing: maybe 'jumbo' is linked to *jambo*, the Swahili word for 'hello', which is pronounced: 'jumbo'. *Jambo* is used all over Africa as a kind of slang term for 'hello' in the same sort of way as 'what's up' or 'sup'. Other English words which may have evolved from *jambo* include **jamboree**, a gathering of people all saying 'hello' or 'jambo' to each other. Or is such a party a bit of a **jam** in which everyone is pressed tightly together? Jamborees can be high-brow too, albeit sarcastically, as the thinker and novelist Aldous Huxley wrote in a letter in 1960: 'Meet me in Boston with the Microbus and drive me ... to Hanover, where you might stay for all or part of the Jamboree (at which I am to receive an honorary degree).' He could have **commandeered** a driver, which is another Afrikaans word. And Huxley was always interested in the effects of narcotics. Would he have considered smoking some *dagga*, from the Hottentot word *dachab*, a name for 'cannabis' or 'hemp' used as a narcotic?

A fistful of Euros

By some estimates, almost a third of all English words are French in origin, and without French, we would be mighty pushed to find the right words or phrases. You may enjoy going **head-to-head** with someone, but would you prefer to have a **tête-à-tête** with them? The English is an exact translation that has been used in writing since at least the days of the dramatist and architect Sir John Vanbrugh (1664–1726), who used it in 1697, but the French phrase implies none of the competitiveness or aggression of the English. Rugby players or golfers go head-to-head: friends – or potential lovers – have a tête-à-tête.

Time and again, when it comes to getting *intime* (intimate), the English language has preferred to hide behind a tree and let French do the talking. After all, if the tête-à-tête goes particularly well, they might exchange the occasional **billet-doux**, even by text or email. Somehow the phrase 'sweet note', which is the literal translation, doesn't seem to do justice to the French words, as writers from Dryden (in 1673) onwards have noticed. The use of language in such circumstances owes something to the heavens: the Latin word *nubes* means 'cloud', which came into Old French as *nue* and thence to Middle French *nuer*, meaning 'to shade'. In 1380 that shading was restricted to colour, but by 1668 it had spread to language – **shades of meaning** – and to music by 1849. The word they all used, of course, was **nuance**, and it fulfilled much the same role in English, ever since Horace Walpole[7] noted in 1781 that 'The more expert one were at nuances, the more poetic one should be.'

----

7 1717–97, fourth Earl of Oxford, politician, writer, former lover of the poet Thomas Gray and others.

The French verb *nuer* has another connection in that it resembles the Latin verb *innuere*, 'to give a nod to'. The verbal noun or gerund is *innuendum*, and the ablative of the gerund, which means 'by nodding at, pointing to, meaning, intimating', is **innuendo**. In medieval Latin this word was used to introduce a parenthetical phrase in a court case, and came to mean 'an indirect or subtle reference' (*CCD*) often, these days, to something indelicate.

Imports from other European languages

Czech – polka, robot, Semtex

Dutch – coleslaw, cookie, deck, easel, freebooter, maelstrom, tattoo, waffle, wagon, walrus, yacht

Finnish – sauna

Hebrew/Yiddish – amen, bagel, cherub, chutzpah, cider, hallelujah, kosher, latke, leviathan, messiah, sapphire, Satan, schlemiel, schmaltz, schmooze, schmuck, schnozz, seraph

Hungarian – biro, goulash, hussar, paprika

Icelandic – geyser

Italian – studio, baloney, fascism, propaganda, bankrupt, paparazzi, umbrella, vendetta

Norwegian* – cog, fjord, kraken, lemming, quisling, ski, slalom

Russian – babushka, gulag, intelligentsia, mammoth, pogrom, agitprop, bolshevik, samizdat, tsar, vodka

Polish – mazurka

Portuguese – auto da fé, cobra, dodo, emu

Spanish – adios, barrio, guerrilla, lasso, machismo, peccadillo, renegade, sherry, siesta, sombrero, tobacco, vamoose

Swedish* – gravlax, ombudsman, smorgasbord

Turkish – kaftan, doner, minaret

* Some Norwegian/Swedish words share a root

Matters romantic and sexual are notoriously tricky to navigate, so should we worry about making a **faux pas**? No, comes the resounding reply, if the alternative is the banality, in straight translation, of making a 'false step'. But are we being a little **risqué**? If so, we are in good company, since the artist Aubrey Beardsley (1872–98) was one of the first to embrace the term in his introduction to *The Yellow Book* (a quarterly journal, still top-shelf in most good libraries) of 1894. 'Our idea,' he wrote, in connection with starting the book, 'is that many brilliant story painters and picture writers cannot get their best stuff accepted in the conventional magazine, either because they are not topical or perhaps a little risqué.' Perhaps it was a little affected to go into French at this point, but *The Yellow Book* was the publishing scandal of its time, and it lasted three years until 1897.

If the French have sex and suggestiveness, the Germans have sausages and doubt. Of the vast number of words that have entered the English language through the German portal, few evoke the streets of Berlin and Munich better than *zeitgeist* (spirit of the time) and *angst* (anxiety, guilt or remorse). Germans have not given us as many words for beauty as the French have, but when it comes to feeling a bit down or confused, they are past masters. Thanks to Sigmund Freud[8] (1856–1939) – OK, he was Austrian, but he spoke German – we can all revel in *schadenfreude* at the expense of our friends, who may well wish that they could revel in it themselves, but since the word means 'malicious enjoyment of the misfortunes of others', why should we care? Of course, we might find ourselves weighed down by *angst*. The first English writer to note the

----

8 The founding father of psycho-analysis, born in Austria, fled to London in 1938. His theories of the unconscious were perhaps his most impressive contribution to the field of psychology.

phrase was George Eliot,[9] who in a letter from 1849 wrote that 'Die Angst' often brought on a pain at her heart.

Still, the Germans can party too, so much so that their word for party, *fest*, derived from similar Greek and Latin words, can now be tacked on to the end of just about any area of human endeavour, sometimes mockingly, sometimes with better intentions. A **gabfest** is a mocking way to describe a conference, and a **rockfest** is a concert – perhaps a form of escape for ageing hippies oppressed by the modern world. If so, they are suffering from *weltschmertz* (literally 'world pain'), a term dating from 1875 that the *OED* defines as 'a weary or pessimistic feeling about life; an apathetic or vaguely yearning attitude'. And if they can't take all that criticism, the world of aviation has given us a new word for it – *fliegerabwehrkanone* (pilot-defence gun), thankfully shortened to **flak** in 1938. Figuratively, it came to mean 'a barrage of abuse', as in the line from Tom Stoppard's 1976 play *Dirty Linen*: 'Isn't that going to cause rather a lot of flak in the … PLP?' But Tom Wolfe had already coined the term 'flak-catcher' in his 1970 book *Radical Chic & Mau-Mauing the Flak Catchers*: 'And then it dawns on you… This man is the flak catcher. His job is to catch the flak for the No. 1 man.'

Above all, though, no one likes to take the flak for someone else's mistakes. It's not fair. Or, as French president Jacques Chirac put it recently, in faultless French, it's not '*le fair play*'. Now where on earth did he get that from?

---

9 Real name Mary Ann Evans, 1819–80, amongst the greatest Victorian novelists. Her work combines high intelligence with an ability to engage in political and social debate, and penetrating psychological insight. *Middlemarch* (1871) is her most famous and influential novel.

Chapter Seven

That's Entertainment

*I*t was the last few days of the 2005 British general election campaign, and the then Conservative leader Michael Howard was staring defeat in the face. With only two days to go, Howard – a lifelong Liverpool football fan – roused his weary troops by claiming that the party was 'two–nil down at half-time'. His chairman, Liam Fox, picked up the analogy by claiming that the election would 'go to penalties' – that, rather than injury time, being the current way to settle a match. The meaning was clear: it wasn't over yet, oh no. In fact, it was, and Labour won comfortably, but the remark shows how often politicians resort to using sporting metaphors rather than – well – political metaphors.

Howard might also have used a metaphor from horse-racing and said that in the **final furlong** he was sure he could find 'an extra yard' or 'catch his second wind', since it was now all **down to the wire** (first recorded use in a horse race, 1901), or that he was predicting a **photo-finish**, a technique first used in a New York horse race in 1936. Of course, he must have been hoping that, in tennis terms, the ball was **in his court**, and that he could now, as if playing rugby, **pick it up and run with it**. Perhaps he could have switched to cricket to say that he intended to **bowl a bouncer** to

Tony Blair or even **hit him for six**. What he couldn't admit, in any sporting metaphor, was that he was **on the ropes**, that Blair had him **snookered** and was about to **checkmate**[1] him.

The problem with leadership is that, in the words of Harry S. Truman (US president 1945–53), '**The buck stops here**,' an expression lifted from poker, in which 'to pass the buck' means 'to shift responsibility to someone else'. In bridge, on the other hand, you want to be able to play a **trump** card (a sixteenth-century corruption of 'triumph'). Having a **joker** or **trick up your sleeve** doesn't always help.

What's the upshot?

Tracing the development of the sporting metaphor 'upshot' from its sixteenth-century origins:

1531: The final shot in an archery match; chiefly *figurative*, a closing or parting shot.

1591: A mark or end aimed at. SPENSER: The onely upshot whereto he doth ayme.

c.1580: An end, conclusion, or termination.

1586: The climax or completion of something.

1669: The extreme limit. ABEL BOYER: A gay Coat and a Grimace is the upshot of what he can pretend to.

1604: The result, issue, or conclusion (of some course of action, etc.). In very frequent use from c.1830. SHAKESPEARE, *Hamlet*: So shall you heare… Of accidentall judgements… And in this vpshot, purposes mistooke.

1639: The conclusion resulting from the premises of an argument. See also the phrase 'A fool's bolt is soon shot', common from the thirteenth to eighteenth centuries, a bolt being 'An arrow; especially one of the stouter and shorter kind with blunt or thickened head, called also quarrel, discharged from a cross-bow or other engine. Often *figurative*.'

1811: *Slang*. A riotous frolic.

1837: *Dial*. A merry-making, a feast.

---

1 Arabic: from *shā-māt*, meaning 'the king is dead'.

The English language is blessed with numerous sporting terms, all of which have reached an audience well beyond the comparatively small number of people who partake in these various sports. On the other hand, the worlds of, say, academia and the Church have a rich and complex technical language too, but fewer words have leaked out into everyday use. Our lexicon is drawn not from a particularly highbrow word base: it is drawn from popular culture – leisure, music, entertainment and sport – the worlds in which we are most interested.

The beautiful game

Football is our national sport, as well as our national phrase repository. To be **on the ball** means 'to be sharpness personified'. **Keep your eye on the ball** is an instruction to concentrate. Football is, in that famously trite phrase, **a game of two halves**, but that wouldn't make much sense to an American football fan because their game has four quarters. The concept of a second half dates from the end of the nineteenth century. Before then, you were more likely to say, 'It's basically a game of all day, or sometimes more'.

The very first written reference to our national game seems to date from 1424 and is suitably vehement, as in this royal instruction: 'The king forbiddes yat na man play at ye fut ball vnder ye payne of iiiid', i.e. 4d, a whopping fine of fourpence, which in those days was about one week's wages for a decent club player. And Sir Thomas Elyot in *The Governour* (1531) writes scathingly of 'Foote balle, wherin is nothinge but beastly furie and exstreme violence'. It was ever thus, it seems. The very first references to football, and already there's crowd trouble.

William Shakespeare liked his football. In *King Lear* (I.iv) the

Earl of Kent is behaving as badly as Sir Alex Ferguson at a post-match press conference:

> **Lear:** Do you bandy[2] looks with me, you rascal?
> **Oswald:** I'll not be stricken, my Lord.
> **Earl of Kent:** Nor tript neither, you base Foot-ball plaier
> (tripping his heels).
> **Lear:** I thanke thee, fellow.

Shakespeare also referred to **foul play** in *The Tempest* ('What fowle play had we, that came from thence?') (I.ii) as well as **fair play**, also in King John ('Shall we upon the footing of our land, / Send fayre-play-orders, and make comprimise [*sic*]?') (V.i). Truly, he would have made a great half-time analyst.

Catches win matches

For a brief period during the summer, the back pages of newspapers yield to **cricket**, another game with an equally illustrious history. The word 'cricket' is mentioned as 'Creckett and other plaies' as early as 1598, fifty years after the death of that great sportsman Henry VIII. It is possible that the game may even have its roots in a French game called *criquet*… But let's not spend too long considering that ghastly possibility.

The names of fielding positions have occasioned many a raised eyebrow, though most seem to derive from the fielder's closeness to the ball and the resultant chances of getting a ball

---

2 A 'bandy' used to be a way, now lost, of hitting a tennis ball (1578). There was also a hockey-like game called bandy (1693), and from the action of driving a small ball back and forth across the ground comes the verb 'to bandy', as in 'to throw or strike' (1577) or 'to give and take' (blows, words, reproaches, compliments, etc.).

in the shins, or worse, hence 'point', 'cover', 'slip', 'silly mid-on' and so forth. But it's our familiarity with other aspects of the game that gives cricket its unique value. **To keep a straight bat**, for example, which is what you do if you're a good batsman, is defined by *Chambers English Dictionary* (*CED*) as 'to behave honourably'. Failure to do so may lead to the Englishman's

---

Cricketing magic

Bernard James Tindal Bosanquet (1877–1936) came from a famous Huguenot family. He scored 120 runs for Harrow against Eton at Lord's in 1896. Oxford picked him as a fast–medium bowler and he became the university's best all-rounder. But his 'greatest conjuring trick in the history of the game', as it was reported, was the 'googly', a ball which, on leaving the bowler's hand, seems to all intents and purposes to be a leg-break (heading for the off-stump) but instead, cunningly, breaks the other way, towards the leg stump. It shocked cricketers the world over, though it was devised as no more than a party piece to amuse the other members of his side. After a few ordinary leg breaks, he would slip in his googly: the batsmen didn't know what had hit them – or their stumps.

In 1902 Bosanquet was picked for Lord Hawke's team to tour Australia and New Zealand. Thanks to his unplayable new delivery, the tourists won all eighteen of their matches in New Zealand, and it was here that the word 'googly' was first used in print to describe Bosanquet's weird off-break[3].

The delivery became the subject of furious debate when the victorious English team travelled on to Australia, where the Australian team suffered a mass collapse. England beat them by 157 runs and regained the Ashes. Of course, someone asked Bosanquet if his googly might be illegal. 'No,' he replied. 'Only immoral.'

---

3 1903 C.B. Fry in P.F. Warner *How We Recovered the Ashes* (1904): 'You must persuade that Bosanquet of yours to practise…those funny 'googlies' of his.'

harshest condemnation, as noted by *The Times* on 17 December 2004: 'IMF says loan deal is **just not cricket**,' though the *OED* can date the phrase to at least 1851. Quite what the International Monetary Fund knows or cares about the rules of cricket is highly debatable, but we know what the sub-editor was thinking.

An unsuccessful batsman may well be out for a **duck** (nothing). Why a duck? Probably because a duck's egg is shaped like a zero. Many other cricketing phrases have entered the language so stealthily that we now use them while being only dimly aware of where they come from. If you have ever felt under-confident, be it in a relationship or a meeting, you might say that you were on a **sticky wicket** or **on the back foot** even if you have never picked up a cricket bat in your life.

Masters of spin

'Spin' is a familiar sporting term used in baseball, cricket, table-tennis and other sports. But the practice of **spin-doctoring** emerged, mainly from the USA in the late 1970s, as a means of controlling the news by giving bad news a favourable tweak. In 1980 the *New York Times* wrote 'President Carter's chief economist … tried to put a "positive spin" on what has generally been perceived as a dismal economic picture.' The *OED* defines this as 'a bias or slant on information, intended to create a favourable impression when it is presented to the public; an interpretation or viewpoint.'

Six years later, the people whose job it was to put a positive (or negative) spin on a story had a name, as recorded by the *New York Times*: 'They won't be just press agents trying to impart a favourable spin to a routine release. They'll be the Spin Doctors, senior advisers to the candidates.' **Spinmeisters** followed.

Punchy language

If you have ever been plucked from danger, just as you thought your luck had run out, you might well describe yourself as having been **saved by the bell**. That's boxing talk, and boxing is one sport that has always **punched above its weight**, since the range of boxing terms extends far beyond the ring. Nelson Mandela has often been described as a **political heavyweight**, as have Gordon Brown and Ann Widdecombe, though you wouldn't fancy their chances over fifteen rounds with Lennox Lewis.

If bids were being sought for the new leader of a political party, someone might **throw their hat into the ring** without pausing to consider that this was the way in which boxers used to declare their readiness to fight. Not surprisingly for a sport that pushes its exponents to their physical limits, boxing has a wealth of terms for that state of mind when your brain feels like mush. **Punch-drunk** is one such phrase that has broken free and taken on a life of its own. First recognized in the *Saturday Evening Post* in 1918, the *CED* defines it as 'having a form of cerebral concussion from past blows in boxing with results resembling drunkenness'. The poet Cecil Day-Lewis (1904–72) even attempted to smuggle it into his translation of Virgil's *Aeneid* in 1954:'So he called an end to the bout, saving the punch-drunk Dares from further punishment.' Nice try, Cecil.

Had you taken a particularly sharp hammering, you probably wouldn't be feeling **up to scratch** either.'To come up to (the) scratch' means to reach the required standard, though it's more common these days to find it in the negative: not good enough, below par.[4] In the past, boxing was an outdoor sport. A line was

---

4 The Latin word for equal, e.g. *Primus Inter Pares* means 'First Among Equals'. The 1897 *Encyclopaedia of Sport* describes a 'scratch player' as 'a good player, who receives neither handicap nor penalty.'

scratched across the ring to which the prospective fighters were brought. In the days when boxing had no ropes, and certainly no bell, the smaller of the two men, on seeing his larger opponent, might suddenly remember an urgent reason for being elsewhere, such as it being his turn to clean out the rabbit hutch, and off he would go, having clearly not come 'up to the scratch'.

Boxing does have certain safety requirements. No self-respecting boxer should hit **below the belt**; that's unseemly and unsporting both in the ring and out. One need hardly add that the original meaning was to whack someone in the **goolies** (from the Hindi word *golí*, meaning 'ball'), and very painful that is too. Among other safety requirements is a mouth-guard to protect the teeth, though this cannot prevent what dictionaries may one day refer to as 'doing a Tyson' (chewing off the opponent's ear). If tempted to make a remark that could be described as **near the knuckle**, that's an allusion to the days when fights were allowed to degenerate into such savagery that bones were exposed. Of course, at that time boxers fought bare knuckle, so the expression **the gloves are off** in a non-boxing context suggests some really brutal behaviour.

The boxing ring is no place for cowards, which is why it has given society some of its most direct phrases. To **pull one's punches**, for example, is defined by the *Collins Concise Dictionary* (*CCD*) as 'to restrain the force of one's criticisms or actions' or, with reference to boxing, not to use quite as much force in the punch as you could, for whatever reason. The verb **punch** used to have a much sharper meaning when it meant (*c.*1440) 'to stab, prick, puncture'. The closed-fist type of punching came a hundred years later. The *OED* thinks 'punch' might derive 'collaterally' from **pounce**, the etymology of which is obscure.[5] Surely everyone knows that to **take it on the chin** means 'to face squarely up to a defeat, adversity, etc.' (*CCD*). **Throwing in the towel** – which is usually white, except when it's covered in blood – is tantamount to running up the white flag. It's a form of surrender, a way of admitting defeat, more humiliating because it's done on behalf of the protagonist, who might not be in the best position to judge whether it's safe for him to carry on. And it doesn't just happen in the ring.

In boxing, but not necessarily in the wider world, there's always somebody in the middle, who is supposed to see fair play. The word **umpire** comes from the late-twelfth-century French adjective *nonper*, meaning 'peerless, without equal, surpassing all others'. The *OED* says that the word was anglicized around 1350 as **noumpere**, and the 'n' dropped off over the next century (the initial letter 'n' of **adder** and **apron** met a similar fate). **Referees**, on the other hand, who were appointed by parliament in 1621 'to examine and report on applications for monopolies or letters patent', seemed not to have turned their attention to sport until 1840.

A big song and dance

While the language of sport is mined for expressions to do with moral rectitude, winning and losing, confidence and the lack of it, the language of music is hijacked[6] for different purposes. And we can command a whole orchestra without even being able to play the triangle. To blow the trumpet, for example, means 'to

---

5 No corresponding noun is known in French or any other Romanic language.
6 A word that, disappointingly, the *OED* gives as 'origin unknown'.

declare or announce', even 'to celebrate something'. But you would not want to be accused of **blowing your own trumpet**. You might **sing someone's praises** but not your own. And you would only **bang the drum** if you were trying to arouse support for your cause from a somewhat resistant audience. Would you be happy to **play second fiddle** to someone? Probably not. And you definitely wouldn't want to **harp** on about it (see page 185).

The media is often preoccupied with questions of harmony or disharmony, and sometimes it takes on sexual overtones. Don't forget the former prime minister John Major urging his Cabinet ministers to **sing from the same hymn-sheet** and display unity at a time when their activities between the bed-sheets were arousing more interest than their policies. Music is a sensory experience. If you are **in tune** with someone, you aren't necessarily playing music together. And if something sounds **out of tune**, it may not be an instrument. **Playing by ear** usually means being able to play a piece of music without reading it off a score, but we also use this metaphor in a situation when we haven't planned in advance how to behave. In the same sense, we might say that we'll **busk**[7] it.

The word **music** has come to mean much more than mere notes. The phrase **music to my ears** – to hear good news – was used before 1586 by one of literature's greatest live-fast-die-young figures, Sir Philip Sidney, in his prose romance the *Arcadia*. And at some time in the 1930s those crazy, sex-mad jazz[8] players started using expressions like **to make sweet music** and **to make beautiful music together** as euphemisms for having sex. The

----

7 1851, Henry Mayhew *London Labour*: 'Busking is going into public houses and playing and singing and dancing.'
8 Many suggestions have been offered for the origin of 'jazz', but none that have satisfied the *OED*.

verbs **rock** and **roll** were used for the same covert purpose in American rhythm and blues of the early twentieth century, though it wasn't until 1951 that disc jockey Alan Freed united the two.

Ever since Freed's immortal coupling, **rock and roll** has been getting steadily louder and louder – and louder. But then, in about 1983, the rock star Nils Lofgren made a significant breakthrough. How about, instead of playing louder, playing… quieter? He achieved this by swapping his electric guitar for an acoustic guitar. *The Washington Post*, which was there to witness this moment, described the event by using the word **unplugged**, as if he had simply pulled the plug on his **axe** – the rock word for guitar since 1967[9] (*Melody Maker*). 'Unplugged' suggested a change in direction: a determination to explore a different side of one's musical personality. It was a back-to-the-land[10] statement.

It could also imply a certain daring. Here, at least, audiences could judge whether the artist really could play, once all that rock posturing had been shorn away. For jazz musicians, playing 'unplugged' never really came into it, since what decided their fate in the first place was how well they played their instruments.

A fair number of words have come into use from the instruments themselves. The word **horn** is cited as a wind instrument by the *OED* as early as *c.*825, but by *c.*1000 had the biological definition 'hard outgrowth' (*CED*), and was often pointed, so it is hardly surprising that by 1785 it had gained inclusion in Francis Grose's *Classical Dictionary of the Vulgar Tongue* (1785) as an erect penis or 'temporary priapism'. As James Joyce so concisely put it in *Ulysses*: 'Got the horn or what?' **Horny**, meaning 'lecherous', has been in use since at least 1889.

----

9 Though prior to that, since 1955, it used to mean 'saxophone'.
10 First attested in *The Times* in 1894.

The piano has also contributed much to our vocabulary. **Putting the dampers** on a project implies toning down its full impact, since the damper is the piano pedal that can be used to make the sound softer. The organ, on the other hand, has given us an expression – **pull out the stops** – that means exactly the opposite. Pulling out the stops means that the organist is using all the various types of pipes at his or her disposal, from the mighty bass pipes to the flutes and treble reeds, to produce the greatest range – not merely the volume – of sounds.

Let's take the word **harp**. As a verb, it originally had the straightforward meaning of 'to play on a harp', but soon it began to imply the slightly irritating noise that someone makes when he or she plucks at the same string all day long. Shakespeare was among those who used the term metaphorically with such phrases as 'Still harping on my daughter?' (*Hamlet*, II.ii) which any wearied father might still use in the same way to this day. Who plays the **clarion** these days? Ever since the fourteenth century, it was a shrill-sounding trumpet, but now it's remembered only for its metaphorical call – rousing people to action.

In the sixteenth century a **drum** was merely something you beat to make a rhythmic noise. In the eighteenth century it became the instrument that was played as a soldier was formally expelled from the army – he was officially **drummed out**, an expression still used today, but in a much wider context. Ever wondered why someone should be as **fit as a fiddle**? That comes from medieval times, when the violin player was supposed to dance about gaily while he performed. He therefore had to be pretty fit.

And what of composers? Wagner is one of the few composers whose name went into more general use during his own lifetime.

Wagnerian first appeared as an adjective in 1873, with the perfectly straightforward definition 'pertaining to Wagner'. Since the great composer's music is almost always grand and solemn, the word soon came to refer to anything that was grand or epic. The word **unison** also demonstrated a shift in meaning from its straightforward origins. It was first used in 1574 as a purely technical description of notes of the same pitch. By 1730 it had come to mean several notes played together to make a harmonious sound. By 1780 the phrase 'in unison' had taken on the more metaphorical tone it has today.

Dance, too, made a contribution to our vocabulary. **Choreography**, from the Greek words *khoreia*, meaning 'dance', and *graphia*, meaning 'writing', originally applied purely to dance, but now almost anyone's behaviour can be choreographed for the press or the public. The verb **to sashay** is first noted by the *OED* in 1836. This American usage is a mispronounced form of the French dance-step *chasse* and, as the *OED* records, it went from that – sometimes as part of a square dance – to 'glide', then to 'move diagonally'. Today it is used, and sometimes over-used, to 'strut': some journalists never use 'move' if 'sashay' can be used instead.

Some people prefer to **waltz** than to sashay, from the German verb *walzen* (1780) which means 'to roll', and which came to mean the dance. Beginning in the Sixties, dance steps became less precise, from where the verb came to mean 'finding something very easy', such that one can these days be said to have 'waltzed' one's way through one's examinations, or into a job.

The expression 'a bit of a **knees-up**' comes from the 1938 song by Harris Weston and Bert Lee, at which dancers raised their knees high in accompaniment. The words – all together now: 'Knees up Mother Brown' – were so memorable that the phrase 'knees-up' took on a life of its own. *The Times* described the song as 'an injunction to apprehend nothing but jollity'. In *London Dossier* (1967), the guidebook to swinging London that had a secret agent theme, to cash in on the first four Harry Palmer novels, the novelist Len Deighton described one experience as being 'As indigenous to London as a Saturday-night knees-up in the boozer.'

In 1928, Louis Armstrong released a record called 'Don't Jive Me', with the sense of 'don't tease me'. The word **jive** was a short-hand expression on the streets of New York for Harlem slang. It is mysterious in its origins, but may be related to that other equally mysterious word, jazz. And, of course, we all know that **it takes two to tango**, referring to the dance that the print world noted in the last decade of the nineteenth century as having sprung from the gipsy or black communities. 'Takes Two To Tango', a song written by Al Hoffman and Dick Manning, was published in 1952. Pearl Bailey made it a hit, whereupon it became proverbial.

Stage and screen

In other fields of performance, theatre in particular has given rise to much gradually extending vocabulary. What exactly is the **limelight**, for example? Originally, it was a very bright light caused by heating a piece of lime in an oxyhydrogen flame – perfect for casting a particularly strong light on the stage. It had been in use since at least 1826, until Wilfred Granville, in his 1952 *Dictionary of Theatrical Terms*, defined **fond of the limelight** as 'greedy for notice' or 'one who claims the centre of the stage'. And the biography of T.E. Lawrence, aka Lawrence of Arabia (1888–1935), was entitled *Backing into the Limelight*, rather appropriate for a man who could steal the show while protesting to one and all that he was doing nothing of the sort.

The plain meaning of to **steal someone's thunder**, according to the *CCD*, is 'to lessen the effect of someone's idea or action by anticipating it'. The *CED*, on the other hand, gives it as 'to make use of someone's invention against him'. But the origin is a jewel of theatrical legend, and, most amazing of all, historically accurate, though the poet and dramatist John Dennis (1657–1734) must have wished it were not so. Dennis's play *Appius and Virginia* was staged at the Theatre Royal in London's Drury Lane in 1709. According to the renowned theatrical historian and gossip Colley Cibber (1671–1757), the play's dramatic intensity at one point required the sound effect of thunder. To achieve this, Dennis had worked out that bashing together large sheets of tin and then thumping them with a drumstick would, fairly accurately, produce the sound required. The inventiveness of the stage thunder was not, alas, matched by the quality of the drama, and the play lasted only four nights. The next production was *Macbeth*, by a certain W. Shakespeare, altogether a more bankable number that also had a fair few storm scenes, and the theatre manager saw no reason why he should not keep the thunder machine and use it for his next production. Dennis, smarting, went to the opening night, heard the thunder and – poor man – was heard to shout, 'Damn them! …They will not let my play run, but they steal my thunder.' Sad but true.

A phrase coined a hundred years later – **old chestnut** – stems from a play being performed in London in 1816. In his book *To Coin a Phrase: A Dictionary of Origins* (1981), author Edwin Radford quotes a character called Pablo in the play *The Broken Sword* by William Diamond. Pablo corrects a reference to a cork tree by saying: 'A chestnut! I have heard you tell the story twenty-seven times.' Whether the popularity of the expression stemmed instantly from the text of the play itself, or from the performers' propensity to use the phrase outside the theatre, is now shrouded in the mists of time, but it entered the language for ever.

Theatre has given us many more expressions that have passed into general currency. Politicians, in particular, are inclined to **play to the gallery**, first making sure that the **backdrop** is flattering. Boring colleagues or in-laws tend to deliver **monologues**, and many of us indulge in **dress-rehearsals** for the real thing, whatever that event might be. We all know people who get a bit melodramatic at moments of crisis, who can't **follow the script** or who need constant **prompting**. Others might simply **fluff** their lines. The word **protagonist** is Greek for 'an actor who plays the first part', and was introduced into English in the seventeenth century to describe the principal character in a play. By 1839 the word had acquired a less specific application, and had come to mean the leading personage in any contest. Of course, after the curtain comes down and the critics are out, the entire play may be **panned**. In 1839, this verb meant 'to wash gravel in a pan' and had been imported from America during the gold-rush of the late nineteenth century. When the gold-rush collapsed, so did the hopes of the settlers, and their dreams failed to **pan out** (1865). Shortly afterwards it took on a figurative sense when critics were accused of **panning** shows.

The TV and film industries in general have brought many technical words into mainstream English. Informed people are **in the loop**, while we regularly leave our mistakes **on the cutting room floor** – and instead give **edited highlights** in a presentation. Reports that are slightly confusing are often referred to as **unfocused**, while an employee may complain that he or she is playing merely a **bit part** or feels like an **extra** in the company.

Of course, the scripts for television and film are also plentiful sources of modern vocabulary, even managing by the alteration of one letter to make a taboo word acceptable during peak viewing hours. The euphemistic alteration of 'fuck' to **feck** was popularized by the novelist Roddy Doyle and the writers of the Channel Four sitcom about three Irish priests and their eccentric lifestyle, *Father Ted*. However, its use as a verb first came to the attention of the *OED* editors in Christopher Nolan's 1987 novel *Under the Eye of the Clock*, when 'fecked', as in 'I'll be rightly fecked if he's not here', was defined as 'to be put into a difficult or hopeless situation, to be in trouble'. But only three years later, when Doyle wrote in *The Snapper*, 'If he'd said it half an hour earlier even I'd've told him to feck off', it's pretty clear that the sense is a little different. And in *Father Ted* (1999), writers Graham Linehan and Arthur Matthews went one further in family entertainment and turned a taboo word into a buzzword:

> **Mrs Doyle**: Now Father, what do you say to a cup?
> **Jack**: Feck off, cup!

Linehan and Matthews have ten quotations cited in the new *OED*. The first four are to be found in the entries Feck (noun), Feck (verb), Fecker and Fecking.

In the UK, the **full monty** once referred either to the purchase of a complete three-piece suit or the popularity of Field Marshal Montgomery (1887–1976), depending on whom you asked. Over the years, and particularly since the film of the same name became such a hit in 1997, the 'full monty' has become an increasingly popular way of saying 'the full amount' or 'to go the whole way in any enterprise'.

TV programmes such as *Goodness Gracious Me* and *The Kumars at No. 42* have had a massive cultural influence on English, and dictionary compilers are now keeping a careful ear out for new programmes from the BBC Comedy Unit, perhaps in the hope of catching the latest Asian words to be brought into everyday use. That chicken tikka masala we're all so fond of may be inauthentic, but there is nothing artificial about the *chuddies* (Hindi for 'underpants') that the characters in these programmes challenge each other to kiss when they feel so moved.

Page-turners

In the nineteenth century, the arrival of greater literacy, combined with the availability of cheap literature, gave rise to the ascendancy of the genre novel. The publication of Horace Walpole's *The Castle of Otranto* in 1764 launched the genre which became known as the gothic novel and inspired Mary Shelley's *Frankenstein* (1818) and – as the century produced ever darker works amid ever more shadowy and collapsing surroundings – Bram Stoker's *Dracula* in 1897. The name **Frankenstein** has been much misunderstood, being taken to mean a man-made creation which gets out of control and threatens to destroy its inventor. In fact, Frankenstein was the maverick scientist who produced the beast.

Dracula was the King of the Vampires and the patron saint of people with fangy side-teeth. The *OED* quotes the *Times Literary Supplement* (1971), which had dug up the information that 'Prince Vlad of Wallachia, who died in 1476, was also known as Dracula', and that his surname was spelt in a variety of ways, but the word **vampire** is of Slavonic origin and means some creature or person that – given half a chance – would suck other people's blood for nourishment. Subsequent biologists used the same 'vampire' word to describe the behaviour of mosquitoes and bats. The word was abbreviated, around 1911 according to the *OED*, to **vamp**, meaning a woman (commonly a character in movies) who goes out to attract men and then sucks them dry of their money.

In the eighteenth century, Samuel Richardson had written the seminal novel *Clarissa*, which, in its own way, led gradually to the rise of what became known, by 1980, as the **bodice-ripper**. This was a literary name for an erotic novel, often set against a distanced but historical backdrop. What had started as a moral treatise on the importance of chastity had become an excuse for some gratuitous sex scenes, lightly strung together with a vaguely plausible plot-line. The 'bodice-ripper', as a term, is quintessentially British: the *Guardian* has over 15,000 references to it on its website compared to the *Washington Post*'s twenty-three.

With very different ends in mind, Gerald Mills (1877–1928) and Charles Boon (1877–1943) formed the publishing house Mills & Boon in 1908 (they were born in the same year: it was meant to be). Mills & Boon set out deliberately to create pure, romantic fiction, and it was no wonder that the company became referred to rather stuffily by authors who would never have dreamt of writing in that style but who could have done with the cash that their leading authors earned. The poet Philip Larkin wrote to his friend Kingsley Amis about the title of his novel *A Girl in Winter* when it was published in 1947: 'though I believe I discarded it on the grounds of sounding **Mills & Boony** (if you know what I mean) [it] does conjure up a more precise image than the present one does'.

Whodunits (literally, 'Who done [i.e. did] it?') is another name for the detective novel and continued a long-standing fascination with crime, murder and the solving of them. The first *OED* reference, in a review in *News of Books*, to a 'satisfactory whodunit' is from 1930. Other 'whodunit' writers include Dorothy L. Sayers (her creation was the delightfully aristocratic detective Lord Peter Wimsey) and Ellery Queen (specializing in tough American cop tales), but the most famous proponent of the genre is Agatha Christie (who gave us Hercule Poirot and Miss Marple). Raymond Chandler, whose novels became classic *film noir* movies, is one of the few detective writers to have become an adjective, albeit one not yet recognized by the *OED*. For a novel to be 'Chandleresque', it has to be sharp, smart and as crisp as a well-starched shirt.

One of the finest exponents of comic fiction was P.G. Wodehouse (1881–1975), a man who was somehow able to invent an enormous amount of words for his chosen field of upper-class twittery (though the phrase 'upper-class twit' has not yet been recognized by the *OED*). Wodehouse personally introduced twenty-three brand-new words into the English language, from **cuppa**[11] to the excellent **lame-brain**,[12] and from **ritzy** (which means 'classy', like the hotel) to **to snooter** ('to harrass', 'to bedevil'[13]). He also experimented with the verb **to what-the-hell** (meaning 'to demand an explanation angrily'), and whereas the Victorian novelist Mrs Gaskell, in a letter written *c.*1855, referred to the normal word for 'drunk' as **squiffy**, Wodehouse coined his own – **whiffled** – in *Meet Mr Mulliner*

----

11 'Come and have a cuppa coffee.' *Sam the Sodden* (1925).
12 'A girl with an aunt who knew all about Shakespeare and Bacon must of necessity live in a mental atmosphere into which a lame-brained bird like himself could scarcely hope to soar.' *Mr Mulliner Speaking* (1929).
13 'My Aunt Agatha ... wouldn't be on hand to snooter me for at least another six weeks.' *The Inimitable Jeeves* (1923).

(1927). He was also the first writer to use **zing** as an interjection in *Damsel in Distress* (1919).

The Washington Post noted in 1917 that **oojah** was a handy word to use in place of whichever word you had forgotten, a little like 'thingummy' or 'whatsisname'. Wodehouse crossed this with 'spiffing' in 1917 to produce the demonstrably silly **oojah-cum-spiff**, to mean either something that one can't remember, or something useful that one doesn't really want to name.

A different type of fiction, which entered the language in the 1970s, is the 'Aga saga'. An **Aga** is defined in the *OED* as the acronym formed from the initial letters of the Svenska Aktiebolag Gasaccumulator, the Swedish Gas Accumulator Company, which was the original manufacturer of the sort of home-heating and cooking system popular among well-off types with solid wood floors. 'Aga sagas' defined a genre of fiction writing set in the country, and described marital infidelity and rolling country hills. Joanna Trollope is the high priestess of the form, and we shall be eternally grateful to her for daring to insert the recently coined word **spoddy** – 'having the characteristics of a **spod**: a dull or socially inept person' (1989 is the *OED*'s earliest usage for the noun) into her 1993 novel A *Spanish Lover* with the immortal lines, 'Remember those French boys we had to have at school? They were utterly spoddy.'

In 1993, *Newsday* magazine noted that the Female Literary Tradition had been renamed **chick lit** at Princeton University. One 'chick lit' heroine is Jackie Collins, author of such works as *Dangerous Kiss, Deadly Embrace, Hollywood Wives, Hollywood Divorces* and – when two-word titles just won't do – *Lucky*. Her sister Joan Collins, who starred as Alexis Carrington in ABC's 1981–89 high-life saga *Dynasty*, was described by *Adweek* magazine in 1985 as a **megabitch**. The novelist Jilly Cooper –

who lies somewhere between writing 'bodice-rippers' and 'Aga sagas' – used the same combining form **mega-** in her 1991 novel *Polo* when she wrote, 'He finally located him in the Four Seasons in New York, closing a mega-deal with some Italians.'

Popular literature has succeeded by building an almost tangible link with the reader. The pop-culture era that feeds it is one of the most dynamic sources of new words, but also one of the most fickle. New words are constantly bubbling up and then down again, which can leave devotees of those words stranded in a vocabulary from which the world has moved on. Such creatures are easily spotted by their archaic language (and clothes), but they should be treated with respect. Many of the words that they still use have had their fifteen minutes of fame and would disappear altogether if some oldsters didn't keep using them. It isn't only literature that has a short attention span, though. The next chapter looks at some of the words produced by the other relentlessly innovative worlds of science, technology and warfare.

Chapter Eight

The Appliance of Science

*I*f you were to take a stick, neither very long nor particularly
sharp, and use it to divide all the words in the English
language into two separate fields, how would you do it? For
generations, society has corralled all our words into two
extremely overpopulated and ill-fitting camps, namely, arts and
science. It's obviously not an ideal arrangement, crammed as it
is with exceptions and words that occupy a shadowy no man's
land,[1] but the worlds of science, technology, computing and
medicine have enriched the language in many ways, and from
many sources. Of course, many of these terms are words that
the non-scientific community will never meet, and the first
editors of the *OED* had to make some hard decisions about
which words to include and which to omit, because if nothing
was left out – every pill, every brand name – the whole book
would have been significantly larger than its eventual size (see
Chapter 3, page 106).

   In this chapter we will join the continuing debate, looking at

----
1 No man's land – the earliest (*c.*1350) usage is defined as '(A piece of)
waste or unowned land; an uninhabited or desolate area'; first military
use 1864.

the relationship between science, technology and the military, which has been crucial throughout history.

Technobabble

The Chinese invented solid-propellant **rockets** (from the French *roquet* or adapted from the Italian *rochetta*) in 1232 during the military siege of Kaifeng, the former capital of Henan Province. Where arrows could not penetrate, rockets set fire to tents and wickerwork fortifications. In Europe and North Africa during the fifteenth century, rockets were used mainly to set fire to the rigging of enemy ships in naval battles, but thereafter the technology was restricted to fireworks. It was several centuries later before William Congreve (1772–1828) resurrected them for use in the Napoleonic Wars.

The naming of things is integral to the process of invention, and whenever inventors have discovered a new thing, they have been careful to give it a name that, in part, is the manifesto of its qualities. When George Stephenson's steam locomotive Rocket won the Rainhill Trials in 1829, its inventor didn't just have the best steam engine: he had the best name for it too (see box). The other competing engines were called *The Novelty*, *The Nonpareil*, *The Cycloped* and *The Perseverance*. The *OED* has six different homonyms for the word 'rocket' – i.e. they're all separate, etymologically distinct words. Nowadays we might say that something 'goes like a rocket', but in the days when rockets were merely fireworks, designed to burst in the air and scatter a shower of sparks, the word didn't pack quite the same punch. The phrase 'like a rocket' only went into circulation when the political theorist Thomas Paine (1737–1809) included it in his seminal work *The Rights of Man*. In 1792 he said of his political rival Edmund Burke (1729–97) that 'he rose like a rocket, he fell like the stick', which became proverbial and was reused by other great writers, including James Joyce (1882–1941) and George Bernard Shaw (1856–1950).[2] Nowadays we talk about 'giving someone a rocket', a synonym for a telling-off. No one, to date, has attempted to coin any phrases that include the word 'cycloped'.

Just as scientific processes work with everyday objects (wood, coal, steam, etc.) to achieve out-of-the-ordinary results, so scientists

---

Other definitions of rocket

1. Rochet. 'An outer garment, smock-frock, cloak, or mantle, sometimes worn by bishops and abbots' (1400).
2. 'Type of lettuce' (1530).
3. 'An apparatus consisting of a cylindrical case of paper or metal containing an inflammable composition, by the ignition of which it may be projected to a height or distance' (1611).
4. 'Bobbin or blunt-headed lance' (c.1440).
5. 'A small rock' (1538).

---

sometimes take or invent names for their discoveries from the world around them. Louis Pasteur (1822–95) was a brilliant chemist and bacteriologist. Alongside his work with **fermentation** – a term originally from the Latin *fervere* (to boil) via *fermentare* – he went on to unravel the complex medical histories behind rabies, anthrax, chicken cholera and silkworm

---

2 1922 James Joyce, *Ulysses*: 'My fireworks. Up like a rocket, down like a stick.' 1950 George Bernard Shaw, *Farfetched Fables*: '"Political adventurers and tin Jesuses" rose like rockets to dictatorships and fell to earth like sticks.'

disease. He also became one of the best-known brands in science, giving his name to the process of **pasteurization**, and also to the Pasteur Institute, the Pasteur flask, the Pasteur treatment, the Pasteur pipette, the Pasteur reaction and the Pasteur effect.

In 1798, several years before any of Pasteur's breakthroughs, the Gloucester physician Edward Jenner (1749–1823) published his research on smallpox, noting that milkmaids who had contracted cowpox appeared to have immunity from the much more serious smallpox. He began to inoculate people with a preparation made from cowpox pustules, and this process became known as **vaccination**, from *vacca*, the Latin word for 'cow'. If Dr Jenner had lived in more modern times and had an agent, the process might have been called 'Jenneration'.

The invention of two Scottish engineers, Thomas Telford (1757–1834) and John Loudoun McAdam (1756–1836), could be described as groundbreaking in the literal sense of the word. Both devised methods of improving road-building, although one proved more enduring than the other. There is one reference in the *OED* to a 'telford road', made from broken stones (1896). McAdam, meanwhile, gave his name to the **macadamizing process**, which is the name given to his tightly packed and symmetrical arrangement of broken stones covered with smaller stones. So sturdy is this foundation that the process is still used in road construction today. The layer of tar laid over the stone surface (first cited 1903) became known as **Tarmac**. When spelt with a small 't' it denotes an airfield or runway, and to appear in the dictionary in both upper and lower cases is a sure sign of achievement.

Science is not sentimental. We know nothing of the tireless experimenters who might have spent years of their lives trying to invent something only to to find that someone has beaten them to it. The world's first patent on a ballpoint pen was issued on 30 October 1888 to John J. Loud of Massachusetts, but though the design was on the right lines, the flow of ink was irregular. Eventually, two Hungarian brothers, László and Georg Biró got the ballpoint technique down to a T (or tee[3]) with a stainless steel ball. The brothers applied for a patent on the pen in 1938 and the world got its first **biro**. The pen was a hit with the Royal Air Force during the Second World War, as the ballpoint didn't leak despite the reduced air pressure at high altitudes. In 1949 a Frenchman, Baron Marcel Bich, introduced a new, improved ballpoint to Europe. The BiC Crystal is currently the world's most popular ballpoint, selling 14 million a day across the world. These days, we tend to write with a BiC but still call it a 'biro'.

Home comforts

There is a saying, 'Necessity is the mother of invention', and this was proved resoundingly true in 1907 when an Ohio department store janitor called James Murray Spangler came up with a device that he hoped would reduce the frequency of his asthma attacks. Suspecting that his carpet sweeper was throwing up too much dust, he devised a crude vacuum cleaner using a soap box, an electric motor, a broom handle and a pillow case. He gave one of the vacuums to a friend called Susan Hoover, who liked it and told her husband, a leather-goods manufacturer called W.H. 'Boss'

---

3 T or tee, first cited 1693. The original sense of 'T' here is unclear. 'Suggestions that it was the tee at Curling, or at Golf, or a T square, appear on investigation to be untenable,' says the *OED*. Maybe it referred to the proper completion of a 't' by crossing it. The phrase 'to a tittle' (i.e. to a prick, dot, jot) with the same sense was in use nearly a century earlier.

Hoover. He bought the patent from Spangler in 1908, kept him as a partner and in 1926 started promoting his product with advertisements such as 'A hoovered room … is … free from dust'.[4] That wasn't the only time the name Hoover became a verb, but 'to hoover' certainly caught on more widely than 'hooverize', a word that H.B. Gross advanced in the *New York Tribune* in 1917 to describe saving food in the way being extolled by future president Herbert Hoover.

'Boss' Hoover and Spangler became wealthy: we could even say they hoovered up loads of cash, and even in these days of Dysons and other brands, the word 'hoover' – whether as noun or verb – got in first and is hard to shift. The novelist H.G. Wells (1866–1946) wrote in *All Aboard for Ararat* (1940), his parable of the coming world crisis, 'I shall feel like a man trying to sell Hoover cleaners to an Arab encampment in a dust storm'. And the magazine *Engineer* pointed out a growing anomaly in 1971: 'How many housewives hoover the carpet with an Electrolux?'

Some other domestic advances have also wormed their way into new contexts. Perhaps you've been in a meeting when a good idea is recognized and heard the boss say, 'Now we're cooking with gas.' Strange how some phrases don't catch on: 'We're really using the hot plate now' or 'Straight out of the microwave' or 'Let's put this on the Primus and see if it boils'. Not yet, it seems.

Inventions, discoveries, the patenting of formulas… all represent a decisive step forward, and the name of an invention can symbolize that process. You could be so proud of your new non-stick product that you might choose to stick forever to its proper scientific name – 'polytetrafluoroethylene'. But if, on the

---

4 From 1926 or 1927 in an advert quoted in the *OED* from the *Army & Navy Stores Catalogue*.

other hand, you give it a snappier name – **Teflon**, say – and the product works, it will have a far longer life. About forty years after it was registered in 1945, when the likes of President Ronald Reagan seemed incapable of getting anything right but always escaped censure, it provided the media with the perfect, pithy description for him: 'the Teflon president'. So maybe it was just as well that the coating's inventor, Dr Roy J. Plunkett, didn't go for immortality on a personal level.

Taking care

Teflon gave us safe cooking: the **condom** gave us safe sex. Is the rise of the condom a testament to the life's work of a Dr Condom (aka Quondam, Condon and Conton), a supposed pox-doctor? The *OED* is in no doubt on the matter. 'Origin unknown,' it says. 'No seventeenth-century physician named Condom or Conton has been traced, though a doctor so named is often said to be the inventor of the sheath.' So poor Dr Condom, if he ever existed, is lost to history, unlike the very real Thomas Crapper, by whose name hangs a different tale.

The Dutch word *krappen* means 'to pluck' or 'cut off'. Mix that with the Old French *crappe* (siftings) and the Anglo-Latin *crappa* (chaff), and you end up with the Late Middle English, fifteenth-century word **crap**, meaning 'the husk of grain'. Even then, though, 'crap' led something of a double life, since it was also a plural word for 'the residue formed in boiling, melting, or rendering fat; crackling'. Within a few centuries, the word had come to mean, by 1879, 'the dregs of beer, etc.', so it is hardly a surprise that by 1898 the *OED* defines 'crap' as 'excrement; defecation', and in the same year as 'rubbish, nonsense; something … worthless…' But sorry, Thomas Crapper fans. He wasn't born until 1836, and he didn't invent the flush toilet, so any confusion with his name is entirely accidental.[5]

The truth can hurt, which is why medicine sometimes helps us by wrapping our symptoms in a protective, condom-like sheath of scientific terminology. You may feel that you have a shocking hangover, for example, but would you hurt any less if you were told that you were suffering from **crapulence**? It has nothing to do with 'crap', being derived from the ancient Greek word *kraipalē*, meaning 'a drunken headache'.

Greek bestows the same aura of respectability on various professions. For example, would you rather talk to a mind doctor or a **psychiatrist**? Whom would you trust more? When you know that *psuchē* means 'breath, life or spirit', and *īatros* is Greek for 'doctor', there's not much to choose between them, yet the word derived from Greek has far greater gravitas. Imagine you go to see your doctor with chest pain and he or she tells you that it's **angina**, a 400-year-old word (first attested from 1590) that means, essentially, 'severe pain'. This technical term makes you feel better, though it might be less reassuring if you know that 'angina' comes from the Latin *angere* (to choke, strangle) and the Greek *ankhonē*, which also means 'strangling'.

Another good example of a word that impresses was used in British Telecom's TV advert from the 1980s featuring Maureen Lipman as 'Beattie', who consoles her grandson over his mediocre examination results. 'An ology. He gets an ology and he says he's failed. You get an ology, you're a scientist!' The word **ology**, from the Greek *logos*, meaning 'word' or 'reason', actually

----

5 Thomas Crapper was, though, a sanitary engineer and successful businessman who went on to invent and patent various improvements to the flush toilet, so you do sometimes find old toilet fittings with his name on them. Was this a case of a man's surname deciding his fate?

has a more respectable history than its use in the TV adverts implied. Charles Dickens in *Hard Times* (1854) wrote, 'Ologies of all kinds, from morning to night. If there is any Ology left … that has not been worn to rags in this house … I hope I shall never hear its name.' The word was, in fact, first used in 1811 for the same effect by writer Edward Nares: 'She … was therefore supposed to understand Chemistry, Geology, Philology, and a hundred other ologies.'

When scientific terms get clinical, sometimes it's more palatable to abbreviate them or turn them into acronyms. Shortenings can soften the stark reality of hospital terms: AKA (for 'above the knee amputation') is a veiled reminder for where an incision should be made or a dressing applied. And if an acronym spells out a new word, such as **radar** (radio detection and ranging, 1941) or **laser** (light amplification by the stimulated emission of radiation, 1960), it can slip into the language very easily. When established, these words can be played with too: having a **gaydar** (1982), for instance, means you can spot someone who's gay a mile off.

Spreading the word

The rise of personal computing has seen the creation of a whole language that was only in its infancy twenty years ago, though the word **geek** is perhaps, says the *OED*, a variant of **geck** – Shakespeare spells it 'geeke' in *Cymbeline* (V.iv) (1623): 'And to become the geeke and scorne o'th'others vilany.'

The language of computers has repossessed certain words that, like 'geek', are probably more familiar to many of us in their new context than in their old. These include: 'virus', 'cookie', 'surfing', 'net', 'web', 'disk', 'memory', 'menu', 'mouse', 'save' and 'mobile'. Let's look at **scroll**. In 1606 it meant 'to write on a scroll of parchment'. In 1730 it meant 'to draft or make a rough copy', and in 1868 'scrolled' meant 'rolled or curled up', and is still used in that way by those writing in an art context: 'The body of the piece is richly encrusted with scrolling ormolu' (*The Times*, 1979). The data on computer screens was being scrolled up or down as far back as 1971, long before the machines were available to the mass market. When we **paste** (first attested 1975) these days, little glue is involved, and the word contains nothing of its original sense (*c.*1425) of pounding or grinding something into a paste. The language is moving on the whole time: invention dictates the need for new language.

Around the year 1200, **cable** was 'a strong thick rope made of hemp'. A variant reading of a familiar phrase in the Gospels of Matthew, Mark and Luke is that 'it is easier for a cable [not a camel] to go through the eye of a needle than for a rich man to enter into the kingdom of God'. One day people may be saying that it is easier for a camel to go through the eye of a needle than it is to get your broadband connection in the same week that you order it.

When we talk about the **web** these days, most of us are not talking about a spider's 'web', first attested around 1220 in the *OED*. The word **text**, a late medieval word from the Old Norman French *texte*, came from the Latin *textus*, which was derived from the verb *texere* (to weave), hence 'textile'. If ever a word has been disconnected from its roots, here is one. And yet technology has also achieved an incredible renaissance for a nineteenth-century word that was virtually dead and buried ten years or more ago. **Wireless** – the name given to early radio, even though the wires were only too evident – was all the rage during the 1890s. 'Wireless' technology might have seemed antiquated a few years ago, when the *OED* noted: 'Now chiefly historical, having been superseded by radio'. And yet wireless is back, and this time it really is wire-less. Way to go.

The **telegraph** was originally 'an apparatus for transmitting messages to a distance, usually by signs of some kind'. Its inventor, Claude Chappe (1763–1805), wanted to call it a **tachygraph**, from the Greek words for 'quick' and 'write', but his friend Miot de Mélito told him it was a bad name, and persuaded him to change it to *télégraphe* (from the Greek words *telos* 'far off' and *graphein* 'to write'), which he did, in 1792. The contraption first consisted of 'an upright post with movable arms', says the *OED*, and the signals were made 'by various positions of the arms according to a pre-arranged code'. Subsequent innovations included 'movable disks, shutters, flashes of light, movements in a column of liquid, sounds of bells, horns, etc., or other means'.

Another Frenchman, Jean-François Sudré (1787–1864), devised a system of telegraphic signalling using musical notes in 1828. (He also came up with a language called Solresol, but that's another story.) He then introduced a sort of foghorn, which was used to send signals to ships and trains by making loud sounds or notes. This device, which he called the **telephone** (first attested in 1835), took its name from the Greek words *telos* and *phōnē* 'sound'. Of course, everyone said it would never catch on.

The grapevine

No one ever heard something 'on the grapevine' until the American Civil War (1861–5), and the phrase is first attested by the *OED* in 1864. The 'grapevine' was the electric telegraph, the wires of which, like vine tendrils, had been spreading across America since Samuel Morse inaugurated the first line (from Washington to Baltimore) on 24 May 1844. The telegraph was a huge success and made a massive impact on how people lived, accelerating communications between communities.

Communications have come a long way since the telegraph. When, in 1611, the German astronomer Johannes Kepler used the term **satellite**, from the Latin *satelles* (attendant, member of a bodyguard), to describe a small planet that revolves around a larger one, he was adapting a word that had been in use from around 1548 to describe a 'royal lackey or flunkey'. The *OED* defines a satellite as 'an attendant upon a person of importance, forming part of his retinue and employed to execute his orders. Often with reproachful connotation, implying subserviency or unscrupulousness in the service.' This is certainly the sense in which the US writer Washington Irving (1783–1859) used it in his 1850 biography of the Irish dramatist Oliver Goldsmith (*c.*1730–74), when he referred to James Boswell being 'made happy by an introduction to Johnson, of whom he became the obsequious satellite'. Nowadays satellite technology has brought remarkable advances in communications, and we receive signals via a **dish**, an Old English word from the Latin *discus* (disc).

Fighting talk

One of the great sources of linguistic innovation has been warfare. Whether we like it or not, fighting is one thing that human beings do particularly well, and it can take something as apparently superficial as a domestic tiff or a boardroom squabble to put our language on a war footing. Whether we end up **digging for victory** and **spearheading** a charge, or closing ranks and waving the **white flag**,[6] it doesn't take much provocation for our thoughts and words to be peppered with the

----

6 Waving a white flag in seventeenth-century France did not mean you were surrendering: it was simply a demonstration of support for the Bourbons.

language of warfare. War has its own logic, and it certainly does not lack for drama. This has been well chronicled by, among others, the sixth- or fifth-century-BC Chinese military strategist Sun-tzu in *The Art of War*, and Niccolò Machiavelli (1469–1527) in his own *Art of War* (1521).

The phrase **theatre of war** seems to have been wheeled out for the first time by the First World War poet Edmund Blunden in his 1928 book *Undertones of War*. This did not seek to suggest that war was anything so vulgar as a box-office smash. On the contrary; after the initial rush, there was certainly no appetite to book front-row seats. But when political correspondents look around for an image these days, they don't have too much time to spend checking the historical accuracy of their references. To some, the mere hint of raised voices in the maze of Whitehall corridors is enough to substantiate an expression such as **trench warfare**, which became a characteristic of the 1914–18 conflict.

For a long time, the source of names for weaponry was the natural world. **Grenades**, named after their resemblance to the pomegranate (*granada* in Spanish), must have been tossed in anger well before they were first attested by the *OED* in 1591 but fell out of military fashion in the eighteenth century. During the sixteenth century a **torpedo** was a ray-like flat fish that emits an electric discharge, but in 1776 an American called David Bushnell[7] turned it into a sea-going **mine** that could be clamped to an enemy ship.

In more modern times, the prettily named **daisy-cutter** – 'a

---

7 David Bushnell (1742–1824) from Saybrook, Connecticut, was an inventor during the American Revolutionary War. He created the first submarine – called *The Turtle* – to be used in combat, in 1775. He proved that gunpowder could be exploded under water and he invented the first time bomb, which, using a clockwork fuse, could be exploded remotely.

horse that in trotting lifts its feet only very slightly from the ground' (1791) – lent its name to something much uglier: one of the world's largest bombs, first used in 1970 in Vietnam to clear undergrowth, which has to be parachuted to its target from a cargo plane. It should not be confused with a cricketing 'daisy-cutter', which is a devilishly low ball, bowled under-arm. Another deadly weapon with a deceptively gentle name was the **cruise** missile, which came from the Dutch word *kruisen* (to cross), and was an American development of German V2[8] technology. The original (1698) meaning of 'cruise' was 'to sail to and fro over some part of the sea without making for a particular port or landing-place, on the lookout for ships, for the protection of commerce in time of war, for plunder, or (in modern times) for pleasure'. 'Cruising' has also been known to imply walking or driving around in search of (usually gay) sex since at least 1904.

Any navy that can call on the services of cruise missile technology has to be said to have a head-start in any looming battle. And if it has enormous big ships with an aversion to sinking, so much the better. The British navy launched the first battleship in the world on 18 February 1906. It was called the ***Dreadnought***, which until then had meant 'A thick coat or outer garment worn in very inclement weather'. The word is cited in Archibald Duncan's 1806 *Life of Lord Nelson*: '"I am lord Nelson," replied the hero … throwing aside his green dreadnought.' Captain Cook, on his voyage towards the South Pole, describes a jacket made from a thick woollen cloth called a 'Fearnought' (1790).

----

8 The V2 was a much-feared German rocket bomb, designed by a team led by the rocket scientist Wernher von Braun, which followed the V1 or 'doodlebug' (1944–5). The V2 was used mostly against British and Belgian targets towards the end of the war.

Both dreaded and feared in wartime was the simply named **shell**, with its military meaning first cited in the *OED* at the twenty-first definition – after crustaceans, pearls, tiles, eggs, coconuts, seeds, tortoises, a racing boat, an armadillo and 'the bottom part of a turnip remaining after the root has been scooped out by sheep' have been dispatched. Then we find 'a case of metal, etc. in which powder and shot is made up, especially for use as a hand-grenade' (1644), followed by 'explosive projectile or bomb for use in a cannon or mortar' in the 1940s. A particular type of shell – 'a hollow projectile containing bullets and a small bursting charge, which, when fired by the time fuse, bursts the shell and scatters the bullets in a shower' – was invented during the Peninsular Wars of 1808–14 by Major General Henry **Shrapnel** (1761–1842). During the Blitz,[9] the period of intensive German attacks on British cities, particularly London, in 1940, the contemporary historical record *Notes & Queries* commented with admirable sangfroid that 'the shell fragments which are at present descending upon its devoted head are unhesitatingly referred to by the public as "shrapnel" and the correct expression, "shell fragments", has begun to verge on pedantry'.

Shell shock, that condition of extreme psychological trauma that the First World War bombardments produced, was first cited around 1915. Ewart Alan Mackintosh in *War, the Liberator* (1918) described how 'The Corporal … collapsed suddenly with twitching hands and staring, frightened eyes, proclaiming the shell-shock he had held off while the work was to be done'. The phrase has since been cleansed, rubbed down and sent to fight

----

9 'Blitz' is a shortened form of the German word *Blitzkrieg* (lightning war). On 9 September 1940 the *Daily Express* reported: 'Blitz bombing of London goes on all night.'

again, though this time in mufti (see Chapter 6, page 158). When Graham Lee won the 2004 Grand National on Amberleigh House, he was said to be 'shell shocked', but in a good way.

Paul Fussell in *The Great War and Modern Memory*, his cultural study of the years 1914–18, points out how our language has been militarized since that conflict, which was the first time for centuries that warfare had seemed close to home. Much **sabre-rattling** had preceded it, although that term was not attested in the *OED* until 1922. It means 'to threaten military action without actually committing troops', and it isn't only generals who practise it. Anyone who indulges in this with more seriousness of purpose might find himself described as a **warmonger**, which the *OED* defines as 'One who traffics in (or) seeks to bring about war'. Since early Old English times (*c.*598), the word **monger** has lived a dangerous double life, both as a 'person engaged in a petty or disreputable trade or traffic' (scandalmonger, whoremonger) and as an otherwise respectable 'dealer, trader, or trafficker in a particular commodity', such as fishmonger and ironmonger. They may be a bit noisy at times, but that's no reason to stigmatize them.

Still, it could be that it's just too late to rehabilitate the monger's stained reputation; it would be like mounting a **rearguard action** – 'defensive stand by the rear-guard of a retreating army' – which, as the *Westminster Gazette* first pointed out in 1898, is 'the worst of all battles to fight'. Since then, many others have tried. In 2005 it was deployed by the *Daily Telegraph*'s film critic to describe George Lucas's latest *Star Wars* film: 'a two-hour rearguard action against encroaching tedium'. These days it means an ultimately futile effort, but one that is worth it nonetheless. A similar tactic, perhaps more wily, could be called a **Parthian shot**. Parthia was a region of the Achaemenian Empire and later a kingdom in what is now the Khorasan region of Iran. Parthian horsemen had a fascinating, possibly mythical way of fighting, which those people reluctant to use a classical allusion – or unfamiliar with its classical origins – also call a **parting shot**, which sounds similar, but misses some of the point. The Parthians used to confuse the enemy by continuing to shoot arrows while appearing to run away. This must have baffled their foes, who assumed the battle won, only to see that the retreat was tactical and the danger was still very much alive. For a modern equivalent, imagine your partner has just chucked you and you let yourself back into the flat to cut holes in his or her clothes. That's a form of Parthian shot. It's not recommended, but it has been known to happen.

There are levels of defeat in warfare, and certainly there are levels of victory too. A **pyrrhic victory** is named after Pyrrhus of Epirus (319–272 BC). Pyrrhus was a Greek king, famed for taking on the Romans. In 281 BC he took a commission to do so from the people of Tarentum. He fought and beat the Romans, with the help of elephants, first at Heraclea and again (in 279 BC) at Asculeum, but his casualties were massive. When someone congratulated him on his victory he is said to have replied – in one of the great satirical utterances of classical civilization – 'One more victory like this will be the end of me.' Ever since the remark came into circulation, a 'pyrrhic victory' has meant just that; a victory in which the price paid is so high that it's debatable as to whether the 'winning' side has achieved anything useful.

War is hell, however **battle-hardened** you are – whether you've been **manning the barricades** with **all guns blazing**, or **battening down the hatches** so as to sit it out, or facing troubles in true **Dunkirk spirit**.[10] Sometimes, though, there is an alternative to fighting. These days, if you said you had **spiked somebody's guns** or **seen them off at the pass**, you would be indicating that you had anticipated and thereby nullified the harm you were expecting them to do you. Had you attempted the same manoeuvre in the seventeenth century, you would have had to drive nails into the touch-hole of the enemy's gun so that it could not be fired. In this way the enemy would be **disarmed**, a word that William Caxton, the first English printer, used in this sense in 1481, when it also meant 'to dismantle a ship' and 'to strip an animal of its horns, claws or teeth'. Chaucer used it even earlier, around 1374, to mean 'deprive of power, to injure or terrify', until Thomas Beale, in *The Natural History of the Sperm Whale* (1839) described how someone (not the whale) 'Beckoned us to approach with winning and **disarming** smiles'.

Equally disarming was the late Lord Scarman's visit to Brixton after the race riots of 1981, when he earned respect among the black population by referring to them as 'living on the **front line**' – a phrase dating back at least to the First World War. He might also have described the events as **snafu**, a Second World War acronym used by American troops, which stood for 'situation normal: all fouled (or fucked) up' (1941).

If you have ever been sent on a **hopeless mission**, you might like to recall the **kamikaze** ('divine wind') that supposedly destroyed the ships (and 100,000 men) of the invading Mongols at Inari Bay in August 1281, and then passed into Japanese

---

10 Dunkirk: 'French Channel port, scene of the evacuation of the British Expeditionary Force in 1940 ... [by] a host of small boats while under constant attack from the air.' In 1961 a writer in *The Listener* magazine observed that 'The Dunkirk spirit of only starting to try hard when it becomes really necessary is deeply ingrained in the British character.'

folklore as a miraculous victory. The word 'kamikaze' (*kami* means 'divinity' and *kaze* means 'wind') took on a horrific significance in the Second World War when Japanese pilots crashed their own planes on to the decks of US and Australian ships in the sea around the Philippines, a tactic first used in 1944 but not recorded in print until 1945.

The word 'kamikaze' was obviously much in evidence after the attacks on the World Trade Center and the Pentagon building on 11 September 2001, but it can also be used on altogether more flippant occasions, as when it was used to describe the Sri Lankan cricket team's disastrous running between the wickets against the West Indies in 2003. 'Kamikaze' is, of course, a euphemism: the more violent the attack, the more deceptively civilized the language. **Carpet bombing** sounds like 'carpet slippers', but has a much harsher reality: it was coined in 1945 to describe laying waste to a large area of land. And the term **collateral damage** – meaning 'Whoops, looks like we hit some civilians' – was used first by the Pentagon/CIA in August 1988, after an air attack on the Al Shifa bomb-making plant in Sudan. Nowadays, it's not uncommon to hear it used to refer to any unintended victims, such as children in a divorce case.

If that is one case of military hardware **impacting**, as they say, on flesh and blood, we should not forget the mother and father of all civilian air-raids: on Hiroshima and Nagasaki. The first **atom bomb**, called 'Little Boy', exploded over Hiroshima on 6 August 1945, killing over 60,000 people. The second bomb, called 'Fat Man', exploded above Nagasaki on 9 August, killing about 42,000 people. The Americans claim that using the atom bomb was the least worst option, and they could be right, but a new word, **fallout**, entered the language. This refers to the contaminated particles thrown up by the explosion that then fall back down to earth. That word, so shocking in its true meaning, is now used simply to mean 'consequences' in far less serious situations, as in 'Net weathers WorldCom fallout'. Similarly, you might read that Thierry Henry remains Arsène Wenger's **nuclear option** at Highbury. And when a pop diva such as Diana Ross can have a hit with a song called 'Chain Reaction' (1985), you know that we have, to some extent, become desensitized to the horrific images that used to accompany these words.

Language can protect us from many horrors, but it can also expose us to many more. It's in our nature that we want to take a look: that is the appeal of **taboo** (see Introduction, page 29). Soldiers on active service traditionally find out more about the seamy side of life than they would have done on **civvy street** (in civilian life). For them, it's a process of discovery equivalent to the greatest efforts of scientists and surgeons. Science flourishes in times of danger, soldiers behave like superheroes in battle conditions, and language is rarely so inventive as when it is under constraints of one kind or another. Some colourful examples of language under stress are contained in the next chapter.

Chapter Nine

Mind Your Language

Swearing is a strange thing: it often expresses two contradictory conditions simultaneously. We swear to show fear, and also to show that we're not afraid. We take the name of God in vain at precisely the moment when we should be most circumspect ('Jesus, sorry I didn't recognize you, Vicar'). Swearing can help to release tension. We swear when we are angry, or to emphasize a point, or when we feel that we've lost control of a situation. We swear in order to shock, to impress or to flirt. We swear to show that we care, and to show that we couldn't give a **toss**.[1] Bad language is called 'transgressive'[2] because it goes beyond or steps over a line of general acceptability.

But the use of language as a weapon need not just be about four-letter words. As we shall see, many communities have been marginalized or discriminated against on account of their race,

---

1 Toss: 'In negative contexts: a jot, a whit, a very small amount.' The first written use comes, amazingly, in George Eliot's *Daniel Deronda* (1876): 'I don't care a toss where you are.'
2 Transgressive – from the French *transgresser*, ultimately from the Latin *trans* ('across') and *gradi* ('go').

gender or sexuality by mainstream society, which uses language to keep them in an inferior position. When these groups seize back the initiative, it is often language that helps them to recover lost ground and status within society.

**** words

Courtesy was introduced into Britain by the Norman invaders, who came over with William the Conqueror in 1066. Discourtesy had existed for centuries before, though not under that name. The idea of courtly behaviour overrode the much coarser ways and language that had held sway until then, which is why the vast majority of swear-words are Old English or Anglo-Saxon. There might not even have been a corresponding term in the French spoken by the barons; and Latin, which they introduced to this country (see Chapter 1), was likely to have been considerably more genteel. **Wank**, for example, is Old English, while the more upmarket 'masturbate' is Latin. 'Fuck' is Old English; 'coitus' and 'intercourse' are Latin. 'Fornication' has splendidly classical roots, arising from the Latin word *fornix*, meaning 'arch, vaulted chamber' but also 'brothel'.

Swearing can be shocking, but it has always been central to our behaviour as human beings. Even the Greeks and Romans let rip now and again. Essentially, swearing takes three forms:

- Words to do with excretion
- Sexual language or imagery
- Religious or blasphemous[3] vocabulary

---
3 Blasphemous – from the Greek *blasphēmos*, meaning 'evil speaking'.

Excretion-related swearing starts early because small children are naturally curious about it. They quickly learn the taboo nature of certain bodily functions, and they continue to experiment with that knowledge in conversation. In the case of sexual imagery, it is hardly surprising that our thoughts turn to swearing when hormones start us raging towards puberty. And we invoke the name of the divine either to call upon or challenge them: either to call upon their strength for our aid or, more commonly these days, to disdain their perceived omnipotence.

Who swears? Pretty much everyone, it seems, if the circumstances are appropriate. Each society has its own sign language for obscenity, such as the V-sign, the single finger, the finger inside the circled fingers, but this is extremely limited in comparison with the spoken language, which offers a vast number of options. We swear in public, in private, on our own, with friends, at work, and sometimes in front of our own family. But swearing is status-dependent. You would be more likely to swear at a fellow worker than at your employer, and you might not want to swear in front of an employee because swearing implies a sort of intimacy, and that exists only at certain social levels. You do it when you know you can get away with it. But how have attitudes to bad language changed over the centuries, and why have certain languages, such as English, developed such a multiplicity of ways in which to keep an uncivil tongue?

Historical swearing

When people give evidence in court these days, they have the option of swearing on the Bible that the evidence they are about to give is the truth, 'so help me God'. This is the oldest sense of the verb **to swear**, to which we find references in the laws of

King Alfred (*c*.900) and the Lindisfarne Gospels (*c*.950), as the *OED* defines it, 'To make a solemn declaration of statement with an appeal to God or a superhuman being, or to some sacred object, in confirmation of what is said; to take an oath'. The sense of 'to swear at', as in 'to imprecate evil up by an oath; to address with profane imprecation' dates from the seventeenth century. The implication is that one would never commit perjury if the result was a lifelong sentence of eternal damnation.

Among the earliest blasphemies on record are Middle English ones that refer to parts of God's body, such as **'slids** (God's eyelids), **'sfoot** (God's foot), **'steeth** (God's teeth) and **zounds** (God's wounds). Referring to His bones, people were likely to exclaim **God's bodskins**, **odsbodikins** or **gadsbudlikins**. Another exclamation was **gadzooks** (God's hooks), which might refer to the nails that pierced Christ's flesh. As swearing has evolved, the body parts have remained, as in '**My arse!**'. In these days of secularization, with fewer and fewer people attending conventional church services, expressions invoking the Godhead (Jesus, God, Christ) have lost some of their power to shock, but practising Christians are still likely to find them offensive.

The Church was all-powerful during the Middle Ages, but after the Reformation[4] its authority began to diminish. As people emerged from under its shadow, **devil** began to be used more as a term of abuse – proof that the very mention of Satan's name was no longer guaranteed to make everyone turn to stone. And as words such as **damn** and **hell** slowly lost their power to shock, there were always other words you could use if you had

---

4 The Reformation – a Protestant movement that, emerging in the sixteenth century, attempted to reform the all-powerful Roman Catholic Church.

hit your thumb with a hammer, from **shit** to a handy new word that began with 'f'.

It was the Carmelite friars of Cambridge who were the first targets of bad language in writing. In a document written some time before the fifteenth century we find a line in cod Latin that reads, *Non sunt in coeli, quia gxddbov xxkxzt pg ifmk*. The first five words mean 'They are not in heaven because...' The next four words are written in a simple code: step back one letter in each case and you get *fvccant vvivys of heli*. The 'v' is pronounced 'u': take off the –ant third person plural ending and you are left staring at the word *fucc*, or **fuck** in modern parlance. The rest of this sentence is more or less English: 'they fuck the wives of Ely'. It's the sort of sentiment that you might expect to see scratched on a toilet door, and yet this disgraceful slur was made about the friars of Cambridge and the womenfolk of Ely.

The word 'fuck' is an ancient Germanic word. The Middle Dutch *fokken*, the Norwegian *fukka* and the Swedish *focka* mean roughly the same thing. However, it did not always occupy the hottest seat in the history of copulation. The apparently blameless noun 'swivel', which today is guilty of little more than helping an office chair to rotate, has something of a shady past, unconnected to its meaning as 'a simple fastening or coupling device made so that the object fastened to it can turn freely upon it'. 'Swivel' was derived from the Old English 'swifan', which also gave us **swive**, a word that, from our earliest (fourteenth-century) records onwards, meant 'to copulate'. The impolite associations were certainly not lost on English speakers around 800 years ago, and Geoffrey Chaucer, for one, never missed a chance to insert a 'swive' when the situation arose: 'Thus swived was this carpenter's wife' is one example from 'The Miller's Tale'. The word continued to perform indelicately for centuries, although with more appetite north of the border, until it dropped pretty much out of sight in the eighteenth century. The *OED*'s last sighting of it is from a publication called *Secreta Secret* (1898): 'Don't bathe on a full stomach: nor swive.'

X-rated words

The shock value of 'fuck' has lessened a great deal over the years. If you still doubt it, ask a twelve-year-old wearing a French Connection UK T-shirt. Maybe this is because the British have found the word so fucking useful – excuse my French[5] – in normal conversation. Indeed, it has peppered so much of our speech that the French refer to us – when they can bear to – as 'Les Fuckings' because that's the word they keep hearing us use when we're *en vacances*.

'Fuck' is an incredibly hard-working word, with multiple grammatical uses. It is a noun: 'Frankly, my dear, I don't give a fuck.' A verb: 'Fuck me, I'm knackered' or 'I'm fucking off home now, OK?' An adjective, or a verbal adjective: 'It was just a fucking joke, right?' An adverb: 'That was fucking hard work.' A past participle: 'Fucked if I know.' And, of course, an interjection: 'Fuck off!' It's a strange thing to urge someone to do, since it's probably a fate that most people would gladly accept, but terms of abuse don't always obey the laws of logic. This taboo word may have lost some of its potency, but there is another four-letter word that still has the power to shock.

Language scholars have been speculating for years about the etymological history of the 'c-word' – or 'the female external

----

5 *Harper's Magazine* 1895: 'Palaces be durned! Excuse my French.' Used as a euphemism for bad language ever since.

genital organs', to quote the *OED*. Francis Grose in his 1788 *Dictionary of the Vulgar Tongue* defined 'c**t' [*sic*] as 'a nasty name for a nasty thing'. Eric Partridge (1894–1979), the famous linguist and author of *The Dictionary of Slang*, found something of 'quintessential femineity' (i.e. femininity) in the opening two letters of the word **cunt**.

Some writers who have traced the word's classical routes may be following their hopes, or a political agenda, or a pure coincidence, more than strict linguistic practice, since it's much more likely to be Germanic than from Greek or Latin. But just to see where this curious trail leads, certain academics have taken the Latin *cognosco* (I know) and derived from it words such as 'connote', 'canny' and 'cunning'. Then they take a noun such as *cuneus*, which means 'a wedge', and the related *cunnus*, which does (finally) mean the 'female pudenda' or, in Horace's words, an 'unchaste woman'. A little bit of *cognosco* and a lot of *cunnus* imply, they say, that **cunt** combines quintessential femininity and some Earth Mother-know-it-all wisdom. These examples might help explain why Geoffrey Chaucer sidesteps the obvious in 'The Wife of Bath's Tale':

> *For certeyn, olde dotard, by youre leve, Ye shul have queynte*
> *right y-nough at eve.*

The word 'queynte' was a familiar euphemism for 'cunt', though later on the bawdy wench alludes to her sexual prowess more fulsomely when she says:

> *And trewely, as myne housbondes tolde me, I had the beste*
> *quoniam mighte be.*

'Quoniam' is the Latin word for 'whereas', so the euphemism here is 'whatever' or 'whatsit' or, as some might say, 'thingy'. There have been other variations right up to the modern day, from the nineteenth-century 'hootchie-cootchie' to a suggestion of sexual gratification in the Small Faces' psychedelia-soaked hit 'Itchycoo Park' (1967). Elsewhere, cunts have featured on the British landscape as far back as the year 1230, usually based near red-light areas. There was a Gropecuntelane in London and in Oxford (where it was later renamed Magpie Lane), a Grapcunt Lane in York (which became Grape Lane), a Cunte Street in Bristol (later renamed Host Street), and a *Rue Grattecon* (scratchcunt street) in Paris. London's Gropecuntelane was later shortened to Grope Lane, then Grub Street in the eighteenth century, then Milton Street in 1830. All this street renaming is probably just as well in purely commercial terms: it wouldn't look too good on a business card to have your office based in Gropecunt Lane.

The language used by the characters in Geoffrey Chaucer's *Canterbury Tales* was among the fruitiest[6] in early English literature, but elsewhere bad language was not necessarily bad. 'Svmmer is icumen in' was written in approximately 1240. It was a Middle English chart-topper, and it runs as follows:

Svmer is icumen in	Summer is a-coming in
Lhude sing cuccu!	Loudly sing cuckoo
Groweth sed and bloweth med	Groweth seed and bloweth mead
And springth the wude nu.	And springs the wood anew
Sing cuccu!	Sing cuckoo!
Awe bleteth after lomb,	Ewe bleateth after lamb,
lhouth after calue cu,	Calf loweth after cow,
Bulluc sterteth, bucke uerteth.	Bullock starteth, buck farteth,
Murie sing cuccu!	Merry sing cuckoo!

----

6 Fruity, 1. mid-seventeenth-century adjective, Of or pertaining to or resembling fruit. 2. 1844. Of wine: having the taste of the grape. 3. *colloq.* Full of rich or strong quality; highly interesting, attractive, or suggestive.

Bullocks start and bucks fart, and nobody seems to care. It wasn't obscene, of course: barely even bawdy. It was merely a frank expression of rustic life, close to the earth, the animals, the elements. If the Victorians objected to the odd word, that was in part because of the genteel horror of bodily parts – or farts – which was a reaction to the loucheness of the eighteenth century. Queen Victoria's prudery was not intrinsically religious, but muscular Christianity had never been as strong as in the nineteenth century. And of course, there are no rude words in the Bible, are there?

Biblical bad language

The Bible, which has had so much effect on our turns of speech (see Chapter 4), also contains strong words and (as TV announcements occasionally warn us) scenes of a sexual nature. Take the cities of Sodom and Gomorrah: their destruction in approximately 2000 BC, graphically delineated in Genesis 18–19, was linked to their reputation for 'immorality'. 'Sodomy' has been a byword for homosexual sex since records began – 'vile sunne of sodomye' (according to Robert of Gloucester's *Metrical Chronicle* (1297), cited in the *OED*). Gomorrah, on the other hand, seems to have got off lightly. (Gonorrhoea? No, different story: that means 'flow of seed' in Greek.) A similar flow of seed connected the brothers Er and Onan (Genesis 38:9). Er was the first-born son of Judah, and when he died childless, Judah ordered Er's brother Onan to marry the widow Tamar. Onan, though, seems not to have fancied marriage to Tamar, so he 'spilled [his seed] on the ground'. He tossed himself off, in other words. This, we are told, 'displeased the Lord: wherefore he slew him also'. It was a German writer who first coined the term 'onanism' in 1649. Since then, the term, sometimes translated as 'self-pollution', has spread around the world, and Onan's name, if not his seed, lived on long after him.

Within the books of the Bible there is prostitution (Ezekiel 23:8, Hosea 1:2), rape (Genesis 39:7–23, 2 Samuel 13:1–14), incest (Genesis 19:30–38), testicle-squeezing (Genesis 24:2–9, 47:29), as well as flashing (by David, 2 Samuel 6:14 and 16:20–23) and mass foreskin-slashing (David again, Samuel 18:27). In the second book of Kings (18:27) and Isaiah (36:12) the Assyrian Rab-Shakeh asks if his men are expected to 'eat their own dung and drink their own piss'. A phrase uttered in wrath and that (politely) translates as 'every man-child' but actually means 'he that pisses', is sprayed across six places in the first book of Samuel (25:22, 25:34), the first book of Kings (14:10, 16:10–11, 21:21) and 2 Kings (9:8).

After the Reformation, literary censorship was undertaken by the Privy Council,[7] and theatrical censorship by the Master of the King's Revels. Writers such as William Shakespeare had to find subtle ways of inserting earthy words. An example of how he did this appears in *Measure for Measure*, when he used 'counsellors' as a pun on 'cunt-sellers': 'Good counsellors lack no clients' (I.ii). In *Twelfth Night* Malvolio spells it out: 'By my life, this is my lady's hand! These be her very C's, her U's, and her T's' (II.v). If the 'and' were pronounced distinctly enough as 'en' (N), the audience would have been left in no doubt as to the reference. The most famous Shakespeare 'cunt' pun is when Hamlet asks Ophelia: 'Do you think I meant country matters?' (III.iii), emphasizing the first syllable of 'country' in case the matter is at all ambivalent. He had

----

7 Formerly the inner cabal of the sovereign consisting of princes, archbishops and specially chosen ministers, past and present.

tried this before, in *The Comedy of Errors* (1590): 'she is spherical, like a globe; I could find out countries in her' (III.ii), and in *Henry IV Part Two* (1597): 'The rest of thy low-countries have made a shift to eat up thy Holland' (II.ii). The punning reference is to Holland, one of the Low Countries, and also to the position of the vagina, low down the body.

Despite the word's ubiquity in the past, 'cunt' is still the ultimate taboo utterance. When a Tony Harrison poem containing it was broadcast on Channel 4 in 1985, the *Daily Mail* splashed its front page with the banner headline 'FOUR-LETTER TV POEM FURY'. And two years later, amid the sometimes unendurable tension of one of the worst-tempered Test series in cricket history, Pakistani umpire Shakoor Rana went several steps further than lifting one finger in the air when he called Mike Gatting a 'fucking, cheating cunt'. The *Independent* was the only newspaper that printed his tirade uncensored.

'People who swear,' say disapproving parents, 'are just displaying their lack of vocabulary.' In fact, there is an absolute wealth of swearing vocabulary to choose from, some of it 'disguised' to conceal its roots. Few maiden aunts would be thrown into a flutter at the sound of the word **berk**, for example, surely an innocuous word for a 'fool'. In fact, it came into the language during the 1930s (first attestation 1936), and is cockney rhyming slang: 'Berkshire (or Berkeley) hunt' – 'cunt'.

Thomas Bowdler and the Victorians

The Obscene Publications Act became law in 1857, in a bid to keep us all safe from unprotected (i.e. uncensored) literature. Someone who would have been among its most enthusiastic proponents, had he not died before it was passed, was the

Edinburgh doctor Thomas Bowdler (1754–1825). Bowdler made it clear that he loved Shakespeare, but nevertheless believed that nothing 'can afford an excuse for profaneness or obscenity; and if these could be obliterated, the transcendant [sic] genius of the poet would undoubtedly shine with more unclouded lustre'. He proved so zealous at expurgating texts that 'to bowdlerize' means just that. His ten-volume *Family Shakespeare*, 'in which nothing is added to the original text; but those words and expressions are omitted which cannot with propriety be read aloud in a family', went on sale in December 1818. Every reference to 'God' is replaced by 'Heaven'. Bowdler's main tool, however, was a pair of scissors – not the most agile editing device – so many speeches were simply hacked and ended up resembling a hedge that has been ruined by an incompetent gardener.

Having struggled with many of Shakespeare's passages, as it were, he gave up altogether on *Othello*, advising that as it was 'unfortunately little suited to family reading', it should be transferred 'from the parlour to the cabinet'. Bowdler's work was successful during his own lifetime, and went through five editions by the 1860s. He even attempted to work a similar magic with Edward Gibbon's *The History of the Decline and Fall of the Roman Empire* (1776–88). Luckily, he never got his hands on John Cleland's *Fanny Hill*, or *Memoirs of a Woman of Pleasure*, which came out, to titillate literate adults, between 1748 and 1749.

As society grew ever more genteel during the nineteenth century, more and more effort went into ensuring social delicacy. This purification process lasted for some time, as indicated by a 1959 edition of Chambers's *Twentieth Century English Dictionary*. Its editor, William Geddie, MA, B.Sc., described his aim as 'to include all words in general use in literary and conversational English', but he acknowledged that he had cut out 'some dead slang'. The chances are, therefore, that Dr Geddie did not use the words 'fuck', 'cunt' or 'wank' in his conversational English, since they certainly appear nowhere in his dictionary. Nor do we find any mention of the lesser horrors **shit**, **crap** or **bollock**. One of the chinks in his lexicon is the noun **twat**, which he had to admit came from a line of verse by Robert Browning in which it referred to nuns' head-gear. (The great poet seems to have misunderstood the 1660 poem *Vanity of the Vanities* by Sir Henry Vane the Younger: 'They talked of his having a Cardinall's hat, They'd send him as soon an Old Nun's Twat.') The coy entry in Chambers for 'twat' reads 'pudendum muliebre: (*Browning*, blunderingly) part of a nun's dress'. The Latin words mean 'female organ'. Browning's poem, *Pippa Passes* (1848): 'Then owls and bats / Cowls and twats / Monks and nuns in a cloister's moods / Adjourn to the oak-stump pantry.'

Translators and editors went to great lengths to avoid causing offence to readers, some of whom might be ladies, and who would be genuinely scandalized by ripe language or indelicate scenes. Half of the nineteenth-century editions of Jonathan Swift's *Gulliver's Travels* (1726) were bowdlerized, writes Noel Perrin in his book on Thomas Bowdler (see Further Reading, page 293). Swift writes of the younger members of the tiny Lilliputian army looking up, as they marched through his legs, to catch a glimpse of his genitals – but not in the Victorian classroom editions. When the tables are turned and Gulliver is a homunculus amid the giants of Brobdingnag, Swift recounts visiting the boudoir of a lady, one of whose breasts 'stood prominent six Foot, and could not be less than sixteen in Circumference. The Nipple was about half the Bigness of my Head, and the Hew both of that and the Dug so varified with Spots, Pimples, and Freckles, that nothing could appear more nauseous.' Again, the description rarely remained to trouble Queen Victoria's schoolchildren.

These days, the Lord Chamberlain's Office (LCO) attends to such matters as state visits, investitures, garden parties, royal weddings and funerals. But the LCO used to be the official censor for all theatres in Britain. So long as theatre companies produced licensed plays, no problem arose. But increasingly during the 1960s, independently minded writers and directors were looking to put on more controversial work. It is not uncommon when looking at manuscripts of plays presented during that period to see the Lord Chamberlain's blue pencil striking out lines that were considered unsuitable. The Royal Court Theatre in London often fell foul of the LCO, one notable occasion being when it wanted to stage *Saved*, Edward Bond's 1965 play about urban violence, in which a baby is stoned in a pram. The theatre frequently resorted to declaring itself a private club so that it could perform works without fear of prosecution.

Curiously, it wasn't just groundbreaking new theatre to which the Lord Chamberlain objected. Classical works, such as

---

What a load of bollocks

Has any other part of the body acquired so many alternative names? Here are just a few:

Apricots; Balls; Bollocks; Cobblers (Cobbler's Awls); Cods; Cojones; Conkers; Family jewels; Goolies (see Chapter 7, page 181); Henry Halls; Knackers; Love-apples; Lunchbox; Maracas (knackers); Meat and two veg; Nadgers; Nads; Niagaras (Niagara Falls); Orchestras (Orchestra Stalls); Nuts; Packet; Plums; Privates; Pills; Rocks; Stones; Taters; Town Halls; Unmentionables.

Lysistrata by Aristophanes, *Mrs Warren's Profession* by George Bernard Shaw, and *Hedda Gabler* by Henrik Ibsen all fell foul of the LCO, until the institution was abolished under the Theatres Act of 1968. The fact that the Lord Chamberlain's Office was once considered necessary, however, is further evidence of the power of language.

Rude words and euphemisms

As well as hard-core, X-rated[8] words, there has never been a shortage of boorish[9] words with which to abuse others or oneself. The Middle English word 'pillicock' meant 'penis' around 1300–25. By 1598 it meant 'young boy'. The *OED* cites a sixteenth-century use of **pillock** in the sense of 'the penis', spelt 'pillok'. The 'pillock' spelling dates from the 1970. The child's term **willie** also appeared in the early twentieth century, but that was long preceded by **dick**, the shortened version of Richard, which began to appear in the mid-sixteenth century, and had hardened into a familiar term for the male private parts by the late eighteenth century.

The *OED* lists eight separate nouns all called **cock**, as well as one, almost certainly a mistake, in Dr Johnson's *Dictionary*, meaning 'the notch of an arrow'. But there is really only one which concerns us: the first. Its twenty-three definitions begin with King Alfred referring to the domestic fowl, around AD 897.

----

8 A government committee reported in 1950: 'We recommend that a new category of films be established (which might be called "X") from which children under 16 should be entirely excluded.'

9 Boor, *c.*1430: 'Husband, peasant, countryman, a clown.' 1598: 'A peasant, a rustic, with lack of refinement implied; a country clown … Any rude, ill-bred fellow.'

Definition number twenty, in language redolent of the *OED*'s first edition, reads 'Penis', followed by: 'The current name among the people, but, *pudoris causa* [i.e. to spare our blushes] not admissible in polite speech or literature; in scientific language the Latin is used.' The first citation is from A*mends for Ladies* by Nathaniel Field (1597–1619): 'Oh man what art thou? When thy cock is up?' The most recent citation is from *Landfall* (1969) by A.S. Byatt: 'She had her hand on his cock.' 'There's no need to be crude.' **Cocksucker** is attested from 1891. The same work, a scrap book by one Edward Farmer, defines 'cock-teaser' or 'cockchafer' as 'a girl in the habit of permitting all familiarities but the last'.

And then there's **prick**, which has only one entry for the noun. Around AD 1000 it meant 'an impression in a surface or body made by pricking or piercing; a puncture.' The fifth sub-heading, and by far the fullest, concerns 'Anything that pricks or pierces; an instrument or organ having a sharp point.' (We're getting closer.) There are five further definitions within this but the seventeenth definition, in the 1989 second edition of the *OED*, is more up-front: 'The penis. *coarse slang*,' it says simply. The first citation is from 1592: 'The pissing Boye lift up his pricke.' The late Ed McBain (1926–2005) gets the last citation, from his 1976 novel *Guns*: 'Jocko had … a very small pecker … Blood on the bulging pectorals, tiny contradictory prick.' The word 'prick' as 'vulgar term of abuse for a man' is wholly twentieth-century. Eric Partridge noted 'prick-teaser', akin to 'cock-teaser', in the supplement to his *Dictionary of Slang* (1961).

It is a curious fact that the rudest letter in the alphabet, measured in sheer numbers, may well be B. The word **bastard** entered the language via Old French from the medieval Latin *bastardus*, though, appropriately perhaps, we are not quite sure of that word's parentage. The Old French *fils de bast* meant 'packsaddler's son', and was used, incredibly, to describe 'the offspring of an amorous itinerant mule driver', who stopped for long enough to use a packsaddle for a pillow but was gone again by sunrise. Extraordinary if true.

There is also **bloody**, of course, which these days hardly raises an eyebrow, but was once considered ruder than 'fuck'. It has been used to add emphasis since the mid-seventeenth century, and may have some sort of aristocratic connection, given the 'bloods' (a word for aristocratic rowdies) and their inability to hold their drink without serious consequences for lawns, windows, chambermaids and so on. **Bloody drunk** was another way of saying 'as drunk as a lord'. 'Bloody' was held in high esteem as a swear-word, and frequently went unspelt when quoted until quite recently. Perhaps people believed that the blood in question was that of Christ; some thought the word was a truncated version of 'by Our Lady'.

A different type of b-word, **bugger**, was used originally to refer to heretics, especially Bulgarians formerly belonging to the Orthodox Church. Around the tenth century, many left the Church, attracted to the creed of Bogomilism. Possibly named after a Bulgarian priest called Bogomil, this sect was popular with the hard-up peasants. Because it distrusted man-made institutions, it was regarded as heretical (which it certainly was) and morally dubious (which was harder to prove.) The movement moved East, reaching France, from where the Old French word for Bulgarian, *bougre* came to mean a 'heretic'. By the sixteenth century, the term had come to be equated with sodomy, on the grounds that forbidden sex was synonymous with heresy, and from the early 18th century onwards the word 'bugger' became a term of abuse directed at homosexuals. Casually, or 'In low language', says the

OED, 'bugger' has since 1719 also been a term of affection: 'silly bugger', 'clever bugger', etc. **Bugger all**, first cited in 1937, means 'nothing'. The twentieth century transferred the meaning of the verb from sex to, simply, 'to mess up or spoil', or 'to be tired out'.

Those wanting to refer to sex in a vernacular way, but who dislike the words offered so far, have several less offensive terms at their disposal. **Bonk** is what people say when they can't bring themselves to say 'fuck'. A listlessly upper-class word, first attested in 1975, it probably comes from the sound made when two SUV vehicles have a minor collision in a Fulham side-street. 'Oh, sorry, did I bonk you?' says one driver, who then realizes, as the colour drains from his cheeks, that the comment could have been misinterpreted.

Earthier by far is the eighteenth-century use of the verb **to shag**. Even if you weren't aware of its origins, this reeks of the farmyard: you can really imagine two shaggy-haired dogs getting down and having a good rut. Perhaps, for that reason, it wasn't the most romantic description ever coined for the act of union, though it may be why we forgive Mike Myers for naming his 'love interest' Heather Graham 'Felicity Shagwell' in the second Austin Powers film, *The Spy Who Shagged Me* (1999). 'Shag' is a word that demands not to be taken too seriously. In fact, it was hijacked for sexual purposes in the late eighteenth century: prior to that, the *OED* compared it to the Scots and Late Middle English 'shog', meaning 'to shake or roll from side to side'. **Screw** is another word that, since the early eighteenth century, has meant 'to have sex'. It also shares with 'fuck' the sub-meaning of implied clumsiness, as in 'I really fucked/screwed that up.' However, 'screw' turns in two directions at once, as it can also be used in approbatory expressions, such as 'He's got his head screwed on right, that boy.'

One other erotic 'b' is the everyday word for 'fellatio': the **blow-job**. Back in the 1970s, about the only place you could find language like that was in the controversial magazine *Oz*, which had started in Australia in 1963. 'Blow-job' is first noted in 1961 as the Anglo-Saxon term for 'fellatio' (from the Latin *fellāre*, 'to suck'). So where does blowing come into it, and why isn't it called a 'suck-job'? Does 'suck-job' just sound wrong? The explanation is unclear, especially since the *OED* has not, so far, stepped into this particular fray. But given that slang terms for sexual activities can be highly figurative (compare the verb 'to eat' as US slang for 'to practice fellatio or cunnilingus…', cited first in 1927), if we look at some of the other meanings of the verb 'to blow', some ideas emerge. One is that the action of blowing is like the water and air ejected through a whale's blow-hole, to which ejaculation is compared. The action of blowing bellows or the coals of a fire (both 1596) is figurative for stirring up passion or anger, which could be of a sexual nature. When something 'blows up' into an argument, it's clear that feelings are running high. When a soldier turns his 'blow-lamp' on to something, the object becomes extremely hot. Jazz musicians blow their horn, and the action of putting an instrument in the mouth could provoke comparisons. According to *Cassell's Dictionary of Slang*, 'blow-job' arrived from 'basket-job', which was a gay term in the 1940s, 'basket' being a slang word for the male genitals.

The journey of **come** towards sexual fulfilment has been eventful. The *OED* doesn't get round to it until the seventeenth definition, dating it as mid-seventeenth-century, by which time we have already met usages such as 'come to pass', 'come about' and 'come into being'. Be warned: the rules are different in other languages. If you're at the end of a meeting in Spain and you try to say, in Spanish, '*tengo que correr*', hoping it means 'I've got to run', you could be announcing that you're about to have an orgasm, or that you're, in hippy-speak, 'turned on', which would be unfortunate, whether you are or not.

Such simple words denote such energetic activities. 'Get', for example, had to wait until the twentieth century before to **get off with** meant 'to have sex with'. In *Iolanthe*, Gilbert and Sullivan wrote: 'I heard the minx remark / She'd meet him after dark / inside St James's Park / And **give him one**!' What was it that she was going to give him? We in the twenty-first century know, but did they? The draft material from the revision process for *OED3*, published June 2004, says that '...the mention of St James's Park (which at the time had a reputation for being frequented by prostitutes) may glancingly suggest the later sexual sense.' And as for the adjective 'hard', given its meaning, what chance did it stand, whether transmuted into a **hard-on** or **hard porn**? Perhaps we should leave it there and move on.

Hot to frot

To the comedian Chris Morris we owe: 'I love to go frotting, with Louise Botting.' The blameless Ms Botting had the misfortune to present Radio 4's eminently worthy *Moneybox* programme at around the same time as the roguish Morris was on the up. 'Frotting' refers to the practice of rubbing oneself, clothed, against another person, also clothed, to achieve sexual arousal. (And cursed be he or she who tries to visualize Ms Botting in any other state.) Originating in the verb 'to frot', meaning 'to rub, polish, stroke', it was only a matter of time – albeit several centuries – before 'frottage' was stripped of its innocence and recast, fully clad.

The language of hate

Racist words can still send a shiver down the spine. At the beginning of the nineteenth century in America, there was a little-used word that meant 'to divide logs into sections by burning them'. The word in question was **nigger**, whereas the word 'coloured' was not considered to be offensive to black people until the late twentieth century. By the middle of the nineteenth century, 'niggerdom' was in wide circulation (though it is marked by the *OED* as 'offensive'), and the word 'niggerize' could be used to mean 'to oppress or treat with contempt in a manner reminiscent of the oppression of black people'. A little later – either as a compliment or an insult – it meant 'to subject to the influence of black people; to assimilate to black culture'. When the respected black academic Cornel West said that the USA had been 'niggerized' after the attacks of 9/11, he was comparing its new national trauma with African-Americans' long history of coping with terror and death. In 1894 'niggering' seemed to have become an alternative for the term 'busking' (see Chapter 7, page 183), as performed by black and white minstrels. In the second half of the nineteenth century we find examples of the word meaning 'to behave or live supposedly in the manner of a black slave; to work very hard, do menial work'. And all this from a process which goes back, via the 1568 French word *neger*, to the humble Latin adjective *niger* (black).

Between 1574 and 1833 the word 'niger' (or 'nigre' or 'nigor'[10]) is used frequently to refer to black people, 'possibly with no specifically hostile overtones', says the *OED* cagily. In 1932 the Harlem intelligentsia were known as the 'niggerati',[11] and 'nigger'

----

10 The range of spellings recorded by early explorers and other curious observers is awesome. A quick scan finds 'Neigers' (1568), 'neegers' (1587), 'Neagers' (1599), 'Negars' (1624), 'neger' (1686), 'Niegors' (1776), 'neegger' (1827), 'negre' (1866), 'naygars' (1913) and 'neegur' (1961).
11 The coinage of the term is usually attributed to Zora Neale Hurston, a member of the group.

went through many other derogatory changes of clothing, so it is with something approaching relief that, after a period in the 1980s when it was customarily referred to (from 1985) as the 'n-word', we find the rap and hip-hop community reinstating 'nigger' on its own terms as a political gesture. They appropriated the spelling too, so that it comes out as 'nigga' or 'nigguh', as in bands such as Niggaz with Attitude and the rap song 'Mnniiggaah'. In this, it resembles the soul/rap community's adoption of the word – and the spelling of – 'gangsta', 'sista', 'brutha' or 'mutha'. As the *OED* notes: 'The resurgence of the form *nigga* (plural often *niggaz*) and other forms without final *-r* in late 20th-century use (especially in representations of urban African-American speech) is probably due to its deliberate adoption by some speakers as a distinct word, associated with neutral or positive senses.'

Another racial group that has been the target of a large amount of denigratory[12] language is the Jews. European Jews have been speaking Yiddish since at least the thirteenth century – two-thirds of its vocabulary is German – as well as referring to themselves as 'Yidden' in the plural, or a singular **Yid**. But among those hostile to the Jews – and there have been one or two over the years – variations on the word 'Yid' became a term of abuse in whichever European country they congregated. In Britain, large numbers of Jews entered the country in the late nineteenth century, and it wasn't long before 'Yid' became widely used, though not always with abusive intent. But, in a triumphant turnaround, modern, secular Jews have reappropriated the word, most notably in the case of the fans of Tottenham Hotspur Football Club, who have been referring to

---

12 Denigrate: 'To blacken (especially a reputation)' (*CED*). The word is derived, again, from the Latin *niger*.

themselves proudly as the 'Yid Army' since the 1970s. It's now almost synonymous with 'Spurs fans' – certainly among rival supporters – even though Jews are not demographically dominant on the terraces.

Pride and prejudice

When Oscar Wilde's *The Importance of Being Earnest* opened in London on Valentine's Day, 1895, he was a national treasure. And yet within 100 days, Wilde, aged forty, was ruined and facing a court case. The reason was that for the previous two years Wilde had been having an affair with Lord Alfred 'Bosie' Douglas. When Bosie's father, the Marquess of Queensbury (originator of the rules of boxing), found out, he was apoplectic, and left a calling card at the Cadogan Club with the words: 'To Oscar Wilde, posing as a Somdomite' [*sic*]. Although he misspelt it, perhaps owing to his heightened emotions that day, we know what he meant.

Sodom, as discussed earlier (see page 226), was a man's town that loved to party. But homosexuals have had almost every term of abuse thrown at them over the years. The word **poof**[13] was just starting to be used in Oscar Wilde's time, and **faggot** came into widespread use in the USA after the First World War. In 1966 the *New Statesman* wrote that 'The American word "faggot" is making advances here over our own more humane "**queer**".'

Several others are used in Frederic Raphael's 1960 novel *The Limits of Love*: 'Great thing about **gay** people...' 'Gay?'Tessa said. 'Bent, queer, you know. Homosexual.' The word 'gay' was obviously unfamiliar at the time, but had been prison slang for

----
13 Probably a corruption of 'puff': 'An effeminate man; a male homosexual.'

'homosexual' since the 1930s. Christopher Isherwood (1904–86) used 'queer' in his classic 1939 novel *Goodbye to Berlin*:'Men dressed as women? ... Do you mean they're queer?'

The first person to try to return control to the hands of the host community may have been the radical writer Paul Goodman with his 1969 essay 'The Politics of Being Queer'. Lesbians, meanwhile, were reassessing terms such as **dyke**, and these days that word can be a term of abuse or a simple declaration of identity, depending on the motivation of the speaker. After the shock of Aids, a greater sense of solidarity entered the gay community, and cheaply derisory terms, such as **carpet-muncher** and **pillow-chewer**, began to lose their capacity to hurt.

'Queer' has come into its own as Channel 4 proved with its screening of *Queer as Folk* (2002) and the US series *Queer Eye for the Straight Guy* (2004). At the time of writing the Amazon website has fifty-four books with 'queer' and 'politics' in the title. Not so **bent**.[14] **Coming out** used to describe the ritual of a young woman being launched into society and thus on to the marriage market.'Miss Price had not been brought up to the trade of coming out,' wrote Jane Austen in *Mansfield Park* (1814). Towards the end of the 1960s,'coming out' began to mean 'stating publicly' that one was homosexual.

In 1990 the *Los Angeles Times* and the *Guardian* newspapers were reporting that some gay activists in both the USA and the UK had instigated a campaign of outing prominent homosexuals who might not want their sexual preferences to be made public. But a year later,'outing' had spread to, for example, the Bald Urban Liberation Brigade of New York City, whose shock tactics

----

14 First cited in the *OED* in *c.*1374, by Geoffrey Chaucer. With homosexual meaning in 1959.

(posting flyers) threatened to expose celebrities with toupées that they refused to acknowledge. Marketing and advertising companies are keen to catch some of the pink pound, a term first used in connection with the economic clout of the gay community in 1984.

Sticks and stones...

The words in this chapter represent language at its sharpest. Even typing some of them feels strange. Many have been created deliberately to cause maximum offence. And yet, as the last section shows, words, unlike missiles, can be sent back to their place of origin with their meaning completely rewritten. This represents the final act of revenge by the supposedly injured party, and it happens when the word is embraced and defused by the whole community. The world of abuse is one of the most dynamic and changeable in linguistics: new formations are coming and going with amazing speed because they depend on novelty to achieve their effect. Once we have got used to them, they lose their sting.

We haven't dealt at length with the cadre of words that has been turned on society's handicapped people, but one example is **spaz**, a shortened form of 'spastic', which was hurled at unfortunate victims, able-bodied or not. The word has, of course, been reappropriated by disabled people. A few years ago, society decided that the word 'spastic' was too hurtful, though, and we were encouraged to use alternatives, such as 'differently skilled' and 'mentally or physically challenged'. At the same time, the British Spastics Society lent its authority to the campaign by changing its name to Scope. It was a brave effort, but it didn't take some playground wag long to come up with a new term of abuse: **scope**.

Some of our favourite terms of abuse have a more matey lyricism about them that reduces the force of their invective. Take the word **wazzock**. No one is going to take someone to court for calling them a 'wazzock': it's not a high-octane term of abuse. It just means someone who is a little bit silly or annoying, or both. Its northern bluntness is appealing, and it achieves its effect through its combination of familiar sounds. The 'wazz' contrasts ironically with the swiftness of 'whizz', and the ending '–ock' reminds us of other words like **pillock**. You might think they were equally ancient terms of abuse, but whereas 'pillock', as we have seen, is first attested from 1535, 'wazzock' is first attributed to the comedian Mike Harding ('you cloth-eared wazzock') in his 1984 book *When the Martians Land in Huddersfield*.

Subsequently, the word has spawned the verb **to wazz**, rhyming with 'has', i.e. 'to piss'. The *OED* writes 'Origin unknown' against 'wazzock', but this author's private theory is that if you scrunched up the word **wiseacre** – first noted in 1595, meaning, among other things, 'a foolish person with an air or affectation of wisdom' – and then straightened it out again, it might make a sound very like 'wazzock'.

'Wazzock' is one of those words whose sound defines - or limits - itself. It's a silly-sounding word (you wouldn't want your plane flown by a wazzock, even if you didn't know exactly what it was). F-words and C-words sound shocking: that's their job. Daft words *sound* silly. Occasionally one gets away, such as **wrangler**, which might not immediately suggest its eighteenth-century meaning of an undergraduate with a first-class honours degree in Mathematics from Cambridge University, but that's one of the exceptions. Most words do a pretty good job of meaning exactly what they sound like. The next chapter tests that statement, to an even more extreme degree.

Chapter Ten

To Er ... is Human

Some dogs look like their owners. Some words sound like their meanings. When you make a twig **snap**, or hear leaves **rustling**, the verbs that describe those activities have an uncanny knack of copying the activity that is taking place. Snaps have been around for just over 500 years: rustles for a hundred years longer. Both fall into a vaguely slapstick category of English language words. Not content with meaning whatever they mean, they have to go and act the word out for you with their very sound. There is, mercifully, one word that embraces all this strenuous activity rather more efficiently than I have been able to express so far, and it would be the literal truth to say that the Greeks have a word for it: in fact they have two words. The noun *onoma* means 'name', and the verb *poiein* means 'to do'. Put them together (in ancient Latin) and filter them through a little mediaeval French and you come up, in around 1553, with the word **onomatopoeia**. It's a word that gets out there and explains itself. We shall be exploring many such words in this chapter.

Sounds like

Onomatopoeic words are the most touchy-feely class of words in the language. They get out on the campaign trail and work for their usage, which is why so many of them are firm favourites among young and old. But there are many different elements of a word that make us like it. In some cases our response to a word may be purely emotional (mama), perhaps cultural (Picasso), or even professional (client contact). In other cases, it's just the sound that appeals to us, and onomatopoeic words are particularly pleasing in this respect. These are words such as **squelch** and **thud**, which, according to the *CCD*, are 'imitative of the sound of the noise or action designated'. Perhaps onomatopoeic words are the ones they give to L-plate lexicographers, since their etymology takes them on a stroll through the alphabet, from **boohoo** (*c*.1525) to **pop** (*c*.1386) and **whizz** (pre-1547). It's also nice to see so childish a word as 'boohoo' (spelt 'bo ho, bo ho!') admitted to the language via the works of an early poet laureate, John Skelton (*c*.1460–1529).

Cat lovers might be interested to know that **miaow** has twenty-one alternative spellings, and that the sound cats make is roughly the same everywhere in the world. If only other animals were so consistent. Pigs go **oink** in Britain, but *groin groin* in France, *knor* in the Netherlands, *xrju-xrju* in Russia, *chrum chrum kwik* in Poland, *röf-röf* in Hungary and *būbū* in Japan.

Did onomatopoeia help us to speak? This is the 'ding-dong' theory favoured by some linguistics experts, which claims that we make sounds that mimic those of the natural world around us. We hear the rain and say **pitter-patter**; we hear birds and say **tweet-tweet**; we hear a snake and say **hiss**. It must apply the other way round too. A dog's world is also onomatopoeic, or – as it's shorter – echoic. Dog wants to go for a walk: **woof woof**. Master not interested: **shhhh**. Master gives in: **sighs**, gets up, opens door (**creak**), closes door (**slam**), feet and paws **crunch** on the gravel, dog does a pee (**tinkle-tinkle**). A car **zooms** towards them. Dog sees cat (**yelp/yowl**), gives chase and – **beep** – **screech** – very nearly ends up as a nasty **squidge** in the road.

It sounds like something out of a children's comic, and if you look at one, it's patently true that the writers can't get enough of strange sounds. The *Dandy*, *Beano* and many other well-known comics have produced some of the finest interjections ever written. The great 'Desperate Dan', for example, experiences or gives voice to a broad range of exclamations, including **niff**, **sploosh**, **whoosh** and **yarf**. Whenever he produces or provokes these sounds, however interchangeable they might seem, they perfectly complement the illustration that they accompany. In reality, few will end up in a dictionary. They're one-offs that light up the page for a moment before sinking and dying. Perhaps the writers have a library of exclamatory sounds that they can turn to, but making them up is probably half the fun of the job. In fact, it's also fun to imagine how they came up with such gems as **krung**, **foosh**, **phft** and **mumph**.

We don't know how many of these letter-sounds are coined each year, but there are many, and some have actually made it into dictionaries. The provenance of 'niff', for example, meaning 'to emit an unpleasant odour'), is discussed at some length in the *OED*. Is it formed by removing the first letter of **sniff**? But 'sniff' doesn't have the same meaning as 'niff'. Perhaps, then, it's from **whiff**? We can't be sure, though the *OED* adds: 'It is also remarkable that *niff*, as a verb, is first recorded from a school in Derby, but as a noun, is attributed by Joseph Wright's *English Dialect Dictionary* to Sussex. This perhaps points to wider, undocumented distribution in regional English.' The source in which the word was found is John S. Farmer's *Public-School Word Book* (1900), which lists it as '*Niff*, verb (Derby), to smell'.

The British public schools[1] have contributed their own very special stock of favourite words to the English language. The following series of exclamations appeared in the *Magnet* comic for boys in November 1909:'Oh!' roared Bunter, as Bulstrode's heavy boot biffed on him. 'Ow! Yah! Yarooh!' The *OED* decided that the word **yarooh** was 'A humorous stylized representation of a cry of pain', and they correctly identified it as being pretty much the unique property of the 'Fat Owl of the Remove', aka Billy Bunter. For less expensively educated children, a simple **ouch**, dating from no earlier than 1838, would have to do.

Linguistics experts are still trying to understand why some groups of letters affect us in different ways. Slip, slide, slither, slouch, slant, slash and others sound as if they are being dragged downhill by their own weight. Snag, snarl, sneak, sneer, snide, sniff (that word again), snigger and snivel all sound a bit dodgy. Swagger, sway, sweep, swing and swoop sound as if they can't stop shifting from side to side. And glamour, glare, glaze, gleam, glimmer, glint, glisten, glitter, glossy and glow are all a bit shiny: the Essex words of the language.

Feels like

It's amazing what difference a letter can make. Take three vowels: A, E and O and add an H to each of them. **Eh**, 'An ejaculation of sorrow', was first noted in 1567, but it is ante-dated by **Oh** (pre-1525), which could indicate, among other things, 'surprise, frustration, discomfort, longing, disappointment, sorrow, relief,

---

1 More often called 'independent schools' these days, most of them date back to the eighteenth and particularly the nineteenth centuries. They were called 'public' to distinguish them from 'private' education, which was done either with home tutors or through the church.

hesitation'. The *OED* even goes to the trouble of speculating that the word Ah[2] may be derived from the French A or A*b*.

If we wrote down an accurate typescript of our daily speech, 'eh', 'oh' and 'ah' would be among our most common expressions. They are the true favourites of our working minds. But how would you define **mm** in a context such as, 'Mm! What's that smell?' 'Expressing satisfaction, approval, or assent' opines the *OED*. And how about 'You really want this job, mm?' The *OED* would classify that as 'expressing hesitation, reflection, or inarticulate interrogation'.

Nonsense words

The sounds of the world are reliable: they're our stabilizers. Perhaps they remind us of a time when, as babies, we knew what things looked like and what sound they made, but not their names: clocks still go tick, even with a quartz crystal inside. Spike Milligan's nonsense poem 'On the Ning Nang Nong' was funny and unsettling because straight from the first line – 'In the Ning Nang Nong where the cows go **bong**' – we knew that we were in a strange world where things didn't make the sounds we expected them to make. No doubt that was partly due to Milligan's harrowing experiences during the Second World War, when he and his fellow soldiers never knew what they were going to hear next. When peace came, he incorporated some of those wartime sounds – **wheeeh**, **boom**, **owwww** and others –

---

2 'An exclamation expressing, according to the intonation, various emotions, as (1) Sorrow, lamentation, regret, passing into the regretful expression of a vain wish (2) Surprise, wonder, admiration (3) Entreaty, appeal, remonstrance… (4) Dislike, aversion… (5) Opposition, objection… (6) Realization, discovery, inspiration.'

into *The Goon Show* (1951–1960), a radio programme that was a sort of adult aural comic.

Some silly noises have been put to use in the commercial world, with highly successful results. Think of Rice Krispies going **snap**, **crackle** and **pop** and Alka-Seltzer going **plink plink fizzzz**. In these contexts the words are amusing, but they must be chosen with care. 'Snap' is funny in a breakfast cereal: not so funny with a broken wrist.

Many English Victorian eccentrics had a language of their own too, though none so well developed as that of the Oxford mathematician Charles Lutwidge Dodgson, better known as Lewis Carroll. In fact, the nearest to an everyday word we have inherited from his made-up lexicon is the verb **to chortle**, which is probably a blend of 'chuckle' and 'snort', from the poem 'Jabberwocky'.[3] He did the same with 'slithy' (lithe and slimy) and 'mimsy' (flimsy and miserable), acknowledging in the text that these were 'portmanteau words', i.e. two meanings packed up into one word.

The first stanza of 'Jabberwocky' is as follows:

> 'Twas brillig, and the slithy toves
> Did gyre and gimble in the wabe:
> All mimsy were the borogoves,
> And the mome raths outgrabe.

Carroll's nonsense verse is pure, inspired poetry. It also goes to the heart of the nature of lexicography. How, after all, can anyone properly translate the verses if none of the essential words has any literary precedent?

Compared to the Jabberwocky, the adventures of Bilbo

----

3 From *Through the Looking-Glass* (1871/2)

Baggins, Gandalf and company, first in *The Hobbit* (1937) and then *The Lord of the Rings* (1954–5), were very serious indeed: the fate of the world was at stake. J.R.R. Tolkien's experience in the First World War, and his in-depth knowledge of the vocabulary of Middle English, which had been put to such good use during the preparation of the first edition of the *OED* (he worked as a staff member from 1917–20), must have helped him ensure that the word-frame of his two most famous works felt so authentic. His language is a mixture of studied elaboration and pure invention. For example, when he writes that the Great Ring was 'hot when I first took it, as hot as a **glede**', he is spot on, since 'glede', also spelt 'gleed', is an archaic word for a 'live coal or ember', which had fallen from use by the nineteenth century, but was first seen in the Lindisfarne Gospels from around the year AD 950. But does the word, as used by Tolkien, have a life outside the books, or will it merely fade away, like the **kerplatz** and **yubyubyub** of Desperate Dan's victims? That is the question facing most dictionary compilers, and they resolve it simply by waiting – usually five years, maybe a bit less these days, to see what's left when all the noise has died down. A word has to bed itself into the language. Usage is what counts.

Words, like cats, go missing. They fall from grace and drop out of sight. We miss them, of course, but only the most hardened lexicographer would think of sticking a note to a tree with the message 'MISSING, in print, since 1827. Answers to the name **Humdudgeon**. Means "an imaginary illness". If found, please return.' Humdudgeon has dropped from sight and is unlikely to return, because words are lubricated by usage. Like humans, they need proper exercise to keep fit. Sometimes, too, another word comes along that seems to do the job better. Maybe this explains the more recent success of **Munchausen Syndrome**, named after Karl Friedrich Hieronymus, Baron von Münchhausen (1720–97), the original inventor of extravagant stories. His talent for fabrication is recorded as far back as 1823 in *Harper's Magazine* ('What a Munchausen tale!..') But it received official medical backing – 'a symptom in which a person feigns injury of illness in order to obtain hospital treatment' (CED) – in *The Lancet* in 1951. The next chapter will cast its net ever wider, in search of words that have dropped into, and out of, fashion.

Chapter Eleven

Changing Times, Changing Terms

*T*his chapter traces the development of some words that have come to be associated with a particular era. Using a dictionary, it's easy to see when they came within the radar of the editors for the first time, but sometimes a different story emerges. Many fall into predictable patterns: during times of war, it's inevitable that certain words crop up. But words continue to surprise us: they're older – or younger – than they appear. Why do certain words keep developing, when others are dead and buried within a matter of months?

We love it when we get a new word: it's a new toy to play with. And linguistics experts get very excited when a word can be dated precisely. Take the word **dude**, which has been cited by the *OED* from in the *North Adams* (Massachusetts) *Transcript*[1] of 24 June 1883: 'The new coined word "dude" ... has travelled over the country with a great deal of rapidity since but two months ago it grew into general use in New York.' When first introduced, it meant 'a name given in ridicule to a man affecting

----
1 **A** local newspaper.

an exaggerated fastidiousness in dress, speech and deportment'.
A bit of a **dandy**,[2] in other words, and most certainly not from
the West Coast, although he might have enjoyed staying on a
ranch for his holidays. The term 'dude ranch' (pre-1921) was
developed specially to accommodate this sort of person. Since its
coining, the word 'dude' has lost some of its fashion-
consciousness. Popularized through black culture in the 1930s, it
has become a general term of affection. Some would say that
there is no greater compliment than being described as a **cool**
'dude', an adjective given a new currency by the jazz saxophonist
Charlie Parker (1920–55) when he released the song 'Cool Blues'
in 1947. Parker was one of the key figures in **bebop**, 'a type of
jazz characterized by complex harmony and rhythms' (*Oxford
Encylopedic Dictionary*). 'The bebop people have a language of
their own,' wrote a dazzled *New Yorker* writer in 1948. 'Their
expressions of approval include "cool"!'

Buzzwords impress themselves on our minds by
encapsulating a topical interest or fashion in a memorable way,
perhaps from the sound.[3] The current media obsession with
celebrity – a very broad church, encompassing everyone from
superstars[4] to **wannabes**[5] means that the word **celeb** is

----

2 The *OED* has 'jack-a-dandy' from 1659: maybe this was a shortened
form. Cited in a song around 1780, defined 'A man greatly concerned
with smartness of dress.' (*CCD*)
3 The *OED* defines a 1616 citation of the verb 'to buzz' as 'To spread as a
rumour, with whispering or busy talk.' The word 'buzzword' was first
used in Harvard Business School in 1946.
4 Superstars were invented by the Hollywood movie industry. The
earliest *OED* citation is from 1925.
5 The first *OED*-cited wannabe is not what you might expect: it comes
from a 1981 *Newsweek* article about people who want to be (i.e.
'wannabe') surfers. This was followed by 'wannabe gang members'
(1985) and the pop-star 'Madonna-wannabes' (1986).

ubiquitous. Interestingly, though, it was first spotted in a Nebraska newspaper in 1913. Perhaps it was something to do with the burgeoning Hollywood film industry, which coined the term **It-girl**[6] a few years later ('it' being a euphemism for 'sex' or 'sexy'). But it transpired that Rudyard Kipling (1865–1936) had beaten them to it in 1904, when he wrote in *Traffics and Discoveries*: "Tisn't beauty, so to speak, nor good talk necessarily. It's just It. Some women'll stay in a man's memory if they once walk down a street.' It-girls have been with us in one form or another ever since, and like some of them, certain words don't show their age. Let's take a quick tour through the last 100 years or so to see which words may be older than we think and which ones had a relatively short use-by date (like certain other It-girls).

The Twenties

During the 1920s, many of Britain's favourite words were transatlantic imports. This was no accident, since the axis of geopolitical power was turning that way too, but cinema and music were the biggest sources of new words. The **bee's knees**, like the **sparrow's kneecap**, used to mean something so tiny as to be almost invisible, but the 1920s changed all that. The 'bee's knees', like the **cat's whiskers** (or **cat's pyjamas**) came to mean 'an excellent person or thing' (*Oxford Encyclopedic Dictionary*). To which one could add 'the vicar's knickers' or, less delicately, 'the donkey's knob', two phrases widely used in Sheffield and perhaps elsewhere. It also gave us

----

6 Clara Bow (1905–65), the American actress, sex symbol and archetypal Twenties flapper (see page 258), was the first It-girl. When she starred in the film *It* (1927), the *LA Times* and others dubbed her 'the "It" girl'.

the phrase **blind date** (1925) and to **carry a torch**, which *Vanity Fair* magazine defined that same year: 'When a fellow "carries the torch" it doesn't imply that he is "lit up" or drunk, but girl-less. His steady has quit him for another or he is lonesome for her.' Another of America's most famous writers from that period, Dorothy Parker (1893–1967), is credited with creating the phrase **scaredy-cat**[7] in 1933.

The first reference to **pop music** dates from 1921, though Bill Haley and the Comets didn't 'Rock around the Clock' until 1956. **Wizard**, in the sense of 'good', was first spotted in 1922, in *Babbitt*, the acclaimed novel by Sinclair Lewis about the moral hole in the middle of middle America, and the British writer J.B. Priestley (1894–1984) used it in 1943, when he wrote: 'The roofs are nicely camouflaged, and the stiff coloured netting ... is a wizard show'. William Brown, the wonderfully naughty boy created by Richmal Crompton,[8] exclaimed in 1954, 'Gosh, that party of Ginger's last Christmas was wizard.' It was also a favourite word of Jennings and Derbyshire in the delightful school series by the late Anthony Buckeridge (1912–2004). The opposite was 'ozard'. How different, you might think, from a much more recent expression of approval: **wicked**. A term coined on the streets of the Bronx, Harlem or South Central LA? Well, this quotation is certainly American: 'Tell 'em to play "Admiration"!' shouted Sloane ... 'Phoebe and I are going to shake a wicked calf.' That line comes, in fact, from a stalwart of preppy – as opposed to homeboy – America: F. Scott Fitzgerald in *This Side of Paradise*, and it was written in 1920.

---

7 'It's so nice to meet a man who isn't scaredy-cat about catching my beri-beri,' she wrote in *After Such Pleasures* (1933).
8 Real name Richmal Samuel Lanburn (1890–1969), a Classics teacher until he contracted polio in 1923. (*Chambers Dictionary of Quotations*)

The musical show *Nifties* of 1923 by W. Collier and S. Bernard popularized the word **nifty** – 'Smart, stylish, attractive' according to the *OED*. It is a very welcome addition to the language, but it's a shame that its origin is unknown. The 1920s were a time of experimentation, and in 1928 the *Daily Telegraph* reported that a favourite example among high-school children was '**necking** in motor-cars in dark roads with the lights turned off'. The word 'necking', which means 'kissing', was in use until at least 1999 because the *OED* illustrates the word with a quotation ('Toyah is being necked by a hunk'[9]) from, of all places, the *Sunday Sport*.

But there are many other expressions from the 1920s, the decade of the **flappers**.[10] B. Mantle in *Best Plays of 1919–20* wrote that '"Jerry" Lamar is one of a band of pretty little salamanders known to Broadway as "gold-diggers", because they "dig" for the gold of their gentlemen friends and spend it being good to their mothers and their pet dogs.' That was the first metaphorical use of **gold-digger**, a term that probably gave some people the **heebie-jeebies**, though it's not known where these come from. The first written reference to 'heebie-jeebies' is from 1923 and is also, of course, American.

The Thirties

A report in the *New York Times* on 25 February 1933 referred to **supermarkets**, which, it said, had sprung up in the previous two years and were already challenging 'both corporate chains and

---

9 There is an earlier use from 1825, but only in the sense of 'embracing, caressing'. Tongues came later.
10 Flappers were 1920s good-time girls who kicked their legs up when they danced, causing the fringe on their skirt hems to flap.

independent wholesale grocers'. In March it reported that one large supermarket in New Jersey had been taking $100,000 a week. In Britain, the *Spectator* of 25 September 1959 seemed to have got the point in a piece about supermarkets 'whose whole economy depends on people going in to buy a can of beans and coming out with a dazed expression and three pounds' worth of groceries'.

The rise of the supermarket is one of the most striking aspects of modern life on both sides of the Atlantic. In the UK, Marks and Spencer (founded 1926) has been experiencing a series of boardroom crises, though it can always take some comfort from the fact that its nickname **Marks and Sparks** earned its place in the *OED* in 1964 in the *Sunday Times*. It's an achievement that our other major food stores – from Waitrose and Sainsbury to Tesco and Asda – have been unable to match.

At the beginning of the twenty-first century we hear a lot about the growing habit of **dumbing down**,[11] but the expression has been around since 1933.[12] The word **racism** was also coined around that time.[13] On a lighter note, in 1935 American shoppers were the first to enjoy **Muzak**. Its inventor, shop-owner U.V. 'Bing' Muscio, told the *New York Times* in 1974, 'We needed a catchy name and the best-known trade name at that time was Kodak. So we just combined Kodak and music and got Muzak.'

----

11 'To simplify or reduce the intellectual content of (esp. published or broadcast material) in order to make it appealing or intelligible to a larger number of people.'

12 1933: H.T. Webster in *Forum*: 'I can cheer, too, for the Hollywood gag men in conference on a comedy which has been revealed as too subtle when they determine they must dumb it down.'

13 1936: L. Dennis *The Coming American Fascism* 'If … it be assumed that one of our values should be a type of racism which excludes certain races from citizenship, then the plan of execution should provide for the annihilation, deportation, or sterilization of the excluded races.'

The Forties

The 1940s gave us words reflecting changes that were social, technological and political. The first **mobile home** appeared in 1940, the **Wonderbra** in 1947, and the first reference to a **mobile phone** – which was probably the size of a phone box – appeared in 1945. In 1948, worried about television and politics of every stripe, George Orwell published his creepily powerful novel *1984*. From this we got a whole raft of expressions that seem ever more relevant: **Big Brother**, **doublethink**, **Room 101**. The expression 'Big Brother is watching you' came to denote complete authoritarian control. 'Room 101' was the room where dissidents were taken where they were confronted with that which they most feared. 'Doublethink' is an axiom of Orwell's totalitarian state, defined as 'The mental capacity to accept as equally valid two entirely contrary opinions or beliefs.' All these words have been appropriated in other contexts to describe suitably 'Orwellian' situations (such as those he might have devised) – from faceless bureaucracy to a police state.

The *OED* records almost three hundred new words entering the language per year during the Second World War. Many were what you might have expected from a state of war: the first **malfunction** happened in 1939, the first **jeep** appeared in 1941, as did **boffin**. Arty – short for 'artillery' – appeared in 1942, and the word **genocide** dates from 1944. The world's first **loud-hailer** went into service in 1941, and, not entirely unconnected, the world's first **marriage guidance counsellor** also dates from that year. In 1941 a **sprog** was army slang for a new recruit. By 1945, if the marriage guidance counsellor's advice had helped and the marriage had survived, 'sprog' meant youngster, child or baby.

A 1941 travel guide to Havana contains the first reference in print to **nightclubbing**, and, if you could wait just one more year, the *American Thesaurus of Slang* records the first **freebie** from 1942. You might have got in had you been wearing the first **zoot suit**, whose existence is recorded that same year in the song of the same name by Ray Gilbert and Bob O'Brien, 'I want a Zoot Suit with a reat pleat, with a drape shape.' **Smart casual** didn't appear until 1945, in the *New York Times*.

Telly, the shortened version of 'television', appears in print in 1942, three years before **bebop** (see page 256). 'Bebop', originally the name of a recording by jazz musician Dizzy Gillespie, was popular among **teenagers**, and 'teenagers' arrived on the pages of *Popular Science Monthly* in 1941, the same year that **existentialism** was translated into English by the philosopher Julius Kraft.

The Fifties

In the 1950s something irritating was described as **bugging** you, but if things were 'good', they were **cooking**. An enjoyable experience was a **blast**, as the editors of Harold Wentworth and Stuart Berg Flexner's 1960 *Dictionary of American Slang* noted: 'Maybe it's a little early in the day for their first blast,' meaning 'wild party' or 'good time'. They also noted that 'blast' had meant 'a strong gust of wind' ever since around the year 1000, and Chaucer in *Troilus and Criseyde* (1374) had written of a 'Reed that boweth dowen with every blaste'. It also came to mean 'a strong reprimand', but that was fully 953 years after its first use. When not having a 'blast', 1950s teenagers might have thought things were a **drag**. This is actually a fifteenth-century Old English word related to 'draw' that acquired a variety of meanings on its journey to the 1950s. These included a 'bonnet-denting car race', 'to dredge a river-bed', 'a major street or road' (as in 'the main drag'), 'women's clothes worn by men', 'a smelly thing that hounds will follow', 'a deep inhalation of a cigarette', 'a back-spin in cricket' and prison slang for a 'three-month sentence'.

In the 1950s, if you weren't **in the know** (first cited 1883), you were in **Nowheresville**, as a 1959 quotation from the *Washington Post* attests: 'Legally speaking, the Coffee and Confusion Club, the beat generation's contribution to Foggy Bottom,[14] was in Nowheresville yesterday.' It's not known for certain why this should have been the case, and the club no longer exists, but if it had waited another few years, it would probably have become fashionable again and been described – as Jack Kerouac put it in his beat novel *On the Road* (1957) – as **hip** (origin unknown).

For a while in the 1950s we fell in love with U and **non**-U words (U standing for upper class). The distinctions were invented by the British linguistics expert Alan Ross as a serious exercise, the idea being that people revealed their class and social aspirations through the vocabulary they used. Although

U	Non-U
Bike	Cycle
Luncheon	Dinner
Vegetables	Greens
House	Home
Sick	Ill
Looking-glass	Mirror
Mad	Mental
Lavatory paper	Toilet paper
Rich	Wealthy

---

14 One of Washington DC's oldest (nineteenth-century) areas, also the location of – and therefore a nickname for – the US Department of State.

his article appeared in an obscure journal, it came to the attention of the novelist Nancy Mitford (1904–73), who had great fun playing on England's uneasy class consciousness. Not surprisingly, it all went very badly for the middle classes, who fretted about whether they should be holding their 'napkins' or 'serviettes'.

Along with social unease, the 1950s were the decade of the Cold War as characterized by **brinkmanship**, a word coined in 1956 by America's Secretary of State John Foster Dulles: the *New York Times* claimed that the US Democrat politician Adlai Stevenson 'derided [Dulles] for boasting of his brinkmanship – the art of bringing us to the edge of the nuclear abyss.' There is one earlier reference, in fact, from 1840, from the political writer John Stuart Mill: 'They had been brought to the brink of war.'

The Sixties

The Cold War continued on through the 1960s, bringing the world to within spitting distance of nuclear annihilation. Young people responded to the insanities of the adult world by living for the moment and lashing back at the perceived repression of their parents' society. A growing sexual awareness, rock and roll music and the glamour of international fame led to a completely new and different sort of mania: **Beatlemania**. Combining biting wit with tuneful melodies, the Beatles' level of celebrity was unprecedented for a rock group. As well as becoming fashion icons, their thick Merseyside accents only added to their lustre, as did their distinctive vocabulary.

The word **grotty** ('nasty or unattractive' – *CCD*) is credited to John Burke who wrote the novelization of the Beatles' 1964 film A *Hard Day's Night*, though the credit should go to Alun Owen, who wrote the screenplay. (The passage in the book reads: 'I wouldn't be seen dead in them. They're dead grotty.' Marshall stared. 'Grotty?' 'Yeah – grotesque.') The Beatles popularized many other sayings. The expression 'that's the gear' had been used to indicate approval since 1925 at least, but the Beatles made **gear** even more popular. The related expression **fab** – an abbreviation of 'fabulous' – is quoted in the supplement to Eric Partridge's *Dictionary of Slang* in 1961, but in the Beatles' mouths it achieved unprecedented prominence.

When the Beatles first sprang to fame, they were known affectionately as the 'Fab Four'. 'These lovable "**moptops**"', as the *New York Herald Tribune* referred to them – on account of their 'shaggy-dog' hairstyles – in February 1964, were cheeky but presentable. Meanwhile, other groups like the Rolling Stones, and the enigmatic Bob Dylan in America, were of more concern to the guardians of conventional mores. As the decade developed, and hairstyles grew longer, consciousnesses expanded under the influence of the prevailing social, musical and pharmaceutical trends. Trouser legs opened up into **flares**, and **hippy** clothes and **love-ins** came into vogue. **Psychedelia** was first named in a 1967 issue of the music magazine *Melody Maker*. **Pot**, the slang term for marijuana, is pre-war, and **pot-head** dates from 1959, as does the word **trip** – whether good or bad – for a hallucinogenic experience, but **acid**, the slang term for LSD, is cited from 1966. The aim of a drug experience was, of course, to get **high**, a term that had been in use to describe narcotic intoxication since the 1930s. On a 'bad trip', one might experience a **freak-out** (cited in the *Daily Telegraph*, August 1966). Or you might just wake up the next morning with a bad headache.

The Seventies

The 1970s started with **Watergate**[15] and ended with **punk**.[16] In political terms, they began with Nixon and Heath and ended with Reagan and Thatcher. In 1970 the proto-feminist Kate Millett wrote in *Sexual Politics* that 'A **sexual revolution** would require …an end of traditional sexual inhibitions and taboos.' Margaret Thatcher didn't promise that, but she was elected nonetheless after the Winter of Discontent put paid to the Labour government in 1979. Punk was great, **karaoke** was terrible, but punk is more or less dead and karaoke is still very much with us. **Trainers** came in, and so did **hypermarkets**,[17] the better to sell them.

The interest in drug culture led many people to explore eastern philosophies or religions like Buddhism and the Hare Krishna movement. The idea of using meditation to find oneself, and the search for peace (as in the slogan 'Make Love Not War') marked an ironic contrast with the violence and savagery of the war happening at the same time in Vietnam. Few people now use the expression **mind-fuck** to denote either 'an imaginary act of sexual intercourse' or 'a disturbing or revelatory experience' with anything like the frequency that its creators, novelist Erica Jong and rock writer Lester Bangs, used it in 1966 and 1971. But good luck to them if they do.

The Eighties

Sometimes, it seems, we prefer to play safe. In a poll of favourite words by the *Sunday Times* in 1980, first place was won jointly

---

15 The name of a hotel in the Foggy Bottom district of Washington DC.
16 The word meant 'prostitute' in sixteenth-century England.
17 Hyper: the adjective was first cited in 1942. The *Guardian* described the first hypermarket in 1970 as 'a gigantic supermarket'.

by **melody** and **velvet.** Third place was shared between – hankies out now – **gossamer** and **crystal**, followed by **autumn**, **peace**, **tranquil**, **twilight**, **murmur**, **caress**, **mellifluous** and **whisper**. (Honestly, what were these people thinking?) Twenty-five years later, in September 2000, a BBC poll asked the same question. The winning word was **serendipity**;[18] **quidditch**[19] came in second, and – in a bracing victory for Anglo-Saxon straight talk – **bollocks** and **fuck** (see Chapter 9, pages 231 and 222) held joint ninth place. How times change.

In September 1981 the class struggle reared its head again, but this time U and non-U played no part in it. The *Guardian* reported: 'A couple of expressions have only come my way in the last month or so. One is **street wise** (though the *OED* has evidence of this from 1965) and the other **street cred**.' 'Street wise' means 'wise in the ways of modern urban life' (*Oxford Encyclopedic Dictionary*). To be 'street wise' meant that one knew how to look after oneself in an urban environment, originally American. 'Street credibility' was a post-punk version of non-U in which what counted was wearing the right clothes, seeing the right bands and having the right accent. In 1985 the *Sunday Times* claimed that 'Neil Kinnock, the Labour leader, lives in a "street cred" west London semi' (i.e. a road that was close enough to a run-down area to be electorally attractive, but not so close that one's house could be broken into every other night), though it didn't help him much in the election.

'C'mon, we're going out for an Indian,' says a character in a 1982 episode of the Mersey soap *Brookside*, and the rest of the

---

18 'The faculty of making fortunate discoveries by accident' (*CCD*), coined by Horace Walpole from the Persian fairytale 'The Three Princes of Serendip', in which the three heroes possess this gift.
19 After the game invented by Harry Potter creator J.K. Rowling.

nation followed suit. We love **going for an Indian**, and **curry** (see Chapter 6, page 162) has been a favourite part of the British diet for some time, so much so that in 1998 the *Goodness Gracious Me* comedy series turned the tables and created its most famous sketch, called 'Going for an English'. The *OED* notes that in 1290, 'to curry' meant 'to rub down or dress a horse with a comb', and 'the currying or dressing of leather' is attested from 1430. In both these cases it derives from the thirteenth-century French word *corroi* ('preparation' in a later, Anglo-French formation). Since then it has meant 'tickle' (1598) and 'stroke' (with flattery) (*c*.1394). Is this where the phrase to **curry favour** comes from? No, that's simply a mishearing of 'to curry favel'. 'Favel' comes from the French *fauvel*, derived from *fauve*, meaning 'fallow-coloured'. Fauvel is the name of a horse in the allegorical French novel *Roman de Fauvel* (1310), which relates the exploits of a horse that is devious and manipulative and widely admired by the humans in the story, who pamper him in the hope of exploiting his talents to further their own aims. It's not clear if this is the first occurrence of a fallow horse as the symbol of dishonesty or not. In the 1980s you might have been a **yuppie** who liked currying favour over a **power lunch**, or you might have been a Sloane Ranger (in fact coined in 1975) canoodling with your **toy boy**. All were hallmarks of the decade where unfettered capitalism, stock market speculation, privatization and the Tory party resurgence came together. The *Independent* noted in December 1988 that '"Radical" … no longer has rebellious or left-wing connotations but means … wonderful or remarkable'.

The Nineties

In the 1990s we stopped pretending that computers weren't winning and just gave in: they had won, hands down. In came **netiquette** (though first attested in 1982), a new code of **online** manners, **emails** and emoticons, e-conferences, e-cards, e-shopping, e-banking and – it was only a matter of time – e-dating.

In the office we might have been **hot-desking**.[20] In our spare time we might have been tempted to **large it** (enjoy ourselves). This shows how an adjective can be changed into a verb – something that would have made William Shakespeare proud, as he was fond of doing that himself (see Chapter 4, page 127). Contemporary culture first 'larged it' in print in 1995, but we certainly weren't the first to do so. 'The wind larged with us again,' is from 1662, with a nautical sense.

The anxiety about the coming end of the millennium was nicely caught in this quote from the *Independent* in 1990: 'After the Eighties and the Nineties, what should we be calling the next decade? The Noughties?' Lots of people made the same joke, but, then, it was a good joke.

The Noughties

So far, the first decade of the twenty-first century hasn't been that naughty. We'll **sex things up**, refer occasionally to the **axis of evil**, and worry about the phenomenon of **happy slapping**,[21]

---

20 The work practice in a busy office with more people than desks: employees work at a number of desks, instead of keeping to one. Intention: to keep staff on their toes. Result: reduces staff to nervous hysteria. First *OED* reference 1994.

21 Commonly known as the act of striking a stranger – often in a public area – by one or more people while an accomplice records the incident on a camera phone.

but we won't ever mention chavs again: we've already done it too many times. Besides, we're probably too busy **texting** (see Chapter 12, page 284) our friends to see if they've found any good deals on eBay.

When you study the English language you meet words from all over the world and from all periods of recorded history. The words in this chapter have all made their mark. Some may not wear their years too well, but they're still here, and still competing for our attention. And the great thing about language is that the field is still wide open. A word can enter at any time, and if it hangs in there for a few years, there's a good chance that it will be noticed. After that, it's in for good. But what if you're unhappy with a word and don't think it does justice to what it describes? Take **boyfriend** and **girlfriend**, for example. Do they describe the relationship between two people in a way that reflects the modern world? Perhaps you could do better. You might have a word in mind, either worked out on your own or with friends or – just possibly – with your boyfriend or girlfriend. This new word will, you think, sweep away both the other words. You are confident that we will all love your new word because it does exactly what we'd want the new word to do: imply sympathy, acquaintance, sex, intimacy and a system of shared values. But how do you bring it to the attention of the editors of the *OED*? The next chapter has some suggestions.

Chapter Twelve

Origin Unknown

*T*he *OED* contains many words marked 'etymology unknown',
or 'origin obscure' or 'uncertain'. This is either very good news
if you like a chase, or frustrating if you like your ends neatly tied.
While we know what most of these words mean, it's much trickier
to say how they came to enter the language. The uncertainty could
be over which language they came from before entering English,
or quite which language they came from – out of the dark – over a
thousand years ago. Norse? Danish? Icelandic? It's not always clear.

Here are some examples for word detectives. The origin of
toodle-oo (goodbye) is unclear. The *OED* has an illustrative
quotation from a 1907 copy of *Punch* magazine: '"Toodle-oo, old
sport." Mr. Punch turned round at the amazing words and gazed at
his companion.' The next quotation, from 1908, is from T.E.
Lawrence, but he says **tootle 'oo**. The *OED* says: 'Origin
unknown: perhaps from toot'. That meant 'an act of tooting' in
1641, in other words, a blast on a horn. The *OED* compares
'toodle-oo' to the 'echoic' **pip-pip**, which is the sound made by a
motorist on the horn of the car before leaving. Toodle pip may
sound nothing like the French 'à tout à l'heure' meaning 'see you
later' – but toodle-oo certainly does.

Now take **boffin**. 'Numerous conjectures have been made about the origin of the word but all lack foundation,' said the *OED* in its 1989 second edition. We know its definition, however: in 1941 it meant an 'elderly naval officer', but by 1945 it was a back-room boy, 'a person engaged in scientific or technical research'. Could it perhaps be related to the word **buff**? Among the *OED*'s seven entries for the noun 'buff' are a blow, a buffalo, a piece of armour, a fellow and foolish talk, but there is also a mention of the buff-coloured uniform worn by volunteer firemen in New York City, cited from the 1934 edition of *Webster's Dictionary*. And it adds, 'Hence generally an enthusiast or specialist', which it traces back to a 1903 copy of the *New York Sun*: 'The Buffs are men and boys whose love of fires, fire-fighting and firemen is a predominant characteristic.' So we have pinned down one meaning, but without further documentary sources, we can't get much closer to explaining the origins of 'boffin'.

Can someone explain the origin of the word **gimmick**? The *OED* says it's US slang, origin unknown. The first reference is to the 1926 *Wise-Crack Dictionary* by George H. Maines and Bruce Grant. 'Gimmick: device used for making a fair game crooked.' We are then directed towards a November 1936 copy of *Words* magazine. 'The word "gimac" means a "gadget",' says the writer. 'It is an anagram of the word "magic", and is used by magicians the same way as others use the word "thing-a-ma-bob".'[1] Can you do better?

Other twentieth-century words that mystify us include **hype** and **skiffle**. Like 'gimmick', these date from 1926, but we can't pin them down any more accurately than that. **Jive**[2] emerged in

----

1 Variant of *thingumabob* or *thingamabob*: 'A person or thing the name of which is unknown, temporarily forgotten, or deliberately overlooked.' (*CCD*)
2 Jive: 'A style of lively and jerky dance, popular esp. in the 1940s and 1950s.' (*CCD*) See also Chapter 7, page 187.

1928, while **jalopy** (an American slang term for a battered old motor car) and **jitter** came along in 1929, but we don't know where from. Could it be, as the upstart *Online Etymological Dictionary* suggests, that many old American cars were sent to Jalapa in Mexico? To have the **jitters** or be **jittery** meant 'to be nervous', but why? Why should 'jittery' connote nervous energy? Could it be related to **chitter**, an ancient – Chaucer uses it – parallel form to **chatter**? No doubt 'jitter' inspired **jitterbug**, an energetic dance developed to accompany the Cab Calloway song of the same name from 1934.

The derivation of the word **patsy** is also mysterious. It's an American slang term, meaning 'a person who is easily taken advantage of, especially by being deceived, cheated, or blamed for something; a dupe, a scapegoat'. To support this the *OED* cites a book by H.F. Reddall, called *Fact, Fancy and Fable* (1889), which quotes the following story: 'A party of minstrels in Boston, about twenty years ago, had a performance … When the pedagogue asked in a rage, "Who did that?", the boys would answer, "Patsy Bolivar!" … The phrase … spread beyond the limits of the minstrel performance, and when a scapegoat was alluded to, it was in the name of "Patsy Bolivar" … the one who is always blamed for everything.' Despite this detail, the *OED* can't say it's that for sure.

Can it be any more certain about the origin of the 1930 noun **woggle**? This is known to be a variant on the much older **toggle**, but where did it come from? The first 'woggle' was commented on in a 1930 issue of the *Daily News* as follows: 'Woggles have now become an established part of Scout uniform, and I have seen some very good examples made by Scouts.' You would think, would you not, that a man-made organization such as the Scouts would have been able to supply name and rank for all its terms. Evidently, someone was not fully prepared.

We don't know how **snazzy** came to mean 'excellent; attractive; classy, stylish, flashy' in 1932, though it may have come about through a felicitous coupling of **snappy** and **jazzy**. Nor are we absolutely clear on how **calypso** came to mean a 'West Indian ballad or song in African rhythm, usually improvised to comment on a topic of current interest' in 1934. Can this possibility be related to Calypso, the treacherous sea nymph in Homer's *Odyssey*? It seems hard to justify the connection at present. Perhaps we'll have more luck with **pizzazz** – 'zest, vim, vitality, liveliness' and 'flashiness, showiness'. The word was recorded in 1937, and in March of that year *Harper's Bazaar* magazine defined it thus: 'Pizazz, to quote the editor of the *Harvard Lampoon*, is an indefinable dynamic quality, the *je ne sais quoi* of function; as for instance, adding Scotch puts pizazz into a drink. Certain clothes have it, too... There's pizazz in this rust evening coat.' By May 1951, the word's original fizz had become a little coarsened. *Time* magazine was using it to describe new developments in aeroplane technology. 'Rentschler thinks the J-57 has more pizzazz than any other engine,' it wrote. 'Says he flatly: "It is more powerful than any jet engine ever flown."'

Aerospace research is an extremely expensive business that requires a great deal of **moolah** (money). This word was first spotted in 1939 in *Designs in Scarlet* by Courtney Ryley Cooper: 'What about it, baby, is it my fault I forgot my wallet?' says one character. 'I got plenty of mullah.'

Thrillers are, of course, known for their racy, perhaps even **raunchy**, storylines. This US slang term of unknown origin means – according to the CCD – 'lecherous or smutty', 'openly sexual; earthy', and 'slovenly, dirty'. But it also points us, for the purposes of comparison, to the adjective **ranchy**, which means 'dirty, disgusting, indecent', offering the following two quotations as evidence. The first is dated 1903: 'Then they brought the monkey in,' wrote A.M. Binstead in *Pitcher in Paradise*, 'the sad-faced, bare-based, flea-ranchy old monk.' The second is from Lord Kinross's *Innocents at Home* (1959): 'The bridegroom, an Englishman, declared his intention of having the English as opposed to the American marriage service. This included … the worshipping of her with his body. There was an embarrassed pause at this; and then one of the bridesmaids remarked, "A bit ranchy, that." ' The earliest spelling of 'raunchy' is dated from 1939, but these days it's more common.

Should we care about these word mysteries, or should we just give up and rejoice in their mysteriousness? A scientist who has identified a new species of plant or animal must classify the find, and consequently has an unpleasant task: the plant has to be torn from the ground, or the animal, no matter how rare, has to be caught and killed. Only then can the process of classification take place. But linguists face a different challenge. Language is not living in the same sense as plants and animals. Few linguists would relish that uncluttered feeling of certain words, the sense of their rootlessness. These words are born out of linguistic wedlock: we cannot leave them alone to their unhitched status. The classifying part of our brain wants to tie them down. These words are like beautiful, mysterious strangers at a party whom others view from afar, wondering where they have come from. But party guests come and go. Words are different: they're here to stay.

Starting from scratch

The current research team on the *OED* is revising the whole dictionary for the first time since it was published and it wants your help to extend its knowledge and solve some of the most intractable puzzles.

Each *OED Online* newsletter contains an appeal which involves finding an earlier citation than the one quoted at present. Let's take an example: **to piss on from a great height** (to humiliate utterly). The earliest current reference for this is from 1992: can you antedate it? Other examples from the letter P for which help is needed include:

> **pony** *n*. an act of defecation; faeces; nonsense [antedate 1958]
> **pony** *adj*. worthless, useless [antedate 1964]
> **poo(h)** *n*. faeces [antedate 1981]
> **poo(h)** *v*. to defecate [antedate 1975]
> **popular beat combo**³ *n*. [antedate 1990]
> **pork scratchings** *n*. [antedate 1982]
> **post-maritally** *adv*. [antedate 1952]

In addition, the editors also want to know if you can **postdate**, i.e. find a later reference, for **portrayment** *n*. portrayal (1891) and **postless** *adj*. without a postal service (1934). It sometimes happens that there is a large gap between two citations, as with **postlike** *adj*. resembling a wooden post (1617 and 1976). Can you help **interdate** this? The flood of responses to previous requests has allowed the editors to antedate **password** (to 1799 from *c*.1817), **patio** (to 1764 from 1828), **pastry-cook** (to 1656 from 1712), **passionately** (to *c*.1487 from 1590) and **parrotwise** (to 1795 from 1856). These achievements are significant, helping

----
3 Informally defined as the description of a pop group from the early days of rock and roll.

to improve the accuracy of the great *OED*. However, the project is constantly evolving and the search never ends.

The search for evidence could take you along paths that snake ever deeper into the past, or simply lead you into dead ends, but the hunt will never be boring. In the July 1999 newsletter a Washington DC researcher describes how her researches in the Library of Congress could take her from the Newspapers and Current Periodicals Reading Room to the Copyright Office, the Performing Arts Reading Room, the Motion Pictures and Recorded Sound Division, the Manuscripts Division and the Law Library. A search for examples of **garbanzo** (chickpea), for instance, led her to a 1770 letter from the American president Benjamin Franklin (1706–90) to the American botanist John Bartram (1699–1777). Franklin wrote:

> I send … some Chinese Garavances, with Father Navaretta's account of the universal use of a cheese made of them, in China … Some runnings of salt (I suppose runnet) is put into water when the meal is in it, to turn it to curds. I think we have Garavances with us; but I know not whether they are same with these, which actually came from China, and are what the Tau-fu is made of.

The researcher conjectures that **garavances** is a variant of 'garbanzos', but she was particularly pleased to come across this reference to Chinese *tau-fu* (**tofu**) since it antedates the earliest example currently in the *OED* by more than 100 years. 'The editors have not yet considered it for publication, and further research may be necessary,' she adds, but she is optimistic of the outcome.

Widening the net

To a linguist, no matter how many times you pick up a word and shake it, if it is marked 'unknown' in the dictionary, it remains a puzzle. Linguists and lexicographers want to get to know how words work. A word that comes into the language without revealing how it arrived is a mystery. Sometimes words send us on false chases, and yet we have to pursue those leads, if only to eliminate them. Some examples are given below. For each one, as we peer back through history, the outline of the word becomes increasingly vague. Eventually, like a ship surrounded by fog, it disappears and we have to make do with pure conjecture.

By ante-dating words the *OED* researchers are cleaving their way through the fog and, in a way, ceaselessly working to undercut their earlier efforts. Sometimes it seems that they will never rest until every single word is sucked back into one vast **ur-text**[4] (original source *c.* AD 1150), perhaps into a giant word representing a linguistic Big Bang, from which every word in the English language originally spread.

Ante-dating also sheds light on society. For example, the second edition of the *OED* defines the noun **oldie** as 'an old or elderly person; an adult; an "old hand". Frequently in ironical contexts.' The accompanying quotation, dated 1874, is from the writer Laura Troubridge (1858–1929): 'I am now in my seventeenth year – isn't it sad? I shall soon be an "oldy".' That seems reasonable, and we would supposedly accept as fair that the writer was describing her ambivalent feelings towards growing old. Maybe we even feel that the writer invented, or came close to inventing, the term, or somehow picked it out of the air. Looking at other pages in the dictionary, we note the first

---

4 Ur-: prefix, first citation 1889. Denoting 'primitive, original, earliest'.

reference to **old age pension** from 1879, the first recorded use of **old boy** (1868) at Haileybury School, and the use of **old-fangled** by the poet Robert Browning in *The Pied Piper of Hamelin* (1842). We sense that we are slipping back in time, but are content that the process has to stop, or start, somewhere. The March 2004 *OED Online* newsletter reveals that 'oldie' has been sighted further back towards the horizon – as early as 1799, in fact: 'Oldy, you don't understand this. Young people must love, and, of course, whine,' (from *Reconciliation* by C. Ludger, translated by A. von Kotzebue). Suddenly the word, which had been standing on the shoulders of other nineteenth-century words, has upended the pyramid, brought it crashing down, and re-enters the structure at a much lower point, carrying more weight on its own shoulders. We should be pleased: this is how dictionaries work. People were being gently mocking about 'oldies' eighty-five years earlier than we had at first thought.

But the *OED* has been drawing on sources from an ever-widening circle. In its 1972 Supplement it made use, for the first time, of a script from a broadcast programme. Written for the comedian Tony Hancock by Ray Galton and Alan Simpson, *Four Hancock Scripts for Television* contained gems that kept the British laughing throughout the 1950s and 1960s, and also shed light on vernacular speech of the time. One of the words Hancock muttered (in 1961) was **bonkers**, as in 'By half-past three he'll be raving bonkers'. The lexicographer Eric Partridge had defined it in his *Dictionary of Forces' Slang* (1948) as 'light in the head; slightly drunk'. By the 1960s, it meant something more like 'crazy', and it was in this sense that Hancock used it and popularized it. The *OED* also notes the use in the scripts of expressions such as **Charlie** (fool) and **cor[5] blimey**. However, according to the September 2003 *OED Online* newsletter, the scripts also provided a successful ante-dating of **stone me** (from 1967 to 1961), which went into the fourth volume of the *OED* Supplement in 1986.

The use of such scripts is extremely useful to lexicographers, since the expressions they contain gained a wide audience and were therefore bound to influence – or reflect – speech patterns. When Ben Elton and Richard Curtis wrote the TV comedy *Blackadder the Third* in 1987, it was a particularly riotous programme that positively relished its use of anachronistic language. Take **mud-wrestling**, for example, which first burst on to the linguistic scene in a 1981 issue of the *Washington Post*: 'One night a week [we found] women who mud-wrestle for appreciative female audiences.' In 1987 Sir Edmund Blackadder yanked it back in time when he said, 'I'd mud-wrestle my own mother for a ton of cash, an amusing clock and a sack of French porn.'

It's worth noting that **porn** is a low-register abbreviation of a slightly higher register word, **pornography**. (See Chapter 1, page 35 for an explanation of 'register'.) In his book A *History of English Words*, the linguist Geoffrey Hughes lists several words in which the more formal version of the word comes first, such as the Middle English **physiognomy**, then the short one registers its own breakthrough, appearing as the more *déclassé* **phiz** (1688). In the same way, **fanatic** (1553) shortens to **fan** (1889), **obstreperous** (1600) to **stroppy** (1951) and **perquisites** (1565) to **perks** (1869).

Elton and Curtis also made great play of the phrase **big girl's blouse**, which was in conversational use at the time. ('Oh Mr

----

5 Cor – a vulgar corruption of 'God', is first attested from 1931.

Byron, don't be such a big girl's blouse!') The *OED* notes that there was an opinion circulating in internet circles at the time that it had been a catchphrase in the stage act of the comedienne Hylda Baker during the 1940s and 1950s, but without any written or recorded evidence of her in performance, this was hard to substantiate. However, when Hylda Baker went on to appear in a TV comedy series called *Nearest and Dearest* (1968–1972) she imported many of the phrases that had made her one of the biggest box-office draws in Britain. The *OED* contacted an archivist at Granada Television, who was able to provide a camera script of the show, and this furnished the evidence required. The line, from series two, episode one, is as follows:

> **Eli:** Go round talking like that, you'll be hearing from our solicitor.
> **Nellie:** He is our solicitor, you big girl's blouse.

This is a good joke, implying that Eli is 'a person regarded as feeble, cowardly or emotionally over-sensitive; an ineffectual or effeminate man'. But again, it shows how the phrase mulches down in time, how it goes from the smack-in-the-face quality of novelty to something more cosy, almost affectionate. The phrase also occurs in *The Balloons in the Black Bag* (1978) by the late William Donaldson: 'The big girl's blouse was sat seated on the bench, eyes closed, a look of foolish rapture on his face.'

Ever since they were first admitted by the *OED*, television and radio scripts have been an invaluable source of admissible evidence. A camera script from a 1973 episode of *Whatever Happened to the Likely Lads?* by Dick Clement and Ian La Frenais provides an ante-dated use of the phrase the **big E** (big elbow, i.e. brush-off). The film script for the 1956 Ealing comedy thriller *The Long Arm of the Law* contains an early recorded slang use of the word **magic** (as in 'fantastic'). Doubtless this reliance on scripts to trace developments in the language will continue, aided by the spread of electronic databases.

Television also captured the cheeky new meaning that **lunchbox** acquired during the 1990s: 'British slang: a man's genitals, especially when conspicuous in tight clothing'. 'Lunchbox' came into prominence, so to speak, in 1998 when the *Daily Mirror* (amongst others) noticed that the Lycra shorts worn by the British sprinter Linford Christie left little to the imagination and coined the euphemism, though it seemed a rather inept comparison, since a box is flat and rectangular. But that wasn't the first reference. We can backdate the word to an 11 May 1972 (Issue 108) cover photo of a nude David Cassidy on *Rolling Stone* magazine and to the punning caption 'Naked lunchbox', a reference to William Burroughs' 1959 novel *The Naked Lunch*.

Ante-dating is a very exact science, and written evidence is the ultimate proof. It could be that Stone Age man and woman woke up each morning and mouthed exactly the same expression to each other for hundreds of years, but until someone wrote it down in a form that survives to this day, in linguistic terms it never happened.

Old, new and in-between

It remains to be seen how the dictionary deals with the phenomenon of **text messaging** or **chat rooms**, in which new words are thrown up with the same sort of frenzy that the McDonald's corporation opens up franchises worldwide (currently two a day and counting). 'Instant messaging', whether via computer or by mobile phone, may not be very elegant, but its truncated spellings are an aid to rapid communication. Schools are having to drill their pupils extra-hard to prevent this usage spilling over into essays and examination papers as micro-words like GR8 (great) and L8 (late) are now more familiar to most teenagers than their conventionally spelt versions. Two generations ago, people used telegrams to communicate with each other, and modified the rules of grammar, punctuation and spelling accordingly. A similar process is taking place today. When you're **texting**, you can't let long words slow you down, hence the profusion of acronyms like AFAIK (as far as I know), BRB (be right back), BTW (by the way), GR8 (great), IMHO (in my humble opinion), TLK2UL8R (talk to you later) and ROTFLMAO (rolling on the floor laughing my arse off).

At present, though, it doesn't matter whether the word's first use is in a folio[6] edition of Shakespeare, on a page of the *Topper* comic, or in a notice above a public lavatory. What counts is that it was committed to writing. It is we, the non-lexicographical specialists, who can only watch, admire and sometimes add judgements, such as in the case of who *barfed* first. You may not be too interested in the first recorded usage of the verb 'barf', but it matters: every word matters.

In lexicography, every ball is permanently in the air, and no word can ever be declared closed. At present, therefore, the world's first 'barf' is recorded in Wentworth and Flexner's *Dictionary of American Slang*. Would it not have been

----

6 'Shakespeare's earliest published plays are referred to as folios or quartos according to the folding of the printed sheets and therefore the size of the book: folios being large, tall volumes and the quartos being smaller and squarer.' From the *Oxford Companion to English Literature*, ed. M. Drabble (1985)

preferable, though, to have found a non-dictionary reference? The very fact that Wentworth and Flexner had netted it implies that someone, somewhere had used it, written it down and printed it before then. Someone must, in other words, have had a 'barf' earlier than 1960.

Part Two

Part Two

Chapter Thirteen

One Sandwich Short

*T*alking about the condition popularly known as 'madness' is a delicate subject these days because, quite rightly, we are hesitant about offending people who are mentally disturbed – or their families, friends and employers. And yet those deemed mad have always been around us. In pre-Victorian London they were herded into a place called the Hospital of St Mary of Bethlehem, later shortened to **Bedlam**, which was located on three sites around central London between 1247 and 1815. Viewing the inmates cost a penny every first Tuesday of the month, and many and varied must have been the unkind expressions aimed at the wretched residents.

These days, we don't queue to stare at the lunatics in the asylum. Rather, we use language to distance ourselves from people undergoing mental turmoil. Some of us don't know whether to laugh or sympathize, which goes some way to explaining the bewildering variety of terms used to describe it. Quite clearly 'mad' people – however inexactly that term is used – worry us. They threaten our sense of normality and remind us of what we might be. And, as with Shakespeare's Fool, they sometimes tell us things we'd rather not know because they see around corners where we'd rather not look.

The variety of words used is pretty dazzling, and it represents just about every shade of linguistic influence that the English language has ever undergone. Everyone, it seems, wants to get in on the madness-naming game. So of course we find the classical languages involved at an early stage. **Mania** and **psychosis** are Greek; **insanity**, **dementia** and **lunacy** are Latin. Lunacy comes from *luna*, the Latin word for 'moon'. Folkloric wisdom has it that the moon's waxing and waning affects the minds of those afflicted by mental turbulence. Howling at the moon is one symptom of these phases. The word **lunatic** dates from the thirteenth century, while its shortened form **loony** is from the late Victorian period. Since then the studied casualization of our attitude to lunacy in areas such as media and fashion have led to, for example, the cartoon craziness of *Looney Tunes* (from 1930) and the surreally wide flares known as **loons**, which date from 1971. Let us pray that this is one form of licensed insanity not about to make a comeback.

Of course the trousered loons should not be confused with the fifteenth-century **loon**, which means 'scamp' or 'rogue', but which is descended by a different route, possibly from the Old Norse *lúenn*, which means 'beaten' or 'benumbed'.

As for the word **mad**, that has an impressively long record. It is probably descended from the Middle English *amad*, meaning 'demented' or 'distracted', or, to use the modern terminology, 'mad', and disappeared from English around 1315. A*mad* itself seems to have emerged from the Old English *gemæd*, which came from the Gothic word *gamaid(s)*, meaning 'bruised', and it's not hard to see how bruised on the skin might lead to bruised in the head.

Various other meanings of 'mad' have evolved over time, such as 'extravagantly foolish' or 'wild with desire'. And the

African-American use of 'mad' the adverb, as in 'mad scared', sounds contemporary, but is in fact at least five centuries old. It's an intriguing thought that the phrase 'mad drunk' could just as easily have been uttered in a twenty-first-century nightclub as by Sir Thomas Lodge – of whom more later.

This chapter discusses some other ways in which we've labelled mad people or their movements, from mildly odd to downright schizoid, and from children's taunts to in-jokes revolving around sandwiches and picnics.

Idiot

Incredibly, words such as **cretin**, **imbecile**, **idiot** and **moron** were once used as diagnostic terms in the early stages of psychiatry, and have all gone on to be terms of abuse, which is why all of them– apart from 'idiot' – are pretty much taboo in polite society.

'Idiot' now means 'a stupid person', but in previous centuries there was a fair bit of jostling as to its precise definition. In New Testament Greek an idiot is an uneducated person, but around the fourteenth century it could also mean (according to the *OED*) a clown, a layman or a private individual. But the definition that's stuck – perhaps because it was so specific, or because there was a lot of it about – reads: 'A person so deficient in mental or intellectual faculty as to be incapable of ordinary acts of reasoning or rational conduct' – and therefore to be distinguished from someone who was merely temporarily insane, or having lucid intervals.

Idiot is Greek, in origin. It comes from the noun *idiotes*, which really meant 'a private person or an individual'. It was a rude term then, but not in today's sense. In ancient Athens it

meant someone not prepared to take part in the Greek
democratic process because they were too preoccupied with
their private concerns. It certainly adds a layer of meaning to the
phrase 'You'd be mad to vote for them'.

Up until the late nineteenth century an idiot could be a
'natural fool' or half-wit: it was all but a legal term, in fact,
meaning a person on the very bottom rung of the intellectual
ladder, an adult with a mental age of two, incapable of looking
after himself or of being trusted not to hurt himself. When IQ
tests came along the idiot score was given as twenty or under.

Cretin

The term **cretin** is more recent than idiot, and much more
specific. It was coined to describe mentally retarded individuals –
perhaps we should use a more sensitive phrase, such as 'intellect-
ually challenged' – who were found mainly in the Swiss Alps. It
defines a person of severely stunted physical and mental growth,
and some amazingly colourful descriptions of those afflicted in
this way appeared in the February 1858 edition of the *Atlantic
Monthly*. The Hartford physician Linus P. Brockett wrote:

> By the roadside, basking in the sun, he beholds beings whose
> appearance seems such a caricature upon humanity, that he is at
> a loss to know whether to assign them a place among the human
> or the brute creation. Unable to walk, – usually deaf and dumb, –
> with bleared eyes, and head of disproportionate size, – brown,
> flabby, and leprous skin, – a huge goitre descending from the
> throat and resting upon the breast, – an abdomen enormously
> distended – the lower limbs crooked, weak, and ill-shaped, –
> without the power of utterance, or thoughts to utter, – and
> generally incapable of seeing, not from defect of the visual

organs, but from want of capacity to fix the eye upon any object,
– the cretin seems beyond the reach of human sympathy or aid.
In intelligence he is far below the horse, the dog, the monkey, or
even the swine; the only instincts of his nature are hunger and
lust, and even these are fitful and irregular.

That, then, was the first, pitiful sighting of a cretin, and it is
impossible to avoid feeling the shock of the writer as he happens
upon these miserable individuals. The reason for the very specific
citing of cretins in parts of Switzerland seems to have been
caused perhaps by insanitary water and lack of iodine in the diet.
But as the modern world became more sanitary, the symptoms
began to recede. Eventually, as the nineteenth century wore on,
you no longer needed to have a huge goitre descending from your
throat to be called a cretin. As the novelist James Joyce wrote in a
letter in 1933, 'The crétin of a concierge … has misdirected half
my mail.' Cretinism is no longer a general medical term as it was in
the nineteenth and early twentieth centuries, though it does still,
amazingly, refer to a condition known as congenital hypothyroidism, which impedes physical and mental growth. But even if that's
the diagnosis, the word isn't used in front of patients.

Where does 'cretin' derive from? It may have come from the
French word *Chrétien*, meaning 'Christian', as if the very name
were a plea for these afflicted people to be accepted as God's
children. Nonetheless, cretin persists as a term of abuse.

Two other possible routes for the word have been advanced.
Could the ghostly pallor of cretins' faces have inspired a link to
the Latin word *creta*, which means 'chalk' (as in the white earth
of Crete)? There is also an alpine French word *cretira* (from the
Latin *creatus*), which means 'creature' – as if alluding in a
somewhat sentimental way to the fact that, whatever our

intellectual level, we are all God's creatures. Sadly, or happily, none of these derivations is fixed with any certainty.

Moron

Another word with distant roots, **moron** meant 'foolish' or 'stupid' in ancient Greek, and the American psychologist Henry Goddard (1886–1957) propagated it in 1910. In his report to the *Journal of Psycho-asthenics* about his work for the American Association for the Study of the Feeble-minded, he argued for the adoption of 'the Greek word *moron*', which he defined as 'one who is lacking in intelligence, one who is deficient in judgement or sense'. At first it was taken to apply to an adult with a mental age of between eight and twelve – pretty sharp, in my experience. The American humorist Robert Benchley (1889–1945) picked up on it seven years later, writing in the magazine *Vanity Fair* that 'A person entering one of these drawing-rooms and talking in connected sentences ... would have been looked upon as a high-class moron'.

Moron, as noted above, has not made its way that frequently into high literature, though it did feature in one of the Sex Pistols' most notorious songs – 'God Save the Queen' (1977) – as well as in the 1978 one-off hit and anthem of *punk pathétique* 'Gordon Is a Moron' by Jilted John, the onetime persona of Graham Fellows, the comedic genius who gave the world the northern saddo John Shuttleworth. All together now: 'Gordon is a moron, Gordon is a moron, Gordon is a moron, Gordon is a moron.' It sounds better with the music.

The Latin word *imbecillus*, meaning 'feeble in body or mind', led to the word **imbecile**, first noted in 1549, when it tended towards meaning weakness of the body. The mental version of imbecile was defined in Dr Samuel Johnson's 1755 *Dictionary* as 'weak; feeble; wanting strength of either mind or body'. The Latin verb *imbecillare* (to weaken) led some early lexicographers to maintain that this word lay at the root of the verb 'embezzle', though it's now known that it came into English via the fourteenth- or fifteenth-century Anglo-French verb *enbesiler*, meaning 'to make away with, cause to disappear, fraudulently destroy'. Since the Victorian age, an imbecile has meant someone who is inane or stupid. It used to mean a state of mental retardation, but not so great as idiocy, and not inherited. As with the other terms for madness, this word has slipped from the medical text books. You won't hear it in a lot of playgrounds either, as it's quite fancy. These days you'll find it used more often as a form of self-laceration by, among and against middle-ranking business executives.

Most of the words mentioned earlier have lost their medical connotations and are just emphatic terms for 'stupid', but it's interesting how they once defined different, subtle degrees of mental retardation. We now prefer to use more clinical terms, which don't really tell anyone (unless they're a specialist) what they mean. But is this helpful? If a forklift truck were labelled 'Not to be operated by idiots, cretins or morons', would that not be clearer, easier to understand and generally safer than 'Not to be operated by anyone with developmental disabilities, ranging from congenital hypothyroidism to severe or profound mental retardation'?

We may no longer regard lunatic asylums as tourist destinations or sources of amusement, but neither have we become more comfortable with the idea of madness and incapacity.

Barmy

Another word for generally crazy is **barmy**. If you're going to be called mad, or any variant thereof, barmy is probably the one to go for: indeed, it must be one of the most genial insults to be thrown around in any language. The title of David Lodge's novel *Ginger You're Barmy* (1962) comes from a song that was popular in the 1950s:

> *Ginger, you're barmy,*
> *You'll never join the Army,*
> *You'll never be a scout,*
> *With your shirt hanging out...*

Barmy is a formation from the earlier word *barm*, a northern European word, similar to the Swedish *barma* and the Danish (and modern German) *bärme*, which is a type of froth found on the top of fermenting malt liquors. This word came to mean 'yeast' or 'leaven'. The ancient verb **to barm** (*c.* 950) meant 'to leaven or ferment', or 'to mix with yeast' (*OED*). The verb was last spotted in John Galt's 1822 Scots-tinged novel *The Provost* – 'It set men's minds a barming and working' – by which time it had come to mean something more like the process of frothing and fermentation. Not surprisingly, then, the verb first spotted in the year 950 referred to the froth of fermenting liquor. Given its use as a fermenting agent, the adjective 'barmy', as in 'good barmy ale' (1535), means 'covered with barm' or 'frothing'. By the year 1602 barmy could also mean 'excited or jumpy'.

But the next evolutionary stage in this word's journey introduces us to a confusion. How many times have you said 'barmy' and meant **balmy**? Are you sure you could tell a barmy army from a balmy afternoon? To clear up any confusion, we must set our sights on balm and its progeny, and follow that back and forth. **Balm** is an aromatic, resinous substance, a fragrant oil for anointing, as well as being the stuff applied to dead bodies, or for healing wounds. It first oozed on to the page around the year 1200. Sir Thomas Lodge (1558–1625), Lord Mayor of London, wrote many works, including a collection of humorous verses called A *Fig for Momus* (1595), which contained the words: 'To guide the Sages of balme-breathing East'.

Deliciously soft, or fragrant, or mild – 'balmy' had all these meanings between the seventeenth and eighteenth centuries, when it was used by writers from John Milton to William Shakespeare – the latter, in particular, using the word in all its meanings. But then, in 1857, Henry Mayhew (1812–87), the co-founder of *Punch* magazine, and a man who kept his ear closer to the ground than was considered aurally hygienic by polite Victorian society, records the use of 'balmy' on the lips of London's cockney rebels as meaning 'insane'. An 1892 cutting from the *Daily News* refers to 'balmy' criminals, the quote marks around the word perhaps suggesting that the confusion with 'barmy' was still under discussion. By the time the word had entered the twentieth century, its meaning as slightly mad had become widely accepted, and the slippage is clearly from the 'soft' of balm to a more metaphorical weak-minded or idiotic. The *Westminster Gazette* noted the crossover in 1896: 'Should not "balmy" be "barmy"?' it wondered. 'I have known a person of weak intellect called "Barmy Billy" ... The prisoner ... meant to simulate semi-idiocy, or "barminess", not "balminess".'

In the 1980s the term **barmy army** became a term of abuse coined to describe the hard-left rump of the Labour party, which its then leaders, such as Neil Kinnock, were trying so hard to restrain. Then, in the 1990s, it became synonymous with a certain type of jingoistic English football fan. Within a few years it had also come to embrace that squad of raucous, mainly good-natured, largely drunken but surprisingly knowledgeable band of loyal supporters who follow the England cricket team around the world from one sporting disaster to another.

Doolally

War has made many mad over the years, and a climate of war is conducive to the creation of many colourful phrases to express madness, either on civvy street or among those in uniform. Some of these phrases are sympathetic; others, as the military campaign presses on and the longed-for peace seems ever more unattainable, merely cynical.

In India during the Raj (the period of British rule), British troops who were waiting to return to Britain by sea were sent to an army camp at Deolali, 100 miles northeast of Bombay. And there, an awful long way from Tipperary and other home comforts, they waited. And waited. And, in some cases, waited for so long that they came down with what became known as **doolally tap** – English being no respecter of foreign spelling. 'Tap', Persian in origin, is a nineteenth-century word for a malarial fever. 'Doolally tap' was noted first in 1925, and is still in demand as a non-medical synonym for madness, as in 'I went completely doolally with the woman in the call centre when I was complaining about my gas bill'. And since the call centre may recently have been relocated to somewhere around Bangalore, it's nice to think that the phrase is, in some way, going home.

Shell shock

During the First World War, soldiers who had seen too much action on the front line in northern France were said to be suffering from a condition that was first discussed in the *British Medical Journal* in 1915, the second year of the war, and described as **shell shock**. They were invalided out, treated with as rudimentary psychiatric care as was then felt appropriate, and shipped back into the war zone, either to suffer the fate they so dreaded, or to see their colleagues suffer it for them. Shell shock is a horrid and wretched condition, that state of psychological exhaustion produced by exposure to near-constant shellfire. The classic symptoms are exhaustion, indecisiveness and confusion over simple tasks. There could also be nausea, shaking and sweating, bed-wetting, suicidal thoughts, aggressive behaviour… In other words, pretty much any sign of disturbed mental activity.

After that terrible war, psychiatrists were allowed greater access to the army. The term 'shell shock' was seen as one of the many unwelcome hangovers of the 1914–18 war. Sadly, the symptoms that it so accurately described were anything but alien to Second World War soldiers, even though trench warfare was less of a factor. *Soldier and Sailor Words and Phrases* by Edward Fraser and John Gibbons, first published in 1925, claims that the army preferred to latch on to the nineteenth-century and the more medical-sounding term 'psycho-neurosis'.

By 1943, although 'shell shock' was still very much in use among the soldiers themselves (including Spike Milligan, who was struck down with it in Italy and, arguably, never recovered), other terms, such as **combat fatigue** or **war neurosis**, were preferred by the authorities. In more recent years, especially since the Vietnam War, the terms have become ever more psychological. In that war, soldiers on both sides suffered horrendous psychological shock, and that's without even mentioning the Vietnamese civilian casualties. In the 1980s the term **post-traumatic stress disorder** was adopted. But the cruder the terms, the longer their postwar shelf-life. Consequently, 'shell shock' is still very much in use today, although more likely to be used when describing the effect of getting a rocket from the boss than to describe the symptoms of a soldier serving in Iraq. Being shell shocked on civvy street is more akin to surprise than trauma.

Bonkers

Another term for 'mad', popularized in the early years of the Second World War but altogether less intimidating, is the word **bonkers**. This can be taken in two ways. Eric Partridge included it in his *Dictionary of Forces Slang* (1948), with the meaning 'light in the head', but it gradually evolved to mean 'mad'. The *OED*'s first reference to the word in this context comes from 1957, but a *Balderdash* wordhunter has unearthed a cutting from a 1945 edition of the *Daily Mirror* in which a British soldier writing from India laughingly confesses his fear of going 'bonkers' (see also 'doolally', page 294). The *OED* doesn't commit itself on the origin of 'bonkers', but Partridge hazards a guess: 'Perhaps from **bonk**, a blow or punch on the **bonce** or head.' 'Bonce' takes us off in the direction, first of an 1862 word for 'marble', and, by 1889, the head itself. Why head? Possibly because it's similar-sounding to **bounce**, which is what we prefer not to happen to our heads.

Off your trolley

Who remembers Care in the Community, the mental health policy formulated by the Thatcher government in the 1980s? In theory, it meant releasing people from Victorian-style institutions and allowing them to receive better treatment at home. In practice, it led to some extremely disturbed people in bobble hats wandering around shopping centres. It proved to be a short step from 'There should be a reorientation in the mental health services away from institutional care towards care in the community' (official report, 1977) to 'I have already heard my daughter and her friends refer to a scruffy-looking boy as "He looks a bit **care-in-the-community**"' (*Daily Telegraph*, February 1995).

As our attitudes to mental health change, we seem to be releasing more of these words into the community, with mixed results. Often they become terms of abuse, or excuses for comedic digs. The phrase **off your trolley**, for example, means to be a bit simple, or not all there. It meant something similar to **tuppence short of a shilling** (from the days of old money, when there were twelve pennies in a shilling, so being two short meant you were worth only tenpence). It belongs in the category 'Strange Ways of Describing Strange Situations', but the trolley word, perhaps appropriately for a wheeled object, has launched off in several other directions.

The derivation of **trolley** is a bit of a puzzle. The word means the kind of low-sided cart that you'd recognize from any railway station forecourt or yard. One of its possible origins is an Old French verb *troller*, meaning 'to quest, to go in quest of game, without purpose'. There is a fine irony in this, since the trolley that we still associate with manly work is linked closely to the verb **to troll**, which has come, since the early twentieth century, to mean 'cruising for gay sex'.

The American journalist and humorist George Ade (1866–1944) first used trolley in the context of madness in his 1896 play *Artie*: 'Anyone that's got his head full o' the girl proposition's liable to go off his trolley at the first curve'. The phrase is still going strong a century later: in 1983 the *Times* (of London) reported that 'The London college gym mistress who is suing her former lover for libel in the High Court heard a lawyer say yesterday that she had "gone off her trolley" about the affair'.

Fans of the London punk rock band the Clash will recall with a wistful sigh the song 'Lost in the Supermarket' from their breakthrough double album *London Calling* (1979).The phrase certainly seemed of its time: how many of us, pushing our wire trolleys up and down aisles packed with food and other products that we don't really need, begin to feel slightly unhinged? The first **supermarket trolleys** were wheeled out in around 1937, since when they have spread to almost every green- or brownfield site in Europe.

My initial problem with 'off your trolley' was that I couldn't see the picture. How can you *be off* a trolley? You might fall off a trolley, if you'd been waiting for several hours in an under-funded NHS hospital corridor, but that's not what the words say. Of course, it takes a moment to realize that when George Ade talked of going off his trolley, he was referring to a **trolley-car** (what we'd call a tram), a mode of transport introduced in the first half of the nineteenth century, not wheeling what Americans call a 'cart' around Costco.The transport sort of trolley can have very dangerous results when out of control.

Losing your marbles

Another way to go mad is to **lose your marbles**, but whose marbles were they and how and when were they mislaid? It's certainly a phrase with which many dictionary-minded people have had a great deal of fun. Nigel Rees – the inventor of Radio

4's hallowed but hoary *Quote … Unquote* word quiz – runs through the main theories in his book *A Word in Your Shell-like* (2004), including the so-good-it-can't-possibly-be-true one that it's a reference to Lord Elgin and the troublesome Parthenon marbles, whose removal to the British Museum in 1816 so enraged the Greeks that it drove them **round the bend**. Nice idea but unsubstantiated, sadly.

More respectable is the cross-Channel connection with the French word *meubles* (furniture). Marbles was a playful swap for *meubles* in mid-Victorian England in what would now be called mockney parlance. In his novel *Claverings* (1867), the author Anthony Trollope (1815–82) used it to mean 'cash': 'She won't get any money from me, unless I get the marbles for it'. But can losing your furniture turn your head? Rees notes some northern expressions, such as 'He's got all his chairs at home', to denote mental stability. He goes on: 'If someone is a bit lacking in the head, we say that they haven't got all their furniture at home.' But the *OED* puts all further claims to shame with a citation from a North American writer, G.V. Hobart, in 1902: 'I see-sawed back and forth between Clara J. and the smoke-holder like a man who is shy some of his marbles.' This was followed, in 1927, by a citation in a journal called *American Speech*: 'There goes a man who doesn't have all his marbles.' And it's been that way ever since.

Basket case

Depending on how ambitious your trip to the supermarket is, you'll either be loading up your trolley or your basket. A basket-holder could, with impunity, join the 'Five items or fewer' queue, whereas the trolley pusher has to stand in one of the longer lines. So who's crazier: the **basket case** or the person who is off their trolley? Surely a basket case is more disturbed, and here's why: there is a cutting from 1919 about 'basket cases' in US military hospitals, but this wasn't substantiated until 1944, in a journal called *Yank*: 'Maj. Gen. Norman T. Kirk, Surgeon General, says there is nothing to rumors of so-called "basket cases" – cases of men with both legs and both arms amputated.' Ouch.

Naturally enough, the phrase soon acquired metaphorical dimensions: 'Kwame Nkrumah [President of Ghana, 1960–6] should not be written off as a political basket case,' wrote the *American Saturday Review* in 1967. Whether you had a profound physical disability or were in a politically vegetative state, being a basket case was clearly not an enviable position to be in.

One sandwich short ...

Among other expressions to denote madness or eccentricity is **one sandwich short of a picnic**. Perhaps not surprisingly, the phrase began life down under. There is something about Australian national culture – one thinks of Barry Humphries' inspired creation Sir Les Patterson – which is attracted, magpie-like, to glittery verbal expressions. And, indeed, the Australian National University's National Dictionary Centre has a detailed entry on this expression. They agree that to be 'a sandwich short' means 'not very bright', or 'just not with it', which has the additional meaning of being 'somewhat confused'. As well as thoroughly Aussie expressions for madness, such as **to have kangaroos in the top paddock** and the downright bewildering **as mad as a gum tree full of galahs**, they also list **a stubbie short of a sixpack**. This has probably been common knowledge in Australia for several decades, but it was not granted access to the *OED* until June 2005.

The sandwich expression first emerged in print in a book called *Travellers: Voices of the New-Age Nomads* (1993) by Richard Lowe and William Shaw. It's a book about unconventional lifestyles, and, appropriately, includes the sentence: 'I thought either I had something very wrong with me physically, or I was two sandwiches short of a picnic'. Since then, the lunacy threshold has shrunk from two sandwiches to just one.

Out to lunch

Clearly, the madder a situation or person, the greater the temptation to coin a pithy description, especially one that can be muttered under the breath, and that sympathizers might understand more quickly than the person it describes. And, talking of food, we shouldn't overlook **out to lunch**, the first recorded instance of which dates from a 1955 edition of the American monthly magazine *Science Digest*: '"Out to lunch" refers to someone who, in other years, just wasn't "there" – and he is told immediately to "Get with it!"' Its meaning has hardened over the years, but it can still mean anything from a little bit lost to bordering on insane.

Nuts

There are certain words that seem to fall naturally into madness. **Nutty** is one: we can't quite say how 'nutty' went from meaning 'studded with nuts' to meaning 'mad or crazy', but perhaps it happened like this. When the Elizabethan writers Francis Beaumont and John Fletcher were writing their comedies and tragedies around 1625, the adjective 'nuts' could mean something pleasurable or delightful. If, therefore, you did something 'for nuts', it was merely for fun. Being 'nuts' sounds very twentieth century, but it was in use in the eighteenth and nineteenth centuries, mainly in Britain, to describe matters of the heart: you could be **nuts on** (or **upon**) someone. If you were **nutty** about someone in 1825, you were probably in love. And then an American came up with **nutty as a fruitcake**, a nonsensical food simile used to suggest the craziness that accompanied being infatuated with someone. By the very early twentieth century, and largely in the USA, **to be nuts** meant to be really wild about someone or something, so much so that you had virtually lost your senses.

Cuckoo

Other words have slid into insanity in different ways. It may be true, for example, that a bird does not have a large brain, so a person who is **bird-brained** (first spotted in 1922) is generally defined as **not the sharpest knife** in that ubiquitous picnic box. The idea of birds and madness is suggested by expressions such as **strictly for the birds**, but this dates from only the mid-1950s and is American. Maybe we should plunge back into Greek history and consult the works of the playwright Aristophanes, whose play *The Birds* (414 BC) gave us the sublimely perfect world known as *Nephelokokkugia*, literally Cloud-cuckoo-land. This wonderful phrase has survived, hale, hearty and nutty as a fruitcake, into the twenty-first century from 2500 years ago.

The fascinating thing about the **cuckoo** is that it has the temerity to lay its eggs in other birds' nests to avoid the chore of looking after them. This may – the *OED* says 'must' – have given rise to that unhappy word for the husband of an unfaithful wife, a **cuckold**. There is, in fact, no better possible derivation. And since when did being a cuckold not drive certain men towards a state of madness? This is probably also the root of the expression **to be cuckoo**, which means 'not all there in the head'.

Early writers in English, from the mid-sixteenth century onwards, heard the bird's monotonous call – it really isn't that hard to copy – and this seemed to make the poor cuckold's life even more difficult. If the man, like the bird's call, could be so easily substituted, there must be something simple about him. By the late sixteenth century the word had come to mean 'fool'.

Durr-brain

There is no *OED* entry for the sarcastic interjection **durr**. (If you look that up, it suggests, not that helpfully, 'door'.) Nor does it have an entry for **derr**. Other, more reactive dictionaries define 'derr' as **special needs**. The *OED* does, however, list **duh** ('imitative', it explains), first used in 1948 and expressing 'inarticulacy or incomprehension'. This naggingly appropriate expression has gone from being on the lips of the 'stupid' to being said by the clever person in mocking imitation of the 'stupid'. 'Duh' survives today, as have the more emphatic 'durr' or 'derr' (spell it how you will), and thanks to them both, we have the thoroughly pitiless **durr-brain**, which means someone who is, basically, **thick**. Brits, it seems, are condemned to put people down by questioning their sanity. Do Americans do the same? Maybe not quite so much.

Chapter Fourteen

Fashionistas

You can never keep up with **fashion**. The world of fashion is fickle and vain. But the *word* of fashion is much more complicated than hair-raisingly expensive handbags and impossibly skimpy miniskirts might suggest. Ideas that come and go are said to be **in fashion** one minute and **out of fashion** the next. To be **fashionable** could be used as an insult or as a term of praise since the first years of the seventeenth century. *Balderdash* word-hunters have even noted the uniquely awful phrase **on trend**, as if even the fashionable word for 'fashionable' is subject to the whims of fashion. It seems appropriate for the world of fashion that many words to do with being, becoming or appearing fashionable have come and gone and not quite caught on, including **fashionative** (1584), **fashionate** (1593), **fashion-monging** (1599), **fashionly** (1613), **fashionist** (1616) and **fashional** (1617).

It's as though the language was trying on new clothes and forever queuing up at the returns counter to ask for a refund – or, perhaps more accurately, a credit note, since they were traded in for something else. Take that example above from 1616: someone who followed fashion could have been called a 'fashionist'. Add one letter and reach forward over 350 years and you find **fashionista**, first spotted in *Thing of Beauty: The Tragedy of Supermodel Gia* by Stephen Fried (1993). The Gia in question was Gia Carangi (1960–86), the model who became a drug addict and was one of the first celebrity victims of Aids.[1] The term 'fashionista' can be used with greater or lesser degrees of ridicule, whether you're in the industry or not. It's defined as 'a devotee of the fashion industry' or 'a wearer of high-fashion clothing'. The rather fabulous '-ista' ending is an homage to the heady days of Sandinistas (1928), Peronistas (1945), Senderistas (1982) and so on, as if these fashion icons become political radicals merely by putting on a T-shirt. It's, like, ironic?

Fashion has given so many looks to the world, and so many words, especially in the twentieth century. The **fashion industry** has been around since at least 1968; people have been **fashion-conscious** (i.e. fashion-aware) since 1951, and **fashion journals** (magazines about fashion) were first noted in 1905.

In this chapter we are going to perform a striptease[2] by reaching into our fashion wardrobe and trying on – and then removing – a number of items of clothing. These objects reveal a variety of different influences. Culled from all over the world, many are refugees from different cultures. Some are more or less insults, others are compliments. Some items of clothing have been extended to include whole sections of society; others have become different types of metaphor, far removed from their original clothing-based sense. Others are, to put it mildly, mutton dressed as lamb. In this spring collection of well-wrapped words we'll start from the outside of the word and make our way to the middle: and we'll also start with the outer layers first, and work our way down to the skimpiest possible undergarments.

---

1 Read more about her life, addiction and legacy at www.thegiacarangiproject.com
2 A word first noted by *Variety* magazine in 1930, originally in the form 'Girls have the strip and tease down to a science'.

Balaclava

The **balaclava** was named after the village of the same name near Sebastopol in the Crimea (now Ukraine). During the Crimean War (1854–6), knitted balaclavas were sent from Britain to protect the soldiers' faces against the bitter cold. The helmet-type hat can be worn around the head only, or hijab-style, covering the mouth and even the nose, depending on the weather or the amount of stealth required. The men wearing them must have been a fearsome sight, and it's no wonder that an 1892 article on mountaineering referred to the hat as the 'Balaclava (Templar) cap' since the wearer does somewhat resemble one of the Knights Templar. There are no references to the balaclava contemporary with the Crimean campaign: the first is from 1881, a quarter of a century later.

The switch from military to civilian use seems to have been spotted first by *Queen* magazine in an article from 1901. Balaclavas went to war again in 1914, resurfacing in a 1929 copy of *Blackwell's* magazine, when they were restyled for the men's military look together with a woolly muffler. Fashion on civvy street, in other words.

Parka

The *OED* defines a **parka** as 'a long hooded jacket made of skins and sometimes trimmed with fur, worn by the people of the Arctic'. The first written record of it comes from 1625, in a work by Samuel Purchas (?1577–1626). (Purchas's accounts of his intrepid journeys to exotic foreign courts were said to be among the inspirations for Samuel Taylor Coleridge's poem 'Kubla Khan'.) The word 'parka' has an intriguing origin: it is in fact a Nenets word, Nenets being a language of one of the Arctic peoples. It turns out that parka is not the only word that Nenets has given to the English language. There are two more: Nenets itself and an alternative word for Nenets – Nganasan. Not, perhaps, as impressive a list as one might have hoped for. In fact, Nenets is part of a language cluster centred around Finland and the Ural mountain range in Russia. The family name for these languages and their peoples is Samoyed: Russian for 'self-eater' or 'cannibal'. To the Russians, these were obviously just a wild and uncivilized people who lived far away.

The Samoyeds are a Mongolian race, from Siberia. A very helpful Nenets language website suggests that Nenets is spoken by 27,273 people, 26,730 of whom are native speakers. Presumably the other 543 just find it useful for business purposes.[3]

So the parka, that item of clothing no self-respecting Mod would be seen without in the 1960s, and that is currently enjoying a resurgence as high fashion, has its roots in a style of life first reported by one of our most intrepid travellers.

Anorak

You could be forgiven for thinking that the **anorak** and parka are from roughly the same vintage, but they're not. 'Anorak' is a Greenland Eskimo word, defined in the *OED* as 'a weatherproof jacket of skin or cloth, with hood attached … a similar garment in countries other than Greenland'. In fact, we should stop right there because, as a BBC language website[4] points out, the word 'Eskimo' is neither polite nor accurate. It is, they argue, rather like

----

3 Actually, this is a very serious matter. This author passionately supports the survival of these tiny, highly localized language groups that are threatened by big business, pitiless governments and worsening atmospheric conditions. Long live Nenets! Long live the Samoyedic people!
4 www.bbc.co.uk/dna/h2g2/A616268

calling a Scotsman 'a Jock', or a German 'a Kraut'. It's also a bit like calling an Australian 'a Kiwi', or a New Zealander 'an Aussie' – and you know how they feel about getting those terms the wrong way round. The BBC suggests that the word 'Eskimo' may be a corrupted form of a French word for someone who eats raw fish. Best not to linger over these details: we shall in future use a more appropriate term, such as Inuit.

In any event, the first *OED* citation of 'anorak' is from 1924, so since parka goes all the way back to 1625, lexicographically speaking, they're 300 years apart.

In design terms, an anorak – according to the excitingly unregulated Wikipedia know-all website – 'is a waterproof jacket with a hood and drawstrings at the waist and cuffs, while a parka is a knee-length cold-weather jacket or coat, typically stuffed with down or very warm synthetic fibre, and having a fur-lined hood'. It also specifies that an anorak should be a pull-over jacket without a zipper, but that 'this distinction is now largely lost, and many garments with a full-length front opening are now described as anoraks'.

In its early days, the anorak was a 'gay beaded' item worn by Greenland women or brides in the 1930s. It was also given the rather splendid appellation of 'glacier smock' by the writer E.A.M. Wedderburn in 1937. At the beginning of the 1950s it was made of nylon, and by 1959 it had become so much a fashion item that it had been noticed by *Vogue* and was made of poplin.

But then came the 1980s.

A 1984 copy of the *Observer* seems to have been the first to transfer the label 'anorak' from the clothing to the people who wore it: 'At weekends boatloads of Dutch "anoraks" – pirate radio fans – come out to cheer on their latest hero.' From this point on-wards 'anorak' became the term of choice for – according to *The*

Dictionary of Contemporary Slang (edited by Tony Thorne) – 'one of those boring gits who sit at the front of every lecture with their Pringle jumpers asking the lecturer their clever questions'. Perhaps that was a little too participatory or outgoing. In any event, **anoraks** are obsessive characters, who have rightly become identical in the public mind with trainspotters.

Hoodie

When David Cameron, the leader of Britain's Conservative Party, asked, in effect, that we all **hug a hoodie**, he clearly did not have in mind the hooded or royston crow (*Corvus cornix*). That bird became the first **hoodie**, or hoody, in print (1789), in lines written by the Scots poet David Davidson: 'Upon an ash above the lin/ A hoody has her nest'. The next rustle in the linguistic undergrowth came in 1990, when the Irish author Roddy Doyle mentioned in passing a new item of clothing that was gaining popularity in urban Britain: the hoodie. Fifteen years later, journalist Lesley Thomas, writing in the *Daily Telegraph* in July 2005, described her life in Brixton, south London, an area where 'It's jolly cutting-edge to live cheek by jowl with crack whores'. She noted of Brixton's younger population that 'Members of this demographic wear the dodginess of their surroundings as a badge of honour on their Marks & Spencer hoodies'.

One of urbandictionary.com's community of self-appointed lexicographers defines 'hoodie' as a 'sweatshirt with a hood and a very large pocket in front, capable of carrying, but not limited to, Walkman and headphones, candy being smuggled into movie theatres, pencil and notebook, pet snake that your parents don't know about, and certain less-legal substances that you don't want people finding'. Thanks, guys.

The hoodie has come to define the person inside it in the same way that anorak does and the negligee (see page 322) doesn't. Certain items of clothing, it seems, come value-laden. No one ever *was* a leather jacket or a Stetson. Today, the wearers of hoodies are a defining symbol of every school, youth club, shopping centre, fast-food joint and concert in every town, city, village, field or beach in the country. They don't define themselves as hoodies, of course, but that doesn't stop us designating them as such, and even banning them from places where they make us feel threatened.

The word **hood** has meant a covering for the head and neck ever since the year 700, and probably since some time before then. In fact, the two other senses of the noun 'hood' play very well in the mind of any self-respecting hoodie: it's a shorter form of **hoodlum**, as well as a shortened form of **neighbourhood**, as in the 1991 film *Boyz N the Hood*, taken from the song of the same name (see page 384). But back in 1871 in Cincinnati a 'hood' was 'a youthful street rowdy'. Either of these senses could still come within the cultural arc of today's hoodies.

It might be asking us a bit much to hug a hoodie, but if you're confronted by one of these strange creatures, why not try and *bug* a hoodie by pointing out to him that the word 'hoodie' is an example of a metonym? As you stare into the blank depths of his eyes, you could point out hastily, but with growing confidence, that a metonym is a way of referring to something by one of its attributes. So when we say 'hoodie', we mean 'a sweatshirt with a hood and also the person who wears it'. The same goes for 'suits', which is a metonym for 'men in suits', while 'skirts' is a metonym for 'women (who wear skirts)'. By now the hoodie might be desperately texting his mates, seeking reinforcements. Alternatively, it might have been a positive learning experience for you both.

Swaggering, dodgy, preoccupied with sex, unlikely to win the best attendance record at school … how far we have travelled from an earlier 'hoodie', the folk hero **Robin Hood**. Bear in mind Robin's ethos of 'Steal from the rich, give to the poor'. That's sort of how hoodies see it too, especially in Robin's native Nottingham, a city that in 2005 had one of the worst criminal records in the country, at 115.5 crimes per 1000 people.

Jumper

Before we start unravelling the etymology of knitwear, it's worth mentioning that **knitting** is related to **knotting**, and our lexico-graphical top brass reckon that both derive from the very old Dutch verb *knutten*, which is very similar to the Old English *cnyttan*, to knot. Like knotting, knitting is all about making knots, or just connections. In the USA groups that gather to knit and gossip are known as 'stitch and bitch' sessions, and it's catching on in the UK too. After all, 'knit happens', as it says on the website www.bust.com.

The names of our favourite items of knitwear all have ancient and fascinating verbal histories. **Jumper** is a good jumping-off point, since we need to know what the verb **to jump** came from, and why the action of springing into the air has anything to do with a woollen item that is lowered over the head.

Jumpers were originally worn by rowers or athletes in the nineteenth century when doing exercise, and the garment was defined as a 'loose outer jacket or shirt reaching to the hips'. It seems to come from the earlier noun **jump**, a short coat worn by men in the seventeenth and eighteenth centuries. It may have been formed as a corruption of *juppe*, the medieval French word for 'jacket' (see also 'gyp', page 388). Over the years *juppe* lost a 'p', sank to the hips and in modern French became *jupe*, meaning 'skirt'.

There have been other types of jumper. The term was also applied around 1760 to Welsh Methodists, who used to jump about while they prayed. At around the same time, there were also Quakers, a Christian sect who 'rejected sacraments, ritual and formal ministry' (*Collins Concise Dictionary*) and concentrated on more important things, such as making porridge oats and quaking when the spirit moved them.

Pullover

We all know that a driver will **pull over** to the side of the road at the behest of a police officer, but what could possibly be the connection between that activity and another item of knitwear? Well, add a hyphen if you wish (or close up the gap later) and you will find four pullovers: and not one, but two of them, refer to items of clothing.

The most interesting of the earlier references is a dialect usage, an eastern counties phrase from an 1883 copy of the *Lincoln Chronicle*: 'The sea swept over the **pull-over** at Sutton'. This is not some poignant tale of the discovery of a lost child's abandoned article of clothing. A pull-over, then, and there, was defined as 'a gap in the coast sand-hills where vehicles can be pulled over to the beach; a cart-road over a sea-bank'.

In 1875 a **pullover** was a hat that you pulled over your head. (Perhaps this was an early name for the balaclava? The *OED* doesn't say.) In 1907 the first mention is made of the pullover (in its current sense of a woolly jumper) as one of the few items of clothing to get its name from an instruction for putting it on. This is the fashion equivalent of the picture on a tin of chick-peas showing a serving suggestion – a picture of some chick-peas in a bowl.

Cardigan

James Brudenell, 7th Earl of **Cardigan** (1797–1868), was one of the commanders of the Charge of the Light Brigade at the aforementioned Battle of Balaclava. The item of knitwear to which he gave his name is 'a knitted woollen over-waistcoat with or without sleeves'. The testament to his military prowess is the very first line of the *OED* entry: 'Named from the Earl of Cardigan, distinguished in the Crimean war (1855)'. The presence of Lord Cardigan at Balaclava was one of the last times in British military history when two really great trends in knitwear came together, although with calamitous consequences: by some estimates, Lord Cardigan lost 110 men out of the 674 under his command. Tragic for the men, but at least it put cardigans and balaclavas on the map.

Muffin top

The entertainment 'industry' manufactures a huge number of new words and expressions. Many of these phrases are particularly expressive of a certain type of fashion tragedy, and they spare little in the way of tact. Unlike the expressions we have encountered so far, very few describe actual items of apparel: rather, they shine a merciless light on the lengths many of us are prepared to go to in order to cram our increasingly unsylph-like figures into clothes that fail to flatter.

In the hands of comedy scriptwriters, the joke is not so much about what we wear, as why we wear it, and why on earth we don't get serious and slip on something more appropriate to our age, weight and looks. In fact, they don't bother to name clothes: their wit is reserved for those who wear inappropriate ones. Scriptwriters, a tribe that doesn't generally give a toss about dressing in 'this year's black', excel at observing the quirks of the fashion industry – quirks that renew themselves every season. (Just for the record, the *OED* first lists the phrase **the new black** from a 1986 copy of the *New York Times*. In those days it was 'gray'.) The fashion commentators write drooling copy, while the scriptwriters behave as if they are the only people in the room to notice that the king is completely naked, or that he's wearing ridiculous clothes. Respect, then, to Australian ABC's comedy series *Kath & Kim*, which seems to have popularized the expression **muffin top**. This may not yet be gracing the online pages of the *OED*, but when Maggie Alderson in the *Sydney Morning Herald* defines it as 'the perfect way to describe that small waterfall of midriff fat that cascades over the top of your low-cut bootleg jeans', it's enough to make a good many readers swallow uncomfortably and disdain a second helping of trifle.

There have been **muffins** since the early years of the eighteenth century, but this new use of 'muffin' as a fashion term is very much a twenty-first-century development. Other phrases from the *Sydney Morning Herald* survey of 19 March 2005 are even less flattering. The first is **camel toe**, which seems to have entered the language from the USA. This term, which has also not yet made an impact on *The Oxford English Dictionary*, could be defined as a more intimate version of **visible panty line**, in which, so sharp-eyed claimants maintain, 'a lady's too-tight trousers unfortunately bifurcate her private parts'. The similarity to a camel's toe is, well, unfortunate, but for a male version the reader is directed to **moose knuckle**, which, allegedly, describes a similar phenomenon. And since we're in the region, we might also tick the box marked **hanging gardens of Babylon**, which refers to – can you believe this? – 'wayward pubic hair emerging from swimwear'. All right, that's quite enough of that: let's move on.

Sequins

Perhaps concealing your muffin top (if you like a bit of glitz) you might have a top decorated with shiny coloured discs known as **sequins**. This word conceals an exotic tale, beginning with the Persian or Arabic word *sicca*. Trying to catalogue all that word's linguistic twists and turns takes us on a journey through Renaissance Italy's narrow, bustling streets and into British trading history, but let's start with the Arabic verb *sakka*, meaning 'to lock or bolt' (a door) and 'to mint or coin' (money). The coins produced were known as *siccas*, and you don't see a lot of them these days. They're certainly nothing to do with the Latin adjective *siccus* (dry), which we find in words such as 'desiccated'.

The **sicca rupee** was a traded coin, much used by the East India Company as British influence was expanding into the subcontinent during the seventeenth century. In addition, the government of Bengal referred to new coins, which were not smoothed or tarnished by frequent use, as 'sicca rupees' from 1793 to 1836.

But what has this to do with shiny metal discs on clothing? Here's the next clue. *Sicca* passed into Italian as *zecca*, and into Spanish as *ceca* or *seca*, depending on which dictionary you consult. In both cases it means 'the mint'. In seventeenth-century Venice there was a gold coin called a *zecchino*, which passed into English, via French, as **sequin**. This sequin was worth a mint: in 1788 the writer Thomas Jefferson estimated its worth at £27,000. (The name was also used during the years of the Ottoman Empire to refer to a Turkish gold coin called a *sultanin*, though this was worth only about eight shillings [40p], so obviously it was handy to know what sort of sequins you were dealing with.)

Clearly, no Venetian man or woman was going to be very popular at home if they ventured out on to the streets carrying a coin worth £27,000 and returned without it. (It's amazing that such valuable coins existed in those days, especially when the highest denomination these days is worth only £2.) If such a coin had slipped from their fingers, or through a hole in their bag, it might not have been worth their while to go home at all, so measures were adopted to safeguard it. These days, we hear a lot about tying up money in investment funds and so on. It could be said that the inhabitants of eighteenth-century Venice did this quite literally, since the custom arose of sewing the coin into a headdress or gown to keep it safe. Eventually, sequin values dropped, but not before the sewing of coins to garments had become a decorative feature. By the late nineteenth century, at least in Britain, the sequin was more fashionable than monetary. 'Never before, probably,' wrote the *Daily News* in 1882, 'have dress trimmings been more artistic than they are now. Sequins are the newest.'

Well heeled

Some phrases enter the language appearing to be connected with fashion, but then go on to tell a very different story. Take the phrase **well heeled**. We all pretty much know what it means. *Chambers Dictionary* defines it as 'comfortably supplied with money' and states that it comes from the word **heeled**, meaning 'provided with a heel'. At first glance – even at second glance – this seems a little odd. Why should the state of your heels be a useful indication of your wealth? Most of the time heels are the last thing observers see, and to get a good look you would either have to be standing behind someone and crouching on the floor, or peering at them from, say, the slats in some stairs. A pretty inferior position, in other words.

'Heeled' could also mean 'loaded', in the sense of 'armed with a revolver'. Mark Twain, in his collection *Letters from Hawaii* (1866), wrote that 'In Virginia City, in former times, the insulted party … would lay his hand gently on his six-shooter and say, "Are you heeled?"' Earlier still, in 1862, it meant to be furnished with a **set of heels** (guns), and the person carrying them would be described as **long-heeled**. The *OED* does not anywhere define 'well heeled' as meaning 'well dressed'. They date it back to 1880, when it meant well-off in terms of money, and cite it from an American journal. But eminent word-sleuth Michael Quinion says that originally it had no connection with wealth or even dress sense. His source – though not acknowledged by the *OED* – was cockfighting.

Cockfighting was – and still is where it continues – a nasty sport, with much blood and flying of feathers, particularly since the cockerel combatants were equipped with sharpened spurs to add potency to their blows. When conducted without these extra weapons, it is called **naked-heel** fighting, and is an even more drawn-out business. So, the theory goes, if you attached a spur or heel to your cockerel, you were at an advantage, though there can surely not have been a game in which both birds were not equally equipped. From this practice, at any rate, comes the expression 'well heeled', first spotted in print in a story – again by Mark Twain – from 1866. Nowadays someone described as well heeled can be either 'well off' or 'well dressed', and few people are aware of the phrase's bloody origins.

Stiletto

As we continue our progress down the body, we come to something that has, at different times, been the epitome of **style**: the **stiletto**. In fact, the two words are connected. The word 'stiletto' is a diminutive of the Italian *stilo*, which means 'dagger'. *Stilo* is descended from the word *stylus*, which itself comes from the word *style,* both of which mean 'pin' or 'stalk'. It's easy to see how *stylus* came to be applied to the needle on record players. It's also easy to understand how, between 1300 and 1600, 'pin' took on the meaning of 'knife'.

The *OED* lists twenty-eight meanings for the small but perfectly formed 'style'. At first it was a physical object that had a pointy end for inscribing and a flat end for erasing what one had written on a tablet (1387 and onwards). But at the same time (1300 and after) 'style' also meant a manner of writing: later (by 1587) it meant the manner of speaking too. And during the fifteenth century it grew from a way of speaking into a whole way of being.

So when you stick the stiletto in, you're not digging the pointy heel of your shoe into something (or someone): you're actually puncturing them with a small knife. The first printed record of a 'little sharpe dagger called a stiletto' dates from 1611. Thereafter it wasn't always used literally as a dagger, but even when being used metaphorically, it always retained the sense of a knife. The **stiletto heel** was first described in the *New Statesman* magazine in 1959: 'She came ... smooching forward, her walk made lopsided by the absence of one heel of the stilettos.'

Mules

Having kicked off our stilettos, we might feel like slipping on something more comfortable, such as a pair of **mules**. But what are mules and where do they come from? Ask at any good shoe shop these days and you will be shown an array of backless shoes, high- or low-heeled, usually for women, but not exclusively. If you get chatting to the staff they might know that Marilyn Monroe made them popular in the 1950s. In fact, mules go back way beyond Marilyn to the *mulleus calceus*, a reddish or purple-coloured shoe worn only by the three highest magistrates in ancient Rome.

Language plays tricks on us all. Who would have thought that in French *mules* referred not to fancy footwear but to chilblains, that itching or swelling you get in the hands and feet from having poor circulation. It sounds like a schoolroom joke, but when it first surfaced in English via the French word for chilblains about 700 years ago, 'mules' meant exactly that. The word limped on with this meaning until the mid-twentieth century, albeit in regional dialects. Meanwhile, its application to 'slippers' crept into use during 1562, although it was then spelt **moyles**. (Is this where Radio One DJ Chris Moyles gets his name from?)

Mules, as in chilblains, used to refer to sores on a horse's pastern (between the hoof and the fetlock). But how nice it is to see that the other mules, the ones with four legs, get a revised reputation from the Oxford lexicographers. In *The Concise Oxford Dictionary* this amounts to a definition of the mule as 'beast of draught and burden and undeservedly noted for obstinacy'.

Pumps

So there are mules and mules. But there are also pumps and pumps. The *OED*'s main entry for **pump** describes the item that is useful for getting bilge out of ships and other places that we'd rather not contemplate. But the derivation of **pumps** – the sort of low-cut shoes worn by dancers and acrobats – remains a mystery. Is it an 'echoic' word deriving from the sound they make when smacking more lightly against the ground than big heavy shoes? It seems that all offers are open on this, but they've been around since at least 1555. There are possible links with the word **pomp** (as in circumstance), but these are too tenuous to expound. At times like these the dictionary compilers have to hold up their hands and admit defeat. And not just defeat: de hands, de legs and sometimes de arms too.

Flip-flops

Who would have thought that **flip-flop** is such a variable word? It can mean anything from 'a flighty woman' to 'a football move', the latter devised by the 1970s' Brazilian player Roberto Rivelino. This manoeuvre, also known as the 'Elastico', involves the player moving to play the ball one way and then, bafflingly, flicking it in the opposite direction, leaving the other player for dead. Nor let us forget the 1970s' word for sandals that flap up and down at the back as you walk. These **flip-flops** have moved from cheap and cheerful rubber beach shoes to high fashion statements in recent years. Just to confuse us, Australians refer to them as **thongs** (see page 325).

Within the last few years 'flip-flop' has been dragged into the political world, and in February 2006 Tony Blair and David Cameron were accusing each other of **flip-flopping** (changing their minds) over policy. The origin of this term is nothing to do with footwear, and everything to do with the acrobatic flip-flop or **flip-flap** (in use since 1902), suggesting that a politician is flipping first one way and then another. In fact, it was an

American term, first applied in 2004 to John Kerry, the Massachusetts senator and Democratic presidential candidate. Throughout his campaign he was accused by opponents of going back on his word, especially on the wisdom or otherwise of military action in Iraq. It's a good way to describe how politicians adjust their views to suit the prevailing mood, much as fashion is said to reflect the times in which it is created.

Negligee

In Eric Partridge's edition of one of the great works of English lexicography, A *Classical Dictionary of the Vulgar Tongue* by Captain Francis Grose, the word **negligee** is listed as 'a woman's undressed gown, vulgarly termed a neggledigee'. There is abundant evidence here of the Englishman's reluctance to tackle French at its most intractable, while nonetheless being alert to the erotic possibilities offered by the French language.

I don't think I'm reading too much back into the word when I say that the interplay of vowels and consonants in the word 'negligee' implies an article of clothing that was intended not so much to be put on as to be taken off shortly afterwards. Indeed, wearing a negligee at all seems somehow to be missing the point. A negligee fulfils its destiny by lying in a crumpled heap on the floor while its owner gets down to it on the nearby bed.

Negligee was an adjective before it became a noun. Its first surviving appearance in print – meaning 'dressed informally' – is in a comic play by John Durant Breval (*c*.1680–1738) called *The Play Is the Plot* (1718), which underlines its sexy credentials: 'Never more like an Angel than at this instant ... thus negligee as you are, if I would not take you before a Dutchess'. In eighteenth-century America it was also the word for 'a loose gown worn by women' (or sometimes men), and in the nine-teenth century it was, says the *OED*, 'a necklace or girdle of (usually irregularly set) beads, pearls, etc.'.

The Latin verbs *neglegere* or *negligere* can mean either 'to make light of' or 'to not care for'. Both meanings suggest a degree of carelessness, which is embodied in the flimsy item of nightwear, found in an 1862 edition of *Harper's Magazine* in what the *OED* defines as 'a woman's light dressing-gown, *especially* one made of flimsy, semi-transparent fabric trimmed with ruffles, lace, etc.'. The word is almost a joke on its properties. It seems to be saying: 'What, this? Oh, it's nothing,' whereas it's definitely something that conveys a mystical allure to the person looking at it.

The *Encyclopaedia Britannica* states that the French root of negligee means 'careless or negligent', and it's certainly meant to imply this, but the negligee has a more complex history than its ruffled translucence might suggest. In that first citation from 1718, it meant 'informally dressed'; the come-hither quality came later. In mid-eighteenth-century America, a negligee was a loose gown worn by women. In fact, according to the *OED*, it has also been 'a type of man's wig fashionable in or shortly before the early 1750s'.

Pants

Now our verbal striptease is really getting down to basics. Whether big pants or flimsy smalls are your preferred option, we'll get to the bottom of them here.

How do you want to be remembered? My guess is that, of all the inscriptions to go on your headstone, the one you'd least like would read, 'Here lies so-and-so: everything he or she did was utter pants'. The word **pants** seems to draw the vigour of its offensiveness from its utter limpness. It is the equivalent of being smacked around the face by a wet fish. If you suggested to a clutch of politicians that their government's policy on Iraq was flawed or dangerous, or even self-destructive, they might debate with you, and even do you the honour of getting steamed up in their own defence. If you told them you thought the government's policies were **total pants**, they might well try to punch you. It's the smack of dismissiveness that makes 'pants' so hurtful.

British pants and American pants went off in different directions during the nineteenth century. Over here they became an undercover matter, while to the Americans they more or less retained their sense of trouserness. In 1904 the British meaning was described sniffily by *The New English Dictionary* (the forerunner of the present-day *OED*) as 'colloquial and shoppy'. The resultant trail of confusion has led many a visiting American comedian to score a few easy laughs on their first gigs in this country. The same goes for British comedians over there. But why do we wear pants, or **panties**, and what have they to do with the heavy breathing that marks the end of a marathon (or just one flight of stairs) or a brief moment of passion or excitement?

Chambers Dictionary cites the French verb *pantoiser* (to tremble), which is what you do when you're out of breath, and which explains **panting**, but it has nothing to do with pants, the underwear item. And if the sound of *pantoiser* reminds you of 'fantasy', you're not dreaming. The Greek verb *phantasoun* means 'to bring images before the mind'. This suggests that Greeks panted more out of passion than they did from physical exertion, which might sound strange coming from the birthplace of the marathon.

'Pants' are descended from a different line altogether. In French **pantomime** the *pantalon* (pantaloon) character was 'an absurd old man, the butt of the clown's tricks' (*Collins*). This character was descended from a fourth-century Venetian saint, Pantalone, which was a popular name in Venice at the time. The Pantaloon character, on which the English harlequin was based, was defined by the **pantaloons** he wore. These ranged from a garment that covered the entire body to a type of breeches or trousers. Pantaloon himself came to represent authority, and was frequently taken to be a bit of a fool.

The use of 'pants' as a put-down seems to have been popularized by yet another (now former) Radio One disc jockey, Simon Mayo. 'It's a **pile of pants**!' was touted as his catchphrase by the *Guardian* in September 1994. A pile of pants: it doesn't strike one as particularly offensive, does it? Amazing what regular airplay can do.

Obviously, pants come into play in other areas of social embarrassment, an experience well captured by the phrase **to be caught with one's pants down**. In fact, it's not as old as you might have thought. This sublimely British phrase owes its genesis to that other well-known popularizer of twentieth-century catchphrases, the Irish writer James Joyce, who first hit upon it in his iconoclastic 1922 novel *Ulysses*: 'Must be careful about women. Catch them once with their pants down. Never forgive you after.' It's not often you get the chance to leap from Simon Mayo to James Joyce.

Thong

Given that any discussion of **thong** these days brings to mind images of near-naked women on beaches, you might have thought that the word was a relative newcomer to the dictionary. You might have placed it in the same vintage as the **G-string**, both clothing and musical versions of which were first spotted – but only just – towards the end of the nineteenth century.

The G-string's origins are hard to locate, unlike the area that it's meant to be concealing. (The **G-spot** would be easier: that's named after a German-born gynaecologist called Ernst Gräfenberg [1881–1957], who pretty much put his finger on the most erogenous area of a woman's body.) 'G-string', first cited in print in the USA in 1878, is baffling, though. Could the G stand for 'girdle'? Or is it because the G-string itself resembles the letter G? We don't know, but if you had to guess on which came first between thong and G-string, I imagine most people would say they were roughly contemporary.

Well, you'd be thwong. In fact the thong has been around since long before records began. Check out the fashion manuals of the year 950, back in the days when we had the perfect clothes for global warming, but lacked the climate – whereas these days it's the other way round. The thong was there, even then, descended from the even Older English **thwang**, and related in some way to the rather nastier **twinge**, which is, I suppose, understandable if you've just executed a hurried turn in your thong. Once it was just a strip of leather. Come to think of it, it's not much more than that these days, unless you're adhering to the dress code of certain private clubs.

If you're in the mood and the night is still young, and atmospheric conditions are right, you might well enjoy wearing just a thong at midnight. But most of us don't get the chance, no matter how relaxed the beach holiday. Still, whether you wear it or not, the thong is unlikely to go out of fashion quite yet. As a result, one is forced, unforgivably, to conclude that, from whichever angle you view it, the thong remains the same. In parts of the world far from the UK, such as Australia and New Zealand, these minimalist underwear items have now become an essential fashion accessory, and visiting rock stars may find the stage piled high with discarded thongs during the course of a successful concert. (If the gig goes awry, they might instead find themselves pelted with the other type of thongs – see page 52.)

Proof of thong's early origins can be found in the Lindisfarne Gospels, now dated at AD 710–20, in a line from the Book of John (1.27): 'Ic ne am wyre ætte ic undoe his uong scoes' (I am not worthy to undo the thong of his shoes). This clearly shows thong's original meaning as 'a narrow strip of hide or leather, for use as a lace, cord, band, strap, or the like'.

Chapter Fifteen

Who Were They?

We are told that we live in an era of people power, but this is not a recent phenomenon. Phrases that have names attached carry an extra punch: they're more colourful. We could, for example, just say **the real thing**, but many of us prefer to say **the real McCoy**. But what or who was McCoy? The trouble is that we don't always keep full records during someone's lifetime, so speculation has centred around a railway locomotive engineer called Elijah McCoy, a rum-smuggling Bill McCoy in Prohibition-era America, and the pure heroin that came from a misspelling of Macao. The truth is that it's most likely to be a mishearing of MacKay, the name of an Edinburgh firm of whisky distillers in 1870.

Every named phrase has a different origin. You might have done something very fast, or for added colour you might say that you did it **as quickly as Jack Robinson**. Jack who? Of the many theories, the most likely seems to be that Jack Robinson was the officer commanding the Tower of London between 1660 and 1679, so the speed alluded to was connected with the downward swing of the hangman's axe. The bloodier the story, the more likely it is to stick.

You might be feeling happy, or very happy, but if you say that you're **as happy as Larry**, that gives your happiness a particular identity. Ah, say the wordhunters among us, but who was Larry? Could it have been a boxer called Larry Foley (1847–1914)? Or was it simply a shortening of the Australian word **larrikin**, meaning 'a rough or hooligan' (see page 382), or 'generally happy-go-lucky individual'. We'd prefer the former, but we'll probably have to stick with the latter.

This chapter offers a selection of first names, surnames, whole names and nicknames that embrace English history stretching all the way back to Tudor times, and coming more up to date with the founder of the world's most respected air-ballooning race and the nephew of one of our most distinguished prime ministers. The honours board of phrase-naming is shared equally by a former English monarch with a taste for persecuting Protestants and an otherwise blameless little girl who was simply playing in the street when she made an unwelcome appointment with fate.

With today's world so fixated on celebrities, we wonder if any will go down in naming history. Will people involved in gruesome or sensational murder trials, such as Myra Hindley, Peter Sutcliffe or even O.J. Simpson, one day suffer the fate of finding their names woven into the fabric of a phrase? The surest way to be immortalized used to be through playground chants ('Lizzie Borden took an axe/And gave her mother forty whacks'). Let's just hope not too many British schools outlaw skipping ropes on health and safety grounds, since that would inevitably reduce the ways in which sing-song references enter the language.

Let's make a few predictions. We predict a new adverb of emphasis: not just **plug ugly** but **Rooney ugly**. Or how about a new scale of beauty, with Wayne at one end and George Clooney at the other? 'Give me the whole thing, from Rooney to Clooney.' We'd like to see a new noun, as in 'to talk utter **Jade**', which means to speak without engaging the brain. How would you like to be remembered? Perhaps, given some of the stories contained here, it would be safer simply to slip away unnoticed.

Gordon Bennett

Some phrases that have names attached to them seem to have existed for ever, as if they appeared from out of the linguistic ether. Others have a shortlist of possible claimants, and one such is the slightly dated oath '**Gordon Bennett**', which is uttered at moments of high surprise. It's easy to see where its appeal lies: you can hear the sound of God – extended to the more expressive Gawd, as in **Gorblimey** or **Gawd Almighty** – in the word 'Gordon', so it's clear that the Lord's name is being invoked via someone else's name.

Gordon Bennett appeared as a cartoon character in the *Beano* comic, though only as recently as 1999. But was that name based on a real character? If so, the main contender to claim this honour is the scion of a famous publishing dynasty. His father, Gordon Bennett (1795–1872), was a newspaperman. Born in Scotland, he moved to America, where he founded the *New York Herald* (1835) and worked his way up from humble beginnings to achieve wealth and fame. But James Gordon Bennett (1841–1918), always known as 'Gordon', threw his money around with unseemly gusto and became one of the most colourful and talked-about characters of his day, a bit like Paris Hilton, except without the leaked Internet sex scenes.

Bennett junior was brought up in France. In 1869 he shrewdly invested some of his father's thousands by sponsoring Henry Stanley's trip to present-day Tanzania. Stanley's famous greeting to the only other white man for hundreds of miles – 'Dr Livingstone, I presume?' – was a masterpiece of understatement, glaringly at odds with the overblown lifestyle of his newspaper sponsor – and, according to a new biography of Stanley, very possibly made up by Stanley after the event. Still, it was a cracking line.

The younger Bennett certainly had a nose for a story: or rather, for a publishing machine that printed stories. He founded the *International Herald Tribune* in Paris in 1887, and he led a lavish and at times dissolute lifestyle that included having his own railway carriages (nineteenth-century-speak for 'private jet'), plus yachts and mansions (nineteenth-century-speak for 'yachts and mansions'). Maybe it was his extravagant behaviour that led to the uttering of his name – frequently accompanied by a despairing shake of the head – becoming synonymous with expressions of amazement or disbelief. In fact, muttering 'Gordon Bennett' could be said to be the quintessential British exclamation, in that it can be used to express either jubilation or extreme disappointment.

Famously, Bennett junior blew his engagement to the New York socialite Caroline May by urinating, when drunk, into a fireplace in front of her family on New Year's Eve 1877. The family was not amused, and before long Bennett was on a ship bound for France, where attitudes to urinating in public were more enlightened. Bennett's drunken feat was recognized by *The Guinness Book of Records* as the 'Greatest Engagement Faux Pas', something that could also be described as the 'Most Spurious Entry for a Guinness Book Record'.

Given the prevalence of Gordon Bennett's name, it's interesting that the exclamation is not recorded earlier in the popular books and journals of the day. The first example, in fact, is from a 1962 episode of the TV sitcom *Steptoe & Son* called 'The Bird'. The exact wording is: 'Gordon Bennett, if you don't know that after all these years'. To a scriptwriter in postwar Britain, the opportunity to sneak in a concealed reference to God was irresistible.

Balderdash wordhunters may be aware of other theories as to the phrase's origins, though none is likely to receive the royal nod from the *OED*. One story refers to the Australian lieutenant-general Henry Gordon Bennett (1887–1962), who was bombarded with criticism on the grounds that after he surrendered to Japanese forces in Singapore in February 1942, he then managed to escape, leaving his men behind. The troops probably aimed a few choice expressions at his departing rear, but would they have included the words 'Gordon Bennett'? Wordhunter correspondents claim that an entire generation of Australian schoolchildren used to call their sports shoes **Gordon Bennetts** because that was what they wore to run away.

Another story comes from the north of England, and concerns a Gordon Bennett who led a foxhunt in the early years of the twentieth century. His name, it is claimed, was shouted to gee up the other hunters. It's a great-if-true story, but so far the documentary evidence has been a bit thin on the ground. The same goes for Gordon Bennett, a hanging judge in Victorian London. The names of these individuals may have been real enough, but we can't prove that anyone uttered their name as an oath.

Returning to our first Gordon Bennett, some readers may have heard about his sponsorship of motor racing, as well as a prestigious air-balloon race that started in 1906 in Paris. Anecdotal evidence has it that a number of wealthy race-goers were lured by Bennett's fame and reputation to travel to County Kildare in Ireland, where the 1903 Gordon Bennett Cup for automobile racing was to be held. Local café and bar owners duly raised their prices, at which point oral history asserts that the locals were moved to exclaim 'Gordon Bennett!' as the price of a pint of stout shot up to reflect the spending power of the visitors. If someone had written their exclamation on the back of a suitably re-priced menu, we would have the vital evidence we need. But, frustratingly, no contemporary evidence exists for this attractive story.

Bloody Mary

A splash of vodka, a squirt of tomato juice and **bob's your uncle** (see page 341) – there's your **Bloody Mary**. Worcestershire sauce? Oh, why not. The Bloody Mary has been propping up people who prop up bars for over sixty years, thanks to the antics of one of the heroes of the early cinema, the actor George Jessel (1898–1981). His latest idea to make a party swing was recorded in a December 1939 edition of the *New York Herald Tribune*, in a cutting that was dug up by a *Balderdash* word-hunter and is included in the June 2005 Draft Revision of the *OED Online*: 'George Jessel's newest pick-me-up which is receiving attention from the town's paragraphers is called a Bloody Mary: half tomato juice, half vodka.' That quotation appears in the entry for **paragraphers**, which was the vogue term for journalists, i.e. those who write in paragraphs. Not a word about optional extras, such as celery, horseradish, cayenne pepper – still less beef consommé, for goodness' sake.

In fact, there are two mysteries about the Bloody Mary: who mixed it first and who it's named after. The second question might be easier to answer. Queen Mary I of England (1516–58) was a woman of strong views. Fourth and penultimate in the line of Tudor monarchs, her stated aim was to shout 'Time, please!' to the tide of Protestantism that Henry VIII had introduced to England during the Reformation. She reigned for a brief five years, but kept busy by executing 300 religious dissenters on charges of heresy – more than twice the number killed during the previous 150 years.

As if that isn't dark enough, there was another Bloody Mary, notorious in folklore and children's street life of the Victorian period. Bloody Mary was the name of a witch invoked during children's games. Sometimes she had a full name, such as Mary Worth, at other times she was just Mary, but always Bloody. Bloody Mary was a real bogey figure. She would appear in a bathroom mirror if you stood in the dark and shouted her name three times, or spun around and rubbed your eyes, or lit a candle. The inspiration for this Bloody Mary may have been a child murderer, and the redness of the tomato juice in a glass of Bloody Mary is clearly reminiscent of the blood of her victims, but was it inspired by the monarch, and – furthermore – was the story of the witch related to Bloody Mary the monarch?

The trouble is we still don't know, which is annoying, but after a Bloody Mary or two, dissatisfaction begins to soften into mere curiosity. So let's try to find out who mixed the first such drink. One popular theory is that it's all down to the barman of Harry's New York Bar in Paris during the 1920s, Fernand Pétiôt. In fact, the owner of Harry's Bar, Harry Macelhone, later claimed to have served the first Bloody Mary to Ernest Hemingway, possibly in 1919, though Hemingway, who wrote most things down, didn't record the event. Hemingway later boasted, in a letter dated 1947, that he was responsible for introducing the drink to Hong Kong in 1941, where it 'did more than any single factor except the Japanese Army to precipitate the fall of that Crown Colony'.

Pétiôt moved to New York in 1934 to become head bartender at the Regis, where he tried to call the drink a Red Snapper, but the name wasn't popular, and the New Yorkers wanted a bit more flavour. He experimented, and this must have paid off because he made the following claim in an interview with the *New Yorker* in July 1954:

George Jessel said he created it, but it was really nothing but vodka and tomato juice when I took it over. I cover the bottom of the shaker with four large dashes of salt, two dashes of black pepper, two dashes of cayenne pepper, and a layer of Worcestershire sauce; I then add a dash of lemon juice and some cracked ice, put in two ounces of vodka and two ounces of thick tomato juice, shake, strain, and pour.

And even he didn't say anything about beef consommé.

As for the name, Pétiôt claimed that 'one of the boys suggested we call the drink "Bloody Mary" because it reminded him of the Bucket of Blood Club in Chicago, and a girl there named Mary'. Elsewhere, it's claimed that the drink was inspired by Bloody Mary, a character in James A. Michener's *Tales of the South Pacific* (1946), the book that inspired the musical *South Pacific*. Bloody Mary was so called because her teeth were stained red from chewing betel nuts.

Quite where the truth lies in this swirl of twentieth-century intoxication is not that clear, but the thread of historical logic seems to connect George Jessel and Mary I, so let's stick there for the time being while we poke around at the bottom of our glass with a celery stick – a refinement invented at the Pump Room in Chicago, according to Joseph Scott and Donald Bain, authors of *The World's Best Bartenders' Guide* (1998).

Jack the lad

If you look up the name **Jack** in Eric Partridge's wonderful *Dictionary of Slang and Unconventional English* (1948), you'd better not have a taxi meter running. There are six columns of closely written type, and it's no wonder why. There is something irrepressible about the very letters of the name, which suggest optimism and a hint of cheek. 'Jack' has had its snappy reputation right from the start of its life as a 'familiar' form of the more formal John. Ever since, it has worn its reputation for flippancy with a definite swagger: it's a man-of-the-people type of name. Hence the plethora of references, from **Jack in the water** ('a handy man at a boat-house or landing stage') to **Jack Weight** ('a fat man').

The *OED* has a reference to the phrase that seems to have been the direct predecessor of **jack the lad**. It's not quite the same – it's **Jack's the lad**, from a song containing the lines 'For if ever fellow took delight in swigging, gigging, kissing, drinking, fighting,/ Damme I'll be bold to say that Jack's the lad'. That song achieved a certain prominence around 1840, but when did we go from 'Jack's the lad' to the simpler 'jack the lad'? At the time of writing, 'jack the lad' doesn't appear in print until a June 1981 edition of *New Society* magazine, by which time the phrase has been shortened, and 'jack the lad' is described as a bit of a chancer – but also a bit of a loser: 'I was always Jack the Lad – the one everyone liked but nobody wanted to know.'

In fact, there may well have been one such Jack, and we even have his dates: 4 March 1702 to 16 November 1724. **Jack Sheppard** was an English robber, burglar and thief, and therefore highly dodgy (see page 373). His parents named him John, but we are told that he was known variously as John, 'Gentleman Jack' and even 'Jack the Lad'. Sheppard's career in crime, including five successful clink breakouts in his *annus criminalis mirabilis* of 1724, lasted only two years before he was hanged at Tyburn. However, his escapades, especially his ability to elude the authorities, gave him an awesome reputation among the poor, similar to that of Robin Hood, though without the same principles of wealth distribution. Plenty has been written about Jack 'the Lad' Sheppard, though, as yet, physical evidence of the nickname 'jack the lad' still eludes wordhunters.

That's one problem with the name 'Jack'. We all love it dearly, but it's a bit of a mongrel. If you survey the columns of Jacks in Partridge's dictionary, from **Jack Muck** (a seaman) to **Jack Shilloo** (a boaster), you wouldn't expect a real Jack to spring up and claim to have given the term its original meaning. Similarly with jack the lad: he can't be a real person, can he?

Jack the lad, then, suggests a certain jauntiness, especially combined with the recent but quintessentially British sense of 'lad'. Lad had a busy time of it in the late 1980s and early 1990s when, depending on your point of view, it either came to represent the acceptable face of post-politically correct sassiness, or merely a sly way by which sexist blokes could say words like 'tits' in public. But it hasn't always been roses for Jack. Its very accessibility as a name meant that when searching for someone to typify selfishness, complacency or a certain dog-in-the-manger attitude (see page 94), the phrase **I'm all right Jack**, first used in 1919, seemed to fit. The famous 1959 film of the same name, starring Peter Sellers as a particularly nit-picking trade union official, has set the pattern for 'I'm all right Jack' ever since.

Nevertheless, we can't believe that there is no printed evidence for 'jack the lad' prior to 1981. Maybe the *Balderdash* wordhunters will come upon buried treasure.

Sweet FA

These days, **Sweet FA** is short for 'Sweet fuck all' and means 'precisely nothing'. It is uttered in a despairing, throw-away tone, as in, 'I paid £25 for that computer manual and what use was it? Sweet FA.' The initials appear first in a 1944 volume of *Penguin*

New Writing: 'Bread – that's about what we got as kids. Bread, and sweet FA.' The expression 'fuck all' was pretty strong language for the first half of the twentieth century, so it was common to commute it to a name: Fanny Adams. The first written reference to Sweet Fanny Adams is from a volume called *Digger Dialects*, written by W.H. Downing in 1919. Fanny Adams sounds like a predictable way of bowdlerizing the letters FA to avoid causing offence, and yet there is cast-iron historical evidence to prove that there was a real Fanny Adams, and it was the horrific story of her excruciating death – still more what happened to her dead body – that led to the phrase's familiarity. Be warned, though: it really doesn't make for pleasant reading.

The gruesome details are contained within the Curtis Museum at Alton in Hampshire, not far from the home of George and Harriet Adams on Tan House Lane in the same village. The date was Saturday, 24 August 1867, and their daughter Fanny, aged eight, and her seven-year-old sister Lizzie were playing with their friend Minnie Warner, also eight, near Flood Meadow, when they were approached by a man.

In a sequence of events chillingly familiar to modern readers, the stranger offered Minnie and Lizzie three halfpence to go off and play, and then offered Fanny a halfpenny to walk with him along a road called The Hollow towards the village of Shalden. Fanny seems to have been uncertain about taking the money, whereupon the stranger carried her into a nearby hop-field. Her two friends went off to play, unaware of the unspeakable act that was taking place near by.

The state in which her body was found, later that very day, is shocking even by today's lurid tabloid standards. Fanny had been murdered, mutilated and then dismembered. Parts of the poor child's body were scattered over a wide area. If you really want to read all the gory details, log on to the website of the Curtis Museum,[1] but be warned: it's pretty gruesome stuff.

The prime suspect was a twenty-nine-year-old solicitor's clerk called Frederick Baker, who had been seen emerging from The Hollow at about five o'clock. Yet he had appeared calm when he was questioned by police. Amazingly, he even went for a drink with a colleague from work that evening, though by now the story was out that a girl had disappeared. When he was arrested later, blood was found on his clothes. Then a stone was found in the hop-field. It had blood on it, together with pieces of flesh and strands of long hair. Baker loudly protested his innocence. The trouble was, he had rather shot himself in the foot because police found his diary entry for that day: '24th August, Saturday – killed a young girl. It was fine and hot.' If *The Guinness Book of Records* had a category for 'Most Incriminating Diary Entry Relating to a Murder', that surely would win the prize by several lengths. After fifteen minutes' deliberation, the jury returned a guilty verdict and Frederick Baker was hanged before a crowd of 5000 – mostly women – on Christmas Eve 1867.

The spectacular and frenzied nature of the attack led to a succession of grim jokes, the most famous of which was in circulation among sailors. In 1869, as a particularly tasteless tribute to the mutilated state of Fanny's sliced and diced body, a consignment of tinned mutton that turned out to taste even more putrid than normal was dubbed 'Sweet Fanny Adams' by the **jack tars** (the name for common sailors since 1781). Fanny Adams was defined in Albert Barrère and Charles Leland's 1889 *Dictionary of Slang, Jargon and Cant* as '(preserved mutton) brought from the ship' and it retained this meaning in W. Granville's 1962 *Dictionary*

---

1 www.hants.gov.uk/museum/curtis/fannyadams/index.html

of Sailors' Slang: 'General nautical slang for stew or hash'.
Sometimes just repeating a name, a word or an idea that has
horrible connotations can deaden its potency. Not that this would
have been of any help to Fanny's family, of course.

Meanwhile, on the other side of the world, our Australian
cousins, with their well-known fondness for colourful expressions,
enthusiastically invested FA, Fanny Adams or Sweet Fanny Adams
with the sense of 'nothing'. This was noted in 1919, and is its
principal meaning today. The combination 'Sweet FA' is first noted
in 1930, and is nowadays a handy newspaper headline, especially
whenever the papers want to bash an organization that is luck-
less enough to share those same initials, such as 'The Football
Association admits it knows Sweet FA about when Wembley
Stadium will be open for business'.

Bob's your uncle

When we say **bob's your uncle**, we are saying 'simple', 'easy',
'no problem' or 'job done'. But how many of us pause for a
moment to ask which Bob/bob we are invoking and why? While
the meaning of phrase may be 'easy' or 'straightforward', bob's
journey to phrasehood is not at all easy or straightforward to work
out. It is beset with complications, in fact, and the *OED* has
refused to wade into the battle, merely marking it as slang. Eric
Partridge's *Dictionary of Slang* recorded it first in 1937, dating it
back to *c*. 1890 and giving a snatch of conversation as an example:
'You go and ask for the job – and he remembers your name – and
Bob's your uncle.' Partridge makes no further comment, but how
telling is it that someone remembers a person's name?

'Bob' has been a pet form of the name Robert since 1721,
but the *OED* has ten entries for it, the meanings ranging from

'a bouquet of flowers' to 'a manoeuvre popular with bell-ringers'. Few of them, though, are relevant to our present investigation. Alongside bob's your uncle, it's worth noting that Partridge quotes **bobby's job**, defining it as an 'easy job', though again we're not told exactly why, nor whether it's connected to Bob and his uncle.

It has been suggested that the Bob in our phrase was a reference to Sir Robert Peel, the man who started the Metropolitan Police Force in 1828, when he was merely Mr Peel the home secretary, and whose police officers were known as **bobbies** from at least as far back as 1844. And yet, can this really be taken seriously? Grateful though Londoners must have been to have a new force keeping the streets safe, there seems no likely reason why they should have transferred their loyalties so far as to think of these police officers as their uncles, no matter how efficient they might have been at apprehending criminals.

In Captain Francis Grose's 1785 *Dictionary of the Vulgar Tongue* – a major early contributor to the field of lexicology – we find the phrase **all is bob**, that word 'bob' being a slang term also cited in the *OED* from 1721 as 'lively' or 'nice'. But, again, it's the word 'uncle' that brings us up short. As a result, we have no option but to draw upon the political career of Lord Salisbury (1830–1903). Also known as Robert Arthur Talbot Gascoyne-Cecil, 3rd Marquess of Salisbury, trading under the name Lord Robert Cecil before 1865 and Viscount Cranborne from 1865 until 1868, he was the last British prime minister to hold that position while still being a member of the House of Lords. For his first two terms in office he rotated the job so frequently with William Gladstone (1809–98) that they must at times have met in the middle. The third time round he was succeeded by Arthur Balfour (1848–1930), who happened to be his own nephew.

In fact, Balfour had been made Chief Secretary of Ireland by his uncle in 1886, a move that provoked a certain amount of muttering on the red and green benches of the Palace of Westminster, in the days before the Ireland job became something of a poisoned chalice. Balfour had also served as president of the Local Government Board and Secretary for Scotland: top jobs. Clearly, then, Uncle Bob had a pretty high opinion of Arthur. Naturally, suspicions arose. Had young Balfour netted these jobs on his own merits or with a little help from his uncle? If, as was widely felt at the time, it was the latter, the charge of nepotism could be applied.

Nepotism, as any classically trained schoolboy would have known in those days, comes from the Latin word *nepos*, which means … 'nephew'? Well, not in classical Latin, where it means 'grandson'. But in post-classical Latin it *does* mean nephew: it's not Latin out of the top drawer, but close enough for the joke to be made by those waggish Victorians. The charge of nepotism can be laid, then, with the mildly waspish 'bob's your uncle', or so the story goes. Unfortunately, none of those waggish Victorians thought to write the remark down in their waggish diaries; nor were any contemporary journalists obliging enough to transcribe it so that we can see the phrase bedding down. This is all very frustrating. Unlike the obliging Frederick Baker, whose diary proved so useful (see page 338), no one wrote down the words 'bob's your uncle' until all the main parties had popped their clogs (see page 423).

Hobson's choice

There are an awful lot of choices around these days, but they don't all get the recognition they deserve. Often they are wrongly labelled. What, for example, would you call a choice between two equally unattractive options? Whatever you call it, don't confuse it with having to make a decision, which appears to be a free choice, but is actually between something and nothing. The origins of the term for this latter choice are both colourful and historically attested, and they relate to a man with a keen eye for a swift shilling, and a stable full of horses of varying speeds. His name was Thomas Hobson (c.1544–1630), and the choice he offered came, in his own lifetime, to be called **Hobson's choice**.

It happened as follows. Hobson was a stagecoach proprietor who ran a mail-carrier company situated outside the gates of St Catherine's College, Cambridge. His horses plied a route between Cambridge and London. When they weren't needed to ferry mail bundles back and forth, they were hired out to the town's students and university staff. Obviously, the faster the horse, the more in demand it was, but Hobson was fearful that his best horses would be run into the ground, so he developed the system for which he became famous. Horses were rented out in strict rotation to allow the swifter ones time to recover, so the would-be rider simply had to take whichever horse was the next one in the queue at the stable entrance. These days it's called the taxi-rank principle; Hobson referred to it as 'this one or none'.

This phrase for a choice between something and nothing is enshrined in *The Oxford English Dictionary* in a quotation from a 1660 work by the Quaker Samuel Fisher: 'If in this Case there be no other (as the Proverb is) then Hobson's choice ... which is, chuse whether you will have this or none'. Alternatives could be **take it or leave it**, or – if you are holding a large mug of tea and sporting a beard like Noel Edmonds – **deal or no deal**.

Hobson achieved a fair amount of fame in his own life. The great English poet John Milton (1608–74) liked him so much that he wrote not one, but two epitaphs after his death, giving people a very unHobson-like choice.

In fact, lack of choice wasn't all that Hobson was famous for. He also built the pipe, known as Hobson's Conduit, that in 1614 delivered clear drinking water to Cambridge. The conduit head is still standing, though it has been moved slightly from its original position, and is now just out of town, past the Fitzwilliam Museum.

The first full-length account of 'Hobson's choice' was recorded in the *Spectator* magazine, a literary but gossipy journal founded by Joseph Addison and Sir Richard Steele. On Tuesday, 14 October 1712 Steele wrote:

> Mr Hobson kept a Stable of forty good Cattle, always ready and fit for travelling; but when a Man came for a Horse, he was led into the Stable, where there was great Choice, but he obliged him to take the Horse which stood next to the Stable-Door; so that every Customer was alike well served according to his Chance, and every Horse ridden with the same Justice.

Steele's pithy conclusion of the practice was that 'From whence it became a Proverb, when what ought to be your Election was forced upon you, to say, *Hobson's Choice.*' In 1688 another writer, Thomas Ward, wrote a poem called 'England's Reformation', in which he noted that 'Where to elect there is but one, 'tis Hobson's choice – take that, or none'.

Take the mickey

Teasing or having fun at someone else's expense is often referred to as **taking the mickey**. The *OED* defines it as 'to behave or speak satirically or mockingly; to make fun of, satirize, or debunk (a person or thing)'. Inevitably, there has been a good deal of discussion over the identity of mickey. One popular theory that has made it into the *OED* claims that it is an offshoot of **taking a mickey bliss**, the name being rhyming slang for a 'piss'; and 'taking the piss', of course, means mocking someone or something. The identity of Mick(e)y Bliss has never been seriously proposed, though the phrase is more recent than one might think.

The *OED* records that the words 'mick' and 'mickey' were both nineteenth-century Australian slang for 'a wild bull' (and therefore a testosterone-fuelled male), as well as Irish slang for 'a penis'. 'Taking the mickey' is first quoted by Joseph Alexander Baron in *From the City, from the Plough* (1948), a British working-class view of the First World War: 'Higgsy,' said the sergeant, 'they think I'm taking the mickey.'

In 1945, buoyed up on hopes of victory in Europe, spirits among Penguin New Writing authors were running high, and there was little room for reverence. 'The corporal ... sat back in his corner looking a little offended,' reads one entry. 'He thought I was taking the piss.'

The variation **to take the mike out of** was in use between the 1930s and the 1970s, and the first recorded instance we have appears in *Mint* (1935), the posthumous memoirs of T.E. Lawrence (of Arabia): 'But, mate, you let the flight down, when he takes the mike out of you every time.' Other variations include the mock-gentrified **extracting or taking the Michael**, the first instance of which comes from Harold Pinter's 1959 play *The Birthday Party*. 'They won't come. Someone's taking the Michael ... It's a false alarm.'

One corking theory is all wrapped up with male pride. The story goes that if a man has a very full bladder, it causes him to have an erection or 'stand proud'. This became known as 'piss proud' – a bit like 'morning glory' – because one's 'pride' is not a macho badge of honour (and where would you wear it anyway?) but is merely to do with an overfull bladder. If you **took the micturate**, or **took the piss**, you dented the person's pride and restored them to normality. So 'taking the mickey' might be a shortened form for the more refined act of micturition (or the less refined act of pissing), though this may be a *post hoc* etymological explanation. In other words, first we started taking the piss, or the mickey, and then someone saw the connection between 'mickey' and 'micturate', and the link was too good to refuse, so on that occasion Bob was your uncle.

Meanwhile, a *Balderdash* correspondent in the United States suggests that **taking the mick** arose from a derogatory term for Irish people (micks), and the fact that they were mocked because people ignorantly assumed that they were insufficiently mentally alert to understand the rudeness of remarks being made around them. This sounds fanciful, however, as well as downright rude. Let's hope our *Balderdash* wordhunter is making his own plans for St Patrick's Day.

The popular historian Adam Hart-Davis is something of an expert in the field, having written a book called *Taking the Piss: The Potted History of Pee* in 2005. He has a very imaginative explanation for the phrase, based on the vast amounts of urine that were used in the wool-dyeing process. He records how huge quantities needed to be transported in barrels, which were loaded on to boats and then shipped from London to Humberside. To spice things up, he adds that the captain used to claim that he was carrying wine, but that when the truth came out, it was acknowledged that, actually, he was only **taking the piss**. And so a phrase grew, though to date we don't have much more than Hart-Davis's word to go on, not that there's anything wrong with that.

Round robin

'This has been a difficult year for us, what with Abigail not quite managing to get an A* in her maths GCSE and our beloved Mr Fluffy finally departing for the great hamster wheel in the sky. On a happier note, however, we had a lovely family holiday in August, returning once again to Fuengirola. Our fifth visit in seven years: some of the locals are even getting to recognize us!' These days, the **round robin** is a pretty derided form of communication, consisting of information about which we care little, emanating from people whom we hardly see. Email has contributed greatly to the alarming proliferation of the medium. The result is that, more than ever, being on the receiving end of a round robin is tantamount to accepting that your friends would rather tell you what they've been up to than see you.

The round robin, though, was not always the confirmation of this social relegation. In fact, at the start of its life, in jarring contrast to the apparent merriness of that shared initial R, putting your name to a round robin could be a way of avoiding the lash of the cat-o'-nine-tails on a ship. Here is a definition from the *Weekly Journal*, January 1730: 'A Round Robin is a Name given by Seamen, to an Instrument on which they sign their Names round a Circle, to prevent the Ring-leader being discover'd by it, if found'. So it was meant to conceal the identity not of the signatory, but of the *first* signatory, who must be the force behind the petition.

Why **robin**? Perhaps because it's a corruption of the French *ruban*, meaning 'ribbon', since the letter goes round in a circle like a ribbon. But why should the names be laid out in this way? A year after the explanation given above the *Gentlemen's Magazine* yielded a further clue: the names go in a circle when the crew mutiny. Little wonder that no single individual was ready to put his hand up first. Was someone called Robin one of the first signatories of that letter of protest? We don't know. It would be nice to think that there was such a person on board. Could this Robin have been a trifle podgy around the waist, hence the play on round Robin? That would fit even better, but until a miraculous discovery puts it beyond doubt, we can only speculate.

The writer Samuel Taylor Coleridge (1772–1834) used the phrase as a metaphor in 1816, referring to 'a round robin of mere lies', but it wasn't until the end of that century that the next evolution in the phrase's meaning took place when the sport of tennis conducted its own mini-mutiny. It arose in the United States, where the *Official Lawn Tennis Bulletin* reported in January 1895 that 'The so-called **round-robin tournament**, where each man plays every other, furnishes the best possible test of tennis skill'. Here it was being taken well beyond its 1731 definition of men 'signing their names in an orbicular manner'.

The sporting round robin exploded the term to the point where – though we don't know exactly when – today's round robin is defined not by the number of people sending the message, but by the number of people receiving it. Who first wrote this meaning in print is still far from clear, but sporting tournaments – tennis, for example – have recently attempted to revive that original round robin method of play in which every player plays everyone else at least once. The formula for calculating the number of possible results for such a competition can be presented as $s(n)\in\emptyset(4^n n - \frac{1}{2})$, where, if your maths is up to it, n is the number of competitors, s is the number of wins scored by a competitor and $\emptyset$ (theta) signifies an asymptotically tight bound. And if that last mathematical expression is giving you a headache, you're not alone because it frightens us too. Those in need of a simpler explanation should think of the s as Maria Sharapova,

n as the grunting noise she makes when hitting the ball, the €
symbol as the amount in euros that the spectators paid for their
seats, and the Ø sign as representing the number of times they'd
like to throttle her. Word has it that traditionally organized round
robin tennis tournaments are haemorrhaging audiences, but the
evidence for that is still anecdotal.

Finally, the delightful and vastly entertaining but not always
absolutely reliable urbandictionary.com offers a few extra
meanings for 'round robin', from 'double penetration of the
vagina and anus' to 'a sexual act which entails a person becoming
dizzy (by any means) and then defecating on their partner's
body'. Whatever happened to curling up in front of the telly with
a pizza and a bottle of wine?

Chapter Sixteen

Man's Best Friend

*T*he word **dog** has made quite a bed for itself in the English language. Altogether the entry for the noun 'dog' takes up a monster 11,000-odd words in the *OED*, running to twenty-two pages. **Hound**, on the other hand, has a mere 1700 words spread across four pages, yet if English behaved anything like most of its linguistic cousins in northern Europe, we would be talking about hounds, not dogs. Quite why remains a mystery, though it's one of the subjects we'll discuss, without, we hope, making too much of a **dog's dinner** of it. And if we can't solve it, we'll just put it aside and say we're **going to see a man about a dog**.

Once you start looking for them, you notice that doggy phrases are strewn all over the English language. That must be one of the positive side effects of being **man's best friend**. We have imputed many of our moods and actions to dogs so that we can see them better in a dog's skin. **Every dog has its day**, of course, and almost every doggy phrase gets a walk in this category, though we couldn't possibly attend to them all because it would by then be **raining cats and dogs** with doggy expressions.

The English national animal, for good or bad, is a British bull-dog. This fierce creature was originally used for baiting bulls. Nowadays, the bulldog might have to be restrained on a lead, as its sometimes aggressive behaviour can illustrate the less likeable

aspects of the British **bulldog spirit**, but – **good dog** or **bad dog** –
it only serves to emphasize that dogs are essential to how the British
see the world. Some have even slipped off the lead and gone out on
their own. If you describe someone as a dog, it's plainly not a
compliment, no matter how well disposed you feel towards dogs.
And when the word **dog-house** comes to mind, you probably think
'someone's in trouble' more than 'a kennel in which a dog sleeps'.

We have, of course, worked hard – **like a dog**, in fact – to get
this selection of words into tip-top shape. We hope there's more
than a **dog's chance** that you'll finish this chapter. In fact, we're
confident that you'll find it all absolutely **top dog**, or even **the
dog's bollocks**.

Dog

When is a **dog** a dog? Or, to put it another way, why is a dog not
a **hound**? The first, perhaps the greatest, mystery about the word
'dog' is how it came to represent man's best friend in the first
place, because in other European countries dog isn't man's best
friend: hound is. So what does a dog have that a hound doesn't?
European languages have that word, but not in our sense. Danes
have *dogge*, the Swedes have *dogg*, Italians have *dogo*, but these
all mean a type of dog, not just dog in itself. 'Dog' seems to have
gone walkies in continental Europe, starting with the Netherlands
in the late sixteenth century, but it always had a label around
its neck, such as 'een *dogghe ... canis anglicus* [English dog]'.
It wasn't just the Dutch. The Germans referred to an '*englische
Dock*' in the sixteenth to seventeenth centuries, while the French
talked of '*le généreux dogue anglais*'. The dog these titles all
referred to was – and is – a specific type of dog: the mastiff. Was
'dog', linguistically at least, the runt of the litter?

It didn't used to be that way. The Old English word for a dog was *docga*, which sounds fairly close to today's word. The roots of this word are hard to trace. We know they're somewhere, but we just can't find them: it's like a bone that we buried and now we can't remember where. In Britain the word *docga* replaced the term *hund*, which remained common across the rest of northern Europe. The *OED* says that 'dog' used to be 'the name of a powerful breed or race of dogs'. Was this dog a bit of a pit-bull terrier, scaring off the hound? We don't know, but we could speculate on the brutish dog word snapping at the heels of the more playful hound until it turned into a **dog-fight**, and dog won.

'Hound' has always been a better European than 'dog'. You will find it or its puppies in old German, Swedish and Danish, even Greek and Lithuanian. In fact, if you go as far back as Sanskrit you'll find the word *çwan*, and if you're an etymologist, you can easily persuade yourself that the two are more or less directly related. The *OED* has tracked 'dog' closely and discovered that its pedigree is extensive: there's almost no field of human activity that dogs haven't poked their noses into.

The *OED* defines 'dog' as 'a quadruped of the genus *Canis*'. A hound, on the other hand, is defined as 'a dog, generally'. In other words, 'dog' is such boiled-down English that you can use it to define 'hound'. As words go, 'dog' really is man's best friend, and pretty much has been since its first written citation in the year 1050. The word has a familiarity to it: if one of our pre-Norman forebears returned to chat to us, amid the embarrassed silence as we thumbed through the dictionary to try to reduce the linguistic gap, 'dog' would be a welcome refuge. On one level, it means exactly the same now as it did then: it does, you could say, exactly what it says on the label.

'Dog' is ur-English – pretty much as old as you get. 'Hound' takes a bit more explaining. The very first reference to 'dog' is by the Spanish-born poet Aurelius Prudentius Clemens, or just Prudentius for short. Sections of his work (in Latin) appeared 600 years after his death, around 1050. We don't know if Prudentius was a dog-lover, but the Latin word *canum* (meaning 'of the dogs') is translated as *docgena*.

'A gentyll hounde ... hath lesse fleshe than a dogge and shorter heere and more thynne,' wrote John of Trevisa in 1398 in an early attempt to differentiate between the two, as if they were different species. There was also the word **cur**, first seen around 1225, but that too is defined in the *OED* as 'a dog' – and is always meant in a 'depreciative or contemptuous' sense, despite a 1530 definition of 'dogge' as 'a mischievous curre'. Evidently not a dog-lover, that man.

The same John of Trevisa (?1340–1402) obviously thought of dogs as hunting animals – 'Brockes [badgers] ... [have] ben huntyd and chassyd wyth hunters dogges' – and there was obviously plenty of evidence from around the country that badgers were indeed being hunted and chased with hunters' dogs. But it was William Shakespeare who upped the metaphorical ante to include the phrase the **dogs of war** in his play *Julius Caesar* from 1601.

'Dog' has been used as a term of insult ('Dogge, ther thou ly!' – Dog, there you lie) since around 1325. But the use of 'dog' to suggest something mediocre or bad can be dated to 1936, when a song described as a dog meant something 'that's kicked around'. It hasn't always been kicks and insults, though. 'Dog' has also been used as a term of affection, as in a letter from Queen Anne to Lord Buckingham: 'My kind Dog...'

Hound

If you go back far enough in Greek and Latin, the words for 'dog' – Greek *kuon* and Latin *canis* – can be seen edging towards each other to the point where they are virtually sniffing each other's bottoms. The word **hound** comes from quite different etymological roots, and in English usage refers specifically to a hunting dog. (Doesn't **riding to hounds** suggest something much more vigorous than 'riding alongside a dog'?) Thus we have fox*hounds* but sheep*dogs*. In German the sheepdog breed is known as Schäferhund, but other dogs used for herding sheep are called Hirtenhund. Both terms use the word *hund*, and for a while so did English, but this eventually stopped and 'dog' took over as the main word.

So closely is the fate of the words 'hound' and 'hunt' intertwined that you could be forgiven for thinking they share a common linguistic ancestor. This is not the case: the very, very Old English verb *huntian* comes from *hentan*, meaning 'to seize'. Hound's etymological roots are equally ancient, though: Old English and Old Saxon both have *hund*, and, since we're in the area, let's greet Old Norwegian (*hundr*) and Gothic (*hunds*).

A later hound that pretty well encapsulated the creature's fearsome qualities was *The Hound of the Baskervilles*, Sir Arthur Conan Doyle's (still scary) Sherlock Holmes novel, originally published in monthly parts in *The Strand* magazine from August 1901 to April 1902. The fact is, however, that 'hound' has been pretty much replaced by 'dog', and is now restricted mainly to archaic or poetic or high literary forms. The 'Baskerville Dog', for example, would not sound nearly as impressive.

Nonetheless, 'hound' crops up in some unlikely places. **Houndsditch**, for example, is the name of a street in the City of London. The original ditch was built by the Romans as a

defensive trough, and then again by the Danes. The name
Houndsditch first appears in the thirteenth century, and alludes
to the waste that was dumped in it: dung, household rubbish,
old clothes, and a huge, huge number of dead dogs.

To dog

'Dog' really is the most obliging of words – always ready to go
for a run. And it's territorial too: it likes to mark its page in the
dictionary, and does it in a variety of ways. We have barely sniffed
the dog's bottom, but it's time to sink our teeth in a bit deeper.

To dog someone, says the *OED*, means 'to follow like a dog;
to follow pertinaciously or closely; to pursue, track (a person, his
footsteps, etc.), *especially* with hostile intent'. The first recorded
use is from a book called *Vulgaria* (1519) by William Horman
(*c.* 1458–1535), an Oxford scholar who went on to become
headmaster of both Winchester and Eton, two of the topmost
jobs in education at the time. The book consisted of handy Latin
phrases or aphorisms, such as *a tergo instabat*, which he translates as 'our ennemyes **dogged** us at the backe'. **Dogging** was
not always by people set on physical assault. A character in
The Plain-Dealer (1676), the last play to be written by William
Wycherley (1641–1715), complains that 'The Bayliffs dog'd us
hither to the very door'.

Dr Johnson was perhaps the first to lament being pursued
by the paparazzi of his day, in a 1750 edition of *The Rambler*
magazine: 'Eleven painters are now dogging me, for they know
that he who can get my face first will make his fortune'. Over a
hundred years later, in 1872, William Dixon (1821–79) wrote a
study of the life of William Penn in which he noted that 'Spies
and informers dogged his footsteps'.

Dogged

How was the dog viewed by our ancestors? With extreme scepticism, it seems. To have **a dogged harte** in 1540 meant 'to rejoyce in another mans mysfortune' according to the humanist and diplomat Sir Richard Morison (*c*.1510–56). It didn't end there. 'Ill-tempered, surly, sullen, morose' is how the *OED* summarizes a rash of bad press for dogs from 1400 to 1852. **Dogged** also shares a sense with the adjective 'crabbed', which dates from the same period and has meant disagreeable, perverse, churlish, irritable and so on. The designation arose in German too, according to the brothers Grimm (great etymologists, as well as compilers of folk tales), apparently 'because these animals are malicious and do not easily let go what they have seized'.

'Crabbed' or 'crabby' are still very far from being compliments, but 'dogged' has turned a corner and now has a much more positive sense. That doggy tenacity is what eventually swung it for the canines, and this rise in the fortunes of 'dogged' must have coincided with an improvement in relations between man and dog. It starts with Dr Johnson commending one of the Dukes of Devonshire for 'a dogged veracity' in 1779, takes a slight dip in 1818 thanks to Sir Walter Scott, in his adventure tale *Rob Roy*, describing 'an air of stupid impenetrability, which might arise either from conscious innocence or from dogged resolution', and then slowly claws its way, paw by paw, to near-respectability thanks to positive dog talk in books such as Charles Kingsley's *Water Babies* (1863): 'He was such a little dogged, hard, gnarly, foursquare brick of an English boy'.

To be dogged is to be persistent, tenacious and to some extent just as cussed and perverse as in the bad old days, but it's won a new respectability through all that hard work. In some hands it even became a national trait. Hilaire Belloc (1870–1953), the writer of cautionary verses, wrote in 1902 of a time when British people started to romanticize Britain's '**dogged determination**, bull-dog pluck, the stubborn spirit of the island race, and so forth'. The phrase 'dogged determination' has become a bit of a cliché. In fact, so closely associated are the two words that using them together is regarded almost as a tautology.

When **doggedness** was less admired, that churlishness also prompted a phrase that recalls one of Aesop's fables. This was the one about the dog who went to sleep in a manger, surrounded by hay. When he was awoken by some of the other animals on the farm, he was so crotchety that he prevented the ox and the horse from coming anywhere near the hay to eat it. The ox was heard to mutter, 'People often begrudge others what they cannot enjoy themselves,' and that was the beginning of the expression **dog in the manger**. The fable was first cited in English in a work by the physician William Bullein called A *Dialogue against the fever pestilence* (1564), where he wrote: 'Like unto cruell Dogges lyng in a Manger, neither eating the Haye themselves nor sufferyng the Horse to feed thereof hymself.'

Doggerel

Dogs are many things to many people, but they are not poets, nor should they claim to be. **Doggerel** is a description applied to 'comic verse, usually irregular in measure' (*Collins*). 'Worthless verses' adds *Chambers*. Pretty compelling evidence, it seems, and once again, who's at the centre of it all? The dog.

The word 'dog' has long been used in a contemptuous sense in certain contexts. We have had **dog-rimes** (it's not a compliment) by the writer and translator John Florio in 1611. And in the nineteenth century many writers were very rude about people writing in **dog-Latin** or **dog-Greek**, which was a sort of public school shorthand for 'not very good'.

In a slightly more elegant way, Geoffrey Chaucer (*c.* 1343–1400) mocked **rym doggerel** in 1386, and George Puttenham (?1529–91), the reputed author of *The Arte of English Poesie,* and a man, therefore, who could be said to know a thing or two about verse, scoffed that 'A rymer that will be tyed to no rules at all … such maner of Poesie is called in our vulgar, ryme dogrell'. The main criticism of such verses, from early times to the nineteenth century, was that their rhythm was irregular; the carping about their contents came later.

John Taylor (?1578–1653), who came from a humble background to achieve a reputation as 'the water-poet' of London's waterways, may have been as honest as his own verses deserved when he wrote: 'In doggrell Rimes my Lines are writ/ As for a Dogge I thought it fit'. All sorts of unflattering descriptions attached themselves to doggerel in later years, from 'bastard' (sixteenth century) to 'bad or trivial' (seventeenth century). The *OED* isn't sure exactly why doggerel comes from dog, but the nineteenth definition of the word 'dog' is 'bad, spurious, bastard, mongrel'. This is the sense that lies behind doggerel, whose mongrel status is underlined by the fact that it can also be spelt 'dogerel, doggerell, doggrell, dogrell, doggril and dogrel'.

This contemptuous sense of dog has, sadly, dogged dog's reputation for years. Somehow the associations with dog are mostly either comical or pathetic. The discarded tip of a spent cigarette, filtered or not, which you'd have to be pretty desperate to try to relight, has been called a **dog-end** since 1935, when Hippo Neville immortalized it in his book *Sneak Thief on the Road*: '"Dog-ends," said Yank. "Dust, funny mixings, ten a pennies, cigarette ends out of the gutter."'

If you don't take proper care of this book, and don't mind it falling into some pretty dodgy company (see Chapter 17), it will end up with crumpled corners, and thus will merit the description **dog-eared**. This rather poetic phrase was first used by William Cowper (1731–1800) in a volume of verses produced in 1784. The reference runs as follows: 'Let reverend churls his ignorance rebuke,/ Who starve upon a dog's-ear'd Pentateuch'. **To dog-ear** a book was originally regarded as an act of conscious vandalism, a grave offence first described in around 1659 by the Hon. Mrs Sarah Osborn: 'To ruffle, dogs-ear, and contaminate by base Language and spurious censures the choicest leaves of a book'. The shameful practice of **dog-earing**, i.e. making an impromptu bookmark by folding down the corner of a page, persists to the present day.

Sleeping dogs

Why are we told to **let sleeping dogs lie**? The phrase is the inverse of the phrase **to wake a sleeping dog**, written first in 1562 in a book of proverbs and epigrams by John Heywood (?1497–?1580): 'It is ill wakyng of a sleapyng dogge'. The *OED* defines that rather laboriously as 'some person or influence which is for the present quiet, but if aroused will create disturbance'. However proverbial that first entry was, it came into sharper, more practical application in 1607 in a statement of Edward Topsell (*c*.1572–1625), who can lay some claim to having been the David Attenborough of his day. His love of animals featured in several volumes, including *The History of Four-footed Beasts* (1607).

Topsell also wrote *The History of Serpents* (1608), which, by pure coincidence, included the line, 'It is good therefore if you have a Wife, that is ... unquiet and contentious, to let her alone, not to wake an angry Dog'. As the phrase moved into the nineteenth century, it was suffused with the deeply dignified joking of the era, as seen in *Frederick the Great* (1864), the last major work by Thomas Carlyle (1795–1881). This includes the remark, 'Friedrich is not the man to awaken Parliamentary **sleeping-dogs**'. Sleeping dogs were, by now, irreversibly metaphorical.

Going to the dogs

There is, perhaps inevitably, a UK blog called **Going to the Dogs**, in which the author gives the government a good roasting every few days. The phrase 'going to the dogs' can mean to wend one's way to a greyhound race meeting, of course, but the proverbial use of 'to the dogs' means 'to destruction or ruin' as in **to go, send or throw to the dogs**.

The phrase is first noted in one of the great early works of British pedantry, the Latin–English *Thesaurus* of Thomas Cooper (*c*. 1517–94). This majestic book, an early draft of which was accidentally thrown in the fire by Mrs Cooper and then painstakingly rewritten, includes the entry: '*Addicere aliquem canibus*, to bequeath hym to dogs'. The idea of someone or something being thrown to dogs was equivalent to tossing a piece of meat at them: the person or thing was as expendable. Shakespeare made use of this in *As You Like It* (1600), in an ill-tempered exchange between Celia and her cousin Rosalind. Celia asks, 'Why Cosen, why Rosalind: Cupid have mercie, Not a word?' Rosalind replies, 'Not one to throw at a dog.' Celia comes back with, 'No, thy words are too precious to be cast away upon curs.' In fact, Jesus used a similar expression just before he expelled a demon from the daughter of the Syrophoenician woman in the

Book of Matthew when he said, 'It is not meet to take the children's bread, and to cast it to dogs.' But this testy use of throwing something to the dogs has influenced all similar expressions since.

The first use of the phrase **gone to the dogs** came in a sermon given in 1619 by Robert Harris (1580–1658), when he preached upon the causes and dangers of drunkenness: 'One is coloured, another is foxt [drunk], a third is gone to the dogs'. The American writer Washington Irving (1783–1859) gave the phrase a further literary twist when, in his book A *History of New-York from the Beginning of the World to the End of the Dutch Dynasty* (1809), he described the behaviour of Peter Stuyvesant, the founder of New York. Angered by the Yankees' constant sniping 'his wrath was terrible. He … threw diplomacy to the dogs … giving them their choice of sincere and honest peace, or open and iron war.' Irving, the Bill Bryson of his day, was feeling so playful with this book that he wrote the work under the pen-name Diedrich Knickerbocker, from which all subsequent knickerbockers derive. From Cooper's hands to Irving's, the phrase has evolved from meaning 'to actively consign something to ruin or destruction' to a more internal, systemic form of decay.

Dog eat dog

It may have been a dog's dinner of a meal, but everyone knows it's a jungle out there, and no creature knows that better than a dog. Really? Well, that seems to be the general view, as the poet Charles Gray put it in a letter in 1858: 'I cannot promise any special instruction, and shall take no fee. "**Dog does not eat dog**" is the saying, you know.'

Gray was paraphrasing Marcus Terentius Varro (116–27 BC),

who was considered by some contemporaries to have been the greatest Roman scholar of them all. Certainly he was a tireless collector of proverbs, and something of a whiz as a bee-keeper too. One of the most famous sayings he collected was Canis caninam non est (**A dog does not eat a dog's flesh**). Brewer's Dictionary of Phrase and Fable (1923) lists '**Dog don't eat dog**' and compares it to 'There's honour among thieves'.

This is, of course, undoubtedly true. Cannibalism is unknown among dogs, and yet the phrase **dog eat dog** has arisen, maybe to emphasize just how mad and bad a world it really is, and the sorts of pressure it puts people under to behave in an uncharacteristic way. Our first sniff of it comes from *The Milk and Honey Route; A Handbook for Hobos* by Dean Stiff (real name Nels Anderson) published in 1931: 'He knows and lives the justice of the jungle as well as he knows and lives the dog-eat-dog code of the main stem.' Evidently, this is one hobo who knows his Varro. The phrase was certainly on the streets by then.

The phrase has also been used ironically, first in the novel *Taxi!* (1963) by Maurice Levinson: 'No woman can call herself weak if she is prepared to throw herself pell-mell into the "dog-eat-dog" kind of driving that goes on in the West End'.

Dog's dinner

In 1934, or perhaps we should say between then and 1954, if you wanted to give someone a mild or slightly backhanded compliment about their appearance, you would probably have said, 'You look like the **dog's dinner**'. The phrase is first cited in C.L. Anthony's play *Touch Wood*, first performed in 1934: 'Why have you got those roses in your hair? You look like the dog's dinner.' This was praise to a woman, as was a sentence from a 1945 edition of Penguin New Writing: 'A dizzy blonde all dressed up like a dog's dinner'. But the tough-guy novelist J.S. Curtis applied it to an overdressed man in his 1936 work *The Gilt Kid*: 'The geezer … was dolled up like a dog's dinner with a white tie and all.'

This usage continued until 1954. What happened then is a slight mystery, but for some reason this use of 'dog's dinner' was sent to the dog-house until it emerged in a different form seventeen years later, by when it had been flipped on its head. Perhaps this lukewarm praise had reached a sort of dead end: maybe we decided to get real. At any rate, when a character in John Wainwright's *The Last Buccaneer* (1971) refers to the north of England as 'a dog's dinner of hovels, dives and drinking dens' there is no longer any ambiguity about whether the phrase is complimentary or not.

In fact there are parallels with another phrase, less used now, but popular in its day. Partridge, in his *Dictionary of Slang*, dates **dog's breakfast** from 1937 and defines it as 'a mess'. The first mainstream quotation is from *The Times* in 1959: 'He can't make head or tail of it … It's a complete dog's breakfast.' As construed then, it's not aimed at a person, but an idea. Or here again from *The Times* in 1963, notably only eighteen years after the cessation of Allied operations in Europe: 'The warders … are very angry and have rejected the latest War Office offer as totally unacceptable. They feel the offer is a bit of a dog's breakfast.'

It may have been the popularity of 'dog's breakfast' that caused 'dog's dinner' to be rehoused under the general heading 'total mess'. Was it accidental, or was dog's dinner mark one originally confined to novels, while dog's dinner mark two was the preferred terminology of newspapers? We're still chewing that one over.

Shaggy dog story

David Low, in the *New York Times Magazine* in 1940, wrote an essay on 'The logical lunacy of "Shaggy Dog"', which may be our first printed reference to that term. The *Penguin Dictionary of Literary Terms* defines it thus: 'An improbable kind of yarn, often long and spun out, which, as a rule, does *not* have a witty or surprise ending; but comes, rather, to a deflating and quasi-humorous conclusion'. Exactly. It's the sense of inevitable disappointment that one finds so dispiriting about **shaggy dog stories**: it's hard not to walk away from them feeling that your time has been wasted and that you would really quite like those five minutes of your life back again. And yet you curse yourself because you couldn't guess where that stupid and, only in retrospect, predictable twist could have come from.

Doggy style

What springs to mind when you see the words **doggy** (or **doggie**) **style**? There is of course the style of swimming (better known as **doggy paddle**) in which the body remains more or less vertical in the water and is propelled forward by paddling with the hands and feet. But there is another sense of 'doggy style' that demands attention.

The *OED*'s only recognition of the phrase is a quotation from 1981 by the late, great rock journalist Lester Bangs, quoted in *Psychotic Reactions*: 'They did it **doggie-style** and rocked so mighty they damn near broke the bedposts', which gives you a fair idea of the intensity of the manoeuvre involved, but not of the nuts and bolts of the technique. However, if you have ever observed two dogs copulating, you will be aware that doggy style is a classic rear-entry position. To put it a little more bluntly, it's a style of sexual intercourse in which the man crouches behind his chosen partner and effects an entrance therefrom. 'Doggy' underlines the difference between this and the face-to-face, human-to-human 'missionary position'. Doggy style is animalistic: the adjective **doggish**, now obsolete, meant 'brutish, bestial, sensual' in 1594. No wonder that the phrase **coming from behind** has such a high snigger factor.

The almost acceptable face of 'doggy style' is the rapper Snoop Doggy Dogg (real name, or the closest we'll get to a real name, Calvin Cordozar Broadus Jr), whose first solo album was entitled *Doggystyle*. In *The Kama Sutra* 'doggy style' is upgraded to the position known as 'the congress of the cow', which is high praise indeed, given the esteem in which cows are held in the Hindu religion. The doggy-style position is not designed for chatting. In fact, the person in front, woman or man, can't even get a good view of their partner without craning their neck, though having a face-to-face chat may not be uppermost in one's mind at the time.

Dog's bollocks

In a society built on aspirations to tabloid excellence, the **dog's bollocks** really is the last word in praise. The generally held view is that it was given to the world by *Viz* magazine in 1989. A strapline on the front cover claimed it was the dog's bollocks, i.e. the best of issues. *Viz* may not have coined the expression, but it has always been such a skilled adapter of whatever was out there on the street – or the pavement – that it's no wonder it picked this one up.

Other theories abound. The eminently respectable Eric Partridge, in his *Dictionary of Slang* has a plethora of expressions to do with dogs, including **dog's ballocks** – note the 'a' rather than 'o' – which is defined as 'the typographical colon-dash' (:-). Partridge also notes the term **dog's prick** for that favourite of women's magazines, the exclamation mark (!).

'Dog's bollocks' outshines, out-booms and generally outsmarts the more sedate **cat's whiskers** or **bee's knees** (both 1923) or **cat's pyjamas** (1925) by a country mile. The *OED* defines 'dog's bollocks' as 'the very best, the acme of excellence', but doesn't venture into the matter of how this came to be, though it's hard not to agree with the assessment of a contributor to urban-dictionary.com that 'It refers to the fact that a dog can lick his own balls, which seems to be an ideal situation for any single dog'.

There is a crucial difference between 'the dog's bollocks' and just 'bollocks' or 'ballocks' – first cited in 'For God's sake, don't talk ballocks, Johnson', from *Mister Johnson* (1939) by Joyce Cary. **Bollocks** were first spotted in 1744, being a playful variation of the older – by about 750 years – **ballocks**, which also meant testicles. It's amazing what a vowel change can achieve. Bollocks still haven't been around for as long as ballocks, but bollocks are everywhere today, while the humble ballocks has retired to lick its wounds.

'Bollocks' is a word you can almost say in front of very small children without feeling that you have **dropped a bollock** (first used in 1970 by Peter Laurie in his book *Scotland Yard: A Personal Inquiry*), or **getting a bollocking** (first seen in literature in the 1950 novel *To the Victors the Spoils* by Colin MacInnes). 'Bollocks' basically means 'rubbish' or 'pants' (see page 323), but **the bollocks** is a term of high praise – and it's a confusion that films such as *The 51st State* (2001) have capitalized on.

So from 'the bollocks' (meaning 'very good') to 'the dog's bollocks' (meaning 'very good to the power of ten'). That juxtaposition of 'bollocks' with the doggy element is a sublime combination. Maybe we like it because dogs are so marvellously unabashed about the amount of time they're prepared to devote – in public – to trying to swallow their own genitalia, an activity that most men would – perhaps literally, perhaps not – give their right arm for.

The only other part of its body that a dog takes as much interest in – and this goes for bitches too – is the tail. No wonder, then, that the postwar twentieth century also gave us the phrase **like a dog with two tails** to express utter joy, the theory being that, given how much dogs enjoy chasing their tails, one-tailed happiness is great, but only half as good as twin-tailed ecstasy.

Doggy business

Dogs are marvellously versatile. Take a phrase such as **dog knot**: in engineering terms, 'dog knot' refers to a section of rod or pipe that enlarges so that it doesn't come out of the hole in which it's inserted. However, the term also applies in doggy love to what is known as 'the inflation of the *carpus cavernosum* of a dog's penis during intercourse'. The truth of this entry is not super-reliable, and some older or less patient readers should fast-forward to the next section, but the source for this definition (the extra-ordinary urbandictionary.com) is worth pursuing since its list of words is, frankly, the dog's bollocks, besides speaking with illiterate, zit-faced articulacy about our continuing love affair with dogs.

As most of urbandictionary.com's contributors seem to be college kids, and American college kids at that, most entries are self-defining, and some, frankly, are a little juvenile. The great majority bring us back time and time again to sex. **To dog nose**, for example, means that 'a male urinates and then wipes his wet cold penis on his partner'. Have you ever tried **dog tubbing**? It means 'attempting to insert one's testicles into a female's ass during sex. So named because it is as difficult to keep the nuts in the butt as it is to keep an unwilling dog in a bath tub.' Doesn't it make you nostalgic for those college days?

Some entries tell us about the beguiling and inviting – is that sarcastic enough? – state of youth culture, as in the apparently inoffensive **dog people**, which actually means 'lads that do piss themselves at parties like raves and punk festivals that do go on all night'. Others betoken a swipe at relations with authority, such as the mysterious **dog roza**, defined as 'a police officer in charge of a police dog'. Others are radiantly inventive. **Dog perch**, for example, is another term for 'beer belly', and an English one at that to judge from the example: 'Have you seen the size of that bloke's dog perch?'

But urbandictionary.com isn't obsessed only with sex, oh no. The other thing for which dogs are famous is excretion, and this subject receives copious attention too. For example, **dog poo sandwich** means 'something that is absolutely rubbish'. Loving (if that's the right word) attention is paid to various types of dog poo: **dog oogie** is defined as 'bright reddy brown dog turds with an orange/yellow center, similar to an onion bahjee', while **dog leg** is – I should have guessed – 'a large turd that sticks up out of the water'. **Dog skidder**, anyone? 'The quarter size … smeared poop dot left by a dog wiping its ass on your carpet.' Verily, all human life, and doggy faeces, is there.

And there are, of course, so many more demure doggy expressions, from **doggone it** and **dogsbody** to **lying doggo** and **hair of the dog**. But for now we must toss this particular bone aside and go chase some other rabbits. Well, actually, there is one other doggy word that we touch upon later. That's the reasonably recent sexual proclivity known as **dogging** (see page 455). Look at if you must, but don't blame us if you're shocked. And don't, for Dog's sake, say we didn't warn you.

Chapter Seventeen

Dodgy Dealings

*T*here is a lot to be said for reading the 2007 edition of *Archbold: Criminal Pleading, Evidence and Practice* if you need a law book. But *Balderdash & Piffle* is no law book, so we're not going to be dealing with the language of formal criminality. The police, the courts, the whole 'Do you find this person guilty or not guilty?' experience relies on a language all its own. We prefer to inveigle ourselves in among the slightly uneasy-looking types hanging around the back of the court, who might be popping out every now and then to squawk on their mobiles, or to light up a Lambert & Butler. These people have their own sub-language, a vocabulary in which crime is condoned more than condemned. It is a colourfully amoral world of slang and phrase-making, the kind of thing you find in the pub, in the press or in the police notebook – but rarely in the court record.

The devil, as we are constantly told, has all the best tunes. The forces of law and order, on the other hand, do not have all the best words. There is, as someone very clever once put it, a morality to geometry. Straight is good because it connects two points directly: a straight line has no wiggles. Euclid, the father of European geometry, defined a line as 'breadthless length', and a straight line as a line that 'lies evenly with the points on itself'.

These straight lines are moral entities: they are described just as you would someone's good behaviour, or their determination to make a new start and clean up their act. There is, as a result, something effortlessly charismatic about badly behaved language. It has verbal charisma far in excess of the action – be it a street mugging or a corporate scam – and the consequences that it describes. The fact is that when you deviate from the true and rightful path, you are, literally, swerving into trouble.

To be **dodgy** or to hold dodgy goods is not a capital offence. It is, though, a deviation from the path of straightforwardness. The language framework of right and wrong is coloured in these terms. If someone is 'straight' or 'direct', he or she is also 'good'. Divert from this and you're in a different terrain altogether. Dodgy sits alongside **bent** (either numismatic or uniformed), **shifty, perverted, off the straight and narrow**. Dodgy words are dodgy because they are not sticking to the path of rightness: they wobble, jump and wriggle off the leash. But dodgy still has enough of a connection to the original path to be potentially a detour, not an actual abandonment of the true way. And that's why we sometimes find it endearing, not downright evil. It's bending the law, not snapping it like a twig.

So far, so dodgy. But the language of dodginess creates another set of opposites. It is unashamedly tribalist, even racist. Words and phrases that have their linguistic roots in English, such as 'jack the lad' (see page 336) have a cheerful, almost playful innocence about them – unless you come home to find them rifling through your drawers. But these words clash with the much less flattering connotations of terms related to foreigners – **Jew, Welsh, Turk, gyp** and **thug** – whose shiftiness almost always used to be linked to their racial background. Nowadays, anti-immigrant feeling can express itself in different ways, but there is less of a tendency for the name of a specific ethnic group to be used as a byword for dodgy behaviour.

Dodgy

The adjective **dodgy** means 'risky, difficult or dangerous' (*Collins*). If you've ever bought a **dodgy motor** or **felt a bit dodgy**, you'll know that the word also means 'shifty, iffy, a bit strange'. But the word itself has played fast and loose with dictionary compilers over the years. 'Dodgy' is not included in Francis Grose's *Dictionary of the Vulgar Tongue*, which contains all the dodgiest lingo from 1785, but Eric Partridge defines **dodge** as 'a shrewd and artful expedient, an ingenious contrivance', and quotes some lines from Charles Dickens's *Pickwick Papers* (1837): 'It was all false, of course?' 'All, sir,' replied Mr Weller, 'reg'lar do, sir; artful dodge.' Dickens, of course, should know: he gave us Oliver Twist's friend the **Artful Dodger.**

The origins of 'dodgy' are suitably arcane. Our first sight of it is from an 1861 book by Andrew Wynter with the unlikely title of *Our Social Bees: or Pictures of Town and Country Life*. The context, curiously, is nothing to do with bees: 'Beggars divide themselves in several classes: the humorous, the poetical, the sentimental, the dodgey [sic], and the sneaking'.

The other words, such as 'humorous' and 'sentimental', are all in the mix too. A **dodgy geezer** will not kill you, but he might not hesitate for too long before separating you from the contents of your wallet if you're silly enough to leave it lying around. 'Dodgy' is a halfway house between good and evil. We tolerate, even admire, **dodginess**, finding expressions such as 'It fell off the back of a lorry' so much sweeter than 'I stole it'. It's the behaviour of a chancer, but not of a hardened felon.

'Dodgy' was in the news in a big way in 2003, when various broadcasters, including Channel 4 and the BBC, discovered that one of the documents underpinning the Blair government's justification for invading Iraq had been 'plagiarized' from an article by the scholar Ibrahim al-Marashi, written for the September 2002 issue of the *Middle East Review of International Affairs*. The discovery led to the item being labelled the **dodgy dossier**, which was as direct a rebuke as you could get. The dossier was dodgy because it had been 'ripped off' (see page 378). In fact, once the war had begun, we discovered that the dossier was just plain wrong because Iraq had no weapons of mass destruction capable of being fired at Britain, let alone WMD that would give us only forty-five minutes to prepare. 'Dodgy', it turns out, was inadequate to the task of describing the level to which we had all been duped. The dossier had, in fact, been **sexed up**.

That term was an Americanism first spotted in 1942 and it meant, fairly obviously, to put a little va-va voom into something, 'giving something a sexual flavour'. In those days it was literally sex, but in 1958 the *Observer* was reporting about 'the business of "sexing up" the titles of foreign films'.

By the way, **dossier** had a slightly dodgy past too, and very different from its ultra-professional image. The French word *dossier*, anglicized in 1880, refers to a bundle of papers bulging so much that it looks like someone's back, for which the French is *dos*. That word gives all sorts of *dos*-related words, such as the late eighteenth-century **doss** and the early nineteenth-century **doss-house**, which was where you rested your **dodgy back** if you didn't have a lot of money.

Underhand

The word **underhand** is a bit of a gent compared to the sort of company kept by other words in this section. *Chambers Dictionary* defines it as 'surreptitious', adding 'with the hand below the elbow or shoulder'. It doesn't say why, but this meaning stretches back to 1592. In terms of the geometry of honesty, if a straight line is totally upfront and pukka, 'underhand' represents a kink, a sudden dive to below the table while your eye is distracted by what's happening above. With reference to people, 'underhand' – defined simply as 'not straightforward' – has been dated to 1842. But its roots lie in a most surprising area: archery. 'Thus the underhande [shaft] must have a small breste, to go cleane awaye oute of the bowe,' wrote Roger Ascham (?1515–68), one of Britain's finest toxophilites or archery lovers. 'To shoot underhand' was a common enough archery term, though it could also mean, as it still does, 'to keep one's hands below the body when doing a certain activity'.

But during the sixteenth century, 'underhand' went three ways: one part carried on working with the sense of 'quietly' or 'behind the scenes'; another part went 'secretive but above-board' (to borrow a seventeenth-century phrase from card play); while a third became 'shady'. We have plenty of evidence from the sixteenth century to support all three of these activities, but it seems that the covert and stealthy underhand snatched the limelight. The Tudor diplomat and scholar Sir Thomas Elyot (*c*.1490–1546) equated underhand with stealing in a 1538 edition of his dictionary. In truth, underhand still has that sense today.

Underhand cricket (i.e. cricket played underarm) was first noted in 1850. These days, underarm bowling is rare, but not unprecedented, and certainly not much loved. Ask any New Zealander about underarm bowling and you may have to take

a few steps back because Kiwi memories are still fresh from
1 February 1981, when the Australian captain, Greg Chappell,
ordered his brother, Trevor, to bowl the last ball of the match
underarm. Chappell, T. bowled a daisy-cutter, right along the ground,
which prevented the New Zealand batsman Brian McKechnie from
clouting the six runs his side needed to tie the third of five games in
the final round of the Benson & Hedges World Cup Series at
Melbourne. Very underhand, and pretty dodgy too.

Swindler

The German word *schwindler* means 'giddy-minded person or
cheat', especially, we are told, 'in money matters'. It stands behind
the English word **swindler**, which means to cheat someone of
money or in some other way defraud them. The *OED* tells us that
the word arrived in England via a boat full of German-Jewish
immigrants hoping to make a new life for themselves and maybe
introduce some of their own words to their new homeland.

In fact, the main waves of Jewish immigration from the
Continent were in the nineteenth century, but the date 'swindler'
arrived is stamped at 1762, which is very early indeed. It was
regarded as a **cant** word, 'cant' being a secret language spoken
by a distinct group of people, whether beggars, thieves or those
belonging to particular religions. (They were, if you like, outcasts,
reacting to respectable society that had said to them, 'You can't
come in.' Can't, cant: oh, never mind ...)

In medieval England the occupations of Jews were regulated
by the Crown, while Christians endured certain restrictions
imposed by canon law. One pursuit open to Jews but not to
Christians (at least not in public) was money-lending. Thus – in
the careful wording of the *OED* – 'the name of Jew came to be

associated in the popular mind with usury and any extortionate practices that might be supposed to accompany it, and gained an opprobrious sense'.

Lots of rude references to 'grasping Jews' continued for centuries. The *OED*'s most recent reference to the verb **to jew** is from *Harper's Magazine* in May 1972: 'Jew the fruitman down for his last Christmas tree'. In that same year and month the British magazine *New Society* used the verb in the same sense of beating someone down or haggling over a price: 'I got jewed down ... over the cheap offer'. Not surprisingly, you won't find the word featured so prominently these days in *Harper's*, or at all in the now defunct *New Society*. Indeed, it is mildly surprising it had a life in respectable print as late as 1972.

Phrase books from former times contain a profusion of phrases that mention Jews, evidence of the – shall we say – lively feelings generated by them. Captain Francis Grose defines **Jew** as 'an over-reaching dealer, or hard, sharp fellow; an extortioner'. His explanation is both geographically and sociologically concise: 'the brokers behind St Clement's Church in the Strand [London] were formerly called Jews by their brethren the taylors'. This wasn't a character reference, but a job description: Jews were fulfilling their historical role as useful but unloved money brokers. Grose says this was in use from around 1600.

But as the Jewish community began to find its feet, so – as with any other community finding itself among the nouveaux riches – its standards of taste became the subject of much vulgar abuse. For example, **Jew's Rolls-Royce** is quoted by Partridge (although he doesn't reveal from where) as a 1938 expression for 'a Jaguar motor-car'. Its prominent features included 'much chromium plating and all that'. We can only guess at what 'all that' refers to.

Rip-off

A **rip-off** is a swindle. It isn't a very old word, but in its first incarnation could apply to both a person – a thief, in other words – and 'a fraud, a swindle; a racket; an instance of exploitation, especially financial'. The verb **rip** has a harshness that adds a sense of outrage to 'rip-off', suggesting that our trust has been abused. Some sweet-talking son of a con-man has been up to his tricks and we're left holding ... Well, that's just the point. He's now holding what is rightfully ours.

The word 'rip-off' first came to our attention in the pages of the *Manchester Guardian Weekly* in May 1970, when an appalled drug dealer, discussing the inhabitants of the Haight Ashbury area of San Francisco, was reported as saying, 'You have burn artists [fraudulent dope peddlers], rip-offs [thieves], and snitchers [police spies]'. But only a few months later *Melody Maker*, that other upholder of left-of-centre views, defined 'rip-off' as 'capitalist exploitation'. A good deal of fudging followed. The person who was a rip-off soon came to operate both within and outside the law. At the same time, the thing that was a rip-off soon came to operate both within the corporate and non-corporate worlds.

The rip-off is fuelled by the violence of that verb 'rip', which in this sense means, and has meant ever since William Caxton printed it around 1477, 'To cut, pull, or tear (anything) away from something else in a vigorous manner'. The *OED* says that 'rip' is 'of somewhat obscure origin and history', though there doesn't seem much mystery about the Frisian verb *rippe*, meaning 'to rip or tear', or the Flemish *rippen*, meaning 'to rip or strip off roughly'.

This verb gives us the 1967 US slang usage 'to rip off', which means 'to steal or embezzle'. In 1967 a **hustler** was described as someone who not only 'burns' people for money, but also 'rips off' goods for money. A **racketeer**, in other words. This was not an impulsive act of street crime: it was planned and organized. Over the years since, it has been applied to people embezzling within an organization, such as former vice-president Spiro Agnew (1919–96), who in 1974 was accused by the Black Panther movement of 'ripping off tax money'. More recently, the verb 'to rip off' has gone from blue collar to white collar: in the 1980s–90s, if your car had been **ripped off**, it had been stolen. In her 1981 novel A *Death in the Faculty* Alison Cross wrote that 'Soldiers are always ripping things off, from their own outfit, from the enemy, everything.'

It has been suggested anecdotally that the noun 'rip-off' has its roots in drug culture. An unscrupulous marijuana seller (as opposed to a thoroughly principled one) selling a brick or key (kilo) of some murky substance that wasn't really the drug required would cover up his unscrupulousness by placing a small amount of genuine marijuana in a corner of the packet. The unsuspecting buyer rips open the corner, finds the real stuff and thinks all is well. Little do they know that the rest of it is actually shoe polish or some other non-narcotic.

Blackmail

There is still something swashbuckling about the sound of **blackmail**. It sounds like a cross between Black Beauty and chain mail, though that noble exterior hides a sordid truth. If you had been eavesdropping on someone and had heard some item of gossip, you might be tempted to contact the people you'd overheard and advise them that unless they made it worth your while to keep silent, you might find yourself with no alternative but to forward the embarrassing information to the last person they'd wish to know it. This is a course of action that, you could argue, puts the threatener in a worse light than the threatened.

Collins Concise Dictionary defines 'blackmail' thus: 'the act of attempting to obtain money by intimidation, as by threats to disclose discreditable information'. There are other definitions to do with putting pressure on or trying to influence people, but that first one is the classic definition. It is not, however, the beginning of the story, which is buried in heather and thistles, with a paper date of 1552 and, no doubt, an oral history long preceding that. It's defined thus by the *OED*: 'A tribute formerly exacted from farmers and small owners in the border counties of England and Scotland, and along the Highland border, by free-booting chiefs, in return for protection or immunity from plunder'.

The picture we have, then, some time in the sixteenth century, is of a big man called Jock holding a club and standing opposite a smaller man, called Jack, and demanding money in return for not hitting him. It was a threat, compliance with which led to something (i.e. violence) *not* happening. Hush money, as it's now known. But as time went on and society became a little less rugged and a little more devious – less *Braveheart*, more *Smarthead* – the threat came to be exacted in a different way, with an ever longer back-story that only began to emerge three or four centuries later.

By the time it had become a popular, if unsavoury, mainstay of twentieth-century detective stories, the picture had changed. Instead of the club, Jock now held something personal to Jack. Jack had done (or become involved with) something dodgy, whether cheating at cards or on his wife, and Jock had found out – perhaps by a spot of eavesdropping. It wasn't simply 'Pay me or I'll hit you'. It was: 'If you don't want the details of this story to emerge, you'd better give me some money', or in some other way comply with my wishes.

This form of menace is, of course, morally equivocal. It cuts both ways, and neither party wins. The initially guilty person thinks, 'Oh, no! Discovered!' But his or her next reaction is to think, 'How dare that person try to extract money with threats!' Morally, it's one of the most twisted ways in which justice can be pursued.

The word **mail** is an early Scandinavian word for 'payment or tax'. To this word were attached qualifying adjectives: either black or, much later – and this time for a good purpose – white. Blackmail can also be emotional – and it can work out more expensive in the long run. And just in case you thought you'd get ahead of the game by merging 'blackmail' with 'blogging' to produce a brilliant new word, **blogmail**, you're too late: Google already has about 83,000 (and counting) instances of that neologism.

Bung

The word **bung** used to be a mid-fifteenth-century term for a stopper to a bottle or cask; a mid-sixteenth-century purse or a pickpocket; a nineteenth-century slang word for a lie, and – as most of us know it today – a twentieth-century word for a huge bribe. Football, ever a sport with its eye on a fast buck, has more or less monopolized the lucrative bung market these days. Thanks to the soft sound of 'bung' and its sonic coincidence with other words more comical than threatening, such as 'bang', it doesn't draw a great deal of popular opprobrium. Perhaps you're more likely to think of it in relation to your bath or sink getting **bunged up**, so it seems matey and convivial. As a result, most of us probably regard it as no worse than a bit of backstreet shenanigans involving a crumpled wad of £5 notes.

The 'bung' has archetypally been located, by the media, in a brown envelope, either because it is seen – mistakenly – as a fair day's tip for a hard day's work or because the shabbiness of the enterprise is so at odds with the super-sleek image that football would like to project (see also 'dodgy-dossier', page 373). In reality, the sorts of sums that have been circulating among Premiership football's top brass could not be crammed inside an envelope smaller than a large suitcase.

The 'bung' nouns have a variety of origins. **Bung-hole** comes from an early Dutch word *bonghe*, meaning 'hole'. It has nothing to do with a **football bung**, even if you likened that hole to the aperture into which a dodgy agent or manager bungs (throws) a cheque. The bung may be related to the Old English (and Frisian) *pung*, meaning 'purse'.

The bribe meaning of 'bung' is marked 'criminals' slang' and 'origin unknown' by the *OED*, but we are advised to compare it with the verb **to bung**. That arose in 1825 as a slang way of saying to throw something with a little extra force. The *Daily Chronicle* from 1903 caught the sense nicely with this lively exchange: '"We are police officers. What have you in that parcel?" Stevens replied, "I don't know; I have just had it bunged on to me."'

In March 2006 Lord Stevens of Kirkwhelpington (no relation to the dodgy Stevens just mentioned), a *News of the World* columnist and former head of the Metropolitan Police, was asked by the Football Association to sort out the mess and start issuing a number of red cards. We do not know how much he was 'bunged' – completely legally, of course – for carrying out this public duty, but in December 2006, with his inquiry not yet complete, he announced the provisional results of his examinations into the transfers of 362 professional footballers. The verdict: corruption in English football was not quite as high as had been predicted, though there remained seventeen questionable deals. More of a yellow card, as it turned out.

Hoodlum

San Francisco in the nineteenth century was not the place to be at night if you were alone, unarmed and fearful. Various words were created to describe the type of tough who used to hang out on street corners, perhaps the most evocative of which was **hoodlum**. An early definition was 'a loafing youth of mischievous proclivities'. In 1871 the correspondent of the *Cincinnati Commercial* was clearly of a mind to run for his life, so eager was he 'to escape the bullying of the San Francisco "hoodlums"'.

The Oxford English Dictionary states that 'The name originated in San Francisco about 1870–72, and began to excite attention elsewhere in the US about 1877, by which time its origin was lost, and many fictitious stories, concocted to account for it, were current in the newspapers.'

So even though the word spread across the States and beyond, its origins remain a mystery. The scholar Dr John T. Krumpelmann suggested in 1935 that it was a Germanic construction, the word *Haderlumpe* being German dialect for 'rags or ragman'. A similar word is *Hudellump* or *Hodalump*, meaning 'a ragamuffin or good-for-nothing'. Perhaps hoodlum was just too mean-looking for anyone to get a straight answer out of it.

The word-sleuth Charles Earle Funk quotes various, gloriously unlikely sources to suggest that 'hoodlum' arose due to a cock-up at the printing press. A journalist reporting on a fight between two gangs became jittery that the gang leader called Muldoon would discover his name and do him over, so he changed the name to Noodlum. This name was mispelt by one of the news-paper's compositors as Hoodlum. A likely story.

The hoodlums were said to have picked on San Francisco's burgeoning population of Chinese immigrants. Albert Barrère and Charles Leland, in their far more respectable *Dictionary of Slang, Jargon, and Cant* (1889), claim that the term can be traced to *hood lahnt*, which means 'very lazy mandarin' in pidgin English.

'Hoodlum' was shortened to the simpler **hood** by 1930, though neither word is linked to the type of hood that is a short-ened form of **neighbourhood**, and emerged in the USA in the late 1960s. Nor is there any connection with Britain's own-brand hoodlum, the **hoodie** (see page 310).

Hooligan

Of all the -isms that you might want to be associated with, **hooliganism** is one of the less respectable. *Chambers English Dictionary* defines **hooligan** as 'a street rough', and our first quotation comes from an 1898 edition of the (US) *Daily News*: 'It is no wonder ... that hooligan gangs are bred in these vile, miasmatic byways'. Indeed, the *OED* brings not one, but four references from that same year, testament to the frisson that this word must have induced back then. The third extract is from the *Daily Graphic*, the first US paper to introduce illustrations, and it features a stab at the group's word origins: 'Mr. White ... stated that every Saturday and Sunday night gangs like the "Hooligan gang" came to his house, broke the windows, glass, &c., and made disturbances'. The fourth extract is from the *Westminster Gazette*, and proves not only that the word had crossed the Atlantic, but also that it was reaching over to senses beyond that of street toughs: 'The Khalifa was, after all, only a sort of Soudanese Hooligan'.

Daily newspaper law reports from the summer of 1898 suggest that 'hooligan' is 'a misunderstanding or perversion' of **Hooley's gang**, but there is 'no positive confirmation of this'. There may also have been a rowdy Irish family at large in the 1890s, who inspired a music-hall song, possibly called 'Hooley's Gang', or that the word is named after an Irish hoodlum called **Patrick Hooligan**.

In 1921 the phrase **hooligan navy** was used by Lehmann Hisey in a book with the catchy title of *Sea Grist: A Personal Narrative of Five Months in the Merchant Marine, a Rousing Sea Tale*. It contains the exchange: 'Haven't even been in the Hooligan Navy? Just land lubbers.' Various rag-tag forces have been referred to as a hooligan navy over the years. The term combines rowdiness with a sense of order.

Trouble loves a crowd, and 'hooligan' soon begat other formations. There were the verbs **to hooligan** and **to hooliganize**, which mean 'to behave like a hooligan', and adjectives such as **hooliganesque** and the frankly unfeasible **hooliganic**. 'The avalanche of brutality,' thundered the *Daily Graphic* in 1898, '… under the name of "Hooliganism" … has cast … a dire slur on the social records of South London.'

W.S. Gilbert, one half of the musical team Gilbert and Sullivan, wrote a play called *The Hooligan*, which was inspired by the execution of Dr Crippen in 1910. Based around the prison musings of a condemned man, it is considered to be one of his most interesting works.

If you decide to throw a party at which your guest list consists of hooligans, the chances are that you will be charged with hosting a **hooley**. This has been the word for a noisy party ever since 1877, which is thoroughly confusing, since the word is 'origin unknown', but gives every suggestion of having derived from the word 'hooligan', even though that wasn't noted until 1898. How maddening.

Hornswoggle

Another, even crazier American word that means to cheat, swindle or bamboozle is the early nineteenth-century **hornswoggle**. The *OED* says its origins are 'probably fanciful', and who could disagree, but at the risk of sounding fanciful, it has been suggested that its origins lie in the combination of 'horns' and 'waggle'. That's to say, it's a gesture. If you place your fingers on either side of the head, like horns, and waggle them – probably sticking your tongue out too for good measure – you are doing or giving someone the hornswoggle. This is untested by the *OED*, which is a shame.

To be frank, it isn't the sort of word that we call on much these days, even though, to this writer's eyes, it looks as gnarled and ancient as if it had first been spoken by Dr Samuel Johnson, but clearly that isn't so. Partridge dates its life cycle as 1860–1905. In fact, the *OED*'s entry, from the Virginia Literature Museum, ante-dates that by over thirty years, taking it back to 1829, with its own definition 'to embarrass irretrievably'. It didn't always mean that, though. 'One practical working theory in advertising circles is that the ad's chief function is to hornswoggle the consumer' – prescient words from the *Boston Herald* in 1904. And in an August 2005 obituary of Lord Lane, a former lord chief justice, it was said that he accused fellow judges of 'making lazy, long-winded speeches which "hornswoggled" juries and delayed trials'. It does feel like the sort of word that only a judge could get away with saying, in Britain at least.

Welshing

It wasn't only Jews who had a reputation for swindling. How exactly, for example, did the verb **to welsh** (or **welch**) fall into common parlance during the second half of the nineteenth century as another term for 'to swindle'? The trouble seems to have broken out down at the race course. A **welsher**, according to the *OED*, arose as a term to describe a racing bookie who took money from a punter for a bet and then did a runner. 'Of obscure origin' says the *OED*. Could the editorial team have felt sheepish about coming down hard on a nation that, historically, had done nothing more controversial than dig for coal and sing like angels? It is, presumably, the same sort of neighbourly chippiness in which, viewed from the comfort of England, the Scots are tight with money and the Irish a bit slow on the uptake. In 1860 Lord William Pitt Lennox wrote a book called *Fifty Years' Biographical Reminiscences*, in which he referred to 'a gang of miscreants called Welchers, who make bets with the unwary, which they never dream of paying if they lose'.

Even in the twentieth century, 'to welsh' had only a slightly less offensive meaning – to fail to keep your word. It means as much in an early citing from 1932, and as late as 1982 in an extract from *Schindler's Ark* (filmed as *Schindler's List*) by the famously irascible Australian novelist Thomas Keneally: 'Across his desk [were] crossed copies of angry SS memoranda addressed to army officials and complaining that the army was welching on its arrangement.' The *OED* has no qualifying comment that the word 'welsh' is offensive, though it clearly is.

Turk

Between the sixteenth and very late nineteenth centuries it was common to refer to a wife-beater as a **Turk**. One states this with lots of flashing warning lights as it has now been consigned to history, but one of the *OED*'s entries for the noun 'Turk', after the various political or ethnic ones, refers to citations drawn from 1536 and defines it as 'a cruel, rigorous, or tyrannical man; any one behaving as a barbarian or savage; one who treats his wife hardly'. It adds for good measure 'a bad-tempered or unmanageable man'.

Some other countries shared this mistrust of Turks, including the Persians. In some of their dictionaries the word 'Turk' is explained as 'a beautiful youth, a barbarian, a robber' – the personification, in other words, of the exotic but dangerous and untrustworthy foreigner who will charm the pants off you and then snatch your purse. In the twentieth century the phrase **Young Turks** entered the language as the name given to a group of bright young things who were trying to modernize the Turkish or Ottoman Empire, and who were of course opposed to **Old Turks**. These days, a Young Turk is someone who tries to ring the changes in a medium that is otherwise hostile to novelty, such as David Cameron trying to persuade the Tory party to be less, well, Tory.

Gyp

Having offended the Jews, the Welsh and the Turks, are we running out of people to upset? Not when we have words like **gyp** at our disposal. It means, says *Collins Concise Dictionary*, 'to swindle, cheat or defraud'. Its first proper citation was in 1899 within the rather marvellous phrase 'Gyp this boob with a deuce', quoted in Louis E. Jackson and C.R. Hellyer's *A Vocabulary of Criminal Slang, with Some Examples of Common Usages*, published in 1914. The word 'gyp' is harsh and has truly unpleasant connotations, but the word **gypsy**, from which it derives, has a rather fascinating history. It was formed through what language specialists call aphesis,[1] a process by which the first part of the word drops away. In this case, it was the 'E' of Egyptian, since when gypsies first appeared in England in the early sixteenth century, it was assumed that they were from Egypt. Other examples of aphesis include the 'e' of esquire dropping away to leave squire, acute to cute, and escape-goat to scapegoat.

In the United States the noun 'gyp' has meant 'bitch', as in young female pup, since 1878. But there are four other definitions: 'gyp' is the name for a college servant at Cambridge and Durham universities; a nineteenth-century term for 'pain', probably from the verb **to gee up**, as quoted in *Funk's Standard Dictionary* (1893): 'To give one gyp – To make one smart for anything done'; it's also US slang for a thief; and finally 'a fraudulent action; a swindle'. The last two of these are clearly insults towards gypsies.

Third degree

Any *Balderdash* wordhunters finding themselves about to be given **the third degree** would know that they were in a spot of trouble. These days we would recognize the latent threat in 'They third-degreed Jimmy Dreek good and plenty'. This comes from the 1928 novel *The Astounding Crime on Torrington*

---

1 Aphesis is formed from the Greek preposition *apo* (from) and the fiendishly irregular verb *hiemi* (I send).

Road by William Gillette, the American actor who perfectly embodied Sherlock Homes in the 1920s. **To be third-degreed** or **to get the third degree** means being subject to an intensive examination that, sometimes with uncomfortable literalness, leaves no stone unturned.

Most of us probably intuit that the word 'third' indicates some greater degree of intensity, possibly the highest of all. Compared to third, the second position would, we assume, involve a very serious talking-to and a modest physical threat. For first position you could probably get away with a written questionnaire, and if you didn't tick the box 'Would you like to be tortured?', you would be on your way within a matter of minutes. But there is a deeper and darker secret behind the third degree.

Third-degree burns, which are the most severe type of skin burn, have been known about since 1866. And if you go back to the phrase's origins, you find writers such as Shakespeare employing it to imply the third or final level of intensity, even of drunkenness. Step forward, if you can, Sir Toby Belch in *Twelfth Night* (1601). Olivia says of him: 'For he's in the third degree of drinke: he's drown'd: go looke after him.' It's clear that he shouldn't be left in charge of heavy machinery.

But then, in the eighteenth century, the phrase acquired an additional but crucial sense. The Freemasons, then beginning to formalize their rituals, used it to mean the highest grade in free-masonry, known as 'master-mason'. The mysteries of Freemasonry are a closed book to outsiders, and members can be punished with great severity for breaching its very strict guidelines of secrecy, so we daren't go into too much detail, but suffice it to say that a friend whose friend's father is a member told us that the third degree is the mystical point at which an initiate can get to use the lodge car park between 5 p.m. and 7 p.m. on a weekday. Or something.

Thug

There are two kinds of thug: the upper-case **Thug** and the lower-case **thug**. The former is defined by *Collins* as 'a member of an organization of robbers and assassins in India'. According to *Chambers*, they also used a poison called datura, which is extracted from the thorn-apple genus of the potato family. Thugs were also known as *p'hansigars*, an Urdu word for members of 'a society or cult of professional robbers and murderers who strangled their victims', from *phasi*, the Urdu for 'noose'. Pretty much the same as a Thug, in other words: if you were being strangled by one, you probably wouldn't be asking if they were a Thug or a *p'hansigar*.

The activities of India's Thugs or Thuggees were first described in the writings of the French traveller and lover of all things exotic, Jean de Thévenot (1633–67). These serial killers (for that's what they were) are estimated to have killed anywhere between 50,000 and 200,000 people. From 1831 the Indian authorities began to clamp down on the Thugs, and they were eventually brought to the point of extinction.

Under its entry for Thug, the classic *Hobson-Jobson: Glossary of Colloquial Anglo-Indian Words and Phrases* (1886) defines the word thus:

> Latterly applied to a robber and assassin of a peculiar class,
> who sallying forth in a gang … and in the character of wayfarers,
> either on business or pilgrimage, fall in with other travellers on
> the road, and having gained their confidence, take a favourable
> opportunity of strangling them by throwing their handkerchiefs
> round their necks, and then plundering them and burying their
> bodies.

And just in case you were in any doubt, the British poet and journalist Charles Mackay (1814–89) wrote the following about their burial rites in a booklet called 'Thugs, or Phansigars':

> Their next care is to dispose of the bodies. So cautious are they to prevent detection, that they usually break all the joints to hasten decomposition. They then cut open the body to prevent it swelling in the grave and causing fissures in the soil above, by which means the jackals might be attracted to the spot, and thereby lead to discovery.

In fact, the Thugs didn't slice people up merely for fun, or profit. They were motivated to do so in order to propitiate the Hindu goddess Kali, to whom all funds were, albeit indirectly, forwarded. So it was religiously inspired gangsterism on a spectacular scale.

Nice people to do business with. The *OED* notes that 'Their suppression was rigidly prosecuted from 1831, and the system is now extinct.' True, except that where once there were Thugs, now we have thugs. This latter group was noted by British journals and newspapers between 1810 and 1897; then, while all that was going on, the term became a byword for a cut-throat or ruffian. 'Glasgow Thuggery' is a headline from Thomas Carlyle's essay on Chartism.

We still use words like **thuggery** and **thuggish**, and most of us are probably only dimly aware of the very deep roots they have. The more one reads about the Thugs, the more extra-ordinary their story is. We should, perhaps, be grateful that our own home-grown thugs are nowhere near as dangerous as this lot, as a further quotation from Mackay demonstrates:

Travellers who have the misfortune to lodge in the same choultry or hostelry, as the Thugs, are often murdered during the night. It is either against their creed to destroy a sleeper, or they find a difficulty in placing the noose round the neck of a person in a recumbent position. When this is the case, the slumberer is suddenly aroused by the alarm of a snake or a scorpion. He starts to his feet, and finds the fatal sash around his neck. – He never escapes.

Chapter Eighteen

Put-downs and Insults

Swearing, we used to be told by our mothers, betrays a limited vocabulary. Well, bollocks to that, because the English language is the beneficiary of a wealth of expressive ways in which to be extremely rude about people. Like a migrating bird spotting a lake from afar, many languages have touched down on British shores and found the land ideal for breeding. From this swirl of cultures, British people have found a plethora of ways in which to use colourful language, and one way is to insult people or put them down. What can be confusing to learners of English, though, is the variety of registers – i.e. the tone of voice – of the insult or put-down. There are significant, if subtle, differences between calling someone a **tosser** and an **arsehole**, and these differences frequently belie their actual meanings. Some of these words you can get away with saying to someone's face. Others are probably better uttered once they're out of earshot.

We're going to be looking at some of our most familiar words, along with one or two others that have dropped off the radar. The word **insult** itself is straight out of the Latin book. *Sulto* meant 'I jump', and *insulto* at first meant 'I leap upon'. Only later did it acquire a more metaphorical meaning. So too in English:

the initial meaning of 'insult', dating from 1603, was physical; the verbal assault came a few decades later.

The verb **to put down**, by contrast, is made up from two Old English elements, but it has to be specially tuned to achieve its aim. You can of course **put your foot down** and insist on something, or you can **put someone's name down** for, say, a school or military service. However, **to put someone down** is usually a calculated snub: it amounts to 'putting someone back in their place', perhaps because they're getting a bit uppity. It's usually more indirect than an insult, which tends to be just a verbal assault. Although a put-down tends to be verbal, an insult can be conveyed by gesture.

In brief, you wouldn't want to get on the wrong side of any of these words. We're going to take a look at some of the snappiest expressions in the language, and examine why the bite went out of some of the others.

Slut

Thomas Hoccleve (?1369–1426), one of the most significant English poets of his time,[1] was famous for two main reasons: for not being as good as the slightly earlier Geoffrey Chaucer, and for describing his own mental breakdown. He gains his *Balderdash* spurs, though, for penning the first evidence we have of a particularly insulting word – **slut**, which means either 'a dirty, untidy woman' (*Chambers*) or 'an immoral woman' (*Collins*). It has German origins, coming from dialect variants such as *schlutt*, *schlutte* or *schlutz*, which mean 'dirty woman'.

---

1 Hoccleve is credited with being the first man to use the word 'talent', as in 'special skill,' though few critics now think his very long poems exhibited much of it.

These days, 'slut' is a rather direct insult when used of someone, but that hasn't always been the case. The sense as used by Thomas Hoccleve in his 1402 *Letter to Cupid* – 'The foulest slutte of al a toune' – although crude, merely means someone who didn't spend too long tidying her room. Even into the late nineteenth century, the word *could* be used as a term of abuse, but not necessarily with a sexual undertone. 'Slut' also crossed over into **slattern**, in use from 1639, which was a slightly kinder way of describing a woman who kept a similarly messy room. In Victorian English, **slut's wool** is the evocative description for the mounds of dust that pile up in a room that rarely sees the dustpan and brush.

St Cuthbert of Lindisfarne, the island off the northeast coast of England, not the 1970s' folk-rock band, used 'slut' to refer to a kitchen maid, albeit a very lowly one, around 1450: 'The quene her toke to make a slutte, And to vile services her putt.' Here 'vile' wouldn't have the same truly odious sense it has today.

How bad was it to be a slut? We have one isolated reference to it from 1460 as being merely troublesome, but even by 1450 it had the pretty heavy overtones of loose morals, though – early on, at least – these were not exclusively female. Geoffrey Chaucer, Thomas Hoccleve's hero, had men in mind when – using the adjective, not the noun – he wrote, 'Why is thy lord so **sluttish**?' in the prologue to 'The Canon's Yeoman's Tale' – one of *The Canterbury Tales* – around 1386. But the general use of 'sluttish' to refer either to men or women didn't last beyond the late seventeenth century, and the sense of slut as a sexually promiscuous woman is now hard to shift.

And yet it could be used playfully, as when Samuel Pepys confided to his diary on 21 February 1664: 'Our little girl Susan is a most admirable slut, and pleases us mightily'. Susan was the couple's maid or 'drudge'.

The first quotation from the amazing urbandictionary.com defines 'slut' as 'a woman with the morals of a man'. The second goes into more detail: 'Someone who provides a very needed service for the community and sleeps with everyone, even the guy that has no shot at getting laid and everyone knows it'.

There are, in addition, dozens of associated entries that attempt to add detail, not always that funny, but almost all written from the viewpoint of sex-obsessed American college kids. Take **slut bagel**: an unflattering description of the shape of the genitalia of a woman who has entertained a large number of male partners.

At some point in the 1990s, 'slut' was reclaimed as a purely descriptive term by those communities that practise 'consensual non-monogamy'. Indeed, members could call themselves **ethical sluts**. A book of the same name was published in 1997, but that meaning has not yet caught up with the *OED*. The word 'slut' in modern Swedish means 'ending'. Be warned.

Pillock

If it's not sex, it's parts of the body that inspire lots of our swear words. A good example is **pillock**, an old word for 'penis'. 'Pillock' dates from 1568, when it appeared in a work by the Scottish poet Sir David Lindsay (*c*.1486–1555). There is no mistaking the point of Lindsay's rather proud comment that 'my pillok will not ly doun'. Pillock, you see, is descended from the even older **pillicock**, which had the same meaning. Nor can there be much confusion about an earlier ballad from around 1325 that states 'My **pilkoc** pisseth on my schone [shoes]'. Just a few decades later the word had become a term of endearment in certain parts of England, with John Florio defining 'pillicocke' in his *Worlde of Wordes* (1598) as 'a darling young lad, a wanton, or a minion'.

In fact, notwithstanding the fact that 'pillock' meant 'penis', in 1608 the word **pill** was a slangy way of referring to 'testicles'. The one was, after all, closely related to the two. That same year, Shakespeare in *King Lear* (III.iv.72) had Edgar, the Earl of Gloucester's son, disguised as a character called Tom O'Bedlam (see page 285) and with a licence to behave very oddly, declare that 'Pilicock sate on **pelicocks hill**'. Etymologists, and anyone else who's had a good look at the line, have suggested that 'pelicocks hill' refers to the part of a woman's body known – with all the grandeur that Latin can bring to bear – as the *mons veneris* (mount of Venus).

'Pill' itself, incidentally, is derived from the Scandinavian word *piller*, which was a common Danish surname and, who knows, possibly the nomenclature of a man with a lot to boast about. By the eighteenth century, therefore, the word 'pillock' triply implied the male member.

By 1719, Thomas D'Urfey – well known in his day as the creator of a country song called 'The Fart' – was writing in *Wit & Mirth* that he was 'bolt upright and ready to fight, And Pillycock he lay there all night'. The superfluity of the triple masculine overtones might reasonably be read to suggest a 'Gosh, what a man you are!' kind of fellow. This definition would also, of course, imply that the word 'pillock' can never be used as an epithet for a girl or woman, but the logic of etymology has never held an English speaker back.

The mystery remains as to how the word persisted as a predominantly masculine adjective for the next 250 years, but then, fairly rapidly, took on its mildly satirical, and much more general, contemporary meaning of 'a stupid idiot'. Perhaps it's the modern decline in masculine notions of self, or, specifically, the rise of feminism during the 1960s, but, in any event, by 1967 the annals of television history reveal a character in *Till Death Us Do Part* saying: 'What are you talking about, you great hairy **pilloch**?' (with an h). Or, in another traditionally male-on-male arena, the football magazine *FourFourTwo* clamoured in 1995: 'What a bunch of pillocks!' The damage to the male ego, let alone the male member, was well and truly complete.

The appeal of 'pillock' as a swear word is that most of us have forgotten what it originally meant. When Johnny Speight revived it in *Till Death Us Do Part*, it was even funnier that the pillock in question was hairy: a clear reference to a testicle, which nobody could deny – nor could they ban it. But in the less profane era of the 1960s, a word such as pillock was a godsend to TV comedy writers, since they could scatter it around and not face censorship from the authorities. In fact, pillock, at source, was a lot ruder than many of the words that really were on the banned list.

A former Northern Ireland secretary, the much admired Mo Mowlam (1949–2005), was in the habit of calling people 'pillocks'. She would drop the term in conversation with cabinet coll-eagues, journalists and members of the public who were wearing silly costumes or who tried to josh her as she went walkabout. But Mowlam's freedom with the term wasn't common among all her government peers: at least, not within reach of a microphone.

Tosser

Has there ever been a better time to be a **tosser**? The earliest definition the *OED* has for this word is 'One who or that which tosses', as in 'tossers of reproaches' (1612) in a work about the

Greek philosopher Proclus by the classical scholar Thomas Taylor (1758–1835). Following that, a great deal more **tossing** took place, from ticket-porters being **tossers-off of beer** (1837) to an innocent American described as a hapless **tosser-up of omelets** (1846). In Scotland, of course, people must have been **tossing the caber** since well before we have written evidence for it (1862).

At one time the word was also applied to a receptacle, as seen in a cookery book called *Hand & Heart* (1884). Cooks were advised to 'Cut the other parts in small bits, put them in a small tosser with a grate of nutmeg'. And not just food. Joan Aiken, in her children's historical novel *Black Hearts in Battersea* (1965), uses it as a consciously anachronistic word for a coin, as in 'I haven't a tosser to my kick'. ('Kick' could mean a sixpence, but it seems to refer here to trousers.)

The remarkable thing is that, until about a hundred years earlier, it had all been going so well for the verb **to toss** (origin uncertain, says the *OED*, but glancingly allied to the Norwegian and Swedish dialect word *tossa*, to spread). We start with 'Howbeit the wroughte seas tossyd and rolled us ryght grevously' in 1506, and the succeeding centuries saw plenty of activity akin to flinging, pitching or throwing, but nothing more suggestive than that. You could **toss a pancake** in 1619, or, a few centuries later, **toss a drink back**. You could even **toss off a book** in 1845 if you were a fast reader. And that seems to be have been where temptation reared its head.

All that flinging and jerking got too much, as in this racy couplet from an erotic Victorian magazine called *The Pearl*, which dates from 1879–80: 'I don't like to see, though at me you might scoff,/ An old woman trying to toss herself off.' That seems to have been our first reference to the masturbatory **toss off**, and the sense was obviously well established by then, though perhaps not widely throughout society. When James Joyce wrote in a 1927 letter that 'The verb "to toss off" [is] an expression for "to masturbate"', it's clear that he was still explaining its meaning – and still enjoying doing so.

'Tosser' was first spotted in an April 1977 issue of a magazine called *Zigzag*, and it was not an auspicious beginning: 'She came on in a big mac and flashed her legs like an old tosser before throwing it off'. Ever since then, it has proved a marvellously adaptable word. You could be an annoying tosser or an amiable one. But the tosser remained, in parliamentary terms, a back-bench swearword until David Cameron's revitalized Conservative party enlisted the word in an attempt to discourage people from over-reliance on their credit cards with a 'viral' media campaign urging young people to 'ignore the tosser inside you' in November 2006.

Predictably, the media were amazed that the Tories had used such a provocative word in an advert, and for days afterwards Cameron tried manfully to steer the conversation back to 'the issues'. He said it was aimed at young people and not made to offend others, but, inevitably, it was also a stick with which to beat the Tories, and one that deputy leader John Prescott seized on in the House of Commons.

Noting the opposition party's use of the word, Prescott repeated it in Parliament, adding, 'I do not know which person on the Front Bench this man is modelled on, but … I always thought that his party was full of them'. Cue laughter from one side of the House. Prescott was not cautioned by the Speaker. Indeed, Labour MPs were reported as having illustrated Prescott's remarks by making hand gestures that were unmistakably identified with the wanking theme, possibly to explain it to the more innocent members in the House.

If Prescott had referred to his opposite numbers as **wankers** or the c-word, he could no doubt have expected to spend a few painful minutes in the Speaker's office with an exercise book down the back of his trousers. But tossers was not deemed unparliamentary, and he might even have got away with calling them **berks** too, even though 'berk' is an abbreviation of Berkeley (or Berkshire) Hunt and therefore rhyming slang for the c-word – a much more offensive epithet. It is the Speaker's job to stop MPs calling each other liars, but if they are merely being called tossers, it seems he is content not to interject. Much ink has been spread since then about this latest threat to civilized society, or is it merely a recognition that even the House of Commons must, just occasionally, move with the times?

Mammet

The words 'now chiefly archaic and regional' appear at the top of the *OED*'s entry on the word **mammet**, and it's easy to see why. It was first defined as 'a false god', and used as such in the thirteenth century. In the sixteenth century it meant 'a hateful person', and in the early twentieth century it was a regional term meaning 'baby or child'. This is clearly a word that has been through several different phases.

Sir Thomas More, Lord Chancellor of England before his run-in with Henry VIII, referred in 1529 to 'The ydolles and mammettes of the paganes'. From the late sixteenth century to the early nineteenth, 'mammet' was flung about as a term of abuse by Protestant writers (and others, no doubt) to describe the images of Christ or the saints used in Catholic churches. And, more metaphorically, it was used between about 1390 and 1593 to describe a person who is the puppet of another, or has moral virtues to match – i.e. not very impressive ones. In fact, between the fifteenth and sixteenth centuries it could even mean 'fairies or pixies', as indicated in John Lyly's *Maides Metamorphosis* (1600): 'What **Mawmets** are these?/ O they be the Fayries that haunt these woods.'

Balderdash readers may have noticed that this word is being treated with unusual delicacy. They're right. The reason lies in the etymology. This is no simple word, but an Anglo-Norman word *maumet*, which was reduced from *mauhomet* and came from the twelfth-century Old French *mahomet* or *mahommet*, meaning 'an idol'. An idol? A contemporary reader would surely see something – or someone – else in it. In fact, its meaning came from the medieval Christian belief – now demonstrably proven to be false – that the prophet Muhammad was worshipped as a god. Hence the profusion of references to it in the literature of the time, and hence too the reason why you don't hear so many light-hearted allusions to it these days.

In these times of sometimes uneasy Islamo-Christian relations, though, it's interesting to pull the carpet back on an earlier time when Christians were portraying their Islamic neighbours overseas in a far from flattering light. (It's a lesson that the current pope might well have pondered more carefully before he was accused of insulting Islam in September 2006.) Nor, indeed, had they finished with it. Once again in the sixteenth century, **mammet** could mean a figure of contempt or hatred, or a weakling, or a mentally feeble person. Shakespeare talks of 'A wretched whyning foole,/ A puling mammet' in *Romeo and Juliet* (1597). And in the twentieth century it still lived on, though, as the good book says, in archaic or regional uses. The poet W.H. Auden (1907–73) complained in his long poem *The Orators* (1932) that 'We're getting a little tired of boys,/ Of the ninny, the mawmet and the false alarm'. And a 1971 volume called *Twenty-Five Welsh Short Stories* contains the line 'His mouth fell open, his eyes glared under the bloody eyebrows, he shook like a mammet'. It's a word that should be used with extreme care.

Spaz

The playground is a breeding ground for terms of abuse. For their 1959 book *The Lore and Language of Schoolchildren* authors Iona and Peter Opie traipsed all over the country to record the revolting expressions children used – behaviour that these days would probably have got them into trouble with the local authority. But the fruits of their labours is endlessly fascinating, and includes childish reflections on eccentricity. Entries for the letters B, C and D alone include **bats**, **batty**, **barmy** (see page 292), **crackers**, **crackpot**, **daffy**, **dippy** and **dithering**. 'You're **daft** and dithering, wipe your chin and stop dribbling,' as they say in Cleethorpes.

One of the most effective verbal swipes among children used to be the word **spaz**, an abbreviation of **spastic**. In Britain the term 'spastic', meaning 'someone subject to muscular spasms that they can't control', dates from 1822: **spastic paralysis** was first recorded in 1877, and refers to the spasms that occur in some muscles, particularly around the neck and spine, resulting in unpredictable movements. The word 'spastic' was adopted as a term of abuse from the 1980s, though it must have been in the air long before, since the word 'spaz' was first quoted by the *New Yorker* film critic Pauline Kael in 1965, albeit with no connotation of physical disability: 'The term that American teen-agers now use as the opposite of "tough" is "spaz". A spaz is a person who is courteous to teachers, plans for a career ... and believes in official values. A spaz is something like what adults still call a square.' The same goes for the related words **spacko** or **spacker** (more popular in northern England) and **spanner**. The popularity of 'spanner' may lie in its association with phrases such as **to throw a spanner in the works**, for which we may be indebted to P.G. Wodehouse's comic novel *Right Ho, Jeeves* (1934).

'Spaz', as the comment from Pauline Kael shows, was not widely known as a term of offence in the United States during the 1960s, nor is it today. When Tiger Woods, master of the plush green, lost the US Masters Tournament in April 2006, he said ruefully that although he had been at the height of his powers when he teed off, 'as soon as I got on the green I was a spaz'. There was such a rumpus in this country that his representative was forced to apologize.

Children, especially, are quick to pin unkind monikers on their contemporaries. Anyone showing signs of physical mal-coordination would, in past years, have been pounced on and called a **retard** or even a **phlid** – an extremely unkind word recalling the anti-morning sickness drug Thalidomide, which caused such dramatic growth abnormalities to arms and legs. Is it better that these terms are used about people who are not necessarily physically impaired? Not really. And it didn't help when a US company brought out a new wheelchair called the Spazz and said it was trying to reclaim the word for the wheelchair-using community. British disability campaigners were not impressed.

Joey

In 1981, the BBC TV children's programme *Blue Peter* decided to do its bit for International Year of the Disabled by focusing on Joey Deacon, who had been born with cerebral palsy in 1920 and who entered Caterham Mental Hospital aged eight. His speech was unintelligible to most people, until he had the good fortune to meet fellow inmate Ernie Roberts, who understood him perfectly. His autobiography, *Tongue Tied*, was published in 1974, and was followed by a memorable, part-dramatized episode of *Horizon*, but *Blue Peter*'s championing of him backfired slightly when schoolchildren all across the country reacted with scant sentimentality, labelling anyone showing even the slightest physical clumsiness as a **Joey**,[2] or even a **Deacon**. This, despite the fact that such behaviour was virtually guaranteed not to win them a *Blue Peter* badge.

Special needs

In today's more sensitive era, a phrase has been resurrected from the early days of the last century that health workers are hoping can be used without any unfortunate side-effects. There are all sorts of reasons why a person might have **special needs**, particularly in a physical or educational context. The *OED* contains examples of its use in official publications dated 1953 and earlier – 'the utmost care is taken to provide them with educational advantages adapted to their special needs' comes from the *Journal of Political Economy* (1913) – but this was not yet evidence of an official policy carrying that name. Its first use in the UK can be dated at 1986. It has yet to suffer the same fate that Joey did, but, as ever with children, you never know.

---

2 In fact, the word Joey had been a byword for 'clown', being a diminutive of the great clown Joseph Grimaldi (1779–1837) since at least 1896.

Plonker

Plink, **plunk** and **plonk**, apart from sounding like an animated cartoon series from Soviet-era Czechoslovakia, are all relative newcomers to the dictionary, and all descriptions of a type of sound. 'Plunk', the sound of a cork escaping a bottle, dates from 1822. The more metallic 'plink' began in 1892, while 'plonk' – a dull, thudding sound – was first noted in print in a 1904 short story by P.G. Wodehouse: 'There was a beautiful, musical *plonk*, and the ball soared to the very opposite quarter of the field,' he wrote in a collection called *Tales of St Austin's*.

In terms of etymology, these words are onomatopoeic, which means they are imitative of the sounds they describe. In the case of plonk, it's the sound made by an object going 'plonk'. This may not be a lexicological masterstroke, but it has the ring – or the plink – of truth to it. **To plonk** means 'to pluck' in a rather, well, plonky way. You could also plonk (put) something down in a casual or heavy-handed way. But the word 'plonk' has meant other things, not least as a generic term for cheap wine. The usage is helped by the assonance of plonk and *blanc*, i.e. white (wine). This rather neat play on words was first effected by Henry Williamson, author of *Tarka the Otter* and many other books. 'Nosey and Nobby shared a bottle of plinketty plonk, as *vin blanc* was called,' he wrote in his 1930 novel *The Patriot's Progress*.

From 'plonk' to **plonker** is a bigger step, but it had already come to light, in the north of England, in the mid-nineteenth century. At first it meant something abstract but significant – what further south might be called 'a whopper'. By the time of the First World War, Australians were referring to artillery shells as plonkers, but by the Second World War, it had become 'penilized' – a *Balderdash* term by which almost any word in the English language sooner or later becomes a synonym for the word 'penis'. The *OED*'s second definition for plonker is 'penis', dated from 1949. It adds 'also in extended use'. We need hardly add that it's not the penis that is extended: merely the expression.

To pull someone's plonker means 'to deceive a person humorously or playfully', and is similar to 'pulling someone's leg'. The first recorded pulling of the plonker is as recent as 1995, in an article in *Empire* film magazine. We are confident that there must be considerable room for ante-dating this expression.

Penises being penises, by the 1960s 'plonker' came to stand for a fool or idiot. But it's fair to say that the biggest fillip that the word 'plonker' ever received was from John Sullivan, writer of the BBC TV sitcom *Only Fools and Horses.* His hero, Derek Reginald (Del Boy) Trotter, referred so often to his brother Rodney as a plonker that it fairly Araldited the word into the British consciousness. If Del Boy had simply said **prick** or **penis**, it wouldn't have been funny in that context. And if he had reused 'pillock', that wouldn't have been funny because the word 'belonged' to Alf Garnett. So Sullivan pulled 'plonker' out of relative obscurity and shot it to prominence because no one knew what it really meant.

Prat

On its first surviving appearance in print, around the year 1000, **prat** meant 'trick or prank'. In fact, in very early Middle English, around 1200, 'prat' could be an adjective meaning 'astute or cunning'. Etymologically, we have the Old English word *praett*, meaning 'guile or trick', the same word that the adjective 'pretty' is descended from. So if it comes to the worst and someone calls you a prat, you could take it as a compliment.

But the chances are it wasn't intended that way, not least because the dismissive way we use it today – as in 'Don't be such a prat' – hangs from a different linguistic thread. The *OED* lists it under 'Origin Unknown', but since 1567 it has meant 'buttocks', as proved by the following line from a comic play, *The Joviall Crew* (1641): 'First set me down here on both my **prats**.' *Both* his prats, you'll note.

'Prat' could also mean 'a trick or a piece of cunning', but this died out in the early nineteenth century. *Chambers English Dictionary* defines it as 'a fool', and the *OED* also includes it in that sense, but this usage is far more recent than one might think. In fact, the earliest evidence the *OED* currently has for it is from the writer Melvyn Bragg in a work entitled *Without a City Wall* (1968): 'He had been looking for the exact word to describe David and now he found it: *prat*.' These days, of course, he's busy presenting arts programmes or speaking in the House of Lords, but he also has twenty-seven quotations in the *OED*, which must surely put him in the running to be the subject of one of his own *South Bank Show* specials.

A **pratfall** is 'a fall on the buttocks'. 'Don't do a pratfall in your first routine' is from *Play Parade* (1939) by Noel Coward, though we can assume that the master himself would never have been caught in such an undignifed position.

Wally

Collins defines **wally** as 'a stupid person'. *Chambers* goes for 'hopelessly inept or foolish-looking person'. Some dictionaries make comparisons with the next word alphabetically: **wallydrag** or **wallydraigle**, which is defined in *The English Dialect Dictionary* as 'a feeble, ill-grown person or animal; a worthless, slovenly person, especially a woman'. Wally is a word that, like 'plonker', was very popular in the 1970s and 1980s to describe an idiot or a fool. It's nice to know that it isn't a codeword for 'penis', even though Partridge lists it as a cockney word for 'gherkin', in use in London's East End since the 1880s.

Where, then, is **Wally**?[3] Anecdotally (i.e. on the Internet) there is talk of a nineteenth-century explorer called Wally Walliams who made a bit of a prat of himself by thinking that he had 'discovered' a new continent. As luck would have it, he had turned up on the coast of Australia. What a wally, in other words.

A more reliable definition is that it's a diminutive form of the name **Walter**, in the same way that Charlie – as in 'a proper Charlie' (from 1946) – is derived from Charles.[4] The *OED* defines 'Charlie' as 'an unfashionable person; one who is foolish, inept, or ineffectual. Also as a mild term of abuse.'

'*Wally*, out of fashion', wrote the *Daily Mirror* in 1969. The *OED*'s examples are culled more from newsprint than from the pages of novels. Take this from a 1974 copy of *The Times*: 'The successors to the flat-earthers … are at present encamped on the perimeter of the great concentric stone circles … They choose to be known as the **Wallies of Wessex**, wally being a conveniently anonymous umbrella for vulnerable individuals.' In 1976 anyone dressing conventionally was a wally. The Bee Gees and Boney M were dismissed as **wally acts** during the years of punk music, and in 1979 Cuban heels were worn by wallies and John Travolta.

So which would you prefer to be called: a prat or a wally?

---

3 The *Where's Wally?* children's books by Martin Handford first appeared in 1987. Their US title was *Where's Waldo?*
4 The alternative spelling 'Charley' was formerly slang for a woman's breasts, from 1874. 'Coo, look at them charlies!' comes from *The Main Chance* by Peter Wildblood (1957).

At least prat has a rather grand – swollen, in fact – ancestry. Wally is probably just a diminutive of the personal name Walter, for no better reason than that it's a rather silly name. But is it really? Go tell that to Wally Disney, Wally Cronkite and Wally Matthau. These are major figures in Western cultural history, their greatness in no way diminished by their silly first name. And if you still disagree, maybe you'd like to take on Sir Wally Raleigh over a roll-up and a sack of potatoes.

The trouble with calling someone a wally is that it makes you sound like a bit of a plonker yourself.

Arsehole

There is surely something almost reassuring about being called – or calling someone – an **arsehole**. It isn't the rudest term of abuse ever uttered; you could probably have thought of something much worse, so it would seem that it's a grumpy put-down rather than a snarled and hateful insult. 'What an arsehole!' is marvellously evocative, though. I am an arsehole, you are an arsehole, he, she or it is an arsehole. It's a quintessentially English word, since Americans have been calling it **asshole** since at least the mid-twentieth century. Stolid, boring, workaday, **arse** has been doing the rounds since the year 1000. It feels utterly Anglo-Saxon, and certainly an Old Frisian would have known his *ers* from his elbow, though in fact it's not a million miles from the Greek word *orros*, which meant the same thing.

The word has impeccable roots. 'They say, he's valiant.' 'Valiant? so is mine arse,' comes from a 1602 play called *Poetaster* by Ben Jonson (1572–1637), a great playwright who died so poor that he was buried standing up, and not lying on his arse. **My arse** has been, ever since, a monumental expression of dignified insolence. Even on its own, 'arse' is a dismissive way of describing a stupid or contemptible person. It feels like it's been with us for ever, though it didn't really come into common parlance until well after the Second World War. But it too changed in form, from the more formal use by the Trinidadian novelist Earl Lovelace in 1968 ('Don't play the arse') to the more familiar 'A couple of stupid arses on motorbikes' by Caryl Phillips from 1986. Phillips is based in the West Indies, so did Caribbean writers pioneer its conversational use? Maybe, since if you have a Trinidadian tinge to your speaking voice, you can really add expression to the word 'arse'.

But 'arsehole', or at least 'arse hole', has been around – if you'll forgive the worthy-of-Jonson pun – for centuries. Since 1379 at least, when it clearly wasn't rude since we have the archives of Gloucester Cathedral to thank for its survival in the form 'The ers hole by egestion' (i.e. the hole from which your poo emerges) followed closely by the word 'schityng' (shitting). Assuming this wasn't some maniac coprophile priest, it seems that such words were fit for, well, a bishop at least. But arsehole's evolution has been almost balletic. When it emerged as slang, in the early 1920s, it was used to describe not people but places – and Los Angeles before all others. 'This place,' wrote the American writer and critic H.L. Mencken in 1926, on what must have been a tough trip for a native of Baltimore, 'is the one true and original arse-hole of creation. It is at least nine times as bad as I expected.'[5] Dylan Thomas (1914–53) described 'fond sad Wales' as 'This arsehole of the universe' in 1950, and from then it's been a bit of a rout, really. Feel the need to slag somewhere off? Just dust down the 'arsehole of the universe' and apply it to the place you wish to dis.

The first application of arsehole to people currently cited in the *OED* comes from an unlikely source. We have already seen the great blow for prats made by the novelist and pundit Baron Bragg of Wigton in the County of Cumbria. Among Bragg's many causes was a campaign he launched in January 2001 to prevent MPs from banning foxhunting. It didn't work, but he would have found favour with the philosopher and right-wing intellectual Roger Scruton, a man seldom seen far from a pair of tweeds. As Bragg was to prat, so Scruton is to arsehole. In 1981, a year before the publication of his book A *Short History of Modern Philosophy*, he enjoyed a foray into fiction with *Fortnight's Anger* in which he wrote: 'He is an arsehole of the first order'. Scruton is mentioned ten times overall in the *OED*. Most of his other words may be rather more uplifting – 'maenad', 'nihilist' and 'platen' to name a few – but they could scarcely be more to the point. Spare a moment though for **podex**, first used by Ben Jonson, and meaning 'buttocks or rump'. By Scruton's time, 'podex' was mainly humorous, as in an extract from the same book, which is also noteworthy for its use of the verb 'to absterge', which means to wipe something clean: 'He made the sign of the cross … and then suddenly cried out "My God, I have forgotten to absterge the podex!"' Podex brings us back to our earlier pratfall, and better still, it can trace its origin back to the Latin verb *pedere*, meaning 'to break wind'.

Chapter Nineteen

Spend a Penny

*E*uphemisms – there's no nice way of putting this – say the things that, for various reasons, we don't want to say. The word 'euphemism' is Greek in origin, *eu* meaning 'well' and *phemi* meaning 'I say'. And saying things well, or at least without bluntness, is what euphemisms are all about. Sometimes, though, so anxious are we not to cause offence that they become oblique to the point of obscurity. No wonder non-native speakers have a terrible time with them.

You can refer to almost anything in an indirect way, but there are several aspects of life that have inspired an unusually large number of euphemisms. These are, traditionally, subjects where we would rather call a spade a tool for digging. We can't talk openly about death because it has always frightened us. Sex, on the other hand, is a subject about which we still have a Victorian hangover. The same goes for toilet-related matters. To these three topics we can also add drunkenness because despite the fact that some of us quite enjoy talking long-windedly about how drunk we were the other night, the rest of the world finds it distasteful. Euphemisms for drunkenness take a wry, somewhat detached view about some of the consequences of inebriation. And certain other nations, it must be said – any passing Australians, take a bow – have bent their elbows to the wheel with great enthusiasm.

Our need for euphemism arises for a variety of reasons. On one level we might feel superstitious about saying something like, 'Your auntie's just **died**', so instead we might say, 'I'm terribly sorry, but your aunt has **passed away**' (in use since the late fourteenth or early fifteenth century) to cushion the blow. At another level, the phrases **snuffed it** or **snuffed out** began to be used in the late nineteenth century. Although these don't include the word 'death', they are so terse that they could hardly be called euphemistic: they're fulfilling another function of euphemisms, which is to demonstrate a sort of bravado in the face of the Grim Reaper.

Other euphemisms operate by concentrating fixedly on a single point, such as bed, when dealing – or not dealing – with sex. Expressions such as **going to bed with** serve to obscure the flailing limbs and grunting noises that would otherwise obtrude. Other phrases mention a non-sexual part of the body, as in **getting your leg over**, and since legs are hardly the most vital limb in the copulatory process, that gets round the thorny question of whether or not we've said something rude. But the joy of such euphemisms is that apparently innocent phrases bedevilled with sexual innuendo can rise up and bite you, as Jonathan Agnew discovered during his commentary on *Test Match Special* in 1991. His observation that Ian Botham, who had just been out Hit Wicket, 'didn't quite get his leg over' reduced him and his co-presenter Brian Johnston to whimpers of uncontrollable hysteria, and produced one of the greatest trophies ever in the display cabinet of euphemism.

Some euphemisms change the focus for comic effect, as in **pointing percy at the porcelain**. This was quoted by no less an organ than the *Times Literary Supplement* in 1965 as one of many 'expressive Australianisms to describe [the] prosaic function' of having a pee. Other toilet euphemisms have their roots in a grain of socio-historical truth, such as the expression **to spend a penny**, which arose from the pay-per-pee installation of the **public convenience** – and that's another euphemism, by the way.

At other times, we punningly call on bestial or animal practices as if, actually, we're all in this together with the entire animal kingdom. This leads to expressions such as **siphoning the python**, another euphemism for taking a pee, and referring to someone **going belly up** (as fish do) rather than dying. Many euphemisms have been generated either to explain certain events to children – 'Fluffy's **in heaven** now' – or in imitation of childish language, such as the inarguable 'I've done a poo'. Since most of us don't want our four-year-olds saying, 'I just shat my pants', we're happy for them to express themselves in this way. But the habit lingers on, hence pseudo-infantile expressions such as **rumpy-pumpy** (from 1968) and **hanky-panky** (see page 421).

Euphemisms contain all these inflections and more, but the crudest black-and-white division is more nuanced than the somewhat labyrinthine *OED* definition, which is 'the substitution of a word or expression of comparatively favourable implication or less unpleasant associations, instead of the harsher or more offensive one that would more precisely designate what is intended'. In fact, we're not always trying to lessen the impact of the thing itself. Sometimes the more elaborate the expression – **hiding the salami** is a popular US term for 'having sex' – the more we seem to be revelling in the act itself.

SEX

Even Casanova would have been hard put to make full use of the formidable verbal array of terms for having sex. We'll inspect as many as we can, but we can't hope to do justice to them all. Most of our examples are home-grown, but we should also delight in the Australian **spear the bearded clam**, and the Black American **bust some booty** ('booty' being a twentieth-century word for vagina or, following another line, buttocks) and **hit skins**, which, says word-sleuth Jonathon Green, is a descendant of the eighteenth-century **wriggle navels**. And that's just the start of it.

The fact is, whenever, however or wherever we talk about sex, we find it almost impossible not to use a euphemism. The only really straight way would be to say something like 'fucking', but that doesn't always do for exploratory conversations with potential in-laws, college or job interviews, and other occasions when a measure of delicacy is required. Welcome, then, to the world of euphemism. Here, even the word **sex** stands for something more than it means. That great family-planning pioneer Marie Stopes described the **sex act** in 1918, but the word 'sex' had barely evolved since its first use in 1382, when it simply meant the gender of the species. It was the writer D.H. Lawrence (1885–1930), who in 1929 thought of combining the words 'have' and 'sex' into **have sex** – after which, of course, he thought of little else. And yet even that was a euphemism because it doesn't explicitly describe the action. In fact, the *OED* entry for the noun 'sex' consists of a mere five sections.

From the biblical expression **to know someone** to the more graphic turns of phrase that developed later, terms for sex are nearly always euphemisms. There are supposedly more technical words, such as **copulate**, which comes from the Latin *copulare* meaning 'to couple together, join or unite'. It's plainer, but it's still circumlocuting the literal truth. And there are good reasons for that.

Bed

The word **bed** may have come from an Aryan root *bhodh* by way
of the Latin *fodio* (I dig), as if it were originally 'a dug-out place'
or a 'lair' of beasts and men. Beds are for sleeping, of course,
but we know that they have also been the scene of some lively
marital and non-marital relations since around the year 1200
when documentary evidence begins, such as 'Thou hast defiled
the bed of him', from William Wyclif's bible of 1382. It wasn't
until the twentieth century, though, that the phrase **to go to bed**
became synonymously – or rather, euphemistically – associated
with sexual activity. The writer Aldous Huxley (1894–1963)
seems to have got there first, in 1945: 'How much less awful the
man would be … if only he sometimes lost his temper … or went
to bed with his secretary,' he wrote in *Time Must Have a Stop*.
From the year 1000 onwards, the verb **to bed** meant 'to put
someone to bed'. Three hundred years later, it meant 'to take
someone into bed', a significant shift. 'A person is said to be **in
bed**, when undressed and covered with the bedclothes,' reads the
OED definition of the noun 'bed'. Not a word about pyjamas
there: what could they be hinting at?

Sleep

Both noun and verb forms of **sleep** are ancient, dating from
ninth-century English. Among these are *slápan* and *slépan*, but
according to the *OED*, all mean 'to take repose by the natural
suspension of consciousness'. Yet by the year 900, the *OED* is
defining that same word as 'implying sexual intimacy or cohab-
itation', as found in the book of laws of King Alfred. It's the word
'implying' that tells you the verb **to sleep with** has grown an
extra skin. It may not be suggesting multi-orgasmic sex at this

point, but it's clear that the word now implies more than the natural suspension of consciousness.

Having it off

There is a slightly less roundabout way of mentioning sex by not mentioning it, and that is with the common Teutonic verb form *habban*, which shook down into English as **to have**. Without beating about the bush, William Shakespeare was the first to address it sexually. When Richard Gloucester, the future Richard III, was ruminating lustfully about Lady Anne and wondering why she wasn't returning his favours (one rather glaring reason being that he had just bumped off her husband, Prince Edward), he says to himself: 'Was ever woman in this humour woo'd? Was ever woman in this humour won? I'll have her; – but I will not keep her long.'

The directness of 'to have' was not toned down until the twentieth century. In 1937 Eric Partridge noted **have it off** as used 'by a man that has contrived to seduce a girl'. There it lay for a few more years until the jazz musician George Melly – not a man to let a euphemism for sex pass by without wanting to jump on to it – completed the act of seduction: 'I derived iconoclastic pleasure from having it off in the public parks,' he wrote in *Owning-Up* (1965). The verb 'to have' continued to draw its admirers, but there was more competition now as more prepositions muscled in. Germaine Greer passed comment on another phrase in her seminal (if you'll pardon the adjective) book *The Female Eunuch*: 'The vocabulary of impersonal sex is peculiarly desolating,' she wrote in 1970. 'Who wants to … "**have it away**"?' To which the answer must be: quite a lot of people over the years.

Hanky-panky

The euphemisms for sex have become both more playful and more crude over the years. One of the funnier ones is **hanky-panky**, which came in from the rear – whoops, there we go again – since it originally meant not sex, but magic. 'Only a little hanky-panky' was first seen in *Punch* magazine in 1841, but it didn't refer to sex. The next use, from 1847, is clearer in context: 'Necromancy, my dear Sir – the hanky-panky of the ancients' comes from a book by Albert R. Smith called *The Struggles and Adventures of Christopher Tadpole*. It could in fact refer to various types of trickery, double-dealing or underhand (see page 375) business. Hanky-panky's sexual awakening only happened in 1939, and George Bernard Shaw (1856–1950) got there first, in his play *Geneva* (1938): 'No hanky panky. I am respectable; and I mean to keep respectable.' In the case of Shaw, this was certainly true: he was one of literature's most famous celibates.

There is always something slightly innocent, or foiled, about 'hanky-panky', as if some landlady is forever hovering in the wings, waiting to stamp it out. And it survives to this day, operating at the 'sex lite' end of the erotic spectrum.

How's your father

Some euphemisms for sex are suggestive for more farcical reasons. **How's your father** is a ludicrously comical way of describing carnal activity, but it came about through the music-hall comedian Harry Tate (1872–1940). In one of his routines he was about to **get it on** (1971 is the date for that particular sexual euphemism) with a young woman when her father entered the room, where-upon he sprang up, saying, 'And how's your dear father?' It thus became a handy phrase that sprang to mind from then on as a knowing substitution for rather more athletic sexual exertions.

Making love

There's falling in love, and then there's **making love**, the latter not necessarily following on from the former. The earliest reference to **fall in love** was the rather beautiful **to be brought into love's dance**, which dates from 1423. To **make love** originally meant 'to pay amorous attention', but 'now more usually', says the *OED* (do we detect a flicker of disapproval?) '**to copulate**'. There was a lot of making love in Shakespeare's time and earlier, but no clothes were removed in the process: it was all done with tongues.[1] In a notorious passage in Jane Austen's *Emma* (1816), the unreliable narrator finds herself in a carriage with the passionate but erring Mr Elton. She had in mind to say something to him, 'but scarcely had she begun, scarcely had they passed the sweep-gate and joined the other carriage, than she found her subject cut up – her hand seized – her attention demanded, and Mr. Elton actually making violent love to her'. Many is the A-level student who, on reading this passage, will have had vivid images of Jane and Mr Elton pulling at each other's clothes on the floor of the carriage. The truth was more genteel. Love-making was an oral skill[2] in those days.

Salami

There are pages and pages of euphemistic expressions for sex, whether full on (such as **hump**, a vulgar expression for sexual

----

1 Please ... no ambiguity intended!
2 Stop it ...

intercourse since 1785), or lighter – such as **slap and tickle**, a thoroughly 1920s' phrase for fairly innocent amorous fun. And the male organ, among its many derisory monikers, has been referred to as a **salami** or **salam** at least since Woody Allen's film *Annie Hall* (1977), where the dialogue goes: 'We should turn out the lights and play **hide the salam**'. However, J.E. Lighter, in his *Historical Dictionary of American Slang* (1997), cites variants of the phrase going back to 1918, such as **to hide the sausage or weenie**. There is a further, post-Aids endorsement from the novel *Kicking Tomorrow* by Daniel Richler (1993): 'I'd steer clear if I was you, dude. **Slap the salami** instead, **pull the pud**, it's disease- free.' Most dictionaries define 'hiding the salami' in terms of sexual intercourse, but this author suggests, from nothing more than a close study of Richler's text, that the emphasis in that last quote is on masturbation.

DEATH

Where death and dying are concerned, our motives for tiptoeing around the subject are more understandable. While sex is something that we might not wish to discuss openly, at least we enjoy it while it's taking place. Not so our appointment with the Grim Reaper. When it comes to the d-word, it's as though if we don't say it, it might not happen.

Pop one's clogs

Take the expression **to pop one's clogs**. On the surface, it doesn't sound final at all. You could almost imagine it meaning to perform a dance or to clap your hands. It sounds rhythmical and light-hearted. But this belies its essential seriousness. 'To pop your clogs' means 'to die'. The verb **to pop** is a hardy English perennial, 700 years old at least, and its original meaning – borrowed from its sound – was to deliver smack or a blow to something. In fact, when you think of a paper bag (rather than a champagne cork) popping, it does seem to have a note of finality. In the eighteenth century 'to pop' on its own meant just that: to die.

So where did clogs come in? Well, they were once everyday footwear in the north of England, and perhaps the most likely item to pop (a slang expression for **pawn**) when people wanted to rustle up some cash. The combination of popping and clogs in the context of death is relatively recent, though, and spotted by no lesser personage than a *Balderdash* wordhunter in a 1970 copy of *Punch* magazine, by which time it could be said to be an analogous expression to **hanging up your boots** (or **hat**). So the phrase harks back from a non-clog era to a much older time.

Clogs were a common item of footwear not only in northern towns, but also in the Netherlands, so it seemed reasonable to ask if that fine country includes references to clogs in any of its euphemistic expressions for death. Luckily, *Balderdash*'s small but fast-growing band of Dutch wordhunters rose enthusiastically to the challenge, and the answer appears to be: absolutely none, though Hollandophiles will enjoy some equally colourful expressions, such as *Tussen zes planken de deur uitgaan* (Leave the door [i.e. house] inside six pieces of wood), and *Er groeit gras op zijn buik* (There's grass growing on his belly). But nothing about clogs.

Kick the bucket

There are plenty of other ways to die, of course. Some offer comfort to the religious – **to be in the arms of Jesus, to go to**

a better place, **to be at rest** – while some adopt an almost
insolent attitude to the brutal finality of extinction. One of these
is the cryptic phrase **kick the bucket**. Why should death result
from a kick to a bucket? Is **bucket** perhaps a medieval expression
for the Black Death? Did buckets collect recently guillotined
heads during the French Revolution? Or did the kick lead to a
fatal toe infection? None of the above, of course, since the great
joy of such euphemisms is that if you stare straight back at them
in search of logical explanation, you won't get anywhere. Nor
is there any etymological help from Dr Samuel Johnson's
Dictionary of English (1755), which defines buckets as 'the
vessels in which water is carried, particularly to quench a fire'.
The *OED* points to the Old French *buket*, which meant 'a washing
tub or a milk-pail', so we still don't seem to be any the wiser.

You might have thought that of all the words in the English
language, 'bucket' was one of the most stolid, reliable words:
never the type to give us the slip. Well, you'd be wrong. There is
another bucket, with a wholly separate life. In part of Norfolk,
in fact, where certain ancient practices persist, they still use this
other bucket pretty much for its original purpose, since it comes
not from the Old French *buket*, but from another Old French
word, *buquet*, which gave us the word **trebuchet**. A trebuchet
was 'a large medieval siege engine' (*Collins*), as anyone who has
sat through the film of *The Lord of the Rings* will already know.
This bucket, then, has nothing to do with carrying water or milk:
it's a balancing operation. The *OED* includes this comment: 'The
beam on which a pig is suspended after he has been slaughtered
is called in Norfolk, even in the present day, a "bucket".'

The theory goes that the condemned pig was suspended by
its heels from the bucket, or the **bucket beam**. Perhaps, during
its death spasms, the poor animal's trotters clanged against this

bucket, giving rise to the phrase. That particular kicking of the bucket is noted by Captain Francis Grose in his *Dictionary of the Vulgar Tongue* (1785). It's a fine story, and it works well, but some people still have a lingering feeling for that other bucket, the one we know better. It suggests, in fact, another series of images – a poor soul standing on an upturned bucket with a noose around his neck, a foot then flying out to knock the bucket away, leaving the body swinging from the gibbet. Could 'kicking the bucket', then, be associated with hanging, either as execution or suicide? It seems possible, but no written evidence attests to this.

Death in combat

As a general rule, those bodies that have pursued war with the greatest zeal have been the most adept at using military euphemisms as camouflage, or sometimes sand-bags, to deaden the shock of their weapons. These days, the US Army is a key player in this theatre of war. Terms such as **collateral damage** have been around for so long – since the Vietnam War – that they even merit definition in the US Air Force's own *Intelligence Targeting Guide*, namely: 'unintentional damage or incidental damage affecting facilities, equipment or personnel, occurring as a result of military actions directed against targeted enemy forces or facilities'. The adjective 'friendly' had been in use since the First World War to describe a missile passing overhead that turns out not to be hostile since it was fired by your own side. The American journalist C.D.B. Bryan wrote *Friendly Fire*, a bestseller about the Vietnam War, in 1976. The phrase **friendly fire** caught on in the UK during the first Gulf War, in 1991, when more American troops were killed by their own firepower – or turned into basket cases (see page 299) – than by Iraqi weapons.

According to a November 2003 report on a Toronto-based website called *Common Dreams*, the new euphemism for death in the army keeps evolving. During the Vietnam conflict, in which 58,000 US soldiers died, the term **body bag** was in common currency to describe the article in which a corpse was wrapped for storage and transport. Perhaps the comparisons with the Vietnam era – when President Lyndon Johnson was accused of hiding the body bags – were regarded as unwelcome. At any rate, during the 1991 Gulf War, body bags were replaced by **human remains pouches**. Perhaps this was a bit close to the bone, for, according to *Common Dreams*, the preferred term among Pentagon briefers is now **transfer tubes**. You couldn't really have a phrase that better embalms the real effects of violent death.

BODILY FUNCTIONS

We can't all be love gods, and very few of us want to be proficient at dying, but if there's one thing we should all have mastered by an early age, it's **going to the toilet**. Yet the subject has always fascinated us, to the point where we are still thinking up new ways of referring to weeing or pooing – these are not medical terms but they'll do for now – with varying degrees of self-mockery. The acute embarrassment that many of us suffer when mentioning our need to use the **rest-room** makes for fertile ground for euphemism. Frankly, most of us would rather say anything than admit that we need to **have a dump**. You don't even have to make a huge attempt to connect the wish with the activity, which is perhaps why a phrase such as **going to see a man about a dog** (see page 86) has achieved its vague and uncertain popularity. The **privy** has for long been the room where one goes to **drain the spuds**, though 'privy' used to mean

– at least in 1225 or so – a circle of intimate friends. It extended its use from people to a private place, a **latrine** in fact, in 1375. Now it's time to meet some more examples of **number ones** and **number twos** (urination and defecation, from 1902).

Toilet

The word **toilet** is, in fact, a euphemism par excellence. It's a diminutive from the French *toile*, which had various meanings according to a Cambridge scholar called Randle Cotgrave who was writing in 1611, including 'a bag to put night-clothes' and 'other stuffe to wrap any other clothes in'. During the seventeenth century, 'toilet' kept retiring to **powder its nose** (see page 434), returning each time with a new definition. Thus we have 'a cloth cover for a dressing-table' from 1682 vying with 'a towel or cloth thrown over the shoulders during hair-dressing' from 1684. To the great diarist John Evelyn (1620–1706), 'The greate looking-glasse and toilet of beaten and massive gold' was an item of furniture used when dressing, as he noted in 1662. By the time Alexander Pope (1688–1744) wrote his famous poem *The Rape of the Lock* (1712–14), his reference to 'The long labours of the Toilet' made it clear that 'toilet' didn't mean squatting over the privy after a curry, but hours spent in pampering and preparing oneself by washing and grooming.

During the eighteenth century, it was fashionable for a lady to entertain visitors as she approached the closing stages of her toilet. Sir Walter Scott (1771–1832), in his romantic novel *Kenilworth* (1821), was one of many nineteenth-century writers for whom 'toilet' referred to a way of dressing, or to the costume itself. But it was Lord Byron (1788–1824) who pipped everyone to the post for giving it the contemporary slant: 'There is the closet, there the toilet' begins stanza 153 of his mock-epic poem *Don Juan* (1819). And so 'toilet' came to mean 'the bowl', and **to go to the toilet** meant 'to empty one's bladder or bowels into a piece of enamel', rather than to fish among the contents of one's wardrobe.

Lavatory

No word for toilet can tell it like it is. What about **lavatory**? It's the place where one washes, from the French verb *laver* (to wash), but in 1375 or thereabouts it meant the jug containing the water that you used to wash your face or have a bath. The actual room called a lavatory, where hands and face were washed, appeared in print in 1656. It wasn't until Europe was on the brink of war, 1913, that this word was shortened in print to **lav**.

The Britain preference for 'toilet' over 'lavatory' marks a peak in the ongoing class struggle, but, characteristically, the war was conducted through language. Class warfare in other countries has seen such horrors as the invention and enthusiastic adoption of the guillotine in France, the purging of the entire royal family in revolutionary Russia, and Pol Pot's genocidal campaign against middle-class Cambodians. In pre-Second World War Britain it took the form of certain people flaring their nostrils on hearing the word 'toilet' as opposed to 'lavatory'.

Loo is a mystery too: is it from *l'eau*, the French for 'water'? The *OED* doesn't even hazard a guess, maybe since printed evidence for it comes, incredibly, not until the twentieth century was well established. James Joyce made a joke about Waterloo or **Watercloset** in his 1922 novel *Ulysses*, but the first incontrovertible evidence – 'In the night when you want to go to the loo' – comes in 1940, in a novel by Nancy Mitford called *Pigeon Pie*.

How appropriate: she, of all people, would have known if loo was U (upper class) or non-U (not upper class): she pretty much invented the terms, after all.

At stool

The word **stool** was, and still is, a very simple chair. Around 1410 it came to mean the humble **privy** or room where you did your toilet activity. The *OED* includes the quotation 'Than go to your stole to make your egestyon' from 1582, at which the stool was the action of either weeing or pooing, though by 1533, the word 'stool' had become solidly – if you'll forgive me – associated with faecal matter. By 1597 it was 'a discharge of faecal matter of a specified colour'. Along the way the stool has had lots of other lives, including 'a stump from which sprouts shoot up' and 'a piece of wood to which a bird is fastened as a decoy' (both *Chambers*), and this is surely a welcome thing: it's good to vary your approach when you don't want to be associated with crapping.

Crap

No one could accuse **crap** of being a particularly delicate euphemism. 'To crap' meant 'to defecate' in 1846. In 1874 it was 'to ease oneself by evacuation', as John C. Hotten's *Dictionary of Modern Slang* informs us with delightful euphemism. As an aside, though, if you were a criminal in Victorian England, you'd probably have something else on your mind if you were over-heard talking about **the crap**: it was an underground term for 'the gallows' until around 1834. And yet, these days, crap, **having a crap** or **sitting on the crapper** are about as base and uneuphemistic as one can get – along with **shit**, **shitting** and

the shitter – for the action of **opening one's bowels**. As for
the origin of the word, the early Dutch noun *krappe* is closely
related to the Dutch verb *krappen*, meaning 'to pluck off'. There's
also the Old French noun *crape*, which means 'siftings', as in 'the
grain trodden under feet in the barn, and mingled with the straw
and dust', which is similar in meaning to the medieval Latin word
crappa. All these meanings have the general sense of residue or
dregs – *Residue Dregs*, great name for a film – and they're all
pretty crappy.

Spending a penny

The origins of **spending a penny** are an object lesson in social
history. The penny in question was the asking price for admission
to public lavatories, which were introduced in this country at the
Great Exhibition of 1851. Charging for admission was common
from then on, it seems, wherever they were built, just as levying
a toll for a newly constructed bridge was also widespread. The
great advantage to saying you were spending a penny was its
non-specificity. You didn't need to go into any detail about
whether it was a **number one** or a **number two**: no further
information was required, or, I'm sure, wanted. Even when prices
rose, the expression remained and seemed set to continue in,
albeit antiquated, use.

The decimalization of Britain's coinage in 1971 brought the
beginning of the end for Britain's pay-as-you-go toilet system,
but that was some time after the phrase 'spend a penny' had
embedded itself in the nation's hearts, minds and bottoms. The
first sighting of the phrase was not until 1945, though, in a book
called *Strange Story* by H. Lewis: "'Us girls,' she said, "are going
to spend a penny!"' Were they really going to visit a **public**

convenience? Surely not. And that's another marvellous euphemism for exactly the same item of street furniture, first noted in print by (Sir) Osbert Lancaster in 1938: 'The cathedral, the Dean's house ... and the public convenience ... are all "architecture",' wrote the great cartoonist, art critic and exotic character.

Call of nature

A need to defecate or urinate has long been known as **a call** or **a call of nature**, and people have been **paying a call** for some centuries now. First off the mark was Laurence Sterne, author of *Tristram Shandy* (1759–67), a novel that was one enormous shaggy dog story (see page 101), so no wonder there were a few exaggerations, such as 'A city ... who neither eat, or drank ... or hearkned [sic] to the calls either of religion or nature for seven and twenty days'. A helpful entry in the magazine *Tailor & Cutter* from 1852 advises that 'The calls of Nature are permitted and Clerical Staff may use the garden below the second gate'. The sequel to Jim Carrey's 1994 comedy film *Ace Ventura: Pet Detective* was called *Ace Ventura: When Nature Calls*. A very funny title: funnier, said some who had seen it, than the script.

Caught short

The staff at the tailors above might have had to **relieve** themselves in a hurry, especially if they were **caught short**. The *OED* doesn't list this, but it has plenty to say on the subject of **to take short**. This means 'to take by surprise, at a disadvantage; to come suddenly upon', and is often to be found in a nautical context. As well as that, **to be taken short** means 'to have an urgent need to urinate or defecate'. For its first instance in English, we are indebted to *Funk's Standard Dictionary*, from 1890, which lists, 'To be taken short (colloquial), to be pressed with the need of evacuation of feces'. For its first use in literature we are directed to consult a poem by Ignatius Roy Dunnachie Campbell called 'The Wayzgoose' from 1928. This includes the line: ''Tis Nature's whim that dogs, when taken short,/ Still to the loftiest monument resort.' So it isn't just people who are taken short. 'To be caught short' is a good phrase, though, and useful in a joking context in cricket, such as 'Their big-hitting number three batsman went for a slog and was caught short by the boundary'. Ho ho.

Relieve oneself

Men and women have been relieving themselves since the dawn of time, but the precise phrasing **to relieve oneself** is no older than 1931 – 'I wanted to relieve myself' – and occurs in a book about the British murderer Alfred Rouse by Sydney Tremayne in 1931. (Rouse gave a lift to a hitch-hiker, whom he murdered by burning him alive inside his car. Nasty story.) The Revised Standard Version of the Bible, published in 1952, renders a line in the first book of Samuel: 'And he came to the sheepfolds by the way, where there was a cave; and Saul went in to relieve himself'. The original Hebrew is **to cover his feet**, but this was evidently a euphemistic expression in itself, so one euphemism was being translated with another, which gives one a nice warm feeling. (Did they do it to keep warm?) The *Collins* definition of 'relieve oneself' is 'to urinate or defecate'. Presumably there was no ambiguity this time.

Vladimir Nabokov (1899–1977), one of the greatest text-teasers in the English language, wrote in his 1960 novel *Invitation* to a *Beheading* about 'The bliss of relieving oneself, which some hold to be on a par with the pleasure of love'. And if you're tempted to dismiss that as stuff and nonsense, just bear in mind that Nabokov was also a world-famous lepidopterist: his collection of male blue butterfly genitalia holds pride of place at the Harvard Museum of Natural History.

To powder one's nose

W. Somerset Maugham (1874–1965) was the first person we know about to put the words '**I must powder my nose**' into a woman's mouth, but there have been many since then. In a way it's the ultimate toilet euphemism because there is nothing in it that remotely refers to defecation or micturition, merely an acknowledgment that, outside the cubicle, a woman might take a few moments to retouch her make-up. Certainly if one were to suggest that she was going to **take a leak**, one would get a very dirty look indeed, perhaps because that phrase is even more recent. In fact it comes from a writer at the very opposite end of the scale of gentility from Maugham: Henry Miller (1891–1980), and his novel *Tropic of Cancer*, which was published in Paris in 1934. The novel was eventually published in the United States in 1961, prompting a furore similar to that generated by *Lady Chatterley's Lover* in the UK. If only Miller had shown more interest in euphemisms, there wouldn't have been any such fuss. In fact, 'I stood there taking a leak' is one of the most respectable lines in the whole book. Such an activity, of course, like many such instances of toilet euphemism, is more likely to apply to a lady than to a gentleman. It's a bit like the old adage that 'horses and soldiers sweat, men perspire; women merely glow'. So bulls shit, men obey calls of nature … and women powder their nose.

DRUNKENNESS

Every generation remembers its first drink, and likes to record the moment with a series of memorable phrases that always tell us much about a particular society and a particular age. So, for example, variations of the phrase **in one's cups** have, since Thomas Hoccleve used it in 1406, referred to the drinking of intoxicating liquor or drunkenness. A 1611 translation of the Book of Esdras, one of the Bible's apocryphal works, contains the line 'And when they are in their cups, they forget their love both to friends and brethren'. Around the same time, the word **legless** meant 'having no legs'. Flip forward three centuries, and it means 'drunk'. The first reference is from the pop song 'Wide-eyed and Legless' by Andy Fairweather Low, which rose to number six in the Christmas charts back in 1975.

A 1946 study of current English records that 'Synonyms for **drunk** now current in England ... [include] **tiddley**, **oiled** or **well oiled**, **sloshed**'. The origin of 'tiddley' (or 'tiddly') – meaning mildly intoxicated – is mysterious, especially since, from the 1920s onwards, 'tiddly' was used in the services to mean 'smartly dressed or well-presented' (perhaps from tidy), which is quite the opposite of **pissed as a fart**.

It's interesting to compare these genteel expressions – like tiddly and so on – with today's barrage of more explosive terms for the same state, such as the not yet *OED*-listed **bladdered**, **twatted** and – heaven help us – **wankered.** Whereas the old-school euphemisms are designed to draw a discreet veil over what can be fairly anti-social behaviour, adjectives such as **arseholed** (1982) and **rat-arsed** (1984) are, if anything, more like dysphemisms – i.e. the deliberate crudities of an age that delights for satirical purposes in putting an ugly gloss on stuff and calling a spade a bloody great mechanical digger.

Three sheets

The joy of being drunk, unless you're doing it every day before breakfast, is that you can pretend not to be. Hence the barrage of phrases that unite to persuade the drinker that he or she can, variously, dance, sing or in some other way entertain someone who is clearly not very interested.

Think of the word **sheet** and you'll think ... bed? That's from the Old English word *scíete*. Now change your location so that you're on board a clipper, snaking its way over the sea to Java in search of spices and exotica. 'Sheet' also meant 'a rope on a ship' (or, if we're going to get technical, 'a line on a ship' – in nautical speak, ropes have to be made of metal, and any other cord is a line). The key point being that if your mainsheet, your jibsheet and your spinnaker sheet all become detached, your ship is **three sheets to the wind**, and unable to control itself or be controlled. Spinning around like a **piss-head**, in other words. Some of our most imaginative and colourful expressions denoting the intake of excess alcohol have come out of the army and navy, which for centuries have housed and trained many of our most successful and enthusiastic drinkers.

The expression **three sheets in the wind** was first recorded by Pierce Egan (1772–1849), a chronicler of London life who had his ear very close to the (under)ground on account of the many slang expressions he noted. 'Old Wax and Bristles is about three sheets in the wind' comes from his book *Real Life* (1821). Sixty years later, Robert Louis Stevenson (1850–94) noted, 'Maybe you think we were all a **sheet in the wind's eye**'.

The navy also gave us the archaic and much less well-known phrase **half-seas-over**, or simply **half-seas**. When originally transcribed, in the mid-sixteenth century, it meant literally 'halfway across the sea'. Then, in the seventeenth century, it meant 'caught in two minds' and was used by such distinguished writers as the playwright Sir John Vanbrugh (1664–1726) and the poet Lord Byron. In between times A *New Dictionary of the Terms Ancient and Modern of the Canting Crew* (1700) explained 'half-seas-over' – perhaps connected to seasickness, though I can't state it with confidence – as 'almost drunk'. This has not survived into the twentieth century.

Cut

Another phrase whose meaning is not immediately apparent is **half-cut**, but one of the meanings of the word **cut**, when used as a participle, is 'lessened or reduced'. In 1624 this could refer to something being diluted or even castrated; then, in 1673, we find 'He is flaw'd, fluster'd, Cup shot, cut in the leg or back', which appeared in a marvellous slang dictionary called *The Canting Academy* by Richard Head, a seventeenth-century rogue who probably knew from first-hand experience every euphemism for drunkenness he collected. A popular book of the time, *Chrysal, or the Adventures of a Guinea* by the Irish lawyer Charles Johnstone (?1719–1800), contains the wonderfully forgiving line: 'Your excellency was a little cut, but you broke up much the strongest of the company.'

'Three sheets' and 'half-cut' are among our best expressions for drunkenness, but there is no shortage of other ways of saying **pissed**. (That term, by the way, evolved from meaning 'splashed with urine'. It appears first in Ben Jonson's 1616 play *The Alchemist* and is an occupational hazard for the inebriated.) And how appropriate that it was first spotted in a volume called *The Tyneside Songster* in 1889: 'Sit still, you pist fool'.

Tired and ...

One of the most successful twentieth-century phrases for drunkenness was born in 1967, care of the satirical magazine *Private Eye*. It owes its creation to the antics of first deputy leader of the Labour party, George Alfred Brown (1914–85). Brown, or Lord George-Brown as he became better, if mockingly, known upon being elected to the peerage by Harold Wilson in 1970, was an effective politician and campaigner, and an inveterate drinker. Unfortunately, when he'd been **at the bottle** (Scotland's most famous poet Robert Burns seems to have hit upon this phrase first, in 1789) his behaviour became unpredictable and often unacceptable. This habit increased when he was under pressure, which was so frequent in the 1960s that his colleague Anthony Crosland referred to the 1963 leadership election campaign as 'a choice between a crook and a drunk' (respectively, Harold Wilson and George Brown).

Of course, as Patrick Marnham recounts in his book *The Private Eye Story* (1982), it was 'quite impossible in those days for the press to say that a cabinet minister was drunk'. Instead, *Private Eye* produced a spoof report of a memo from the Foreign Office (FO): 'Following the appointment of Mr George Brown as Foreign Secretary, I am reliably informed that a special memo has been dispatched by the F.O. to embassies and consulates abroad.' The memo, it went on, 'is intended as a guide to ambassadors and embassy spokesmen when dealing with the Foreign Press.' There followed a list of English words that were obviously intended to be helpful when dealing with Brown: 'Tired, Overwrought, Expansive, Overworked, Colourful, Emotional'. Translations were provided in French, Italian, German and Russian. Thus the phrase **tired and emotional** tottered into the language. By the time Peter Paterson came to write the biography of Lord George-Brown in 1993, the phrase was so well established that it was used as the book's title. How very different from our own dear politicians of today.

Chapter Twenty

X-rated

*T*he usual definition of **X-rated** implies that the material described thus is suitable only for adults. In practice, adults are some of the last people who should be exposed to such material. It's not as if we don't think about sex too much anyway. Feeding X-rated material to an audience that's perpetually hungry for more may not be such a great idea.

Society is still struggling with its attitude to **adult** matters. Indeed, the word 'adult' is something of a euphemism itself, having evolved from meaning 'a mature person', most often a man (1531), to 'a grown-up attitude' (as late as 1929). From there, according to the *OED*, it came to be 'applied euphemistically to premises or productions ostensibly restricted to adult access, such as **adult cinema**, entertainment, movie, etc.; pornographic, sexually explicit'. That usage originated in the fleshpots of North America, naturally, but it has travelled to places as far apart as Kent and Burnham-on-Sea, as we shall soon find out.

The joy of dictionaries lies in witnessing the utter demo-cratization of language. There are no priorities in this system of headwords: each word gets the attention it deserves, and just that. Thus, the etymological roots of 'sublime', 'beautiful' and 'culture' (none of which you will find in this book) are investi-gated just as passionately and scrupulously as the stories that lie behind **wank**, **jerk** and **dogging** (all of which you *will* find – and in this very chapter).

The democratic nature of lexicography is evident in the dating process that lies behind every word, for without that information, no word is properly 'dressed'. Britons may grumble that their society is obsessed with bureaucracy and form-filling these days, but it was the Victorians who really set the ball rolling with their learned disquisitions on every – well, nearly every – English word that had ever been.

And yet, for all the *OED*'s unparalleled, unrivalled, unapologetic and unshakable intellectual excellence, anecdotal evidence suggests that it's not just the common people – the hoi polloi – who enjoy luxuriating in the detail of rude words. You might think that all those highfalutin types in their libraries would have eyes only for posh words, but you'd be wrong. Whisper it not in the reading rooms of the British Library and the Bodleian, but there is evidence that the *OED Online*'s wordsearch tool receives a disproportionate number of enquiries for its X-rated words. Surprising? Perhaps not. Maybe it's because the dictionary is just the place from which to examine some of the language's most dangerous elements. Seeing these words on the screen, you can inspect them at your leisure. Downloading child porn is, of course, illegal, and rightly so – even if you're writing a book about it. But examining **pornography**, the word, is not a crime, and rightly so.

Seeing how different centuries have dealt with X-rated issues – mostly, in some form, to do with sex – is as important a part of our shared social history as any other. Did Victorians wrap up difficult words in Latin just as they encased 'naked' piano legs in satin? Was Geoffrey Chaucer's readiness to use a word such as **cunt** an act of daring, or merely frankness?

Our aim is not to tiptoe around the long shadow cast by some of our most shocking words, so be warned: this chapter starts with **kinky** and ends with **fluffer**. In other words, it goes from bad to worse.

Kinky

The *OED* tells us that the word **kink** is probably from the Dutch word *kink*, meaning a 'twist or a twirl'. (German, Danish and Swedish all have the same word.) The *OED* speculates that it comes from a root *kink-* (which seems logical) or *kik-*, meaning 'to bend or twist'. That's hypothesis, but we are fortunate to have physical evidence from contemporary Icelandic, which uses the verb *kikna*, meaning 'to bend at the knees', or *keikr*, meaning 'bent back'. The word 'kink', when first used in English in 1678, meant 'a short twist or curl in a rope, thread, hair, wire, or the like, at which it is bent upon itself'.

Kinky was first attached exclusively to hair. More specifically, and since 1844, it was used to describe Afro-style curls. In fact, it seems to have been a traveller's term because references to **kinky-headed** and **kinky-haired** Africans were most often used by nineteenth-century voyagers. But in that same century it also began to acquire a more figurative sense. This is clear from John Russell Bartlett's *Dictionary of Americanisms* (1860) in which he defined kinky as 'queer, eccentric, crotchety'. In his 1907 novel *The Longest Journey* E.M. Forster (1879–1970) described a jaundiced young philosopher as having a 'kinky view of life'.

'Kinky' became kinkier as the twentieth century progressed, and varied according to where on the planet you were standing. In the USA, until the First World War, 'kinky' could mean 'lively or energetic': 'You seem to be feeling pretty kinky to-day' comes from a US publication called *Dialect Notes*, dated 1914. The next twist in the story of kinky comes in 1927, when it appeared in *Collier's Weekly*, a magazine that published a mixture of fiction and investigative journalism in a distinctive narrative style. This has to be fiction: 'Why, you can't tell me that you didn't know those five big cars were kinky.' 'Kinky?' ... 'Those cars were bent.' This suggests that the word was popular with the criminal fraternity and could also mean 'dodgy' (see page 373). This sense continued, certainly until 1954, as the *OED* includes the citation 'kinky gambling paraphernalia' from that year. But kinky could also be used in its original sense of 'curled': for example, the offspring of an artificially irradiated mouse in 1956 had tails that were 'kinky'.

From criminality, kinky then became associated with **perverted** behaviour, as it was then called. It first broke through in that touchstone novel of postwar London *Absolute Beginners* (1959) by Colin MacInnes. The unnamed nineteen-year-old narrator has a girlfriend called Crepe Suzette. 'Suze ... meets lots of kinky characters ... and acts as agent for me, getting orders from them for my pornographic photos.' Thus 'kinky' became associated with the seamier side of sex. A **kinky advert**, reported the *Daily Telegraph* in 1963, implied 'irregular sexual practices', but there is evidence from a variety of novels, films, journals and other memoirs of the time that people were capable of feeling kinky towards teapots (1960), sweetbreads (1964) or Black Russian cigarettes (1967). They probably thought that these objects were – to use a popular word from the time – exceptionally 'groovy'. These uses of 'kinky' seem to have pretty much flushed out any earlier ideas about innocent fun or simple liveliness.

'Kinky' could also connote **gay sex**, though it more often meant – and still does – what is nowadays called **fetishism**. This is illustrated in an extract from the *Daily Telegraph* (again) in 1971: 'In a moment of excessively kinky passion a husband strangles his mistress'. We're not told, of course, whether a husband's urge to strangle his mistress with his bare hands would be called deranged or perverted. Perhaps he (or she) was wearing **kinky boots** at the time: made of leather, these were first spotted in 1964.

The last part of kinky's journey has been from 1960s' **creepiness** to late 1990s' **funkiness**. Where the word was once a synonym for 'perverted' or **deviant** behaviour, these days couples of all types are being urged to inject a little **kinkiness** into their lives. Esther Freud wrote a bestselling novel called *Hideous Kinky* in 1992. Cinema audiences also enjoyed a British comedy called *Kinky Boots* in 2005. And, of course, there's also the detective writer Kinky Friedman, still ploughing his lonely but entertaining furrow as the world's only Jewish cowboy. Being kinky is now seen as pleasantly eccentric, and is certainly inclusive. Kinkiness no longer means skulking around the edge of society in a pair of rubber trousers. In fact, we seem to have got to the point where being kinky has fused with being **sexually adventurous** and can now be worn as a badge of pride to show that the 'romance' or 'fun' hasn't gone out of your love life. These days there's a global design agency called Kinky, a Ghent-based record label called Kinky Star, and over in San Francisco the Kinky Salon is building 'a community dedicated to sex-positive self-expression'. Wherever you look the world seems to be pointing in an ever-kinkier direction.

Marital aids

On the surface, **marital aids** sound vague and respectable enough. Like 'athletic support' or 'passing wind', they get away with masking their actual function, but the *OED* tells us that a marital aid is 'any device for the production or enhancement of sexual stimulation'. The first printed reference to the term – 'We sell a wide range of marital aid appliances ... Send for our ... catalogue – it'll help you put more life into loving' – is from the *Burnham-on-Sea Gazette*, dated April 1976. That definition strains the link between 'marital' and 'marriage' to bursting point, but maybe that's the intention. If it's 'marital', goes the thinking in Burnham-on-Sea, it must be all right. No doubt that rather windy area of Somerset in 1976 was not the sort of place whose news-agents' windows were full of adverts for ticklers, dildoes, leather straps and butt plugs, but the successful mass marketing of marital aids is attributable to the fact that the words contain a wink and a discreet nod. The term sounds wholesome, but we sense that there is something else going on too. It's post-Philip Larkin, who claimed that sexual intercourse began in 1963,[1] but *before* the anything-goes era of today. It's a prime example of a euphemism (see page 156).

To understand the attraction of certain words, you need first to read the manual. Take the **Wartenberg wheel**, for example. This device, designed by Dr Robert Wartenberg (1886–1956), is made of stainless steel and has a rotating head studded with evenly spaced pins. It can still be found in most medical catalogues. In the field of neurology it is rolled across the skin to test nerve reactions, but it is also popular within the **BDSM community**.

---

[1] From 'Annus Mirabilis' in the collection *High Windows* (Faber & Faber, 1974).

BDSM? The letters refer to **B&D** (Bondage and Discipline), **D&S** (Domination and Submission) and **S&M** (Sadism and/or Masochism). The Wartenberg wheel enhances sexual pleasure for a consenting community with a distinctive approach to pain and sensitivity. The wheel, along with the use of a **vaginal speculum**, are employed to heighten pleasure. In the online world the Wartenberg wheel is listed more prominently as a sex or marital aid than as part of orthodox medical practice.

The fact that certain groups are finding sexual gratification from items more usually found in a medical context reflects a blurring of social divisions, and crossover at its most inventive. In fact, electrical **vibrators** were invented in the 1880s as a means of treating 'hysteria' in women. In her book *The Technology of Orgasm* (1999), Rachel P. Maines begins with her own shock at finding an advertisement for such vibrators within 1906 copies of *Modern Priscilla, Needlecraft* and *Woman's Home Companion* – all respectable women's magazines. These days, however, women are not being prescribed genital massage by their physician: they are shopping online and buying the necessary equipment for themselves, batteries not included.

The rise to near-respectability of what has long been called the marital aid is either a miracle of marketing or an acceptance that a quick shag (see page 456) is not the only means of relaxation after a hard day's work. Unusually, the *OED* seems rather coy about defining **dildo**: 'a word of obscure origin, used in the refrains of ballads'. Now you don't need to be making a living from writing about words to know that *that* is not a definition – it's more a historical note. It's only in the small print, written underneath, that we learn it is 'also a name of the penis or phallus, or a figure thereof; *spec.* an artificial penis used for female gratification'. As well as Dr Wartenberg and his wheel, the dildo has been pleasuring women – and men too, whatever the *OED* might say – for centuries, and was originally made of stone, wood or other materials.

The commercial success of the 'Jack Rabbit Vibrator', along with a plethora of other **ticklers** and **teasers**, is evidence of the **sex toy** as a form of home entertainment, though the topic of 'marital aids' is still some way from becoming chatter around the dinner party table. The main difference these days is that this category of marital aid is made from rubber or latex rather than wood or stone.

Nowadays you don't have to be married to enjoy the improvements that a marital aid can bring to your sex life. The term was once a kind of code encompassing **butterfly strap-ons**, **vibrating panties**, **love eggs** and suchlike, but it's now 'out there' in common parlance. Where Burnham-on-Sea led the way, the rest of the country has followed. It's almost as if women are claiming that they can do perfectly well on their own, thank you very much, or with just a little help from their battery-operated friends.

Jerk

While Philip Larkin's tongue was firmly in his cheek when he wrote his now-famous lines about sexual intercourse beginning in 1963, there had long been another type of sexual act that, if it came to a contest, would have triumphed, one-handed, over intercourse. It was masturbation. We know for sure that people were **jerking off** in the nineteenth century because they have told us. The extracts in the *OED*, listed under the word 'off', introduce us to the verb **to jerk off** – the jerking in this case being to the point of orgasm. One is from a rare 1865 work called

Love Feast by a writer who took the pen-name Philocomus: 'I'll jerk off, thinking of thee'. That's the earliest, but a pantomime called *Harlequin Prince Cherrytop* was performed in 1879 and this contained the line 'To the privy I would repair, And **toss it off** in the basin there'. The *OED*, admirably thorough as ever, also suggests we look up **bring**, **jack**, **pull**, **suck**, **toss**, **wank** and **whack**. By adding the word 'off', all these verbs can be extended to the point of orgasm, though not on the same evening.

The noun/verb 'jerk', along with its Scots cousin **yerk** (1509–1871, but not much since), is assumed to have arisen in imitation of the sound of a whip or rod. 'Jerking' has implied masturbation since the Victorian era, according to Barrère and Leland's 1889 *Dictionary of Slang*, but, like adolescence in its later stages, the word seems to have shed its obsession with self-abuse and can be applied to the wider world. The implication is never kind, of course, but **a jerk-off** could mean 'a simpleton' in 1968 or 'a fool' according to a 1970 edition of *Playboy*. These days, **a jerk** or a jerk-off is more likely to be a time-waster, especially in the States, than someone engaged in what used to be called **self-pollution**.

'Jerk', like many of our X-rated words, lost its impact after a while and began popping up in less threatening environments. Who knows: perhaps it's time for 'jerk' to return to the meaning it had 300 years ago – 'to lash with satire or ridicule'. There is no shortage of institutions that richly deserve the sting of its lash.

Meanwhile, 'jerk' should not be confused with the cured meat known as **jerky**, since this latter word comes from the Spanish-American verb *charquear*, which means either 'to dry' (of meat) or 'to carve up' (of a person). Hmm… There is also the Peruvian dialect word *charqui*, which means 'dried flesh, unsalted, in long strips'. It's hard to see how any confusion could arise between jerking off and laying out long slivers of tender meat, isn't it?

Pole-dancing

In 1992 the *Chicago Tribune* reported on 'girls soliciting, performing naked **pole dances** and erotic carnival tricks in the bars that blanket the area'. And yet, in October 2006, the *Guardian* newspaper reported that 'The country's biggest supermarket chain [Tesco] has upset parents by selling a pole-dancing kit in its toys section'. The BBC would evidently have approved, judging by this comment, made two years earlier: 'In recent years, pole dancing has been attracting a steady stream of women keen to improve their fitness, flexibility and have fun at the same time'.

Just a bit of fun? Fun and fertility, more like. Dancing around the **maypole**, as it was originally known, was originally a Germanic custom and has long inspired ambivalence among northern Europeans about what that pole represents. It combines springtime fun and a much older, darker, pagan-influenced adoration of the male member. Put it this way: if, instead of a maypole, there were a giant carved wooden phallus plonked down on the centre of village greens, would the churches, the girl guides and the morris dancers be so keen to endorse it?

Of course, there are theorists – or spoilsports – who deny the pagan or penis/pole connection, and insist that sometimes a pole is simply a pole, or a tree, but not a penis. Whatever form the ceremony takes, though, it has long been a central feature of May Day celebrations, but evidence suggests that even some Victorians were growing weary of it, as this quotation from *Appletons' Journal* – a magazine devoted to literature, science and art – reveals: 'When next a **May-pole dance**, that long since worn-out and always wearisome affair, is introduced in a drama, the exasperated audience will rise *en masse* … and exterminate the May-pole.'

Our earliest reference to the May Day maypole is from 1529. Eighty years later, the royalist journalist John Crouch had already carved out a more ribald idea of it in his 1655 'newsbook' *Mercurius Fumigosus*: 'Wee'l Increase and Multiply, and may with any man. You may, indeed good Sir, you May, your May-pole stiff and strong.' That doesn't leave much doubt about how he viewed the pole.

Pole-dancing can be done with varying degrees of sensuality, and either fully clothed or butt-naked, but that isn't the key to the commercial success of, for example, the telescopic X-pole (with its own carrying case and nylon strap). For the fact is, to pole-dance your way to success, you need the sort of upper thigh muscles that would not look out of place on a bucking bronco rider, and the fitness industry has not been slow to spot the potential health benefits from the activity.

That's what pole-dancing has in common with its maypole ancestor. Raunchier aspects have been deliberately played down in favour of something more wholesome. It used to be about crowning the Queen of the May, the embodiment of the Earth's energy. These days, no doubt helped by movie stars such as Angelina Jolie having their own poles installed at home, it's more about having well-toned bums and tums.

Wanking

Etymologically, **wanking** is a huge anti-climax. It gives the impression of having impeccable baggage from northern Europe, and we turn to the dictionary, expecting to find references to similar words such as *wenken*, Icelandic for 'to squeeze', or *wengen*, very Old German for 'to tug', or possibly the Old Norwegian *wanka*, meaning 'to stand up'. Alas, no such history exists. The word **wank** seems to have embedded itself in the (largely British) lexicon of self-abuse as recently as 1948, and is the bastard offspring of a Mr and Mrs Slang, according to Eric Partridge.

The *OED* doesn't support this comparison in any way, but we couldn't help our eyes wandering over to the noun **whang**, a 1536 variant of **thwang**, meaning 'thong' (see page 325). *Chambers English Dictionary* defines whang as 'a leather thong; a thick slick; a penis'. The *OED*'s last reference to it in this form is from Robert Louis Stevenson's *Travels with a Donkey in the Cévennes* (1879): 'With a glass, a whang of bread, and an iron fork, the table is completely laid'.

The next thing we know is that 'whang' has indeed morphed from a hunk of cheese into a penis. It sounds like an early feminist joke in reverse. 'Leave them horses alone or I'll cut your whang off' is a line from *Honey in the Horn* (1963), a novel of pioneer life in eastern Oregon by Harold Lenoir Davis, which drew a lot of praise at the time. In sightings since then, 'whang' has been used, mostly by admiring male writers, about well-endowed men.

Again, though, 'wanking' and its associates have turned a sort of corner. Granted, it's unlikely to turn into a euphemism for a bouquet of roses – although you never know with the English language – but it has developed a further array of meanings in recent years, beginning in 1970, when Peter Laurie's book *Scotland Yard: A Study of the Metropolitan Police* contained the unedifying comment that 'Fred's counsel is a fat wank'. The use of 'wank' as a synonym for 'rubbish' continues to this day, as do more recent coinages, such as 'Oh, do stop **wanking on**' – which is merely a request for someone to talk less. At this point it seems entirely appropriate to move on, though not before we pause to pay tribute to some of the proliferation of entries on the urbandictionary.com site for 'masturbation'. These include: **buffing the banana, holding your sausage hostage, jackin' the beanstalk, rounding up the tadpoles, spanking the frank** and on and on and on …

To wap

Amid the profusion of words for the sexual act these days, and despite marvelling at every college kid's eagerness to include his own well-rehearsed – physically and verbally – neologism on the latest list, it's also fascinating to wander back into the past to see which words have come into and then fallen out of fashion. One such is the verb **to wap**, evident around the year 1400, and with a meaning similar to throw or pull. Between 1567 and 1725 it was a slang term for **copulation**. We owe its first reference in this context to the irrepressible Mr Thomas Harman, a Kentish gentleman active during the sixteenth century. His one book was called A *Caveat or Warning for Common Cursitors, Vulgarly Called Vagabonds*. It was first published in 1566, and – from later copies – we know that Harman was a dab hand at chatting to many of the ne'er-do-wells and itinerants (frequently failing to distinguish between the two) who passed his door. Harman writes of a man who 'tooke his Iockam in his famble, and a wapping he went', which means something like, 'He took his penis in his hand and went away copulating (or jerking off)'. **Iockam**, incidentally, lingers on in the members-only area of the jockstrap.

The activity of **wapping** is not to be confused with Wapping, the part of London named after a Saxon called Wæppa, even though, given the area's dodgy reputation, it probably saw a fair amount of wapping over the years. Now, of course, since Rupert Murdoch moved his newspaper operation there, the area enjoys unrivalled respectability, especially the lorries driving bundles of the *Sun* and *News of the World* with headlines screaming 'What a **whopper**!' This word, marked 'colloquial or vulgar' by the *OED*, is defined in *Chambers Dictionary* as 'one who whops; anything very large, especially a monstrous lie'. It began its career in print in 1785, thanks to Captain Grose and the *Dictionary of the Vulgar Tongue*, when it meant 'a large man or woman'. To study it further, etymologists direct us towards the verb **to whop**, a variant of 'to wap'.

More recently, 'wap' went all upper case, in which style it stands for Wireless Application Protocol, an international standard for applications that allow you to connect to the Internet from your mobile phone or PDA (Personal Digital Assistant). WAP technology dates from 1997, though in some circles it is regarded, for various reasons, as a failure, leading to its rebranding as Worthless Application Protocol. It would be nice to think that some wag had 'wap' in mind when WAP was conceived, or that if WAP achieves universal admiration, 'wap' will also return to fashion. Maybe that's too much to hope for. After all, it's not as if we have don't have enough words for having sex.

Porn

In between **porn** and **porny**, the *OED* stops at twenty-one other headwords along the way, like a British tourist taking a wide-eyed stroll on his first night in Amsterdam's red-light district. These

entries include freakish one-offs from serial neologists such as
James Joyce: he invented **pornosophical** in 1922 – it didn't
catch on. Nor did Arnold Toynbee's **pornographico-devotional**,
which means 'both pornographic and devotional'. ('Rare',
comments the *OED*. Unique, you might wish to add.) Along the
way, we are exposed to all the various shapes into which the
word **pornographic** has been squeezed, the very earliest of
which appears to be the noun **pornography**. This seems to
have entered English from an 1800 French (who else?) treatise
on *la pornographie*, though it took until 1842 to make the
transition. How would we define it? The depiction of sexual
subjects or activities 'in a manner intended to stimulate erotic
rather than aesthetic feelings', says the *OED*. And then, of
course, there's the **hard** or **soft porn** split, depending on how
explicit the material is.

Sir William Smith's *Dictionary of Greek and Roman
Antiquities* (1842) distinguishes between 'rhyparography,
pornography, and all the lower classes of art'. **Rhyparography**:
there's a word to conjure with. It's Greek in origin, as is 'porn',
in fact. The Greek word *rhuparos* means 'filthy'. Add the verb
grapho (to write) and you have someone who writes about filthy
things. Of course the Greeks didn't just write about sex: they
drew it, painted it, sculpted it and – sometimes telling us more
often than we need to know – had it. Turn it into English and you
have 'a painter of mean or sordid subjects'. Rhyparography is a
lovely-looking old word, first spotted in 1656, which did not
survive into the twentieth century.

As for 'porn', it's from the Greek work *porne*, meaning
'prostitute' – simple as that. A *pornuboskos* was 'a brothel-
keeper', and someone described as *pornophiles* was 'fond of
prostitutes'. In English, 'porn', as the shortened form of 'porno-

graphy', dates from 1962 (mentioned in the 10 May issue of *John o' London's Weekly*, where a character called the Captain, a seedy but not at all unsympathetic individual, is described as making a precarious living by writing 'porn'). It took 120 years for us to drop the -ography bit, but it is interesting that we are habituated enough with porn now to settle for the simple word. Here's hoping one day soon we'll all be into 'lexico', rather than having to spell out our passion for lexicography.

It's striking how many of these early references to pornography are taken from the world of classical Greece and Rome. It seems that Victorian scholars had quite enough on their hands weighing up what to do with the recently discovered treasures of Pompeii, and doubtless preferred to immerse themselves in that world, rather than pass comment on contemporary porno mores. Given the subsequent history of porn, from soft to hard – from rumpled knickers to aggrieved-looking mongrels – and given that distinction between material stimulating erotic rather than aesthetic feelings, it's interesting to see how pornography has turned something of a corner in recent years. Onlookers can see a hint of it in non-sexual writing, such as Kathryn Flett's description of the BBC's remake of *Dracula* – 'more **property porn** than an entire series of *Grand Designs*' – in the *Observer* newspaper in December 2006.

If you love reading cookery magazines, but prefer gazing at beautiful images of food to making it yourself, you are participating in **food porn**. If you like reading about exotic places rather than actually visiting them, you're indulging in **travel porn**. All tastes are catered for: **gastro porn**, **disaster porn**, **war porn**, even **weather porn**. The *OED* has been on to this trend since 1973, when an article in the *Journal of Pop Culture* mentioned **horror porn**. In fact, almost any activity that seduces its audience with glamorous images – emphasizing 'the sensuous or sensational aspects of a non-sexual subject' as the *OED* says – can now be said to have its own style of porn, and this may be where the word is going. Alongside this is the still depressingly rapid spread of **Internet pornography**.

Dogging

The verb **to dog**, as language buffs never tire of telling us, reveals a sizeable linguistic shift, made possible because English verbs had begun to shed themselves of their grammatical constraints from the time of Geoffrey Chaucer and onwards. In 1519 'to dog' (see page 356) meant what it still means: 'to follow closely and not a little menacingly'. These days the verb **to stalk** has partially supplanted it, though that has – or had – more obviously sexual undercurrents.

If you were a spy (or espie) in the seventeenth century, as a snippet from Randle Cotgrave's *Dictionarie of the French and English Tongues* (1611) shows, you would have indulged in 'ambushes, waylayings … treacherous dogging, of people'. The term was also applied to the sport of grouse-shooting, where dogs, rather than human drivers or beaters, were used to stir up the birds. (You can imagine the Royal Family and half the toffs in the country going to that kind of dogging.) A good **dogging moor**, in the first seventy or eighty years of the twentieth century, was a moor fit for this activity. What happened next?

What happened next has not yet been documented by the *OED*,[2] though if its lexicographers could get their hands on the network of closed-circuit TV cameras that is slowly tightening its

---

2 The revised entry was being prepared as this book went to press.

grip on all aspects of life in Britain, they might begin to see how many people are engaging in semi-public sexual activities. This new form of alfresco sex is known as **dogging**. The BBC reported on it in September 2003: 'Dogging is an extension of "swinging" parties – and involves exhibitionist sex in semi-secluded locations such as car parks or country parks'.

It is indeed a strange mixture of back-door sexual exhibitionism, voyeurism and yet another excuse for forming a queue – an old English habit that takes going to the dogs in quite a different direction. Like a cross between a cockfight and an orgy, it involves groups of people watching two others having sex. The Internet is used as a message-board, alerting people, very often at the last minute, about locations. An NHS team in Kent noticed a rise in hepatitis cases towards the end of 2002, and they put it down to dogging. It's interesting to note where the locations for illicit sex have moved to. It used to be a sea-front hotel – or its rustic and more romantic alternative, the shady copse. These days it's supermarket car parks and motorway lay-bys. *O tempora!* as the Roman orator Cicero observed in 63 BC, *O mores!*

While the health risks are worrying hospitals, the etymology is causing concern to wordsmiths. Is it called 'dogging' because dogs have no objection to **shagging** in public? Or is it playing with the idea of the innocent and morally unobjectionable practice of taking the dog for a walk? Maybe it's linked to the sense of tracking, which dogs have been doing since at least the sixteenth century. After all, aren't contemporary **doggers** meant to follow a trail that ends with them watching couples making out in a car or on the ground?

Wherever 'dogging' comes from, it will be interesting to see where it goes now that the cat – so to speak – is out of the bag.

The activity received an intense blast of publicity in March 2004, when the former England international footballer Stan Collymore was pursued – dogged, in fact – by reporters from the *Sun* until he is said to have admitted: 'I've been to dogging sites maybe a dozen to fifteen times and, yes, I have taken part and had sex'. Whether it was preferable to being a Five Live match commentator – since he was sacked from that post forthwith – poor Mr Collymore hasn't so far revealed in public.

It seems likely that the publicity generated for dogging will lead to its gaining greater acceptance, since it was always destined to take place on the threshold of society. An explosion of cold sores and hepatitis infections will tell its own story, but the questions that bother *Balderdash* wordhunters – would 'word-doggers' have made a greater impact? – is whether outdoor sex enthusiasts felt more inclined to indulge in this activity once it had a name, and whether the welter of references in the media has legitimized or even encouraged the practice. 'There's nothing wrong with dogging: it's in the dictionary.' Is that really how social licence works?

Fluffer

The word **fluff** is surely one of the skimpiest words in the language. It feels like a gentle breeze could simply knock it over. Just the thing, in other words, to describe 'downy particles that separate from dressed wool', or 'the fluff of a peach' as Captain Francis Grose wrote in his 1790 *Provincial Glossary*. Given its wispy nature, it is perhaps not surprising to see the term **a bit of fluff** used to describe a young girl in a little-known novel called *Fluff-hunters*, written in 1903 under the pseudonym 'Marjoribanks'.

And there, as blameless as the skin of a peach, matters would have rested, had not the world of filmed pornography ruptured the purity of this innocent tableau. The *OED*, in a draft entry dated September 2004, defines **fluffer** thus: 'In the pornographic film industry: a person employed to stimulate a male actor to ensure that he has an erection when required. Hence: a person employed to prepare or warm up an audience for another act.' The first quotation to back this up is from a 1979 issue of the magazine *Screw*: 'One of the black guys was nearly demanding a warm-up, some contrivance to stiffen his johnson before the main event ... "No fluffers," screamed someone.'

It is rather extraordinary, isn't it, that this sordid term is sharing the same pages – well, online pages – with some of the noblest and most uplifting sentiments ever translated into words, from Shakespeare to the King James Bible and onwards? It illustrates the *OED*'s absolutely rapacious appetite for all words. One might almost say they're promiscuous for words, but they're not: they're simply wholly and non-judgementally democratic. There is no censorship or discrimination, no matter how unsavoury.

Fluffers were also the people employed by London Underground to clean the railway system at night. They were 'the char-ladies of the Underground' as a Pathé film from the 1950s referred to them, flossing the railways lines with knives and brushes. Perhaps they got their name because of the huge amount of fluff and dust – and human hair – that was sucked into the tunnels every day.

The verb **to fluff** was by no means lacking in experience before. It has been around, one way or another, since 1790, but it had never known times like these. It could mean 'to pant' or 'to knock the breath out of someone', as if literally to wind them. To these nineteenth-century meanings could be added a rare sense that ran similar to 'flash in the pan': a **fluff in the pan** (1825) was what you did to gunpowder to cause it to ignite. So there at least the word had a bit more backbone.

To fluff someone in the nineteenth century also referred to the practice – evidently quite common among railway clerks – of giving passengers the wrong change, presumably in those scrambled moments when the train was pulling into the station and people were thinking more about racing to catch it than whether they had been given the right change. (I might suggest a link with 'to fleece', but I'd be alone.)

If you mis-speak your words on stage or on air you have **fluffed your lines** – a meaning extant since 1936. 'Fluff', at its most fly-away, came to mean something utterly insubstantial, as in this 1906 letter from the Bloomsbury Group art critic Roger Fry: 'Having to see reporters … and being careful to give them a lot of fluff with nothing inside it.'

You could also, of course, **fluff your hair**, which may have influenced – ironically of course – the porn usage, since the porn world's fluffer is, albeit contemptibly, something of a make-up artist.

And all the actions involved in these centuries of cleaning, scrubbing, primping, rejuvenating and lifting somehow coalesce on the set of a **blue**[3] movie, converging and dancing upon the tip of a man's penis in a series of pampering manoeuvres carried out by someone who, one at least hopes, might find themselves

---

3 'Blueness', as first described by the writer Thomas Carlyle in 1840, can refer to indelicacy or indecency, perhaps because of its connection to blood or the equally sensual colour purple. 'Blue-blooded' dates from 1853: 'The old blue-blooded inhabitants of Cranford', in the novel *Cranford* by Mrs Gaskell. Blue can go either way, it seems, from classy and upmarket to seamy and downmarket.

referring rather vaguely to a certain period on their CV in years to come.

It's notable how, perhaps because of its somewhat arcane job specifications, the fluffer of the porn industry has not pushed the other types of fluffing out of the way. Fluff, for all its apparent flimsiness, is not as insubstantial as you might think.

Wordhunt Results

The First *Balderdash & Piffle* Wordhunt

In June 2005 *The Oxford English Dictionary* and the BBC jointly launched a national Wordhunt, asking the public to seek out ante-datings and information about the origins of fifty words and phrases. Although this was a twenty-first-century campaign, conducted largely online, it was very much in the traditions of the *OED*'s original 'Appeal to the English-speaking and English-reading Public' back in April 1879.

More than 1500 emails and letters arrived in response to the BBC/*OED* Wordhunt. Many of the correspondents were utterly convinced they knew an earlier use of a word, or offered attractive, exotic and sometimes downright implausible theories as to its origins. All fascinating stuff, but not always of much help in rewriting the dictionary. However, among these tall tales and adamant correspondents were hundreds of offerings giving clear evidence of the sought-after words in books, newspaper articles, sheet music, records, TV programmes and handwritten diaries. These were used to make the six programmes of the BBC2 series *Balderdash & Piffle*, first broadcast in January 2006. Each programme focused on a different letter of the alphabet – P, M, N, C, S and B being the favoured ones.

A tribunal of senior editors from the *OED* (associate editor Peter Gilliver, etymologist Tania Styles and chief editor John Simpson) sat in judgement on the submissions of wordhunters. And over the course of the series, they agreed to revise a whopping twenty-one entries in the dictionary – all thanks to the new evidence.

While the series was broadcast (to an average audience of 2.7 million viewers), 4500 more emails came flooding in. The quality of the evidence supplied by this ever-growing band of keen wordhunters was such that the BBC sprang into action and commissioned a one-off follow-up programme, *Balderdash & Piffle* – The Results Show, to demand further action by the judges. Yet more rewrites followed – twenty-two of them to be exact – fourteen of which were for words and phrases that had stumped the original wordhunters.

Perhaps the most distinctive feature of the first *Balderdash* Wordhunt was the nature of much of the evidence we were sent. While the *OED*'s editorial teams and reading programme members have ready access to mainstream books and newspapers, that doesn't always help them. Many modern words and phrases are first recorded in sitcoms, football fanzines, local newspapers and classified advertisements, and, increasingly, online. Our wordhunters could lay their hands on this type of material where professional lexicographers could not. They also offered handwritten evidence, which presented a challenge to the dictionary's bibliographers. How reliably was it dated? How could future scholars consult it? Ultimately, thanks to *Balderdash* wordhunters (now honoured on the 'Wordhunt Wall of Fame' on the *OED*'s website), thirty-six of the *OED*'s 300,000 or so entries have had a makeover. And here they are.

Balti

Thanks to *Balderdash & Piffle*, there is now a corner of the *OED* that is forever Balsall Heath in Birmingham. Journalist Tazeen Ahmad found a perfectly preserved copy of a magazine called *The Balsall Heathan*, dated July 1982, which contained an otherwise unremarkable advertisement for a restaurant boasting

'Specialists in Kebab, Tikah, **Balti** Meats, Tandoori Chicken and all kinds of curry'.

That was a two-year ante-dating of **balti** for the OED, and as crucial as garam masala is to a curry chef. What it didn't settle, however, was the question of where the balti was born. Wordhunter Harry Bell watched the programme and also came forward with evidence from 1982, of 'Balti mince' on a special menu for a sci-fi fans convention – held not in Birmingham, which has long claimed paternity of the balti, but Newcastle! In any event, it seems that one place the balti definitely didn't originate in is the Indian subcontinent.

Beeb

Apart from **Auntie**, the most common nickname for the BBC is the **Beeb**. The OED calls it a 'colloquial contraction', but evidence of its use in print hadn't come any earlier than the 1970s. Now surely someone must have been using it earlier than that? In fact, Jeff Walden of Caversham came across an interview with the colourful and eccentric disc jockey Kenny Everett. Here, surely, was a man who wouldn't hesitate to use the affectionate colloquial contraction. And his hunch was right. Everett obliged in an *Evening News* interview from September 1968. The journalist writes, 'He gives the impression he doesn't worry about anything: least of all "Beeb", as he calls the BBC.' Those inverted commas suggest that the nickname was pretty new back then.

Boffin

The boffins at the *OED* – splendid chaps that they are – had two senses of **boffin** in the dictionary, dated just a few years apart. The first sense, from 1941, is 'an "elderly" naval officer'. The second sense is 'a person engaged in "back-room" scientific or technical research', first encountered in *The Times* in 1945 with reference to the early pioneers of radar. But surely, historian and uber-boffin Felipe Fernandez-Armesto asked in *Balderdash & Piffle*, the word has now moved on, being the denigration of choice to describe people who are frightfully clever but can scarcely tie their shoelaces. The *OED* judges were persuaded, and have unveiled a whole new sense for 'boffin': '3. Brit. colloq. In weakened use: an intellectual, an academic, a clever person; an expert in a particular field; esp. such a person perceived as lacking practical or social skills. Cf. EGG-HEAD n.'

Bog-standard

Mark Edwards from Coventry may have had to put up with years of mickey-taking (see page 345) for not disposing of his large pile of *Personal Computer World* magazines, but in the end the clutter proved its worth. The *OED*'s first use of the term **bog-standard** was dated 1983: *Balderdash & Piffle* just knew there had to be something earlier, and, more importantly, so did Mark Edwards. He rifled through his pile and dug out a copy from 1978 that had the very phrase we were looking for.

However, Gerald Dawson in Bristol could go not one, but five years better. His example, culled from a review of an Escort racing car in *Hot Car magazine*, is dated to October 1968, so we've pulled the bar back a whole fifteen years. What a Triumph! (Or an Escort.)

Bomber jacket

If the US-style **bomber jacket** was based on American flying jackets from the Second World War, why was there no textual evidence earlier than 1973? Is it possible that, as the *OED* suspected, the term was applied retrospectively, and only after they became a fashion item?

In a classic case of 'The Yanks are coming', Bill Mullins in the USA came to our rescue. He found an advertisement from the Los Angeles Times for December 1940 – 'This three-piece outfit for junior consists of a bomber jacket, drape trousers, and squadron cap' – which ante-dates the original front-runner by thirty-three years! Bill: Britain salutes you.

Bonk

The *OED* couldn't find anyone who had been **bonking**, sexually speaking, prior to the year 1975. Despite much frantic activity, Balderdash wordhunters could find no earlier reference to it either. But it was more than a consolation prize when Gerald Donovan from Bristol found us an ante-dating for the noun **bonk**, as in the sound of being hit on the head (see page 296). He uncovered this in a risqué little number from 1934 called Cannibal Quest by Gordon Sinclair, subtitled 'The Racy Record of a Cannibal Quest from Sydney to Afghanistan'.

Chattering classes

The originator of the term **chattering classes** was thought to be the journalist and quintessential chatterer Clive James. But we were sure that a certain section of the middle classes had been described in that way before 1985. In fact, it fell to a former editor of the *Spectator*, Frank Johnson, to offer one of his own cuttings from James Goldsmith's short-lived *Now!* magazine, dated March 1980. Sadly, Frank Johnson died in December 2006. He will be remembered as one of the wittiest journalists of his day, and could have few better memorials than to be quoted in *The Oxford English Dictionary*.

Cocktail

The model Jerry Hall went searching for the origin of **cocktail** in New Orleans, just days before Hurricane Katrina hit. Despite her efforts to find the answer at the bottom of a martini glass, she couldn't push the date back. After the broadcast, news came in from wordhunter David Barnhart of a sighting of 'cocktail' that predated the *OED*'s first 1806 reference. As a result, we now have evidence from a New Hampshire newspaper called *The Farmer's Cabinet*, dated April 1803: 'Drank a glass of cocktail – excellent for the head … Call'd at the Doct's … drank another glass of cocktail …' Not such good news for the bicentenary celebrations of the cocktail, which were held in 2006, but we hope the world of mixology will forgive us.

Codswallop

It feels like it's been around for as long as other silly-sounding words, such as 'nincompoop' or 'popinjay'. In fact, **codswallop** is a twentieth-century newcomer. The *OED*'s first recorded use of it was from a 1963 correspondent who wrote to the *Radio Times* to complain that some programmes were rubbish. (No doubt they'd revise their opinions if they experienced today's output.)

Thanks to Joe Cunningham, a resident of Canada, we have an earlier citation from those kings of radio and TV comedy – who never wrote a word of codswallop in their lives – Ray Galton and Alan Simpson. The extract is from a 1959 script for Hancock's Half Hour. Sid James is, as usual, upbraiding Hancock: 'Don't give me that old codswallop. You were counting your money.'

There is no proof, says the *OED*, for the attractive but sketchy story that the name came from a real person, a British soft drinks manufacturer called Hiram Codd (1838–87), who produced several designs for mineral water bottles in the 1870s, and that it became a derogatory term used by beer drinkers to refer to soft drink. No, says the *OED* severely: no evidence for that.

Cool

Jazz saxophonist Courtney Pine went hunting for the roots of **cool**, as a term of approval or sophistication, certain that it must pre-date 1948. Sure enough, thanks to a tip-off from wordhunter Kate Carter from Putney, he found a reference to that kind of 'cool' in a short story of 1933 by Zora Neale Hurston, a writer who recorded dialect terms from the exclusively African-American Florida town she grew up in.

But that was just the start. Alan Dobson of Sheffield put his hand on the lyrics to a travelling minstrel show performed by white people in black-up with the very of-its-time title *Evah Darkey Is a King*. That was from 1902, and included the line 'de way we dress is **cooler**'. And then the phrase 'Dat's **cool**!' was found as an interjection from as far back as 1884. Dat is indeed cool – a sixty-six year ante-dating for such a ubiquitous and magnificent word.

Full monty

This has to be one of the most mythologized phrases ever used. Did it arise from Field Marshal Montgomery or Montague Burton the tailors? The most recent citation was 1985: *Balderdash* wordhunters resolved to do better. The *OED* had – and still has – a slight preference for the term as a shortening of Burton, the tailor: the Montgomery theory is described as 'popular but unsubstantiated'. The *OED*'s damning verdict on the latter was that 'the sheer variety of often vague, purely anecdotal, and mutually contradictory explanations for the connection – ranging from his wartime briefing style to his breakfasting habits – renders this less credible'.

Balderdash may not have settled the argument, but wordhunters did send in several references to fish and chip shops called *The Full Monty* from before 1985, which made it into the *OED*'s revised etymology, albeit with a pinch of salt (and a dash of vinegar). Could the 1982 edition of the Yellow Pages: Manchester North (where these shops were listed) be the most boring cited work in the entire *OED*? And that's saying something, since there are 2,436,600 quotations.

Gay

The *OED* appealed for help with pinning down when **gay** started to mean 'homosexual'. Their earliest evidence for the word in this sense was 1935 (as an adjective), and 1971 (as a noun), though the word goes back at least as far as the 14th Century in English in its original sense of 'light-hearted, exuberantly cheerful, merry'. Establishing a precise meaning is a challenge for even the most pernickety etymologists in the shady period when the word was used first in a homosexual context (pre-1940s) and then came to be used explicitly with reference to homosexuals.

The Wordhunt came up with two great examples of this. Noel Coward's song from his 1929 musical, *Bittersweet*, had camp lyrics referring to Oscar Wilde's trademark green carnation – one of the first symbols adopted by homosexual men to identify themselves: 'Faded boys, Jaded boys, Come what may, Art is our inspiration, And as we are the reason for the 90s being gay, We all wear a green carnation...' With our modern perspective it seems to be an obvious nod and a wink to sexuality, but the *OED* were not convinced - it *could* simply be referring to the original light-hearted sense of gay.

Lesbian writer Gertrude Stein's short story "Miss Furr and Miss Skeene" was from even earlier – 1922 – and contains surely the record number of gays in any published English sentence: 'Georgina Skein and Helena Furr lived together then. Helena Furr did not care about travelling, she liked to stay in one place and be gay there. They were together then and travelled to another place and stayed there and they were gay there, not very gay there, just gay there, they were both gay.' Again, although the innuendo seems obvious, the *OED* cannot be sure of the meaning and could not accept it as a straightforward citation for the homosexual sense.

Nevertheless we can claim a victory and be gay ('disposed to joy and mirth'). Both the Wordhunt's examples *have* gone into the dictionary in square brackets, as examples of how the word evolved towards its modern meaning, and also proof of how tricky it can be for etymologists to pin down meaning. The dictionary has now given their entry for the word a thorough review, and curiously the earliest recorded date for gay meaning homosexual has travelled forward in time. Noel Erskine's *Underworld and Prison Slang* which included the word 'geycat' in 1935 has been expunged, and now sits correctly in the entry for 'gay cat', meaning a young or inexperienced tramp (a term which dates back to 1889). The earliest date for gay in the homosexual sense is now 1941, whilst the earliest noun usage has been brought back from 1971 to 1953.

Mackem

The word **mackem** has long been a nickname for a fan of Sunderland Football Club, or more generally for someone who lives in Sunderland or the Wearside. It recalls the days when ships were made there and taken back for repairs (hence 'We mack 'em and we tack 'em'). Local radio DJ Mike Elliott was outraged that the *OED* had no record of this word in between **mackelerage** and **Mackenzie bean**, so he set out on a quest for the grail of printed evidence. Answers came in thick and fast, and 'mackem'ly as far back as 1980–1.

In fact, it was Jerome Borkwood of London who supplied the earliest printed evidence of the word 'mackem'. It comes from – what an irony! – *The Magpie*, a Newcastle United Supporters Club fanzine. Now that Sunderland fans claim 'mackem' as their word, it might be better for them to remain in denial that it was probably coined by their arch-enemies.

Made-up

The term **made-up** is a regional expression for being happy, originally from Ireland, and now distinctive of Liverpool. The wordhunt for it led, via a dose of Beatlemania, to a first for the *OED*. Professor Stephen Fletcher of Loughborough University remembered 'made-up' from the mid-1960s, and tracked down its use to the wedding day of Ringo Starr to Maureen Cox on 11 February 1965. In an ITV News interview, Starr said, 'John and George were at the wedding, and they were made up, you know. They're happy.' Tania Styles of the *OED* enjoyed that: 'He's even glossing it,' she said excitedly.

This was the first time in the *OED*'s history that it had cited a TV interview, as opposed to something scripted. And it's Ringo's eighth appearance in the *OED*: he'll be made-up about that too.

Management-speak

It seemed to fall naturally to Ian Hislop, the editor of *Private Eye*, to investigate **management-speak**, which (curiously) hadn't yet made it into the *OED*. *The Sunday Times* dates the phrase back to 1986, and *Balderdash* submitted its own definition to the dictionary's top team: 'a load of balderdash and piffle, spouted by self-important morons in an attempt to feign intelligence and authority, has the effect of rendering the most simple concepts completely unintelligible; the bastard son of newspeak, coined by George Orwell for the lies of corrupt politicians'.

The *OED* team seemed reluctant to buy that wholesale, so they had a bit of a think and came up with: 'a form of language considered typical of business managers or consultants, esp. in being obfuscatory, needlessly complex, or empty of useful meaning'. Well, that's their job, after all.

Mark/Gas mark

These unlikely candidates actually provoked the greatest number of entries to the first Wordhunt. It seems that cookery books are the one type of publication that people never throw away.

We were seeking uses prior to 1963, and entries for both **Mark** (noun 1, sense 34) and **Gas mark** – both used in relation to ovens – came in by the ladleful. For 'Gas mark' the first prize was won by *The Berkshire Cookery Book*, published by the Berkshire Federation Women's Institute, and the date was pushed back to 1958. We trust that their 2007 jam output will be of a particularly high quality. For 'Mark', the alarmingly titled *Radiation Cookery Book* from 1929 took the honours.

Minger

As the *Balderdash* Wordhunt heated up, the *OED* judges were put to the test on the type of material they would accept, especially in the case of **minger**. This rather rude word for 'an ugly or unattractive person, especially a woman' had been dated at 1995, but that was before *Balderdash* was inundated with poetry from teenage Goths.

The trump card came in from Clare Washbrook of Derbyshire, who'd dug up her own teenage poetry-filled notebooks. One, entitled 'They Ming Therefore They Are', contained the lines, 'They bandy around the tag of minger/ Slap it on teacher, pupil, parent, singer.' The *OED* team wrestled long and hard over this one. Did this handwritten poem, albeit date-marked 1992, count as evidence? John Simpson, reigning chief of the *OED*, finally delivered his verdict: yes. Rejoice! (Note to Goths: that means 'be happy'. Try it some time.)

Moony

The moon has been a synonym for the buttocks since 1756, but **mooning**, or doing a **moony**, is of more recent vintage. Will Weaver of Eastbourne overcame his natural embarrassment and showed us a comic that he and his childhood friend Ben, then aged ten, had created in 1990, replete with references to buttocks, **moonies** and other pre-teenage thrills. Respect also to the editors of the Leicester University student magazine *Ripple* for re-creating an attack by 'The Moonie Squad', in which a lecture-hall is invaded by a gaggle of students who run in, expose their buttocks and run out. This activity was first glimpsed in print in 1987. Some students are still in therapy.

Mullered

The trouble with words for drinking is that they don't tend to come up in a situation where one is armed with pen and sober enough to use it, so written evidence is often thin on the ground. One such is **mullered**, a word for 'drunk' that the *OED* sought before 1995.

Our wordhunters must have been too busy getting mullered to better this, but then Paul Davies found a reference to another sense of the word, meaning 'to destroy or comprehensively beat another team on the sports field'. This came from *All Played Out* written by Pete Davies just after the 1990 World Cup, and beating (mullering?) the *OED*'s first entry by three years. As Davies wrote, 'It had been a dreadful game. Macca asked Gazza, had he heard? – they were getting "mullered" back home…' Gazza is, sadly, now more familiar with both senses than he was in 1990.

Mushy peas

As most people know, **mushy peas** are a northern delicacy. Not to everyone's taste, perhaps, but whatever you think of their nutritional value, we were sure wordhunters had encountered them before 1975. In fact, we might have known that Roy Clarke, writer of *Last of the Summer Wine* and identifier of so many northern traits, would have bettered that, or indeed battered that, as he did in 1973, with a serving of fish and chips.

One group of hopefuls felt that it could do better – but, failing to find any evidence, decided to make it up. These scoundrels, who shall remain anonymous, produced a *Guide to Tenby* (Pembrokeshire) from 1950. On closer inspection, the cover turned out to have been Photoshopped (yes, that's in the *OED*) to include not only the fake date, but also the term 'mushy peas' itself. Nice try, chaps, but we weren't fooled! It just shows the lengths people are prepared to go to in order to gain *OED* immortality.

Ninety-nine/'99'

We asked Daniela Nardini, whose family have connections with the catering business, to try to find out why a **'99' ice cream** is so called. If we'd known the controversy that it would unleash, we might never have gone there. Ante-dating it from 1977 to

1935, thanks to a price list in Cadbury's archives, was the easy bit. It was exploring pre-war ice-cream history that turned things ugly. The Arcari family, purveyors of fine ice cream from 99 Portobello High Street in Edinburgh since the 1920s, said they invented it. But so did the Dunkerleys from 99 Wellington Street in Gorton, and Marino Bianco from Barrow-in-Furness. Not to mention two other ice-cream dynasties.

To complicate matters, what exactly was a ninety-nine originally? This is an important matter for a historical dictionary like the OED. The definition as 'an ice-cream cone made with soft ice cream with a stick of flaky chocolate inserted into it' would no longer suffice. Thanks to *Balderdash*, there was now also evidence of '99' meaning a short Cadbury's flake (on its own, without ice cream or cone); a sandwich of ice cream and wafers with flake in the middle (but no cone); and, most challenging of all, a cone (manufactured by Askeys from 1937) called the '99', despite the absence of either ice cream or flake! All of these needed to be encompassed in the new post-*Balderdash* OED definition.

As to why it's called a ninety-nine, the arguments continue. The *OED* judges were persuaded to distance themselves from suggestions that they had previously quoted uncritically – 'that something really special or first class was known as "99" in allusion to an elite guard of ninety-nine soldiers in the service of the King of Italy'. But they were unpersuaded by several *Balderdash* wordhunters' ingenious suggestion that the letters IC stand not only for ice cream, but also – and here's the clever bit – that they make the number ninety-nine in roman numerals. Nice theory, said the *OED* top brass, licking their lips. But it wasn't good enough to think of the answer first and then work your way back.

Nip and tuck

The September 2003 *OED* entry for **nip and tuck** reads: 'minor cosmetic surgery, especially for the tightening of loose skin' and comes from 1980. US-based wordhunter Katherine Flynn thought this was showing its age a bit, though, so she got out her scalpel and took it back to 1977. Result: it looks years older, which is just how ante-dating ought to look.

Nit comb

Where would the **nit nurse** be without a fine **nit comb**? In the process of tracking down the former, we also improved the *OED*'s entry for the latter. Fiona Bourne from the Royal College of Nursing in Edinburgh came up with a citation from 1917, in the British Journal of Nursing, beating the previous reference by twenty-six years. Job well done, we thought. But proving that nits have been irking us for a very long time, the *OED* has subsequently rooted out a 1662 quote – from Giovanni Torriano's Proverbial Phrases. 'To enter into the Nit-comb, viz. to sift and examine strictly and impartially, sparing none'. This reads as if it's lifted from the *OED*'s own mission statement. We were proud of our ante-dating, but a further 255 years really is astonishing.

Nit nurse

A nit nurse is a colloquial British term for 'a school nurse who periodically checks children's hair for lice'.

The first recorded use of 'nit nurse' in the *OED* was from the *Guardian* in January 1985. But since this said, 'Whatever happened to the **nit nurse**?', it seemed manifestly to miss the itchy spot by several decades. Anton Dil of Milton Keynes scratched his head and found a reference to 'nit nurse' from a

1942 copy of *The Lancet*. But once you find one, you have to deal
with the whole damn lot ...

Nutmeg

There may not be a lot of footballers who know this, but a
nutmeg is actually 'the hard, oval, aromatic kernel of the seed of
the evergreen tree Myristica fragrans'.

The usage known to most Premiership players (not, it would
be fair to say, usually avid *OED* readers) is of a football manoeuvre
in which the ball is cheekily played between an opposing
player's legs (see also 'flip-flop', page 321). Author Giles Milton
went on a surreal journey, aided by the hallucinogenic properties
of nutmeg, to try to better the OED's first reference. It was
Michael Parkinson who came to the rescue. Delroy Gayle of
London spotted a reference in his biography of George Best –
a player who certainly drifted past a few opponents in his time –
from 1975. Best, ever obliging, even glosses the phrase himself: 'I
love taking the piss out of players too. Like "**nutmegging**" them.
That's sticking it between their legs and running round them.'

Pass the parcel

This game must have been doing the rounds at children's parties
for donkey's years, but whereas people have been pinning the
tail on the donkey since 1887, paper evidence for **pass the
parcel** as the name of a game wasn't unwrapped earlier than
1967. In the rush to clean the room afterwards, it all seemed to
have been swept away. *Balderdash* got it back to 1953, but the
OED was worried about that citation because all the people
playing seemed to be grown-ups.

Step forward Vivian Clear (née Smith), who was sure she'd
written a story about the game in 1955 when she was all of

seven and a half. She consulted her carefully preserved exercise book and there it was – 'Then the party began. Molly, who always had good ideas said to everyone "Should we have **pass the parcel**?" "That's what we're going to play," said Mr. Brown.' Vivian can now lay claim to being the youngest contributor to the *OED*. The dictionary now says 'V. Smith Bk. about Browns (MS story) (O.E.D. Archive) xxi. 46.' If you didn't know other-wise, you'd think it was a reference to some classic of English literature.

Phwoar

Most of us probably know what **phwoar** implies, but how many of us could define it? It's a word that positively begs for an exclamation mark afterwards, as the *OED* acknowledges: 'an enthusiastic expression of desire, approval, or excitement, especially in regard to sexual attractiveness: "cor!" "wow!"' But who first wrote it down? Naturally, *Carry On* … aficionado Graeme Johnston went to the spiritual home of the word, *Carry On Doctor* (1967), but the *OED* team was not convinced whether a wiggling Barbara Windsor had elicited the comment 'Phwoar!' or, as typed in the script, 'Cor!' from the man under the car.

More satisfying, though, was the ante-dating of the word from 1980 (an entry in Viz comic) to c.1976. Why only circa and not exactly 1976? Because the citation came from the autograph book of Michele Grange, formerly of Scunthorpe, and the remark was made about a very shapely pair of legs belonging to her school gym teacher: 'We love Mr Blackburn's legs. Phwor! Cor! Wow!!! Phew! Get Em Off!' This entry caused considerable discussion within the *OED* trinity: could they really accept a teenager's autograph book? An affidavit from Michele finally swung it, and her autograph book has now gained lexicographical immortality, referred to in the *OED* as 'MS

Inscription in Autograph Bk.' But given the unusual
circumstances, the *OED* felt it safer to make the date c. 1976.

Ploughman's lunch

The delightfully specific definition of **ploughman's lunch** is:
'cold snack, usually including bread, cheese, and pickle, and
frequently served in a public house at lunch-time'. But the *OED*
had found no evidence for it before 1970. There is a citation from
1837 regarding a **ploughman's luncheon**, but this wasn't eaten
in pubs, and hardly ever included pickled onions, so it was ring-
fenced with square brackets in the *OED*.

One wordhunter found a reference to a **ploughboy's lunch**
from a 1958 copy of *The Times*, which was close – but not quite
close enough to cut the mustard (or pickle). It fell to
Balderdash's own crack research team to uncover some minutes
at the National Archives from a meeting of the English Country
Cheese Council in 1960, referring to 'Ploughman's Lunch
Showcard[s]' and proving that, far from being traditional fayre,
the ploughman's lunch was the clever invention of cheese
marketers. The big cheeses at the *OED* were duly impressed.

But a Wordhunt is never over. More than two years later, the
OED updated their entry yet again with a reference from the
Monthly Bulletin of the Brewers' Society from 1957: 'There
followed a '**Ploughman's Lunch**' of cottage bread, cheese,
lettuce, hard-boiled eggs, cold sausages and, of course, beer'. Cold
sausage? No self-respecting ploughman's would include that any
more, but at least it pushes the date back three more years.

Pop one's clogs

There are many ways of referring to the act of dying (see page
423), of which to **pop one's clogs** is among the most colourful.

It was David Johnson of Wembley who produced a copy of
Punch from 1970 that couldn't have been plainer. 'He was forced
to retire in 1933 after a disastrous Catholic/Protestant punch-up
among the bugs,' reads the entry in that lightly witty style Punch
was so renowned for throughout the 1970s and before. 'He's just
popped his clogs.' This was a whole six-year improvement on
what had come before.

Pull, on the

The phrase **on the pull** is defined in the *OED* as 'intending or
hoping to attract a partner, especially for sex'. Until wordhunters
got busy, the earliest evidence the *OED* had was from a 1988 copy
of *Jackie* magazine: 'Poor Dave, on the pull, as usual'. But thanks to
David Parkins and Geoffrey Cunnington, we were able to backdate it to a Dick Clement and Ian La Frenais 1975 screenplay. Their
film, released as *The Likely Lads*, included this line from one of
Rodney Bewes's exhausted girlfriends: 'The answer to all your
problems – look up the lads and go on the pull – isn't that the
expression?' That's a massive thirteen-year ante-dating.

Inspired by the Wordhunt, the *OED* boffins went back to the
BBC television series which inspired the film, *Whatever
Happened to the Likely Lads?* And found an even earlier
reference to 'on the pull' in a script for episode 10 in 1972. A
Clive James TV review from 1972 compared the immortal pairing
of Rodney Bewes and James Bolam to Damon and Pythias, Castor
and Pollux, perhaps even Butch and Sundance, 'but never – not in
a million years – *Alias Smith and Jones* (BBC2), which is typical
American TV in that the buddies have no past.' Even then, the
great Clive recognised that Bob's mate Terry's main
preoccupation had been 'trying to pull the birds'. So that settles
the matter.

Ska

The term **ska** had music-lovers reaching for their old 45s, which is fine because that's what most music-lovers love doing anyway. Poet Benjamin Zephaniah's explorations took him – where else? – to Jamaica, where he eventually tracked down the word in a copy of the Gleaner newspaper from 1964, ante-dating the *OED*'s previous first citation of 'ska' by a precious six months.

London-based record collector Dave Edwards went one better, digging out an Island Records recording from 1963 by saxophonist Tommy McCook with the title on the label 'Ska-ba'. Thanks to this, the *OED* was able to issue an improved etymology, suggesting that ska was 'probably imitative of the distinctive guitar sound typical of this music'.

Smart casual

The challenge for wordhunters here was to find a reference to **smart casual** earlier than the New York Times in 1945. They responded, and lo and behold, 'smart casual' has been traced even further back in the annals of fashionable acceptability, to a 1936 advertisement from the Toronto Daily Star. In fact, an even earlier use – from the Davenport (Iowa) Democrat & Leader in 1924 – was found, but the *OED* remained sceptical that it was exactly the right sense, and put it in square brackets – the lexicographical equivalent of purgatory.

Snazzy

A bit passé these days, but **snazzy** was the word to describe something stylish and attractive throughout the 1950s and 1960s. The first reference in the *OED* was from 1932; could wordhunters do any better? The *OED* defines it as 'excellent, attractive; classy, stylish, flashy', but, apart from saying it comes from the United States, gives its origin as 'unknown'. We pulled it back by one year, to the Los Angeles Times of 1931. This was spotted by eagle-eyed Bill Mullins (he of earlier 'bomber jacket' fame). Only one year, but every day counts. Snazzy work, Bill.

Something for the weekend

Certain phrases slip through the net, especially when they refer to our foibles and sexual antics. We were in no doubt that something for the weekend predated 1990, but finding documentary evidence proved unusually difficult. Balderdash wordhunters Michael Glass, Timothy Freeman, James Barrett and Mrs E. Blatherwick provided helpful evidence that the *OED* drew on in composing the first-ever entry for this word. The earliest reference came, funnily enough, from a 1972 Monty Python record, which referred to 'a herd of zebras visiting the same chemist to ask for **something for the weekend**'. But of course.

Square one, back to

This was one of those phrases where we were berated by numerous wordhunters for our apparent ignorance – many were utterly convinced that its origins lay in BBC radio commentary of the 1930s, with its numbered grid system for following football and rugby matches. However, it was back to square one with them, for none was able to furnish us with any evidence of this. Nor, in fact, could anyone find a board game – a more likely origin of the phrase – where you really did go **back to square one**. In the end, American wordhunters Darren Hick and William C. Waterhouse trumped the *OED* by finding the phrase in a 1952 issue of the Economic Journal, so they definitely get another turn on the board.

The Second *Balderdash & Piffle* Wordhunt

Following the success of the first Wordhunt, the *OED* and BBC
decided to join forces again, and in January 2007 appealed to the
public for help with a new list of 40 words and phrases. Once
again there was an outstanding response, with thousands sending
in letters and emails. These were used for another television
series on BBC2, first broadcast in May 2007, in which each of the
eight programmes focused around a different theme [also
adopted as the structure for Part 2 of this book]. Once again
Balderdash & Piffle presented all the evidence to the *OED*
tribunal, and as a result a grand total of thirty-three dictionary
entries were revised. And here they are:

Bananas

We all know what is meant if you say that someone has **gone
bananas** – the *OED* describes it as to go 'crazy mad or wild (with
excitement, anger, frustration etc.)' – but nobody knows where the
phrase came from. Wordhunters came up with some pretty bananas
theories – from enthusiasm at tasting the yellow fruit for the first
time in the austere days of rationing, to people smoking them to get
high – but none of these theories could be proven. The dictionary
had also appealed for evidence that people went bananas before
1968. The Wordhunt found it in George and Ira Gershwin's
unforgettable 1930s hit song *But Not For Me*, in the couplet:

> I never want to hear from any cheerful Pollyannas
> Who tells you fate supplies a mate, It's all bananas…

A famously irreverent rhyme – but didn't this beat the
dictionary's date by 38 years? Alas not. The *OED* tribunal rejected

this evidence, because it wasn't bananas clearly meaning 'mad, crazy' in the sense they were looking for. But it's also clear that we are not talking about fruit salads - so we seem to have come across an entirely new meaning of the word. *OED* Chief Editor John Simpson explained why this new sense wasn't going to get a mention in the dictionary: 'It's sometimes claimed that we collect more instances of words and meanings that don't make it into the *OED* than we do for terms that do finally find a place in the dictionary. The problem with these excluded terms is that there simply isn't enough documentary evidence available to be sure that they have (or had) a significant place in the language. English is full of outliers or borderline cases, which sparkle for a moment and then disappear, leaving no appreciable effect on the language. The Gershwin example seemed to represent a slang use of the word earlier than the 'mad' sense, but even after hunting around in various files and dictionaries we were unable to collect together enough evidence to illustrate that the use had had any real longevity. That's not to say that it'll never be included in the OED, but just that at present it has to go back into the files waiting for more evidence to come to light.' You or I may consider that decision bananas, but that's the way the cookie crumbles, or the banana mushes. Wordhunter Fred Shapiro did, however, manage to find the word in a cartoon strip about a not-very-bright policeman 'Fearless Fosdick', which antedated it by eleven years, back to 1957.

Bloody Mary

Many Wordhunters knew the story that the **Bloody Mary** was both created and named by 1920s movie star George Jessell. The story of the cocktail's creation, and how it came to be named after society girl Mary Warburton, was, after all, told in Jessell's autobiography… which unfortunately wasn't published until 1975, twenty-one years after the *OED*'s first evidence for the drink in a 1956 issue of *Punch* magazine. But the Wordhunt can crack open the Worcestershire sauce and start celebrating, because an article in the *New York Herald Tribune* by Lucius Beebe, the famous food and drink critic, from 1939 reveals all at last: 'George Jessel's newest pick-me-up which is receiving attention from the town's paragraphers is called a Bloody Mary: half tomato juice, half vodka.' Pretty much a perfect citation – it defines the drink, it confirms George Jessel's role in its creation, and it antedates the drink by a full seventeen years. Chin chin. Well, it should be trebles all round for the Wordhunt except for the curious fact that this citation was *already* in the *OED*. The only trouble was that it wasn't in there as evidence for 'Bloody Mary', but for the word 'paragrapher'. Of course the dictionary contains nearly two million quotations. But it is ironic that the Wordhunt for Bloody Mary could have been solved by looking in the dictionary itself.

Bonkers

Although the *OED* did have evidence of **bonkers** being used as early as 1948 in Navy slang, to mean drunk or lightheaded – perhaps from **bonk**, a blow or punch on the bonce or head (see our efforts on **bonk** in the first Wordhunt above) – the first evidence for the word in its modern sense of mad dated to almost a decade later in 1957. Wordhunter Martin Pitt thought that was completely bonkers, and proved that bonkers meant mad first – by finding it in The *Daily Mirror* from 1945. Now that more British newspaper archives are becoming searchable on the internet, finding antedatings from old newspapers seems set to show an upwards spike.

Daft (or mad) as a brush

Daft as a brush is one of those phrases that, once you stop to think about it, seem, well, pretty daft. What is so ridiculous about a brush, anyway – why don't we compare people with the lunacy of a mop or a feather duster? The *OED*'s first evidence for this curious phrase was from the novelist Henry Williamson (most famous for writing *Tarka the Otter*) – he'd used it in a 1945 novel, *Life in Devon Village*: "**Mazed as a brish**', declared Mrs. 'Revvy'…' Pleasingly, *Balderdash* could beat this date by thirteen years, finding it in a novel from 1932, *Labouring Life*, by the very same Henry Williamson. This time the citation helpfully glosses the meaning of brish, for those of us too daft to work it out for ourselves: 'Jealous as a rat. Slow as a toad. Mazed as a brish (brush)…'

Der-brain

Children's jibes are often cruel, but the *OED* do their best to keep up with the playground lingo; if a word has stayed around long enough, it deserves a place in the dictionary. Deep in the archives in Oxford was a file on **der-brain**: building on from the much earlier word **duh** (1948), der-brain had gathered enough citations to justify a whole new dictionary entry. But the earliest was from *Just 17* magazine in 1997 – which seemed implausibly late for the many Wordhunters who recollected using it – no one admitted to being called one - in the 1980s. Andrew Dickens proved them right – he remembered der-brain appearing much earlier, in an episode of the sitcom *Fathers' Day* – another vehicle for the great John Alderton - from 1983, and *Balderdash & Piffle* found the original script to prove it. No der-brains at Wordhunt HQ, then.

Dogging

Never ones to dodge a challenge, the *OED* team turned their attention to **dogging** and wrote a new entry for the sense which means 'the practice of gathering with other people in a public place, typically a car park, to watch or engage in exhibitionist sexual activity'. Wordhunter and sex expert Tuppy Owens helped by providing the earliest citation, from her *Sex Maniac's Diary* published in 1986. And the Wordhunt proved that the word had an even older precedent in the noun **dogger**, found in an interview with singer Marc Almond for *Kicks* magazine in 1982, describing his childhood in Southport:'Parts of it were always so empty and desolate – full of what we used to call "old doggers" – men lying in the bushes spying on couples – staring and messing about with themselves'. This article added weight to the numerous examples of anecdotal evidence that were sent in by Lancashire-based Wordhunters, convinced that the word originated as regional dialect before going mainstream. Most memorable of all was the story of an eighty-nine year old from the Wirral, who remembered first hearing the word in the 1930s. As young teenagers, he and a friend accidentally chanced upon a canoodling couple and were accused of being doggers. Not knowing what was meant by this, they were unable to deny it, nor, perhaps understandably, did they have the presence of mind to ask the couple to write down the terms of their grievance… At any rate, the term made a lasting impression.

The dog's bollocks

It was the connoisseurs of creative crudity at *Viz* magazine who provided the dictionary's first evidence for **the dog's bollocks** from 1989, but though many people credited the magazine with having coined the phrase, its editors insisted that they did not. Step forward Wordhunter and playwright Peter Brewis, who told us of a play he wrote called *The Gambler* (along with Mel Smith and Bob Goody) which includes the immortal line 'when it comes to Italian opera, Pavarotti is the dog's bollocks'. This was first recorded in 1986, beating the dictionary by three years. But it didn't stop there. In the search for the dog's bollocks, numerous leather-clad bikers wrote to the Wordhunt about the days when the Yamaha TZ750 cruised onto the scene. Nothing like it had been seen before – what language could suffice to describe the glories of this new machine? According to *Superbike* magazine from September 1981, "When superlatives fail, get crude". The bike is described quite simply in a headline as "The Absolute Bollocks". Crude indeed – but lexicographically fascinating. Does this mean that '**the bollocks**' pre-empted 'the dog's bollocks' as a superlative? It's difficult to say, however this new evidence prompted the *OED* to create a whole new sense for the word bollocks.

But the phrase was older still than that. Wordhunters also came forward with anecdotal evidence that the term was used by printers many years earlier to refer to a particular set of punctuation marks – a colon followed by a dash :- This usage, sometimes also called the **dog's ballocks**, was recorded in Eric Partridge's *Dictionary of Slang* in 1949. Whilst it's clearly a wholly different meaning, it's hard to think that the printers' slang was unconnected to the later phrase. The *OED* were persuaded, and now also include this wholly different sense in the dictionary entry.

Domestic

The *OED* was keen to find earlier evidence of the Police slang for a violent quarrel between husband and wife – euphemistically

called a **domestic**. Their earliest evidence was from 1963.
Wordhunt detectives got on the case, and a retired policeman
sent in his old notebook, which listed that in 1957 he went to
attend a 'domestic' in Buckley. The policeman wanted to stay
anonymous, because he wasn't supposed to have kept his old
notebook, but *Balderdash* was thrilled by the five-year antedating
– though obviously we hope that the raised voices have calmed
down and that the couple now see eye to eye. Still this didn't cut
the mustard with the stern judges at high court *OED*. They were
concerned that the single word 'domestic', written without any
context around it, was insufficient to prove unambiguously it
meant the noun euphemism they were looking for. With this
evidence flung unceremoniously out of court the Wordhunt
continued the investigation, and found domestic, unambiguously,
in the script for the first episode of BBC series *Z Cars*, in 1961.
Case over – for the time being.

Flip-flop

The humble **flip-flop**, footwear for all fashion-conscious
etymologists, kicked up two of the Wordhunt's most unusual
pieces of evidence. First of all Dot Strong beat the dictionary by a
decade, with her diary entry from 2nd July 1960: 'Worked. Lil set
my hair. Bought flip flops'. A mundane day for Dot perhaps, but
lexicographical gold dust to the *OED* who don't usually have
ready access to the nation's teenage diaries. Then P.D. James (not
the distinguished lady of letters, but a Wordhunter in his own
right) sent in a handwritten Customs and Excise Declaration
form, dating back to when he transferred from RAAF
Butterworth, Penang, Malaya to the UK in 1958. The form records
'1 pair of "flip flops"' – the quotation marks perhaps indicating
that the term was relatively new, little known or colloquial. We're

proud to add that this is the very first time a Customs and Excise Declaration has made it into the *OED*.

Glamour model

The word glamour originally meant magic or enchantment, sharing its root with the word grammar, which originally meant 'all learning'. But the *OED* – and, we suspect, a lot of readers too – wanted to know when this erudite word lost its innocence and became linked to a euphemism for soft porn. Their first evidence for the adjective **glamour**, as in topless model, was from 1981. Never ones to turn up their noses, and with the purest of possible motives, Wordhunters searched high and low – mostly low – to find a range of examples from the 1960s but nothing could top the evidence of Pamela Green. In the 1950s Pamela was Britain's most famous **glamour model** – and she can now add membership of the Wordhunt hall of fame to her accolades. She still had a 1958 *Glamour Guide*, which clearly used the word in its euphemistic sense. No need to avert your eyes – that's a twenty-three year antedating.

Glasgow Kiss

Affectionate as it might sound, a **Glasgow kiss** is no amorous embrace – it's a headbutt. The *OED* couches this in suitably cautious terms by telling us this is 'in humorous allusion to the reputation for violence accorded to some parts of the city' – though the dictionary also contains the rather similar 'Liverpool kiss' which is a blow delivered to the head or face. Archaeologist Neil Oliver went digging for evidence to prove that the word was older than 1987. Glaswegian memories pointed to the 1950s or earlier, but – perhaps as a result of excessive head-butting – no written evidence was found from the 1950s, nor for the next two decades. In fact the best written citation to be found was in the *Mirror* from 1982 – in an article about the Pope's visit to Glasgow that year. His Holiness may have been better known for kissing the ground than administering headbutts, but evidence is the Wordhunt's holy grail and straight it went into the dictionary.

Gordon Bennett

Despite a wealth of anecdotal accounts, the Wordhunt couldn't quite link the exclamation **Gordon Bennett** all the way back to the 19th Century playboy and newspaper mogul of the same name, but it did manage to bridge the gap sufficiently to convince the *OED* that he should get a mention in the etymology. The date to beat was 1967 – an early episode of *Til Death Us Do Part*. Sitcom fans remembered correctly that Gordon Bennett got a mention five years before that in *Steptoe and Sons*. But then Jonathon Green found a novel by James Curtis, *You're in the Racket, Too* from 1937 – a magnificent antedating, well worthy of an interjection.

Hoodie

The OED wanted to know whether **hoodie** was a metonym (see chapter 14) before 1994. Wordhunter David Malone from Mount Temple School in Dublin sent in a copy of their *Spring Magazine* from 1991. He drew our attention to a cartoon picture comparing and contrasting two different fashionable looks – one labeled 'The Rocker', the other 'The Hoodie'. No doubt the magazine's editors were too cool to point out that they were the using the words as metonyms but we're happy to do it on their behalf. A school magazine is a pretty unusual source for the *OED* but the meaning and citation were clear, so the antedating made it into the dictionary. Its Irish origin is also interesting because the earliest citation for the garment **hoodie** (1990) comes from Roddie Doyle, which could well be an etymologically significant hint that this word appeared in Irish English first. Either that or it's a complete coincidence. In any event, hugs all round for hoodies everywhere.

Identity theft

The *OED* were pretty sure that **identity theft** was a relatively new phrase, as it's a relatively new crime – but they wanted to know whether people were fraudulently acquiring personal information to perpetrate fraud, and calling it identity theft, before 1991. No fewer than three Wordhunters (whose identities shall remain anonymous for security purposes – you never know who is reading *Balderdash & Piffle*) found the reference in Florida newspaper the *Sun-Sentinel* from 1989: "Identity theft besmirches victims' records". Bad news for the victims; good news for the Wordhunt – an antedating of two years.

Jack the Lad

Who else could *Balderdash & Piffle* ask to search for the original **Jack the Lad** than loveable rogue, Madness singer Suggs? To help him along the way he had one of the Wordhunt's most bulging postbags – it seemed that *every*body outside the hallowed walls of the *OED* could prove that it was older than 1981. The phrase seemed to pop up particularly often in popular culture – songs by Elvis Costello, punk rockers Sham 69, folk singer Frankie Armstrong and Ian Dury all referenced Jack the Lad. There was even a folk rock band called Jack the Lad, formed in 1973, which featured a former member of Lindisfarne and other musicians from the north-east of England. Their first album, in a bold attempt to familiarise us with their name, was called 'It's Jack the Lad' (1974).

And huge numbers of Wordhunters remembered the phrase being used in the cult classic film *Performance*, released in 1970. Just as that was going into the dictionary as the earliest citation, out of the woodwork dashed a 1969 reference, in the autobiography of British communist and trade unionist Jack Dash. One still can't help but suspect that he wasn't the original Jack the Lad either, but for the moment the title is all his.

Loo

Loo is one of those words that has had etymologists puzzling for decades. There are so many theories for why a toilet is called a **loo** that it's advisable not to try and read them on a full bladder. Was it 'Gardyloo' – a misspelling of guardez l'eau (mind the water) yelled by chambermaids as they poured the chamber pot out the window? Or perhaps it was related to the leeward side on a ship, or a pun on Waterloo? Or perhaps it was named after a prank played on one Lady Louisa Anson, also known as Lou. The word has long been associated with upper class circles, and the *OED*'s first evidence from 1940 was from a Nancy Mitford novel. The Wordhunt flushed out some more aristocratic evidence – a letter from Lady Diana Cooper to her husband Duff Cooper, from 1936, in which she describes her dwellings in Tangier. 'We've come to this very good hotel – your style, with a pretty Moorish bath in an alcove in every room and a lu-lu à côté.' While the word 'loo' is not used in Lady Cooper's letter, 'lu-lu' implies the same meaning and is a very similar word, so the citation has gone into the dictionary inside square brackets. *OED* etymologist Tania Styles was convinced that 'it couldn't possibly refer to anything else'. It has long been suspected that this euphemism for toilet was born in a blue-blooded setting and this high-born evidence adds weight to this theory.

Marital aid

Burnham-on-Sea (which has the shortest seaside pier in Britain, ahem) can heave a sigh of relief – no longer is this most respectable of towns tainted with being the source of the first **marital aid**. The Burnham-on-Sea Gazette from 1976 is no longer the earliest citation in the *OED* for this rather prim euphemism, as thanks to the Wordhunt we now know it dates at least back to 1969 and a newspaper in Long Beach, California – much more racy.

Mucky pup

The Wordhunt for **mucky pup** – '*colloq.* a (habitually) messy or dirty child or (*humorously*) adult' – threw up one of *Balderdash & Piffle's* biggest antedatings, a full fifty years back from 1984. It was a search that provided some unconventional evidence, including a 1977 punk song with the poetic lyrics "I pick my nose… I'm a mucky pup", Ruth Miller's school exercise book from 1954 in which the teacher had written "Mucky pup! Material… very carelessly expressed", and the printed lyrics of Harry Hemsley's song *Dirty Little Tinker* from 1934: "Dirty little muck-pot! Dirty little tyke! That's what Daddy calls me… Dirty little Mucky Pup, But he loves me just the same". Not to be outdone, after the series finished on television, the *OED* themselves started hunting again and managed to push the date back even further still – to 1925 in Roger Dataller's *From a Pitman's Notebook*: "Tha mucky pup! Ah'll bet tha's ad ter coomo doon't chimbley this mornin'.

One sandwich short of a picnic

The *OED* were pretty sure that **one sandwich short of a picnic** came from Australia, and their earliest evidence was from a book from down under from 1993. But the Wordhunt found a British citation in a BBC programme from 1987 – *Lenny Henry's Christmas Special*, in which the comedian spoofed Michael Jackson's song 'Bad' as 'Mad', and sang along with the backing singers in a pleasing falsetto: 'one sandwich short of a picnic!' But it didn't stop there. Earlier evidence also arrived from a 1985 edition of the Brisbane *Courier Mail*: 'He's got one oar out of the water… the light is out… he's one sandwich short of a picnic'. Maybe having one oar out of the water will catch on too one day…

Plonker

As a result of the Wordhunt, **plonker** has acquired a new sense in the dictionary. Whilst *Balderdash & Piffle* appealed for evidence for the sense in which a plonker means 'a foolish, inept or contemptible person', Wordhunters noticed that the *OED*'s earliest two quotations in their entry were misplaced. In the original 1966 citation from *All Neat in Black Stockings* by J Gaskell, the word refers not to a Del Boy type plonker, but to 'a man who sanctions sexual relationships between his girlfriend and his male friends', which is now the definition for this new sense of the word. As an *OED* staff member remarked, it's always good when the public teach the *OED* a thing or two about the way our language is used!' Having moved the misplaced citations of plonker into their new sense, the earliest citation for the foolish person sense is now 1981, from an episode of *Only Fools and Horses*.

Pole dance

Pole dancing can be a dangerous occupation – one of the *OED*'s citations for **pole dancer**, from 1952, is a headline recording 'Pole dancer dies in 137-foot fall'. That was one long pole. But it was **pole dance** in the erotic sense that was on the *Balderdash*

& *Piffle* appeal list, and Wordhunter Stephen Bond pushed the word back by one year, finding evidence from 1991 on the internet (if you must know, a dated chat forum in a user net newsgroup thread). Accepting evidence from the internet is a relatively recent change of policy for the *OED*, a decision they didn't take lightly. The dictionary still do not cite from the internet if there is an acceptable traditional alternative, and much prefer 'archived' online sources which are more reliably datable. But in the 21st Century it's impossible to ignore the web – often new terms appear on the internet long before they arrive in print, so it's too late to view internet citations as not properly, lexicographically-clothed. It's also common to discover recent uses of words which, according to the dictionary's rules, would have had to be labeled as 'obsolete', or no longer in use, but which were still attested online.

Prat

Melvyn Bragg can no longer list, amongst his many claims to fame, the earliest citation in the *OED* for **prat** (in the sense of 'An idiot, a fool; an ineffectual or contemptible person'). Wordhunter Toby Forward made a tantalizing discovery in a modern biography of Sir Richard Burton, which quoted a letter from India in 1876. The adventurer described the place that he was staying as a 'rotten hole full of middle class and respectably pious water-swilling pratts'. Was this really an antedating of nearly a century – and was that the sort of term of abuse that Sir Richard might have reached for? We know that he spoke 29 languages including several African and Asian dialects, but we still found it hard to believe that the word prat ever left his lips – or nib. The Wordhunt tracked down the original handwritten manuscript of the letter to show to the *OED* tribunal. Alas, Richard Burton's handwriting was not as neat as professional lexicographers require – from his scrawl the *OED* could not make out 'pratts'. They decided that it instead said **mull** – quite a different-looking word, you'd think! A Mull was a European official serving in the former Madras Presidency in southern India – a context fitting perfectly with Burton's letter. Not the antedating *Balderdash* was hoping for, but it did prompt the *OED* to update their entry for Mull.

The Wordhunt didn't stop there with **prat** though. The date *was* brought back first of all to 1965, in Joe Orton's play *Entertaining Mr Sloane* – with the marvelous and underused insult 'you superannuated old prat!'. And then, after the *Balderdash & Piffle* programme was broadcast, further evidence came in from a full decade earlier – E Trevor's 1955 book *Big Pick-up*: 'Come dahn aht of it, Milly, you stupid prat!'.

Regime change

Euphemisms have always found particularly fertile ground in the military – sometimes it's just nicer if we all pretend we're not really at war, and talk about **friendly fire** or **collateral damage** instead of straightforwardly discussing killing each other. The expression **regime change** has been in existence since at least 1925, but in those days it was just a simple expression meaning the replacement of one ruling group in a country by another. Later on, this neutral term started to acquire a new twist in its meaning: it wasn't just the replacement of one regime by another, but a change of regime which was brought about intentionally by an external power for political ends. The challenge for the Wordhunt was to work out when the term turned this corner – the earliest euphemistic use of the phrase the *OED* had was 1990, the time of the Nicaraguan conflict. A *Washington Post* article revealing an American plot to topple

Colonel Gadaffi and create 'regime change' in Libya got the phrase back to 1987. Wordhunt hits the target once again – and without any further loss of life.

Shaggy dog story

The *OED* define a **shaggy dog story** as "a lengthy tediously detailed story of an inconsequential series of events, more amusing to the teller than to his audience, or amusing only by its pointlessness". Valerie Stewart found near-perfect lexicographical evidence for the phrase in a 1937 edition of *Esquire* magazine – nine years earlier than the dictionary's first record.

Better still, the dictionary wanted information on the phrase's origin, and our antedating helps with that too. We now know it's called a shaggy dog story because of a particularly long, bad joke about a shaggy dog. The magazine piece, *Don't Laugh Now* by JC Furnas, tells a story which may well be the original joke, and similar versions with minor variations were found by Wordhunters in several slightly later publications from that era, suggesting that it was widely circulated at the time. It is a long and involved narrative – it really does not repay close reading - in which an Englishman loses his dog while holidaying in New York, and places the following advertisement in a local newspaper: 'Big, white, shaggy dog lost. Reward of £500 offered to anyone who safeguards its return to London'... Enter the American hero of the tale, who finds a shaggy dog on the street, takes it by ship across the Atlantic, encountering all sorts of long and tedious adventures along the way, finally tracking down the Englishman in London. The Englishman takes one look at the dog and coldly remarks: 'My dog is shaggy, Sir, but not so damn shaggy as that.' Woof woof.

Shell-suit

When they weren't gallivanting about in frockcoat and tails,
Victorian gentlemen were apparently wearing **shell-suits** – the
OED's first citation of the word is from 1893, and this first sense
was defined as "a suit of clothes consisting of a tight-fighting
trousers buttoning on to a tunic" – and not a chav in sight. It
sounds almost as attractive as the modern version: 'a lightweight
casual outfit, similar to a tracksuit, consisting of loose fitting jacket
and trousers with a thin inner lining and water resistant shell of
shiny polyester'. The dictionary's earliest evidence for this
apotheosis of clothing hell was from a home shopping catalogue
from 1989 (well it's not the sort of item you'd want to buy in
public, is it) – but the Wordhunt, ever with its fingers on the pulse,
unveiled a shell-suit from sixteen years earlier, in an advertisement
from the 1973 *Charleston Daily Mail*, showing a dapper looking
fellow (in what looks rather like a pair of pyjamas) described as a
'comfortable nylon shell suit'. One more victory for Wordhunting;
one more blow on the cheek for fashion.

Sick puppy

No, not a young dog – still less a mucky pup - in need of
veterinary attention, **sick puppy** is an American slang term for
an individual who acts a little strangely. The *OED* were preparing
a draft entry for this term, and wanted to know if it was older
than 1985. No Wordhunter could possibly be considered an
'abnormal, deviant, or deranged person', as the dictionary now
defines sick puppy, but never liking to shirk a challenge, the
archives were scoured and evidence found two years earlier in
the *Boston Globe*.

Spiv

The dictionary lists the etymology of the flashy, wheeler-dealer **spiv** (1934) as obscure, suggesting it might come from spiff and spiffy, meaning to be smartly dressed. But other suggestions include the Romany word for sparrow, V.I.P.s backwards, or a police abbreviation for 'Suspected Persons and Itinerant Vagrants'. Searching for spivs, the Wordhunt came up trumps twice over. Wordhunter and slang expert Jonathon Green found a 1929 book *Crooks of the Underworld* which referred to railway fare dodgers as 'spives'. The *OED* team scratched their heads long and hard over this dodgy spelling and decided that, despite the extra 'e', it is the same word as spiv. The meaning was the same and, after all, words like 'give' and 'live' are pronounced that way. So spiv was antedated by five years.

But Martin Pitt from Sheffield sent in four earlier uses of spiv, all from the *Daily Mirror*, mentioning an intriguing character named Henry 'Spiv' Bagster. The earliest was from 1904.

'"Spiv" Bagster, the Victoria Station newsboy, is back to his old haunts again. Between eleven and twelve on Saturday night he was seen dodging about the station yard stopping people, to whom he offered a ring which he made a pretence of picking up... A police sergeant heard Bagster say to one gentleman that he had just found a good ruby ring, which he would sell for 6s... He found on him a brass ring, marked 18 carat 'cold', set with red glass... Bagster was remanded.'

A dodgy fellow indeed, and behaving just as you would expect a spiv to behave. It's possible that Bagster was the original spiv, giving the word to the language for ever after. Perhaps more likely, the existence of his nickname in 1904 suggests that our word spiv was already in use at that early date. The *OED* were intrigued, and whilst they couldn't include Bagster as an antedating, because the citation records a name not a common noun, they did conclude that he deserved a mention in the etymology – so Spiv Bagster does get eternal fame at long last.

Stiletto

The Wordhunt walked this one. **Stilettos** aged by six years, from 1959 back to 1953. But **stiletto heel** did even better, first of all with an example from 1952 about "the new stiletto heel *Vogue* raves about", which combination of high fashion and novelty suggested that we had got as close to the birth of the expression as we were ever likely to. But then an unexpected antedating submitted later showed the term in use over twenty years earlier in an Indiana newspaper in 1931. Perhaps stiletto heels were a frivolous trend that fell victim to the Depression – but they certainly had a longer pedigree than the *OED* thought.

Trainer

Nothing defines the coolness of a fashionable youth more than his or her **trainers**, but rather alarmingly the *OED*'s first evidence for the soft running shoe was about a women's morris dance side in 1978: 'no trainers or pumps: it's clogs or nothing.' One doubts that passed for cool even in the seventies. The dictionary wanted to find out whether the trainer was really older – or did everyone call them sneakers, pumps or plimsolls before that?

The competitive Wordhunters at the British Olympic Association did some legwork in the archives of their own official magazine *World Sports* and found an advertisement placed by sports shoe manufacturer Gola – which includes a shoe called the 'Gola Trainer', from 1968 – a decade earlier. The sticklers at the *OED* were reluctant to hand round the gold medals, pointing out that this was a trade name, not a generic usage of the word trainer, and so the citation in the dictionary would be in square brackets, suggesting etymological significance but not an earlier usage of the word. But following up the Gola lead, Wordhunter Ben Shuttleworth unearthed a Gola Catalogue from 1977, which described the 'Junior Cobra, Ideal for youngsters – a popular trainer in black leather. Padded collar, insole, tongue and raised back'. This time trainer was clearly being used as a word, not a brand, and it is currently in the *OED* as the mother of all trainers.

TWOC

The *OED* was pretty sure that the crime **TWOC** (taken without owner's consent, usually applied to car theft or joy riding) was older than 1990 but until *Balderdash* took on the challenge, there was no evidence to show whodunit or when. Out of the murky shadows emerged Wordhunter Philip Creed, with *Murder Ink*, a murder mystery companion from 1977 and a thirteen year antedating. But several lawyers and policemen wrote in to tell us that they thought the word must be even older, as it came about from a change in the laws concerning vehicle theft in the late sixties. Sure enough, the relevant section of the Theft Act of 1968 discusses the offence of 'taking a conveyance without the owner's consent', and the *OED* now quote this in their account of the word's etymology. And then to cap it all, in came a policeman's notebook, recording a 'suspected TWOC' on 20th October 1972. This pushes the history of the word back close to where we think it began, and is the first policeman's notebook to make it into the dictionary.

Wazzock

This word provoked the biggest response of the entire Wordhunt
– a wealth of weird and wonderful theories about the origin of
wazzock poured in, and nearly all of them were from Yorkshire.
After all, the *OED*'s earliest citation from 1981 referred to
Sheffield born actor Tony Capstick, and there's even a Yorkshire
climb named 'The Wazzok'. Sadly for Yorkshire though, the
Wordhunt finally crossed the border over into Lancashire to find
the earliest evidence – a 1976 recording of comedian Mike
Harding's *One Man Show*. No doubt Yorkshire's finest are
rummaging their attics even now in a bid to restore country
pride before the next black pudding throwing competition.

Wolf-whistle

As far as we're aware, wolves can't whistle – they just don't have
the right kind of lips. (Which is one reason why there were no
parts for wolves in *Bridge on the River Kwai*.) The *OED* define
wolf-whistle as 'a distinctive whistle from a man expressing
sexual admiration for a woman'. But curiously their early citation
for the word suggests that it might be the woman doing the
whistling: 'Some vulgar female let out a low wolf-whistle as she
passed him' (1953). Whistles all round for the Wordhunt, which
managed to push the date of the word back to 1944, with an
article in Californian publication the *Fresno Bee*. And once again
it's clear that it isn't necessarily a gender-specific activity: 'A
group of Fulton Street 'scientists' report that at last they have
identified and isolated the female version of the wolf whistle—
that often heard call used by men of the armed forces when their
trail crosses that of the opposite sex'. So now you know.

Could do better ...

You might be able to trump any of the findings described in this section. You might also be able to make some progress with those words and phrases that, despite the best efforts of Balderdash wordhunters, still managed to get away. The search goes on. Can you trace any of them back to an earlier date? For those marked with an asterisk, the *OED* is also somewhat mystified about the word or phrase's origins.

Bouncy castle (1986)	**Bung*** (1958)
Crimble (1963)	**Cyberspace** (1982)
Cyborg (1960)	**Dog and bone** (1961)
Kinky (1959)	**Minted** (1995)
Mullet* (1994)	**Naff*** (1966)
Nerd* (1951)	**Pear-shaped*** (1983)
Pick and mix (1959)	**Porky** (1985)
Posh* (1915)	**Round robin** (1988)
Take the mickey* (1948)	**Tosser** (1977)
Wally* (1969)	**Whoopsie** (1973)

Find out more about the series at www.bbc.co.uk/balderdash

Visit *The Oxford English Dictionary* online at www.oed.com and explore the *OED*'s own *Balderdash & Piffle* section at www.oed.com/bbcwordhunt/

Further Reading

USEFUL GENERAL REFERENCES

Brewer's Dictionary of Phrase and Fable (1923)

Chambers English Dictionary (1988)

Collins Concise Dictionary (2nd edition 1988)

David Crystal, *The Stories of English* (Allen Lane, London, 2004)

J.A. Cuddon, *The Penguin Dictionary of Literary Terms and Literary Theory* (1977, 3rd edition 1992)

Susie Dent, *The Language Report* (Oxford University Press, 2005) An editor and translator, Susie Dent appears regularly on TV's *Countdown* quiz as the resident dictionary expert. Her annual *Language Report* covers the year's latest crop of new words. The 2005 edition is called *Fanboys and Overdogs*.

Fowler's Modern English Usage, revised by Sir Ernest Gowers (1965)

Funk's Standard Dictionary (1890 and subsequent editions)

Jonathon Green, *Slang Down the Ages* (1993)

Albert Jack, *Red Herrings and White Elephants: The Origins of the Phrases We Use Every Day* (Metro Publishing, London, 2004). Also available at www.albertjack.com. Contains explanations of phrases such as 'above board', 'Bob's your uncle' and 'scratch my back and I'll scratch yours'.

Paul McFedries, *Word Spy: The Word Lover's Guide to Modern Culture* (Broadway Books, New York, 2004). Also available at www.wordspy.com. This book is an entertaining introduction to the explosion of new words, from 'affluenza' to 'zoo rage'.

Iona and Peter Opie, *The Lore and Language of Schoolchildren* (1959)

The Oxford English Dictionary (1st edition 1928, 2nd edition 1989, 3rd edition 2004)

Eric Partridge, A *Dictionary of Slang and Unconventional English* (1949)

Eric Partridge (ed.), A *Classical Dictionary of the Vulgar Tongue* by Captain Francis Grose (1931, original edition 1785)

Eric Partridge, *A Dictionary of Forces Slang* (1948)

Michael Quinion, *POSH* (2004)

Hugh Rawson, A *Dictionary of Invective* (1989)

Nigel Rees, A *Man About a Dog* (2006)

Nigel Rees, A *Word in Your Shell-like* (2006)

Tony Thorne, *Shoot the Puppy* (2006)

David Wilton, *Word Myths: Debunking Linguistic Urban Legends* (Oxford University Press USA, 2004)

Sir Henry Yule, *Hobson-Jobson: Being a Glossary of Colloquial Anglo-Indian Colloquial Words and Phrases and of Kindred Terms* (1886)

OTHER WORKS CITED

PART ONE
Introduction – The Power of Words

Frederick Bodmer, *The Loom of Language* (Allen & Unwin, London, 1944)

Susie Dent, *Larpers and Shroomers* (Oxford University Press, 2004)

Michael Quinion, *POSH* (Penguin, London, 2004)

Lynne Truss, *Eats, Shoots and Leaves* (Profile, London, 2003)

Chapter 1 – Our Mongrel Tongue

Melvyn Bragg, *The Adventure of English* (Hodder & Stoughton, London, 2003)

Geoffrey Chaucer, *The Canterbury Tales* (1386) (Penguin, London, 2003)

David Crystal, *The Cambridge*

Encyclopedia of Language (Cambridge University Press, 1987)

Richard A. Firmage, *The Alphabet Abecedarium* (Bloomsbury, London, 2000)

Geoffrey Hughes, A *History of English Words* (Blackwell, Oxford, 2000)

David Sacks, *The Alphabet* (Hutchinson, London, 2003)

Chapter 2 – Dr Johnson's Big Idea

James Boswell, *The Life of Samuel Johnson* (H. Baldwin, London, 1791)

Samuel Johnson, *Dictionary of the English Language* (Papermac, London, 1982)

Samuel Johnson, *Dictionary of the English Language*, ed. Jack Lynch (Walker & Company, New York, 2003)

Samuel Johnson's Dictionary: Selections from the 1755 Work That Defined the English Language, ed. Jack Lynch (Atlantic, London, 2004)

Henry Hitchings, *Dr Johnson's Dictionary: The Extraordinary Life of the Book that Defined the World* (John Murray, London, 2005)

Chapter 3 – From 0800 Number to Zyxt

The Concise Oxford English Dictionary, eds. H.W. and F.G. Fowler (Oxford University Press, 1911, 2004)

Jonathon Green, *Chasing the Sun: Dictionary Makers and the Dictionaries They Made* (Jonathan Cape, London, 1996)

Lynda Mugglestone, *Lost for Words: The Hidden History of the Oxford English Dictionary* (Yale University Press, New Haven, 2005)

K.M. Elisabeth Murray, *Caught in the Web of Words: James A.H. Murray and the Oxford English Dictionary* (Yale University Press, New Haven, 1977)

A New English Dictionary on Historical Principles, eds. Frederick Furnivall, James Murray (Oxford University Press, 1884-1928)

The Oxford English Dictionary, eds. Frederick Furnivall, James Murray, Henry Bradley, William Craigie, C.T. Onions, Robert Burchfield (Oxford University Press, 1928, 1933, 1989)

OED Online (www.oed.com) (launched 2000)

The Oxford English Reference Dictionary, eds. Judy Pearsall and Bill Trumble (Oxford University Press, 1995, 2002)

The Oxford School Dictionary of Word Origins, ed. John Ayto with Jessica Feinstein (Oxford University Press, 2002)

The Pocket Oxford Dictionary, first edition eds. F.G. and H.W. Fowler, 1924; 10th edition ed. Catherine Soanes, with Sara Hawker and Julia Elliott (Oxford University Press, 2005)

The Shorter Oxford English Dictionary, eds. William Little, H.W. Fowler and Jesse Coulson (Oxford University Press, 1933, 2002)

The Visual English Dictionary, eds. Jean-Claude Corbeil and Ariane Archambault (Oxford University Press, 2002)

Simon Winchester, *The Meaning of Everything: The Story of the Oxford English Dictionary* (Oxford University Press, 2003)

Chapter 4 – Desert Island Texts

The Holy Bible, pref. the King James version (Nelson Bibles, Nashville, 2003)

Frank Kermode, *Shakespeare's Language* (Allen Lane, London, 2000)

Alister E. McGrath, *In the Beginning: The Story of the King James Bible and How It Changed a Nation, a Language, and a Culture* (Doubleday, New York, 2001)

William Shakespeare: *The Complete Works* (Oxford University Press, 2005)

George Steiner, After Babel (Oxford University Press, 1975)

Chapter 5 – Local Lingo

The New Shorter OED (Oxford University Press, 1993)

Iona and Peter Opie, *The Lore and Language of Schoolchildren* (Clarendon Press, Oxford, 1959)

Harold Orton, The Linguistic Atlas of
England (Croom Helm, London, 1978)
John Walker, *Critical Pronouncing
Dictionary and Expositor of the
English Language* (G.G. and J. Robinson
and T. Cadell, London, 1791)
Joseph Wright, *English Dialect
Dictionary* (Henry Frowde, Oxford,
1898)

Chapter 6 – Global Lingo
Collins Concise Dictionary & Thesaurus
(HarperCollins, London, 2003)
David Crystal, *English as a Global
Language*, (Cambridge University Press,
1998)
Ivor Lewis, *Sahibs, Nabobs and
Boxwallahs*
(Oxford University Press, 1991)
Paroo Nihalani, R.K. Tongue and Priya
Hosali, *Indian and British English:
A Handbook of Usage and
Pronunciation* (Oxford University
Press, 1979)
F. Richards, *Old-Soldier Sahib* (Faber &
Faber, London, 1936)
*The Times English
Dictionary*(HarperCollins, London,
2000)
Sir Henry Yule and A.C. Burnell, A*nglo-
Indian Dictionary aka Hobson-Jobson*
(J. Murray, London, 1886)

Chapter 7 – That's Entertainment
Chambers English Dictionary (Chambers
Harrap, Edinburgh, 2003)
Wilfred Granville, *Dictionary of
Theatrical Terms* (A. Deutsch, London,
1952)
Francis Grose, *Classical Dictionary of the
Vulgar Tongue* (S. Hooper, London,
1785)
Steven Johnson, *Everything Bad is Good
for You: How Popular Culture is
Making us Smarter* (Allen Lane,
London, 2005)
Nigel Rees, A *Word in Your Shell-Like:
6,000 Curious & Everyday Phrases
Explained* (HarperCollins, London,
2004)

Chapter 8 – The Appliance of Science
Edmund Blunden, *Undertones of War*
(R. Cobden-Sanderson, London, 1928)
Paul Fussell, *The Great War and Modern
Memory* (Oxford University Press,
1975)
Ewart Alan Mackintosh, *War, the
Liberator* (J. Lane, London, 1918)
Steven Pinker, *The Language Instinct: The
New Science of Language and Mind*
(Penguin Science, Penguin Books,
London, 1995)

Chapter 9 – Mind Your Language
Paul Baker, *Polari, the Lost Language of
Gay Men* (Routledge Studies in
Linguistics) (Taylor & Francis, London,
2002)
The F-Word, ed. Jesse Sheidlower (Faber &
Faber, London, 1999)
Jonathon Green and Kipper Williams, *The
Big Book of Filth* (Cassell, London,
2000)
Geoffrey Hughes, *Swearing: A Social
History of Foul Language, Oaths and
Profanity in English* (Penguin Books,
London, 1998)
*The Language, Ethnicity and Race
Reader*, eds. Roxy Harris and Ben
Rampton, (Routledge, London, 2003)
Eric Partridge, *The Dictionary of Slang*
(Greenwood Press, New York, 1951)
Noel Perrin, *Dr Bowdler's Legacy: A
History of Expurgated Books in
England and America* (Athenum, New
York, 1969)
Percy Walker, *The Message in the Bottle:
How Queer Man Is - How Queer
Language Is - and What One Has to Do
with the Other* (Farrar, Strauss and
Giroux, New York, 1975, 2000)

Chapter 10 – To Er … is Human
*Fifty Years Among the New Words: A
Dictionary of Neologisms, 1941-1991*,
ed. John Algeo (Cambridge University
Press, 1991)
Leo H. Grindon, *Figurative Language: Its
Origin and Constitution* (James Spiers,
London, 1879)

Patrick Scrivenor, *Egg on Your Interface:
A Dictionary of Modern Nonsense*
(Buchan & Enright, London, 1989)
Robert D. Sutherland, *Language and
Lewis Carroll* (Mouton, The Hague,
1970)

Chapter 11 – Changing Times, Changing Terms

The Cassell Dictionary of Slang, ed.
Jonathon Green (Cassell, London, 2000)
R.W. Holder, A *Dictionary of
Euphemisms: How Not to Say What You
Mean* (Oxford Paperback Reference,
2003)
*The Oxford Encylopedic English
Dictionary*, eds. Joyce M. Hawkins and
Robert Allen (Oxford University Press,
1991)
Harold Wentworth and Stuart Berg
Flexner, *Dictionary of American Slang*
(T. Crowell, New York, 1960)

Chapter 12 – Origin Unknown

George H. Maines and Bruce Grant,
Wise-Crack Dictionary (1926)
Online Etymological Dictionary
(www.etymonline.com)
Eric Partridge, *Dictionary of Forces' Slang*
(Seckler & Warburg, 1948)
H.F. Reddall, *Fact, Fancy and Fable* (1889)
Noah Webster, An *American Dictionary
of the English Language*, 1st edition
1828, 3rd edition (Merriam-Webster,
Springfield MA, USA, 1961), also
available online at www.merriam-
webster.com

PART TWO
Chapter 13 – *One sandwich short*

Joseph Alexander Baron in *From the City,
from the Plough* (1948)
Albert Barrère and Charles Leland,
A Dictionary of Slang, Jargon and Cant
(1889)
W.H. Downing, *Digger Dialects* (1919)
W. Granville, A *Dictionary of Sailors'
Slang* (1962)
Adam Hart-Davis, *Taking the Piss: The
Potted History of Pee* (2005)

T.E. Lawrence, *Mint* (1935)
James A. Michener, *Tales of the South
Pacific* (1946)
Harold Pinter, *The Birthday Party* (1959)

Chapter 14 – *Fashionistas*

Edward Fraser and John Gibbons, *Soldier
and Sailor Words and Phrases* (1925)
John Galt, *The Provost* (1822)
James Joyce, *Ulysses* (1922)
David Lodge, *Ginger You're Barmy* (1962)
Sir Thomas Lodge, A *Fig for Momus* (1595)
Richard Lowe and William Shaw,
*Travellers: Voices of the New-Age
Nomads* (1993)

Chapter 15 – *Who were they?*

Joyce Cary, *Mister Johnson* (1939)
Geoffrey Chaucer, *The Canterbury Tales*
(1386, 2003)
W.H. Downing, *Digger Dialects* (1919)
Stephen Fried, *Thing of Beauty: The
Tragedy of Supermodel Gia* (1993)
Guinness Book of Records (1992)
Joseph Scott and Donald Bain, *The World's
Best Bartender's Guide* (1998)
Sir Walter Scott, *Rob Roy* (1818)
Tony Thorne (ed.), *A Dictionary of
Contemporary Slang* (1988)
Mark Twain, *Letters from Hawaii* (1866)

Chapter 16 – *Man's best friend*

C.L. Anthony, *Touch Wood* (1934)
William Bullein, A *Dialogue against the
fever pestilence* (1564)
Thomas Carlyle, *Frederick the Great* (1864)
Thomas Cooper, *Thesaurus linguae
Romanae & Britannicae* (1565-73)
J.S. Curtis, *The Gilt Kid* (1936)
Sir Arthur Conan Doyle, *The Hound of the
Baskervilles* (1902)
William Horman, *Vulgaria* (1519)
Washington Irving, A *History of New-York
from the Beginning of the World to the
End of the Dutch Dynasty* (1809)
Charles Kingsley, *The Water Babies* (1863)
Peter Laurie, *Scotland Yard: A Personal
Inquiry* (1970)
Maurice Levinson, *Taxi!* (1963)
Colin MacInnes, *To the Victors the Spoils*
(1950)
Hippo Neville, *Sneak Thief on the Road*
(1935)

George Puttenham, *The Arte of English Poesie* (1589)
Edward Topsell, *The History of Four-footed Beasts* (1607)
Edward Topsell, *The History of Serpents* (1608)
Dean Stiff, *The Milk and Honey Route; A Handbook for Hobos* (1931)
John Wainwright, *The Last Buccaneer* (1971)
William Wycherley, *The Plain-Dealer* (1676)

Chapter 17 – Dodgy dealings
Albert Barrère and Charles Leland, *Dictionary of Slang, Jargon, and Cant* (1889)
Alison Cross, *A Death in the Faculty* (1981)
W.S. Gilbert, *The Hooligan* (1910)
William Gillette, *The Astounding Crime on Torrington Road* (1928)
Louis E. Jackson and C.R. Hellyer, *A Vocabulary of Criminal Slang* (1914)
Lehmann Hisey, *Sea Grist: A Personal Narrative of Five Months in the Merchant Marine, a Rousing Sea Tale* (1921)
Thomas Keneally, *Schindler's Ark* (1982)
Lord William Pitt Lennox, *Fifty Years' Biographical Reminiscences* (1860)
Paul Tempest, *Lag's Lexicon: A Comprehensive Dictionary and Encyclopaedia of the English Prison To-day* (1950)
Andrew Wynter, *Our Social Bees: Or Pictures of Town and Country Life* (1860)

Chapter 18 – Put-downs and insults
Joan Aiken, *Black Hearts in Battersea* (1965)
Melvyn Bragg, *Without a City Wall* (1968)
Noel Coward, *Play Parade* (1939)
Joey Deacon, *Tongue Tied* (1974)
Thomas D'Urfey, *Wit & Mirth* (1719)
John Florio, *Worlde of Wordes* (1598)
Martin Handford, *Where's Wally?* (1987)
Thomas Hoccleve, *Letter to Cupid* (1402)
Gwyn Jones and Islwyn Ffowc Elis (eds) *Twenty-Five Welsh Short Stories* (1971)
Ben Jonson, *Poetaster* (1602)
John Lyly, *Maides Metamorphosis* (1600)
G.F. Newman, *Sir, You Bastard* (1970)
Roger Scruton, *Fortnight's Anger* (1981)

Roger Scruton, *A Short History of Modern Philosophy* (1984)
Peter Wildblood, *The Main Chance* (1957)
Henry Williamson, *The Patriot's Progress* (1930)
P.G. Wodehouse, *Right Ho, Jeeves* (1934)
P.G. Wodehouse, *Tales of St Austin's* (1904)
Joseph Wright, *The English Dialect Dictionary* (1898)

Chapter 19 – Spend a penny
C.D.B. Bryan, *Friendly Fire* (1976)
Pierce Egan, *Real Life* (1821)
Germaine Greer, *The Female Eunuch* (1970)
Richard Head, *The Canting Academy* (1673)
Joseph T.J. Hewlett, *Parsons & Widows* (1844)
John C. Hotten, *A Dictionary of Modern Slang* (1874)
Aldous Huxley, *Time Must Have a Stop* (1945)
Samuel Johnson, *Dictionary of English* (1755)
Charles Johnstone, *Chrysal, or the Adventures of a Guinea* (1821)
Ben Jonson, *The Alchemist* (1616)
D.H. Lawrence, *Lady Chatterley's Lover* (1932)
H. Lewis, *Strange Story* (1945)
E. Lighter, *Historical Dictionary of American Slang* (1997)
Patrick Marnham, *The Private Eye Story* (1982)
George Melly, *Owning-Up* (1965)
Henry Miller, *Tropic of Cancer* (1934)
Nancy Mitford, *Pigeon Pie* (1940)
Vladimir Nabokov, *Invitation to a Beheading* (1960)
A New Dictionary of the Terms Ancient and Modern of the Canting Crew (1699)
Peter Paterson, *Tired and Emotional: The Life of Lord George-Brown* (1993)
Alexander Pope, *The Rape of the Lock* (1712-14)
Daniel Richler, *Kicking Tomorrow* (1993)
Sir Walter Scott, *Kenilworth* (1821)
George Bernard Shaw, *Geneva* (1938)
Albert R. Smith, *The Struggles and Adventures of Christopher Tadpole* (1847)

Laurence Sterne, *Tristram Shandy* (1759–67)

Sydney Tremayne (ed.), *The Trial of Alfred Arthur Rouse* (1931)

Chapter 20 – X-rated

John Russell Bartlett, *Dictionary of Americanisms* (1860)

Randle Cotgrave, *Dictionarie of the French and English Tongues* (1611)

John Crouch, *Mercurius Fumigosus* (1655)

H.L. Davis, *Honey in the Horn* (1963)

E.M. Forster, *The Longest Journey* (1907)

Esther Freud, *Hideous Kinky* (1992)

Captain Francis Grose, A *Provincial Glossary* (1790)

Thomas Harman, A *Caveat or Warning for Common Cursitors, Vulgarly Called Vagabonds* (1566)

Peter Laurie, *Scotland Yard: A Study of the Metropolitan Police* (1970)

Rachel P. Maines, *The Technology of Orgasm* (1999)

'Marjoribanks', *Fluff-hunters* (1903)

Colin MacInnes, *Absolute Beginners* (1959)

Sir William Smith, *Dictionary of Greek and Roman Antiquities* (1842)

Robert Louis Stevenson, *Travels with a Donkey in the Cévennes* (1879)

We have done our best to acknowledge all the authors of works cited and apologize for any omissions.

Useful Addresses & Websites

Dr Johnson's House
17 Gough Square
London EC4A 3DE
Tel: 020 7353 3745
Email: curator@drjohnsonshouse.org
Website: www.drjohnsonshouse.org

The Johnson Society
The Birthplace Museum
Breadmarket Street, Lichfield
Staffordshire WS13 6LG
Email: edmanmail-johnsoc@yahoo.co.uk
Website: www.lichfieldrambler.co.uk

The Oxford English Dictionary
Oxford University Press
Great Clarendon Street
Oxford OX2 6DP
Tel: 01865 353660
Email: oed3@oup.com

**http://encarta.msn.com/encnet/
features/dictionary/dictionaryhome.
aspx**
MSN Encarta: Online **dictionary** with over
100,000 entries, definitions, and
pronunciations.

http://portal.unesco.org
Initiative B@bel uses Information and
Communication Technologies (ICTs) to
support linguistic and cultural diversity, and
to protect and preserve languages in danger
of disappearance.

www.collinslanguage.com
The HarperCollins site includes an online
dictionary and a weekly bulletin by Jeremy
Butterfield, editor-in-chief of Collins
dictionaries.

www.oed.com
The website of *The Oxford English
Dictionary*. Comprehensive information
on the *OED*, and home to *OED* Online. Its
archive includes previous newsletters back
to January 1995, much valuable material
from the vaults and an information
resource.

www.en.wikipedia.org
The biggest independently edited
encyclopaedia on the net.

www.ethnologue.com
Ethnologue – Languages of the World: an
encyclopedic reference work cataloguing all
the world's 6912 known living languages.

www.ogmios.org
Foundation for Endangered Languages –
aims to raise awareness and support the
use of endangered languages.

www.phrases.org.uk
Offers word meanings, origins, a thesaurus
and a discussion group.

www.urbandictionary.com
An online slang dictionary, with entries and
definitions supplied and updated by
readers.

www.wordorigins.org
The website of David Wilton, author of *Word
Myths*, discusses commonly misunderstood
words and phrases and includes a weekly
newsletter, A Way with Words.

www.worldwidewords.org
Michael Quinion, author of *POSH and
Other Language Myths* is the nation's
foremost word-sleuth.

www.wordwizard.com
Word site that includes quotations, insults
and neologisms.

Acknowledgements

My thanks go to the staff of the British Library, the London Library (especially Christopher Phipps), and Mount Pleasant writers' retreat, where some sections of this book were written. To the good people of Takeaway Media past and present: Archie Baron, Neil Cameron, Helena Braun, Kate Carter, Kim Lomax, Naomi Zola, Jayne Rowe (and Muffin) and Rob Silva.

To Tim Jackson, for making that initial contact. To Peter Gilliver and Jane McCauley of the Oxford English Dictionary. To Cameron Fitch and Stuart Cooper of BBC Books (volume one) and to Martin Redfern of Random House and Trish Burgess (volume two) – and to Eleanor Maxfield (for combining the two).

Thanks to Andy Davey for his very funny cartoons for volume two. Also to Julian Alexander of LAW (both volumes) and Antony Topping of Greene & Heaton (volume two).

Thanks, finally, to those readers who took the trouble to write in with corrections, suggestions or merely appreciative comments. We hope that all errors have been put right.

Index

Headings in **bold type** indicate words and phrases highlighted in the text.